# PERSIAN G

BY

## ANN K. S. LAMBTON

CAMBRIDGE
UNIVERSITY PRESS

PUBLISHED BY THE PRESS SYNDICATE OF THE UNIVERSITY OF CAMBRIDGE
The Pitt Building, Trumpington Street, Cambridge, United Kingdom

CAMBRIDGE UNIVERSITY PRESS
The Edinburgh Building, Cambridge CB2 2RU, UK    http://www.cup.cam.ac.uk
40 West 20th Street, New York, NY 10011–4211, USA    http://www.cup.org
10 Stamford Road, Oakleigh, Melbourne 3166, Australia
Ruiz de Alarcón 13, 28014 Madrid, Spain

*Persian Grammar* first published 1953
Reprinted with corrections 1957
1960 1961 1963 1967 1971
*Key* first published 1967
Paperback edition incorporating *Grammar*
and *Key* first published 1974
Reprinted 1976 1979 1981
Reprinted with repagination 1984
Reprinted 1986 1988 1990 1992 1993 1996 2000

ISBN 0 521 09124 1 paperback

Transferred to digital printing 2003

# CONTENTS

iv

CONTENTS

# PART II

## The Arabic Element

# PREFACE

This work is intended primarily to meet the needs of the student of the Persian language of the present day, but it is hoped that it will also serve as an introduction to the student who wishes to read the classics.[1] The first part is devoted to a description of the main Persian grammatical forms and their use, without reference to their historical development. These forms have been arranged into classes according to their grammatical function. The terminology used is the traditional grammatical terminology of English. These classes do not necessarily correspond exactly with similar classes in English; as in English, some words belong to more than one class. Exact definitions of the various classes have not been given and an exhaustive division into sub-classes has not been attempted. Part II describes the main Arabic forms used in Persian, a knowledge of which is indispensable for the student of Persian. A standard Arabic grammar should be consulted for a more detailed description of these forms. The usages described in this work are those current unless the contrary is stated. In many cases these do not differ from the Classical Persian usage. It should be remembered that language is in a constant state of flux: on the one hand there is a tendency to drop certain expressions and words or to restrict their meaning, while on the other 'slang' expressions are being constantly incorporated into the literary language. No attempt has been made to include in this work words and expressions which are not already so incorporated. The student should beware of using 'slang expressions' in literary contexts. There is, moreover, a vagueness of usage in Persian; and the student should also beware of supposing that the forms set out in the grammar are always

[1] Literary Persian (Farsi), as its name implies was originally the dialect of the province of Fars, the Persis of the Greeks. It can historically be divided into three main periods: (a) Old Persian, represented by the Achaemenid cuneiform inscriptions; (b) Middle Persian, represented chiefly by the Zoroastrian 'Pahlavi' books, the Sasanian inscriptions and the Manichaean texts recently discovered in Central Asia; and (c) New Persian, by which is understood the literary language of Mohammadan times written in the Arabic script. This work is concerned with Modern Persian, which term is used to mean the language of the present day. Incidental references will be found to Classical Persian, the earliest extant examples of which belong to the tenth century A.D. Broadly speaking the term Classical Persian covers the whole Islamic period down to, and perhaps even including, Qajar times. The best period of Persian prose is, however, considered to be the pre-Mongol period. Lastly, occasional references will be found to Colloquial Persian, which is a form of spoken Persian. This work is not intended to be a complete description of modern colloquial idiom.

strictly adhered to. A transcription has been used to indicate pronunciation. The pronunciation given is that of Tehran. No attempt has been
made to describe local variations of this. An English—Persian and
Persian—English vocabulary for the convenience of the student will be
published as a separate volume, but it is not intended that these vocabularies should enable him to dispense with the use of a dictionary. A full
description of all words is not given: for this the student must refer to
a dictionary. Further, the meanings given are those in current use,
which, in many cases, differs from the classical usage.


## PREFACE TO KEY

My *Persian Grammar*, first published in 1953, was designed as a teaching
grammar. A key, therefore, seemed unnecessary. For students working
on their own, however, the lack of a key has proved a disadvantage;
and it is my hope that its inclusion in the present volume will be of
assistance to such students.

Experience in teaching, using the *Grammar* as a textbook, has convinced me that the incorporation of some additional exercises would
be beneficial to the student. Consequently, a number of exercises and
some passages of continuous prose for translation into Persian have
been added. Words not included in the Vocabulary, which are required
for these translations have been added in footnotes at the end of the
relevant passage, except in the case of the final passage. The Persian
version of this has been taken from a published translation (with a few
minor alterations) and has been included as an example of translation
by one of the leading contemporary translators. In this case I have
thought it best to give the new words, or new meanings for words
already in the Vocabulary, in a list at the end of the Persian version.
I have not included extra passages for translation from Persian into
English on the grounds that such material in the form of readers,
books and newspapers is readily available.

Alternative translations have been put in round brackets, but in
general no attempt has been made to give more than one translation.
Square brackets have been used for words not in the original, the
addition of which is required by the sense.

# INTRODUCTION

1. Persian is written in the Arabic script, which is read from right to left. The letters پ *p*, چ *c*, ژ *z* and گ *g* were added by the Persians to the Arabic alphabet. For the complete Persian alphabet see para. 5 below.

2. VOWELS:

*i*   approximating to the vowel in the English word 'beat' and represented by ی in the Arabic script, e.g.

بید   *bid*, willow-tree.

*e*   approximating to the vowel in the English word 'bed' and not represented in the Arabic script, e.g.

به   *beh*, better.

*a*   intermediate between the vowels in the English words 'bed' and 'bad' and not represented in the Arabic script, e.g.

بد   *bad*, bad.

*a*   approximating to the vowel in the English word 'barred' and represented by ا in the Arabic script, e.g.

باد   *bad*, wind.

*o*   rather more rounded than the vowel in the English word 'book' and not represented in the Arabic script, e.g.

بردن   *bordan*, to carry.

*u*   approximating to the vowel in the English word 'booed' and represented by و in the Arabic script, e.g.

بود   *bud*, he, she or it was.

*i*, *e* and *a* are front vowels; *a*, *o* and *u* back vowels. *i*, *a* and *u* are longer than *e*, *a* and *o*. The latter group, namely *e*, *a* and *o*, are slightly prolonged when followed by two consonants in the same syllable, but their articulation time, even when thus prolonged, is less than that of *i*, *a* or *u*.

A vowel approximating to the vowel in the English word 'bit' is heard in a few words, notably شش *ʃeʃ* 'six' (except in the expression شش و بش *ʃeʃ o beʃ* 'six and five' used in backgammon, when the vowel of شش approximates to the *e* of the English word 'bed'). This vowel belongs, as regards articulation time, to the group *e*, *a* and *o*. Its occurrence, however, is so rare that it has not been thought necessary to represent it in the transcription by a separate symbol, and it will accordingly be transcribed *e*.

In a few words ا followed by ن represents a vowel intermediate between *a* and *o*. Its articulation time is also intermediate between that of *a* and *o*. Again, its occurrence is not so common that it has been thought necessary to represent it by a separate symbol (see Lessons v, para. 2 and xiv, para. 2).

See also Introduction to Part II.

3. The formation of the vowels is shown in the following diagram. In this diagram the tongue positions of the vowels are compared with those of the eight cardinal vowels.[1] The dots indicate the position of the highest point of the tongue.

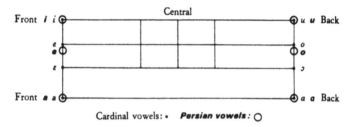

Cardinal vowels: • *Persian vowels:* ○

4. DIPHTHONGS. These are $\widehat{ei}$, $\widehat{ai}$, $\widehat{ui}$, $\widehat{ou}$ and $\widehat{ai}$. The starting-point and direction of the diphthongs is shown in the following diagram. $\widehat{ei}$ and $\widehat{ai}$ are represented in the Arabic script by ـَی; $\widehat{ui}$ by وی, $\widehat{ai}$ by ای and $\widehat{ou}$ by ـَو. In the transcription the diphthongs are shown by a ligature mark; thus in گوی $g\widehat{ui}$ 'ball' the $\widehat{ui}$ represents a diphthong whereas in گوئی $gui$ 'thou sayest' *u* and *i* are separate vowels.

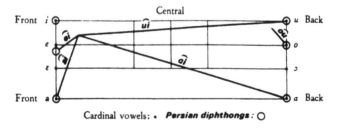

Cardinal vowels: • *Persian diphthongs:* ○

[1] The cardinal vowels are fixed vowel sounds which have fixed tongue positions and known acoustic qualities. Their sounds are recorded in Linguaphone, No. DAJO 1/2 H.M.V. B 804.

5. THE ALPHABET. The majority of the letters of the alphabet have four forms, which are used according to the position of the letter in the word. These forms are initial, medial, final joined and final unjoined. The letters ‌ا, د, ذ, ر, ز, ژ and و cannot join the following letter, hence the existence of two final forms, one joined and the other unjoined. The medial and final joined forms of ‌ا, د, ذ, ر, ز, ژ and و are thus identical as also are their initial and final unjoined forms. The term 'initial' is used to cover the case not only of a letter in an initial position in a word, but also of a medial following one of the letters which cannot join the following letter. The table overleaf shows the various forms of the letters, and gives their Persian names, phonetic description and transcription. The system adopted is a 'transcription' and not a 'transliteration', one symbol being used for all letters having the same sound. Thus ث, س and ص are all transcribed by s.[1]

6. The sign ء is known as *hamẓe*. In Persian words it only occurs in a medial position and is written over a bearer, thus ئ. It is a grammatical mark indicating that there is a junction of vowels and it will not be represented in the transcription, e.g.

پائيز    paiẓ, autumn.

It performs this function in the following cases also:

(a) Between the Present Stem of a verb if this ends in a vowel and the personal endings of the 2nd pers. singular and plural and the 1st pers. plural, e.g.

میگوئی   *migui*, thou sayest.     میائی   *miai*, thou comest.

میگوئید   *miguid*, you say.     میائید   *miaid*, you come.

میگوئیم   *miguim*, we say.     میائیم   *miaim*, we come.

(b) Between a word ending in ‌ا *a* or و *u* and the Indefinite ی -*i* (see Lesson I, para. 2 (c) below), e.g.

پاروئی   parui, a spade.

دانائی   danai, a wise man.

(c) Between the final ‌ا *a* or و *u* of a word and the suffixed Abstract ی -*i* (see Lesson X), e.g.

زناشوئی   ẓanaſui, matrimony.

توانائی   tavanai, power, strength.

---

[1] An exception is made in the case of غ and ق, which are transliterated as ɣ and q respectively.

| Name | Final unjoined | Final joined | Medial | Initial | Transcription | Phonetic description | Remarks |
|---|---|---|---|---|---|---|---|
| alef | ا | ا | ا | ا | — | alef, or alef hamze as it is properly known, represents at the beginning of a word a glottal plosive and may be vowelled e, a or o. In a medial or final position it represents the vowel a. E.g. امروز emruz 'to-day', اسب asb 'horse', افتاد oftad 'he fell', باد bad 'wind', ما 'we' | The vowel a in an initial position is written آ and known as alef madda, e.g. آب ab 'water'. alef is written before the vowels ای i and او u at the beginning of a word, e.g. این in 'this', او u 'he' |
| be | ب. | ب. | ب | ب | b | Voiced bilabial plosive | |
| pe | پ. | پ. | پ | پ | p | Voiceless aspirated bilabial plosive | |
| te | ت. | ت. | ت | ت | t | Voiceless aspirated dental plosive | See also ط below. ت (and ط) differ from the English t, which is alveolar |
| se | ث. | ث. | ث | ث | s | Voiceless alveolar fricative | See also س and ص below |
| jim | ج | ج | ج | ج | j | Voiced post-alveolar plosive | =j in the English word 'John' |
| cim | چ | چ | چ | چ | c | Voiceless post-alveolar fricative | =ch in the English word 'church' |

| | ح | ج | ‍ | ‍ | h | Description | Notes |
|---|---|---|---|---|---|---|---|
| *he hoti* | | | | | h | Glottal fricative | English students should be careful to give *h* (whether this is ح or ه below) its full value in a final position, e.g. صبح *sobh* 'morning', راه *rah* 'road', and also when followed immediately by another consonant, e.g. شهر *šahr* 'town' |
| *xe* | خ | خ | خ | خ | x | Voiceless velar uvular with scrape | Approximating to the *ch* in the Scottish word 'loch' |
| *dal* | د | د | د | د | d | Voiced dental plosive | د differs from the English *d*, which is alveolar |
| *ẕal* | ذ | ذ | ذ | ذ | ذ | Voiced alveolar fricative | See ز, ذ and ظ below |
| *re* | ر | ر | ر | ر | r | Voiced alveolar with weak roll or tap | |
| *ze* | ز | ز | ز | ز | ز | Voiced alveolar fricative | See ذ above and ز and ظ below |
| *že* | ژ | ژ | ژ | ژ | ž | Voiced post-alveolar fricative | =*j* in the French word 'jour' |
| *sin* | س | س | س | س | s | Voiceless alveolar fricative | See ث above and ص below |
| *šin* | ش | ش | ش | ش | ʃ | Voiceless post-alveolar fricative | =*sh* in the English word 'show' |
| *ṣad* | ص | ص | ص | ص | s | Voiceless alveolar fricative | See ث and س above |
| *ẕad* | ض | ض | ض | ض | ز | Voiced alveolar fricative | See ذ and ز above and ظ below |
| *ta* | ط | ط | ط | ط | t | Voiceless aspirated dental plosive | See ت above |
| *ẓa* | ظ | ظ | ظ | ظ | ز | Voiced alveolar fricative | See ذ, ز and ض above |

| Name | Final unjoined | Final joined | Medial | Initial | Transcription | Phonetic description | Remarks |
|---|---|---|---|---|---|---|---|
| ʿain | ع | ع | ع | ع | ʻ | Glottal plosive | ع is a glottal plosive and is represented in the transcription by 'ʻ'. It corresponds to the check in the voice substituted for t in Cockney and other dialects in such words as 'bottle', 'water', etc., e.g. بعضي *baʻʐi* 'some', وضع *vaʐ* 'situation'. In an initial position when it is followed immediately by a vowel it is omitted from the transcription, e.g. عمر *omr* 'life'. The combination of ع preceded by a and followed by i tends to become âi, e.g. سعى *sâi* 'effort' |
| ɣain (yēn) | غ | غ | غ | غ | y | Voiced or voiceless uvular plosive according to phonetic context | See ق below |
| fe | ف | ف | ف | ف | f | Voiceless labio-dental fricative | |
| qaf | ق | ق | ق | ق | q | Voiced or voiceless uvular plosive according to phonetic context | غ and ق are not differentiated by most speakers. Both are pronounced as a voiceless uvular plosive (formed by the back of the tongue coming into contact with the rearmost part of the soft palate), unless between two back vowels when they tend to be pronounced as a voiced uvular plosive |

| Name | | | | | Translit. | Description | Notes |
|---|---|---|---|---|---|---|---|
| kāf | ک | ک | ك | ل | k | Voiceless aspirated palatal or velar plosive according to phonetic context | ک k and گ g (see below) are palatal if followed by a front vowel, i.e. i, e or a or the diphthong ai, or in a final position (whether in a word or syllable). In other contexts ک k and گ g are velar. The palatal k and g are not found in English. They are made by the front of the tongue, excluding the tip, coming against the hard palate |
| gāf | گ | گ | ک | گ | g | Voiced palatal or velar plosive according to phonetic context | See ک above. ک k and گ g followed by ا a are written کا and گا respectively |
| lām | ل | ــل | ـلـ | لـ | l | Voiced alveolar lateral | ل l followed by ا a is written لا |
| mīm | م | ــم | ـمـ | مـ | m | Voiced nasal bilabial | |
| nūn | ن | ــن | ـنـ | نـ | n | Voiced nasal alveolar | ن n if followed by ب b in the same word is pronounced m and will be so represented in the transcription, e.g. انبار ambar 'store' |
| vāv | و | ــو | ـو | و | v<br>u<br>ōu | Voiced labio-dental fricative<br>See para. 2 above<br>See para. 4 above | و can be a consonant, vowel or diphthong. After an initial خ x in Persian words it is not pronounced, e.g. خواستن xāstan 'to want'. Exceptions to this are خوب xub 'good', خون xun 'blood', خوک xuk 'pig', خوشه xuše 'a cluster of grapes', خوزستان xuzestan 'Khuzistan' |

¹ See Introduction to Part II for the use of this sign to transcribe a medial or final hamze in Arabic words.

| Name | Final unjoined | Final joined | Medial | Initial | Transcription | Phonetic description | Remarks |
|---|---|---|---|---|---|---|---|
| | | | | | | | In the words دو *do* 'two', and تو *to* 'thou', and بوه *bote* 'bush' the و is pronounced *o* (see para. 2 above) |
| *he havaz* | ه | ـه | ـهـ | ها | *h* | Glottal fricative | In words derived from Turkish ه is also sometimes pronounced *o*, thus دوفك (دوفه) *dofak* 'mattress', تومان *toman* 'ten rials', توتون *totun* 'tobacco'. یورتمه *yortme* 'trotting, trot'. See ح above. In a final position in certain words when preceded by the vowel *e*, ه is not pronounced. This will be called the 'silent' *h*. This is the case when ه represents a verbal, adjectival or nominal suffix, e.g. گفته *gofte* 'said', نامه *name* 'letter', ماهه *mahe* 'monthly'. The ه of نه *na* 'no' and بله *bale* 'yes' is not pronounced. See also Introduction to Part II, para. 11 |
| *ye* | ی | ـی | ـیـ | ـ | *y* / *i* / *ei, ai* | Semi-vowel / See para. 2 above / See para. 4 above | In certain contexts ی represents the *ezafe* and is pronounced *ye* (see Lesson II, para. 7) |

(*d*) Between a word ending in ‏ا‎ *a* or ‏و‎ *u* and the Relative ‏ى‎ -*i* (see Lesson VIII), e.g.

‏كتابهائيكه‎... *ketabhai ke*, the books which....

‏آدم پرروئيكه‎... *adame porrui ke*, the bold (brazen) man who.....

7. Over the 'silent' *h* a *hamze* represents:

(*a*) The Indefinite ‏ى‎ -*i*, e.g.

‏نامهٔ‎ *namei*, a letter.

(*b*) The 'Adjectival' ‏ى‎ , e.g.

‏سرمهٔ‎ *sormei*, dark blue.

(*c*) The personal ending of the 2nd pers. sing., e.g.

‏گفتهٔ‎ *goftei*, Thou hast said.

(*d*) The *ezafe* (see Lesson II, para. 6), in which case it is represented in the transcription as *ye*, e.g.

‏نامهٔ من‎ *nameye man*, my letter.

8. For the *hamze* in Arabic words see the Introduction to Part II, paras. 8 and 9.

9. The following orthographic signs exist, but are not in common use:

  ‏ˉ‎  *fathe* = a.

  ‏ˍ‎  *kasre* = e.

  ‏ˊ‎  *zamme* = o.

  ‏ˉ‎  *tafdid*, used to mark a doubled consonant.

  ‏ˊ‎  *sokun* or *jazm*, used to show a consonant is not vocalized.

These signs are placed above or below the letter to which they refer, e.g.

‏دَر‎ *dar*, door.

‏كِشت‎ *keft*, cultivation.

‏پُر‎ *por*, full.

The student should note that although the sign *tafdid* is rarely used the doubling of a consonant should be strictly observed in pronunciation (except in a final position).

## READING EXERCISE

| | | | | | |
|---|---|---|---|---|---|
| با *pa* foot | تا *ta* until | با *ba* with | آن *an* that | آش *aʃ* stew | آب أب *ab* water |
| باج *baj* tribute | کی *ki* who (interrog.) | بی *bi* without | رو *ru* on | تو *tu* in | جا *ja* place |
| بال *bal* wing | باك *bak* fear | باغ *baɣ* garden | باز *baʒ* open | بار *bar* time | باد *bad* wind |
| بیش *biʃ* more | بید *bid* willow | بیخ *bix* root | بوم *bum* soil | بود *bud* he was | بام *bam* roof |
| پود *pud* weft | پوچ *puc* futile | پاك *pak* clean | پاس *pas* watch | بیم *bim* fear | بیل *bil* spade |
| پیش *piʃ* before | پیر *pir* old | پیچ *pic* corner | پیت *pit* petrol-tin | پول *pul* money | پوك *puk* rotten |
| تور *tur* net | توپ *tup* ball | تار *tar* guitar | تاج *taj* crown | پیه *pih* lard | پیل *pil* elephant |
| جاه *jah* rank | جان *jan* soul | جام *jam* cup | تیغ *tiɣ* thorn | تیز *tiʒ* sharp | تیر *tir* arrow |
| چاپ *cap* print | جیغ *jiɣ* scream | جیب *jib* pocket | جوش *juʃ* boiling | جور *jur* kind, sort | جوب *jub* irrigation channel |
| چیت *cit* calico | چون *cun* when | چوب *cub* wood | چاه *cah* well | چال *cal* pit | چاق *caq* fat |
| خال *xal* mole | خاص *xas* special | خار *xar* thorn | حین *hin* time | حال *hal* state | چین *cin* pleat |

| | | | | | |
|---|---|---|---|---|---|
| خام<br>*xam*<br>raw | خان<br>*xan*<br>khan | خواب<br>*xab*<br>sleep | خواه<br>*xah*<br>whether | خوب<br>*xub*<br>good | خون<br>*xun*<br>blood |
| خیس<br>*xis*<br>soaked | خیش<br>*xiʃ*<br>plough | داد<br>*dad*<br>justice | دار<br>*dar*<br>gallows | داغ<br>*daɣ*<br>hot | دام<br>*dam*<br>snare |
| دود<br>*dud*<br>smoke | دور<br>*dur*<br>far | دوش<br>*duʃ*<br>shoulder | دوغ<br>*duɣ*<br>sour milk | دیر<br>*dir*<br>late | دیگ<br>*dig*<br>cauldron |
| دین<br>*din*<br>religion | دیو<br>*div*<br>demon | ذات<br>*ʒat*<br>nature | راز<br>*raʒ*<br>secret | رام<br>*ram*<br>tame | ران<br>*ran*<br>thigh |
| راه<br>*rah*<br>road | روح<br>*ruh*<br>soul | رود<br>*rud*<br>river | روز<br>*ruʒ*<br>day | ریش<br>*riʃ*<br>beard | ریگ<br>*rig*<br>sand |
| زاغ<br>*ʒaɣ*<br>magpie | زود<br>*ʒud*<br>early | زور<br>*ʒur*<br>force | زیج<br>*ʒij*<br>almanac | زیر<br>*ʒir*<br>under | زین<br>*ʒin*<br>saddle |
| ساق<br>*saq*<br>shank | سال<br>*sal*<br>year | سان<br>*san*<br>parade | سوت<br>*sut*<br>whistle | سود<br>*sud*<br>benefit | سور<br>*sur*<br>feast |
| سیخ<br>*six*<br>skewer | سیر<br>*sir*<br>garlic | سیم<br>*sim*<br>silver | شاخ<br>*ʃax*<br>branch | شاد<br>*ʃad*<br>happy | شام<br>*ʃam*<br>supper |
| شور<br>*ʃur*<br>brackish | شوم<br>*ʃum*<br>ill-omened | شیر<br>*ʃir*<br>lion | صاف<br>*saf*<br>pure | طاق<br>*taq*<br>portico | طول<br>*tul*<br>length |
| طین<br>*tin*<br>clay | عود<br>*ud*<br>lute | عید<br>*id*<br>holiday | غار<br>*ɣar*<br>cave | غاز<br>*ɣaʒ*<br>goose | غول<br>*ɣul*<br>ghoul |
| فاش<br>*faʃ*<br>divulged | فال<br>*fal*<br>omen | فام<br>*fam*<br>colour | فیل<br>*fil*<br>elephant | قاب<br>*qab*<br>plate | قیر<br>*qir*<br>pitch |
| کاج<br>*kaj*<br>pine | کاخ<br>*kax*<br>pavillion | کار<br>*kar*<br>work | کال<br>*kal*<br>unripe | کام<br>*kam*<br>desire | کان<br>*kan*<br>mine |

| | | | | | |
|---|---|---|---|---|---|
| كاه | كوچ | كور | كول | كوه | كيف |
| *kah* | *kuc* | *kur* | *kul* | *kuh* | *kif* |
| straw | migration | blind | shoulder | mountain | bag |
| گاو | گه | گور | گوش | گول | گيج |
| *gav* | *gah* | *gur* | *guʃ* | *gul* | *gij* |
| ox | place | tomb | ear | deceit | giddy |
| گير | لات | لاش | لاف | لال | لور |
| *gir* | *lat* | *laʃ* | *laf* | *lal* | *lur* |
| caught | vagabond | carrion | boast | dumb | whey |
| ليف | مات | مار | ماش | مال | ماه |
| *lif* | *mat* | *mar* | *maʃ* | *mal* | *mah* |
| fibre | checkmate | snake | a kind of pulse | possessions | moon |
| موم | ميخ | ميز | ميش | ميل | نام |
| *mum* | *mix* | *miʒ* | *miʃ* | *mil* | *nam* |
| wax | nail | table | ewe | rod | name |
| نان | ناو | نور | نيز | نيش | نيل |
| *nan* | *nav* | *nur* | *niʒ* | *niʃ* | *nil* |
| bread | ship | light | also | sting | indigo |
| نيم | وام | هوش | هيچ | ايل | اين |
| *nim* | *vam* | *huʃ* | *hic* | *il* | *in* |
| half | debt | intelligence | nothing | tribe | this |
| ياس | يار | يال | رأس | شان | ياس |
| *yas* | *yar* | *yal* | *ra's* | *ʃa'n* | *ya's* |
| lilac | helper | mane | head | dignity | despair |
| دَور | ذَوق | شَوق | فَوج | خَير | سَيل |
| *dōur* | *ʒōuq* | *ʃōuq* | *fōuj* | *xeir* | *seil* |
| round | taste | enthusiasm | battalion | good | flood |
| صَيف | عَيب | مَيل | | | |
| *seif* | *eib* | *meil* | | | |
| summer | fault | inclination | | | |

# PART I

**3**

## LESSON I

### The Indefinite ی -i. The Personal Pronouns. The Demonstrative Pronouns.

1. There is no definite or indefinite article in Persian.[1] Broadly speaking, a noun becomes indefinite by the addition of ی -i, e.g.

کتاب *ketab*, (the) book.

کتابی *ketabi*, a book.

2. (a) If the noun ends in the 'silent' *h* preceded by *e*, the Indefinite ی -i is not written. The sign ٔ known as *hamze* is written over the 'silent' *h*,[2] e.g.

پنجره *panjare*, (the) window.

پنجرهٔ *panjarei*, a window.

The sign ٔ is usually omitted in writing, the reader being expected to know from the context whether the word is definite or indefinite. (See also para. 15 (e) below.)

(b) The Indefinite ی -i is not added to a word ending in ی i; thus صندلی *sandali* is used to mean '(the) chair' or 'a chair'.

(c) If the noun ends in ا *a* or و *u* a *hamze* over a bearer is inserted between the final ا *a* or و *u* and the Indefinite ی -i to mark the transition between the final long vowel of the noun and the Indefinite ی -i. It will not be represented in the transcription, e.g.

پا *pa*, (the) foot.

پائی *pai*, a foot.

پارو *paru*, (the) wooden spade.

پاروئی *parui*, a wooden spade.

[1] The student must not expect the application of the terms 'definite' and 'indefinite' in Persian to correspond exactly with their application in English.

[2] Words ending in ه *h* take the Indefinite ی in the usual way, e.g.

راه *rah*, (the) road.

راهی *rahi*, a road.

3. If two or more nouns are joined by و *va* 'and' and are indefinite, the Indefinite ی *-i* is added to the final one only, the group being regarded as a syntactical whole, e.g.

كتاب و مداد و قلمی بمن داد   *ketab va medad va qalami be man dad*, He gave a book, a pencil and a pen to me.

4. A noun qualified by the Interrogative Adjective چه *ce* 'what' usually takes the Indefinite ی *-i*, e.g.

چه كتابی   *ce ketabi*, what book?

5. The Indefinite ی *-i* never carries the stress.

6. Persian has no inflexions. When a *definite* noun is the direct object of the verb, this is marked by the addition of the suffix را *-ra*, e.g.

كتابرا بمن داد   *ketabra be man dad*, He gave the book to me.

But

كتابی بمن داد   *ketabi be man dad*, He gave a book to me.[1]

7. If more than one definite noun forms the direct object of the verb, these are regarded as a syntactical whole, and the را *-ra* is placed after the final noun, e.g.

مداد و قلمرا بمن داد   *medad va qalamra be man dad*, He gave the pen and the pencil to me.

8. را *-ra* never carries the stress.

9. The Personal Pronouns are:

| | | | |
|---|---|---|---|
| من | *man*, I. | ما | *ma*, we. |
| تو | *to*,[2] thou. | شما | *ʃoma*, you. |
| او | *u*, he, she.[3] | ايشان | *iʃan*, they.[4] |

[1] There is a third possibility, namely:

كتاب بمن داد   *ketab be man dad*, He gave a book to me.

Here there is no differentiation of number or particularization, whereas in the example above كتابی *ketabi* implies 'some book or other' or 'a particular book, from among the class of articles known as book'. See also Lesson XII, para. 1 (*a*) (iii) and para. 3.

[2] For the pronunciation of تو *to* see Alphabetical Table in Introduction.

[3] There is no gender in Persian. Different words are used to differentiate between male and female animals, or the words نر *nar* or نره *nare* 'male' and ماده *made* 'female' are added before or after the name of the animal, which in the latter case takes the *eʒafe*.

[4] See also Lesson XIV, para. 1 (*a*).

وی *vei* is an alternative form to او *u* but is seldom used in Colloquial Persian.

The Demonstrative Pronoun آن *an* 'that' is used to mean 'it'. Its plurals آنها *anha* and آنان *anan* are used in Colloquial and Literary Persian respectively in place of ایشان *iſan* 'they'.

10. The Personal Pronouns are by their nature definite and consequently take را *-ra* when the direct object of a verb. من *man* 'I' followed by را *-ra* contracts into مرا *mara* 'me' and تو *to* 'thou' into ترا *tora* 'thee'.

11. If the grammatical subject of a sentence is a personal pronoun, this is implicit in the verb and is not usually expressed separately unless it is desired to lay special emphasis on the pronoun.

12. آن *an* 'that' and این *in* 'this' may be either Demonstrative Pronouns or Demonstrative Adjectives. As Demonstrative Pronouns they stand alone, e.g.

آن چیست *an cist*, What is that?

این چیست *in cist*, What is this?

آن *an* and این *in* when used as pronouns may mean 'the former' and 'the latter' respectively.

When used as Demonstrative Adjectives آن *an* and این *in* precede the noun they qualify, e.g.

آن کتاب *an ketab*, that book.

این میز *in miz*, this table.

13. آیا *aya* is a particle used to introduce a question which does not contain an interrogative word, e.g.

آیا این کتاب است *aya in ketab ast*, Is it this book?

In conversation questions which do not contain an interrogative word are usually indicated by a rising intonation at the end of the sentence (see Appendix VI) rather than by the use of آیا *aya*.

14. The normal word order in simple sentences is Subject (unless this is contained in the verb), Object, Indirect Object, Extension, Verb.

15. The following orthographical points should be noted:

   (a) آن *an* 'that' is frequently joined to the following word, provided the initial letter of this is a consonant, e.g.

آنکتاب *an ketab*, that book.

(*b*) The preposition به *be* 'to' is usually joined to the following word, the final ه of به *be* being omitted, e.g.

بمن *be man*, to me.

The following combinations should be noted:

باین *be in*, to this.

بآن *be an*, to that.

باو *be u*, to him, to her.[1]

(*c*) The initial *alef* of است *ast* 'he, she or it is' can be omitted, the ست being joined to the preceding word, provided the final letter of this is not the 'silent' *h*, e.g.

این کتابست *in ketab ast*, This is the book.

If the preceding word ends in ا *a* or و *u*, the initial *alef* of است *ast* is always omitted and the *a* of *ast* elided, e.g.

آنجاست *anjast*, He, she or it is there.

اوست *ust*, It is he, it is she.

Similarly, if است *ast* follows the word تو *to* 'thou' the initial *alef* of است *ast* is sometimes dropped and the *a* of *ast* elided, e.g.

توست *tost*, It is thou.

If است *ast* follows a word ending in ی *i*, the initial *alef* of است *ast* is usually dropped and the *a* of *ast* elided, e.g.

کتابیست *ketabist*, It is a book.

(*d*) چه *ce* 'what' followed by است *ast* is written چیست and pronounced *cist*, e.g.

این چیست *in cist*, What is this?

(*e*) If a noun ending in the 'silent' *h* is made indefinite ای can be written after the word in place of the *hamze* over the 'silent' *h* (see para. 2 (*a*) above), e.g.

پنجرهای *panjarei*, a window.

---

[1] Some writers insert a د *d* between the preposition به *be* and آن *an* این *in*, او *u*, and ایشان *išan*, e.g.

بدان *bedan*, to that.

بدین *bedin*, to this.

بدو *bedu*, to him, to her.

بدیشان *bedišan*, to them.

If such a noun is followed by است *ast* 'is' the *alef* of است *ast* is omitted, e.g.

پنجره‌ایست *panjareist*, It is a window.

16. Word stress falls on the final syllable of nouns and pronouns. Stress is marked in the transcription by an upright stroke preceding the syllable which carries the stress, e.g.

كتاب *ke'tab*, book.

صندلى *sanda'li*, chair.

شما *ʃo'ma*, you.

As stated above, neither the Indefinite ی *-i* nor را *-ra* carries the stress, thus

كتابى *ke'tabi*, a book.

كتابرا *ke'tabra*, the book (acc.).

## VOCABULARY

| | | | |
|---|---|---|---|
| اين | *in*, this. | كاغذ | *kaɣaz̧*, paper. |
| آن | *an*, that; it. | پنجره | *panjare*, window. |
| جا | *ja*, place. | پا | *pa*, foot. |
| اينجا | *inja*, here. | پارو | *paru*, a kind of wooden |
| آنجا | *anja*, there. | | spade. |
| كجا | *koja*, where? | چيز | *ciz̧*, thing. |
| من | *man*, I. | چه | *ce*, what? |
| تو | *to*, thou. | به (بِ) | *be*, to. |
| او | *u*, he, she. | و | *va*, and. |
| ما | *ma*, we. | يا | *ya*, or. |
| شما | *ʃoma*, you. | است | *ast*, he, she or it is. |
| ايشان | *iʃan*, they. | نيست | *nist*, he, she or it is not. |
| آنها | *anha*, those; they. | داد | *dad*, he, she or it gave. |
| ميز | *miz̧*, table. | ديد | *did*, he, she or it saw. |
| صندلى | *sandali*, chair. | بله | *bale*, yes. |
| كتاب | *ketab*, book. | نخير | *naxeir*, no. |
| مداد | *medad*, pencil. | آيا | *aya*, an interrogative par- |
| قلم | *qalam*, pen. | | ticle (see para. 13 above). |

## EXERCISE 1

کتاب اینجاست — مداد آنجاست — آن میز است و این صندلی است — این
قلم است — کجاست — اینجا نیست — این چیست — این کتابی است — چه
کتابی است — کتابی بمن داد — قلمرا بمن داد — شمارا کجا دید — اورا اینجا
دید — این مدادرا بمن داد — میز و صندلی و کتابرا دید — مداد و قلمرا باو
داد — میز و صندلی را بشما داد — مارا دید — صندلی اینجا نیست

## EXERCISE 2

1. This is the book.   2. He saw a book.   3. Where did he see the
pen and the pencil?   4. He gave a book to me.   5. Here is the table.
6. What is this?   7. This is a pen.   8. He gave the pen and the pencil
to you.   9. The book is here and the pencil is there.   10. What is that?
11. That is a chair.   12. Where did he see the book?   13. He saw it
here.   14. He saw you.

## LESSON II

**The Plural of Nouns. The 'Possessive' *ezafe*. Possessive Adjectives
and Pronouns. Interrogative Pronouns. The Verb 'to be'.**

1. The plural of nouns is formed by the addition of ها *-ha* to the
singular, e.g.

مداد   *medad*, pencil.

مدادها   *medadha*, pencils.

2. If a noun denotes a human being the plural can also be formed by
adding ان *-an* to the singular, e.g.

زن   *ʒan*, woman.

زنان   *ʒanan*, women.

In Classical Persian the distinction between the plural in ها *-ha* for
irrational beings and inaminate objects and the plural in ان *-an* for
human beings is usually observed, but in Colloquial Persian there is
a tendency to form the plural of all nouns in ها *-ha*.

3. (*a*) If a noun ends in the 'silent' *h* preceded by *e*, unless it represents the Arabic ة (see Part II, Introduction, para. 11), the 'silent' *h*
is changed into گ *g* before the plural termination ان *-an*, e.g.

بچه   *bacce*, child.

بچگان   *baccegan*, children.

(*b*) If a noun ends in ا *a* a ی *y* is inserted between the final ا *a* and the plural termination ان -*an*, e.g.

گدا    *gada*, beggar.

گدایان    *gadayan*, beggars.

(*c*) If a noun ends in و *u* a ی *y* is inserted between the final و *u* and the plural termination ان -*an*, e.g.

راستگو    *rastgu*, (the) truthful person.

راستگویان    *rastguyan*, truthful persons.

or there is merely an off-glide from the final و *u* to the plural termination ان -*an*, e.g.

بازو    *bazu*, forearm.

بازوان    *bazuan*, forearms.[1]

4. The plural terminations ها -*ha* and ان -*an* carry the stress, e.g.

کتابها    *ketab'ha*, books.

زنان    *za'nan*, women.

5. Possession is shown in Persian by the addition of *e*, known as the *ezafe*, to the thing possessed, which precedes the possessor. The *ezafe* was originally the Old Persian relative pronoun and was an independent word. In New Persian it is an enclitic. It is not represented in writing unless the word to which it is added ends in ا *a* or و *u* (see para. 7 below), e.g.

کتاب آن مرد    *ketabe an mard*, that man's book.

باغ منزل    *baye manzel*, the garden of the house.

If the direct object of a verb is definite and formed by two or more words connected by the 'possessive' *ezafe*, را -*ra* is added after the final word in the group, e.g.

پسر آن مردرا دید    *pesare an mardra did*, He saw that man's son.

6. If the noun to which the *ezafe* is added ends in the 'silent' *h* or in ی *i* the semi-vowel *y* is inserted in pronunciation between the final *e* or *i* and the *e* of the *ezafe* but is not represented in writing. A *hamze* is sometimes written over the 'silent' *h* or the ی *i* to represent the *ezafe*, but is usually omitted, e.g.

بچه این زن    *bacceye in zan*, this woman's child.

صندلی آن مرد    *sandaliye an mard*, that man's chair.

[1] See Lesson XII, para. 5.

**7.** If the noun to which the *eʒafe* is added ends in ١ *a* or و *u*, the *eʒafe* is written as ى and in pronunciation the semi-vowel *y* is inserted between the final *a* or *u* of the word and the *e* of the *eʒafe*, e.g.

كتابهاى آن مرد    *ketabhaye an mard*, the books of that man.

بازوى اين زن    *baʒuye in ʒan*, this woman's forearm.

**8.** The *eʒafe* never carries the stress, e.g.

باغ منزل    *'baye man'ʒel*, the garden of the house.

**9.** The English Possessive Adjectives can be translated by placing the Personal Pronoun after the noun qualified by the English Possessive Adjective and adding the *eʒafe* to the noun, e.g.

كتاب من    *ketabe man*, my book (lit. the book of me).

اسب شما    *asbe ʃoma*, your horse.

**10.** The English Possessive Pronoun is translated by the Personal Pronoun preceded by the word مال *mal*,[1] to which the *eʒafe* is added, e.g.

اين كتاب مال من است    *in ketab male man ast*, This book is mine.

But    اين كتاب من است    *in ketabe man ast*, This is my book.

**11.** مال *mal* is also used to express the possessive case of nouns but only when this case is used pronominally, e.g.

اين اسب مال آن مرد است    *in asb male an mard ast*, This horse is that man's (belongs to that man).

باغ مال پسر اوست    *bay male pesare ust*, The garden is his son's (belongs to his son).

**12.** كه *ke* and كى *ki* are Interrogative Pronouns meaning 'who'. كى *ki* forms a plural كيها *kiha*. Both كه *ke* and كى *ki* take را *-ra*; كه *ke* followed by را *-ra* contracts into كرا *kera*, e.g.

كرا ديد    *kera did*, Whom did he see?

While كى *ki* is more frequently used in Colloquial Persian than كه *ke*, the latter is more frequently written.

**13.** Before describing the Verb and the formation of tenses it will be convenient to introduce here certain tenses of the verb بودن *budan* 'to

---

[1] مال *mal* means 'possessions', 'wealth'. It is also used to mean 'horse', 'mule' or 'donkey'. از آن *aʒ an* (lit. 'from those of', with an implication of plurality), with the *eʒafe*, can be substituted for مال *mal* in the cases covered by paras. 10 and 11.

be' (Present Stem باش *baʃ*), which is used to conjugate the verb (for stress on verb forms see below Lesson III, para. 9 and Lesson IV, para. 8):

### PRETERITE

| | | | |
|---|---|---|---|
| 1st pers. sing. | بودم | *budam* | ⎫ |
| 2nd pers. sing. | بودی | *budi* | ⎬ I was, etc. |
| 3rd pers. sing. | بود | *bud* | ⎭ |
| 1st pers. pl. | بودیم | *budim* | ⎫ |
| 2nd pers. pl. | بودید | *budid* | ⎬ We were, etc. |
| 3rd pers. pl. | بودند | *budand* | ⎭ |

### PAST PARTICIPLE

بوده *bude*, been.

### PRESENT

| | | | |
|---|---|---|---|
| 1st pers. sing. | میباشم | *mibaʃam* | ⎫ |
| 2nd pers. sing. | میباشی | *mibaʃi* | ⎬ I am, etc. |
| 3rd pers. sing. | میباشد | *mibaʃad* | ⎭ |
| 1st pers. pl. | میباشیم | *mibaʃim* | ⎫ |
| 2nd pers. pl. | میباشید | *mibaʃid* | ⎬ We are, etc. |
| 3rd pers. pl. | میباشند | *mibaʃand* | ⎭ |

### SUBJUNCTIVE PRESENT

| | | | |
|---|---|---|---|
| 1st pers. sing. | باشم | *baʃam* | ⎫ |
| 2nd pers. sing. | باشی | *baʃi* | ⎬ I may be, etc.[1] |
| 3rd pers. sing. | باشد | *baʃad* | ⎭ |
| 1st pers. pl. | باشیم | *baʃim* | ⎫ |
| 2nd pers. pl. | باشید | *baʃid* | ⎬ We may be, etc. |
| 3rd pers. pl. | باشند | *baʃand* | ⎭ |

For the formation of the other tenses of بودن *budan* see Lessons III and IV.

---

[1] There is an alternative form:

| | | | | | | |
|---|---|---|---|---|---|---|
| 1st pers. sing. | بوم | *bovam.* | | 1st pers. pl. | بویم | *bovim.* |
| 2nd pers. sing. | بوی | *bovi.* | | 2nd pers. pl. | بوید | *bovid.* |
| 3rd pers. sing. | بود | *bovad.* | | 3rd pers. pl. | بوند | *bovand.* |

This is not used in Colloquial Persian. See also Lesson IV, 1 (*d*).

14. The Negative is formed by adding the prefix نه *na-* to the positive, e.g.

نبودم   *nabudam*, I was not.

نمیباشم   *namibaſam*, I am not.

نباشم   *nabaſam*, I may not be.

15. The Present of the verb 'to be' can also be formed:

(a) By the addition of the following personal endings to the preceding word, except in the 3rd pers. sing., for which است *ast* 'is' is used:

| | | |
|---|---|---|
| 1st pers. sing.   (ا)م   *-am*, I am, etc. | 1st pers. pl.   (ا)ع   *-im*. | |
| 2nd pers. sing.   (ا)ی   *-i*. | 2nd pers. pl.   (ا)ید   *-id*. | |
| [3rd pers. sing.   (ا)ست   *ast*.] | 3rd pers. pl.   (ا)ند   *-and*. | |

If the personal endings are added to a word ending in the 'silent' *h*, the *alef* is written, e.g. بچهام   *bacce am*, I am a child.

In all other cases the *alef* of the personal ending is omitted, e.g.

مردید   *mard id*, You are a man.

The 2nd pers. sing. personal ending added to a word ending in the 'silent' *h* can also be represented by a *hamʒe* over the 'silent' *h*, e.g.

بچۀ   *bacce i*, Thou art a child.

If the personal endings other than the 1st pers. sing. and the 3rd pers. pl. are added to a word ending in ا *a* or و *u* a *hamʒe* over a bearer is inserted between the final ا *a* or و *u* and the personal ending, e.g.

شمائید   *ſoma id*, it is you (lit. 'you are').

(b) By the following form which stands alone:

| | | |
|---|---|---|
| 1st pers. sing.   هستم   *hastam*. | 1st pers. pl.   هستیم   *hastim*. | |
| 2nd pers. sing.   هستی   *hasti*. | 2nd pers. pl.   هستید   *hastid*. | |
| 3rd pers. sing.   هست   *hast*. | 3rd pers. pl.   هستند   *hastand*. | |

16. The Negative of the forms in para. 15 above is formed as follows[1]:

(a)  1st pers. sing.   نیم   *nayam* ⎫
     2nd pers. sing.   نئ   *nai*    ⎬ I am not, etc.
     3rd pers. sing.   نیست   *nist* ⎭

     1st pers. pl.   نئیم   *naim*  ⎫
     2nd pers. pl.   نئید   *naid*  ⎬ We are not, etc.
     3rd pers. pl.   نیند   *nayand* ⎭

[1] They are not enclitic.

(b)      1st pers. sing.     نیستم    *nistam* ⎫
        2nd pers. sing.    نیستی     *nisti*  ⎬ I am not, etc.
        3rd pers. sing.    نیست      *nist*  ⎭

        1st pers. pl.      نیستیم    *nistim* ⎫
        2nd pers. pl.     نیستید    *nistid* ⎬ We are not, etc.
        3rd pers. pl.     نیستند    *nistand* ⎭

The forms in (a), with the exception of the 3rd pers. sing., are rare.

17. If که *ke* or کی *ki* 'who' is followed by the Present of the verb 'to be' given in para. 15 (b) above the following contractions may take place:

        1st pers. sing.     کیستم    *kistam* ⎫
        2nd pers. sing.    کیستی     *kisti*  ⎬ Who am I? etc.
        3rd pers. sing.    کیست      *kist*  ⎭

        1st pers. pl.      کیستیم    *kistim* ⎫
        2nd pers. pl.     کیستید    *kistid* ⎬ Who are we? etc.
        3rd pers. pl.     کیستند    *kistand* ⎭

18. The various forms of the Present of the verb 'to be' are, broadly speaking, interchangeable. هست *hast*, can be emphatic, and is used to mean 'there is' as well as 'he, she or it is'.

After a word ending in ی -*i* the forms هستی *hasti*, هستیم *hastim* and هستید *hastid* are used in preference to ی -*i*, ایم -*im* and اید -*id*, e.g.

        ایرانی هستید    *irani hastid*, You are a Persian.

19. A plural subject, if it denotes rational beings, takes a plural verb. A plural subject denoting irrational beings or inanimate objects takes a singular verb, e.g.

    پدر و مادر من اینجا هستند    *pedar va madare man inja hastand*, My father and mother are here.

    برادران شما آنجا بودند    *baradarane ʃoma anja budand*, Your brothers were there.

    مداد و قلم کجاست    *medad va qalam kojast*, Where are the pencil and pen?

    کتابها آنجاست    *ketabha anjast*, The books are there.

This distinction, however, is less carefully observed in Modern than in Classical Persian.

20. The word منزل *manʒel* when used to mean 'home' or 'at home' does not usually take a preposition, e.g.

منزل بودم *manʒel budam*, I was at home.

## Vocabulary

مرد  *mard*, man.

زن  *ʒan*, woman.

پسر  *pesar*, boy; son.

دختر  *doxtar*, girl; daughter.

پدر  *pedar*, father.

مادر  *madar*, mother.

برادر  *baradar*, brother.

خواهر  *xahar*, sister.

بچه  *bacce*, *bace*, child.

کار  *kar*, work.

اطاق  *otaq*, room.

منزل  *manʒel*, house; home.

باغ  *baɣ*, garden.

گدا  *gada*, beggar.

شهر  *ʃahr*, city, town.

بازو  *baʒu*, forearm.

راستگو  *rastgu*, truthful; a truthful person.

ایرانی  *irani*, Persian (adj.); a Persian.

اسب  *asb*, horse.

سگ  *sag*, dog.

گربه  *gorbe*, cat.

گاو  *gav*, ox.[1]

بیرون  *birun*, out, outside; when used as a preposition it takes the *eʒafe*.

در  *dar*, in (prep.); door.

تو  *tu*, in; inner; inside; when used as a preposition it normally takes the *eʒafe*, thus becoming توی *tuye*.

رو  *ru*, on; outer; when used as a preposition meaning 'on' it precedes the noun it governs and takes the *eʒafe*, thus becoming روی *ruye*.

که  *ke* } who (interrog.).
کی  *ki* }

کدام  *kodam*, which (of two or more; interrog.).

ولی  *vali*, but.

دارد  *darad*, he, she or it has.

آمد  *amad*, he, she or it came.

رفت  *raft*, he, she or it went.

[1] گاو *gav* is also used for cow, though strictly speaking a cow is ماده‌گاو *made gav*.

## EXERCISE 3

این منزل ماست — آن باغ مال کیست — آن باغ مال من است — پدر
این بچه کجاست — این اطاق پنجره دارد — کتاب شما روی میز است — مردی
بمنزل ما آمد — پسر او بیرون است — دختر من گربه دارد — آنهارا در باغ
دید — این زن کتابی بمن داد — کجا رفت — بشهر رفت — کتاب و مداد روی
میز است — مادر شما بمنزل ما آمد — اسب او توی باغ است — این منزل
مال ماست

## EXERCISE 4

1. The room has a door and a window. 2. Whose is this garden?
3. The garden is his. 4. He has a horse. 5. A woman came into our
room. 6. The horse and the cow are in the garden. 7. The child is
in your room. 8. The pen and the pencil are on the table. 9. He came
to your house. 10. Your brother went to the town. 11. He saw the
child in the garden. 12. He gave your book to me. 13. This is their
house.

## LESSON III

### The Infinitive. Tenses formed from the Past Stem. Adjectives.

1. The Infinitive of the verb ends in تن *tan*, دن *dan* or یدن *idan*, e.g.

کشتن    *koštan*, to kill.

آوردن    *avardan* (*avordan*), to bring.

خریدن    *xaridan*, to buy.

2. The Short Infinitive is the Infinitive from which the ending
ن -*an* has fallen away, e.g.

کشت *košt*.    آورد *avard* (*avord*).    خرید *xarid*.

The Past Stem is identical with the Short Infinitive and also with the
3rd pers. sing. of the Preterite.

3. The Present Stem of Regular Verbs is found by cutting off the final
تن *tan*, دن *dan* or یدن *idan* of the Infinitive, e.g.

کش *koš*.    آور *avar* (*avor*).    خر *xar*.

Irregular Verbs undergo certain other changes in the formation of the Present Stem. Their irregularity is confined to the changes made in the Present Stem.[1]

4. The following are formed from the Past Stem:

(a) The Past Participle by the addition of the 'silent' *h*, preceded by *e*, e.g. خريده *xaride*, bought.

(b) The Preterite by the addition of the personal endings, except in the 3rd pers. sing., which is identical with the Past Stem, e.g.

| | | | |
|---|---|---|---|
| 1st pers. sing. | خريدم | *xaridam* | ⎫ |
| 2nd pers. sing. | خريدى | *xaridi* | ⎬ I bought, etc. |
| 3rd pers. sing. | خريد | *xarid* | ⎭ |
| 1st pers. pl. | خريديم | *xaridim* | ⎫ |
| 2nd pers. pl. | خريديد | *xaridid* | ⎬ We bought, etc. |
| 3rd pers. pl. | خريدند | *xaridand* | ⎭ |

(c) The Imperfect by the addition of the personal endings as in the Preterite and the prefix می *mi-*, e.g.

| | | | |
|---|---|---|---|
| 1st pers. sing. | میخريدم | *mixaridam* | ⎫ |
| 2nd pers. sing. | میخريدى | *mixaridi* | ⎬ I was buying, used to buy, etc. |
| 3rd pers. sing. | میخريد | *mixarid* | ⎭ |
| 1st pers. pl. | میخريديم | *mixaridim* | ⎫ |
| 2nd pers. pl. | میخريديد | *mixaridid* | ⎬ We were buying, used to buy, etc. |
| 3rd pers. pl. | میخريدند | *mixaridand* | ⎭ |

If the verb has an initial *alef* with a short vowel, the initial *alef* drops out after the prefix می *mi-*, e.g.

میفتادم *mioftadam*, I was falling (from افتادن *oftadan* 'to fall'),

or the می may be written separately, in which case the initial *alef* does not drop out, e.g.

می افتادم *mioftadam*, I was falling.

---

[1] A list of irregular verbs will be found in Appendix I. In the vocabularies to the lessons the present stem of irregular verbs is given in brackets, but the present stem of irregular compound verbs will not be given if the verbal part of the compound has already been given as a simple verb.

If the verb has an initial آ *a*, the *madde* of the *alef* drops out after می *mi-*, e.g.

میامدم    *miamadam*, I was coming (from آمدن *amadan* 'to come').

If the verb has an initial ای *i*, the می *mi-* must be written separately, e.g.

می ایستادم    *miistadam*, I was standing (from ایستادن *istadan* 'to stand').

(*d*) The Perfect by the Past Participle followed by the Present of the verb 'to be' (see Lesson II, para. 15 (*a*) above), e.g.

| | | | |
|---|---|---|---|
| 1st pers. sing. | خریده‌ام | *xaride am* | I have bought, etc. |
| 2nd pers. sing. | خریده‌ئ | *xaride i* | |
| 3rd pers. sing. | خریده‌است | *xaride ast* | |

| | | | |
|---|---|---|---|
| 1st pers. pl. | خریده‌ایم | *xaride im* | We have bought, etc. |
| 2nd pers. pl. | خریده‌اید | *xaride id* | |
| 3rd pers. pl. | خریده‌اند | *xaride and* | |

The *hamze* in the 2nd pers. sing. is often omitted in writing.

(*e*) The Pluperfect by the Past Participle followed by the Preterite of the verb 'to be' (see Lesson II, para. 13), e.g.

| | | | |
|---|---|---|---|
| 1st pers. sing. | خریده بودم | *xaride budam* | I had bought, etc. |
| 2nd pers. sing. | خریده بودی | *xaride budi* | |
| 3rd pers. sing. | خریده بود | *xaride bud* | |

| | | | |
|---|---|---|---|
| 1st pers. pl. | خریده بودیم | *xaride budim* | We had bought, etc. |
| 2nd pers. pl. | خریده بودید | *xaride budid* | |
| 3rd pers. pl. | خریده بودند | *xaride budand* | |

(*f*) The Subjunctive Past by the Past Participle followed by the Subjunctive Present of the verb 'to be' (see Lesson II, para. 13), e.g.

| | | | |
|---|---|---|---|
| 1st pers. sing. | خریده باشم | *xaride baʃam* | I may have bought, etc. |
| 2nd pers. sing. | خریده باشی | *xaride baʃi* | |
| 3rd pers. sing. | خریده باشد | *xaride baʃad* | |

| | | | |
|---|---|---|---|
| 1st pers. pl. | حریده باشیم | *xaride baʃim* | We may have bought, etc. |
| 2nd pers. pl. | خریده باشید | *xaride baʃid* | |
| 3rd pers. pl. | خریده باشند | *xaride baʃand* | |

18 [III, 4–7]

(g) The Future by the Indicative Present[1] of خواستن *xastan* 'to desire' (Present Stem خواه *xah*) without the می *mi-*, followed by the Short Infinitive, e.g.

| | | | |
|---|---|---|---|
| 1st pers. sing. | خواهم خرید | *xaham xarid* | ⎫ |
| 2nd pers. sing. | خواهی خرید | *xahi xarid* | ⎬ I shall buy, etc. |
| 3rd pers. sing. | خواهد خرید | *xahad xarid* | ⎭ |
| 1st pers. pl. | خواهیم خرید | *xahim xarid* | ⎫ |
| 2nd pers. pl. | خواهید خرید | *xahid xarid* | ⎬ We shall buy, etc. |
| 3rd pers. pl. | خواهند خرید | *xahand xarid* | ⎭ |

5. The Negative of the verbal forms in para. 4 above is formed by adding the prefix نه *na-* to the main verb, except in the Future, when it is prefixed to the auxiliary verb, e.g.

نخریدم *naxaridam*, I did not buy.

نمیخریدم *namixaridam*, I was not buying.

نخریدهام *naxaride am*, I have not bought.

نخریده بودم *naxaride budam*, I had not bought.

نخریده باشم *naxaride bafam*, I may not have bought.

نخواهم خرید *naxaham xarid*, I shall not buy.

6. If the verb has an initial آ *a*, a ی (ـِ) *y* is inserted between the negative prefix and the آ *a* of the verb, which loses its *madde*, e.g.

نیامد *nayamad*, He did not come (from آمدن *amadan* 'to come').

If the verb has an initial *alef* followed by ی *i*, the *alef* is retained after the negative prefix, e.g.

نایستاد *naistad*, He did not stand (from ایستادن *istadan* 'to stand').

If the verb has an initial *alef* with a short vowel a ی (ـِ) *y* is inserted after the negative prefix and the initial *alef* drops out, e.g.

نیفتاد *nayoftad*, He did not fall (from افتادن *oftadan* 'to fall').

7. The verb داشتن *daftan* 'to have, possess' forms its Imperfect without the prefix می *mi-*. Its Imperfect is thus identical with its Preterite, e.g.

داشتم *daftam*, I had, or I was having.

---

[1] See Lesson IV, para. 1 (c).

Certain Compound Verbs formed with داشتن *daſtan* (see Lesson IX) form their Imperfect in the usual way.

8. The verb بودن *budan* 'to be' also forms its Imperfect without the prefix می *mi-*. The Subjunctive Past of بودن *budan* is seldom used.

9. (*a*) Stress in the affirmative verbal forms in para. 4 above is carried on the final syllable of the main verb where there is no prefix, except in the Future, when the stress falls on the final syllable of the auxiliary verb. Where there is a prefixed می *mi-* this carries the stress. E.g.

| خریدم | *xari'dam*, I bought. |
| میخریدم | *'mixaridam*, I was buying. |
| خریده‌ام | *xari'de am*, I have bought. |
| خریده بودم | *xari'de budam*, I had bought. |
| خریده باشم | *xari'de baſam*, I may have bought. |
| خواهم خرید | *xa'ham xarid*, I shall buy. |

(*b*) Stress in the negative verbal forms is carried on the negative prefix, e.g.

| نخریدم | *'naxaridam*, I did not buy. |
| نمیخریدم | *'namixaridam*, I was not buying. |
| نخریده ام | *'naxaride am*, I have not bought. |
| نخریده بودم | *'naxaride budam*, I had not bought. |
| نخریده باشم | *'naxaride baſam*, I may not have bought. |
| نخواهم خرید | *'naxaham xarid*, I shall not buy. |

10. Adjectives normally follow the noun they qualify, an *eʒafe* being added to the noun, e.g.

کتاب بزرگ   *ketabe boʒorg*, the big book.

Adjectives do not take the plural ending,[1] e.g.

مردان خوب   *mardane xub*, good men.

---

[1] Thus آن *an* 'that' and این *in* 'this' when used as demonstrative adjectives do not take the plural ending. When used as demonstrative pronouns they take the plural endings ها *-ha* or ان *-an*, e.g.

اینها   *inha*, these.
آنها   *anha* those.

11. The 'qualifying' *eȥafe* follows the same rules as those given in Lesson II, paras. 6 and 7 for the 'possessive' *eȥafe* if the word to which it is added ends in the 'silent' *h*, ی *i*, ا *a* or و *u*, e.g.

         کتابهای بزرگ    *ketabhaye boȥorg*, big books.

         صندلی نو    *sandaliye nōu*, the new chair.

         بچه کوچك    *bacceye kucek*, the small child.

         پاروی نو    *paruye nōu*, the new spade.

12. If more than one adjective qualifies a noun, the 'qualifying' *eȥafe* is added to each adjective except the final one, e.g.

         کتاب بزرگ نو    *ketabe boȥorge nōu*, the big new book.

13. The noun and its attributes are regarded as a syntactical whole and, therefore, if the noun is indefinite, the Indefinite ی *-i* is added to the final adjective only. Similarly if the noun is definite and the direct object of the verb, the را *-ra* is added to the final adjective, e.g.

         کتاب بزرگی    *ketabe boȥorgi*, a big book.

         کتاب بزرگ نوئی    *ketabe boȥorge nōui*, a big new book.

         کتاب بزرگرا آورد    *ketabe boȥorgra avard*, He brought the big book.

         کتاب بزرگ نورا آورد    *ketabe boȥorge nōura avard*, He brought the big new book.

14. The comparative and superlative degrees are formed by the addition of تر *-tar* and ترین *-tarin* respectively to the positive, e.g.

         بزرگ    *boȥorg*, big.

         بزرگتر    *boȥorgtar*, bigger.

         بزرگترین    *boȥorgtarin*, biggest.

Exceptions are:

         خوب    *xub*, good.

         بهتر    *behtar*, better.

         بهترین    *behtarin*, best.[1]

به *beh* is also used to mean 'better' when it stands alone as the predicate of the verb 'to be'.

---

[1] خوبتر *xubtar* and خوبترین *xubtarin* are also occasionally used.

In the comparative degree of بد *bad* 'bad' the د *d* is sometimes assimilated to the ت *t* of the comparative ending, thus:

بتر    *battar*.

The words کهتر *kehtar* 'smaller, younger' and مهتر *mehtar* 'greater, elder' are seldom used in the positive degree. The Superlative of these forms, کهین *kehin* and مهین *mehin* respectively, is rare also.

15. The comparative follows the noun it qualifies, the *eӡafe* being added to the noun, e.g.

کتاب بزرگتر    *ketabe boӡorgtar*, the bigger book.

کتابهای بزرگتر    *ketabhaye boӡorgtar*, the bigger books.

16. The superlative precedes the noun it qualifies. It does not take the *eӡafe*, e.g.

بهترین کتاب    *behtarin ketab*, the best book.

17. Comparison is expressed by the word از *aӡ* preceding the person or object used as a standard of comparison, e.g.

آن پسر از این دختر بزرگتر است    *an pesar aӡ in doxtar boӡorgtar ast*, That boy is bigger than this girl.

من از شما زودتر آمدم    *man aӡ ʃoma ӡudtar amadam*, I came earlier than you.

Comparison can also be expressed by the word تا *ta* preceding the person or object used as a standard of comparison. This form is used if the person or object used as a standard of comparison is governed by a preposition, e.g.

کتابهای بهتر بمن داد تا باو    *ketabhaye behtar be man dad ta be u*, he gave better books to me than to him.

18. بیشتر *biʃtar* and بیش *biʃ* both mean 'more'. The former is used as a noun, adverb or adjective, e.g.

بیشتر باو دادید    *biʃtar be u dadid*, You gave him more.

اورا بیشتر دوست داشتند    *ura biʃtar dust daʃtand*, They liked him better (more).

مردها بیشتر بودند تا زنها    *mardha biʃtar budand ta ӡanha*, There were more men than women.

When بیشتر *bi∫tar* qualifies a noun it precedes the noun, which is put in the singular, e.g.

بیشتر کتاب داشتید تا او      *bi∫tar ketab da∫tid ta u*, You had more books than he.

بیش *bi∫* is used as a noun, e.g.

بیش از او خوردید      *bi∫ a ̴ u xordid*, You ate more than he.

It can also be used predicatively as an adjective, e.g.

کتابهای او بیش از کتابهای من است      *ketabhaye u bi∫ a ̴ ketabhaye man ast*, His books are more than mine.

بیش از پیش      *bi∫ a ̴ pi∫* means 'more than before', e.g.

اورا بیش از پیش دوست دارد      *ura bi∫ a ̴ pi∫ dust darad*, He likes him better (more) than formerly.

بیشتر *bi∫tar* is also used as a noun meaning 'most', in which case it precedes the noun it qualifies and takes the *e ̴ afe*, e.g.

بیشتر مردها رفته بودند      *bi∫tare mardha rafte budand*, Most of the men had gone.

بیشتر آنها جوان بودند      *bi∫tare anha javan budand*, Most of them were young.

'Most of all' is rendered by بیشتر از همه *bi∫tar a ̴ hame* or از همه بیشتر *a ̴ hame bi∫tar*, e.g.

اورا از همه بیشتر دوست داشتیم      *ura a ̴ hame bi∫tar dust da∫tim*, We liked him best (most) of all.

19. Adjectives are also used as adverbs, e.g.

آنرا گران خرید      *anra geran xarid*, He bought it at a high price (expensively).

20. Adjectives can be strengthened by خیلی *xeïli* or بسیار *besyar* 'very'. These words precede the adjective they qualify, e.g.

این میز خیلی بزرگ است      *in mi ̴ xeïli bo ̴ org ast*, This table is very big.

باغ بسیار بزرگی دارد      *baye besyar bo ̴ orgi darad*, He has a very large garden.

The comparative degree can be similarly strengthened, e.g.

این خیلی بهتر است      *in xeïli behtar ast*, This is much better.

21. زیاد *ʒiad* is used as an adjective, noun or adverb meaning 'much, many, too', or 'too much'. With a negative verb it means 'not very', e.g.

كتابهای زیاد داشت    *ketabhaye ʒiad daʃt*, He had many books.

بمن زیاد دادید    *be man ʒiad dadid*, You gave me too much.

این كتاب زیاد گران است    *in ketab ʒiad geran ast*, This book is too expensive.

این كتاب زیاد خوب نیست    *in ketab ʒiad xub nist*, This book is not very good.

زیاد *ʒiad* may precede the noun it qualifies, in which case the latter is put in the singular, e.g.

زیاد كتاب دارد    *ʒiad ketab darad*, He has many books.

22. Adjectives, like nouns, carry the stress on the final syllable, e.g.

بزرگ    *bo'ʒorg*, big.

بزرگتر    *boʒorg'tar*, bigger.

بزرگترین    *boʒorgta'rin*, biggest.

## VOCABULARY

| | | | |
|---|---|---|---|
| راه | *rah*, road, way. | خوب | *xub*, good. |
| نامه | *name*, letter. | بد | *bad*, bad. |
| بزرگ | *boʒorg*, big. | نو | *noū*, new. |
| كوچك | *kucek*, small. | زود | *ʒud*, early; quick, quickly. |
| جوان | *javan*, young. | دیر | *dir*, late (of time). |
| پیر | *pir*, an old person; old (of persons); پیر مرد *pire mard*, an old man; پیر زن *pire ʒan*, an old woman.[1] | یواش | *yavaʃ*, slow. |
| | | زیاد | *ʒiad*, much, many; too, too much; (with negative verb) not very. |
| مسن | *mosenn*, old, aged. | بسیار | *besyar*, very. |
| كهنه | *kohne*, old, worn-out. | خیلی | *xeīli* very. |
| مریض | *mariʒ*, sick, ill. | چند | *cand*, some; for how much? how many? |
| گران | *geran*, expensive, dear. | چرا | *cera*, why? |
| ارزان | *arʒan*, cheap. | از | *aʒ*, from; than. |

[1] مرد *mard* and زن *ʒan* are used in these expressions to define the sex.

| | | | |
|---|---|---|---|
| همه | hame, all. | گفتن (گو) | goftan (gu), to say. |
| روز | ruz, day. | خریدن | xaridan, to buy. |
| امروز | emruz, to-day. | داشتن | daʃtan (dar), to have, |
| دیروز | diruz, yesterday. | دوست داشتن (دار) | possess; dust daʃtan, to like. |
| پریروز | pariruz, the day before yesterday. | فروختن (فروش) | foruxtan (foruʃ), to sell. |
| افتادن (افت) | oftadan (oft), to fall; rah oftadan, to set out.[1] | رسیدن | rasidan, to arrive; (with the preposition به be) reach. |
| رفتن (رو) | raftan (rav-, rōu), to go; rah raftan, to walk along, about. | کشتن | koʃtan, to kill. |
| آمدن (آ) | amadan (a), to come; zud amadan, to be (come) early. | نوشتن (نویس) | neveʃtan (nevis), to write. |
| | | دیدن (بین) | didan (bin), to see. |
| | | دادن (ده) | dadan (deh), to give. |
| کردن (کن) | kardan (kon), to do; dir kardan, to be (come) late. | ایستادن (ایست) | istadan (ist), to stand (intrans.). |
| | | آوردن | avardan, to bring. |

## EXERCISE 5

کجا رفتید — بمنزل شما رفتیم — این کتابرا چند خریدید — آنرا ارزان
خریدم — این مرد باغرا بآن زن فروخت — نامهٔ باو نوشتم — کرا دیدید — پسر
و دختر شمارا دیدم — بشهر رسیدیم — این گاورا چند فروختید — اینرا گران
فروختم — یواش راه میرفتند — کتابرا باو داد — بمنزل ما آمدند — اسبرا در
باغ دید — اینجا آمدند و مرا دیدند — دختر شما از همه کوچکتر است —
دیروز بیشتر کار کردیم تا امروز — پریروز بشهر رفتیم — منزل شما کجاست —
منزل ما در شهر است — دیروز منزل بودیم

## EXERCISE 6

1. He gave a big book to me.  2. He went to the town.  3. I saw
him the day before yesterday.  4. They bought the house and the
garden.  5. She came slowly.  6. How much did you buy this for?
7. I bought it cheaply.  8. We saw the man, the woman and the children

---

[1] See Lesson IX for Compound Verbs.

yesterday. 9. He was writing a letter to me. 10. We were walking in the garden. 11. Where were you yesterday? 12. I was at home. 13. The woman is older than the man. 14. You had more horses than he. 15. He came early. 16. We were late.


## LESSON IV

Tenses formed from the Present Stem. The Pronominal Suffixes. خود *xod*, خویش *xiſ* and خویشتن *xiſtan*. همین *hamin* and همان *haman*. چون *cun*. چنین *conin* and چنان *conan*. چندان *candin* and چندان *candan*. کسی *kasi* and شخصی *ſaxsi*. هیچ *hic.* طور *tour*.

1. The following forms are derived from the Present Stem of the verb:

(*a*) The Present Participle by the addition of ان *-an*, e.g.

خواهان *xahan*, desiring (from خواستن *xastan* 'to desire, wish', Present Stem خواه *xah*).

This form is not found in all verbs.

(*b*) The Noun of the Agent by adding نده *-ande*, e.g.

فروشنده *foruſande*, seller (from فروختن *foruxtan* 'to sell', Present Stem فروش *foruſ*).

This form is not found in all verbs.

(*c*) The Present by the addition of the personal endings and the prefix می *mi-*, e.g.

| | | | |
|---|---|---|---|
| 1st pers. sing. | میخرم | *mixaram* | ⎫ |
| 2nd pers. sing. | میخری | *mixari* | ⎬ I am buying, etc. |
| 3rd pers. sing. | میخرد | *mixarad* | ⎭ |
| 1st pers. pl. | میخریم | *mixarim* | ⎫ |
| 2nd pers. pl. | میخرید | *mixarid* | ⎬ We are buying, etc. |
| 3rd pers. pl. | میخرند | *mixarand* | ⎭ |

A General Present is formed by the addition of the personal endings, but without the prefix می *mi-*, and is used in Classical Persian for general statements which contain no element of doubt. In Modern Persian the General Present has been confused with the Subjunctive Present (see (*d*) below). The latter, properly speaking, has a prefixed ب *be-*. Modern writers often omit the ب *be-* of the Subjunctive, especially in the case of Compound Verbs, and at times even prefix ﺑ be- to what is properly speaking a General Present. No attempt will be made in the following pages to distinguish between the two tenses; indeed, they have become so confused in modern usage that it would be difficult to do so in all cases.

(*d*) The Subjunctive Present by the addition of the personal endings with or without the prefix ﺑ be- (see above), e.g.

| | | | |
|---|---|---|---|
| 1st pers. sing. | بخرم | *bexaram* | ⎫ |
| 2nd pers. sing. | بخرى | *bexari* | ⎬ I may buy, etc. |
| 3rd pers. sing. | بخرد | *bexarad* | ⎭ |
| 1st pers. pl. | بخريم | *bexarim* | ⎫ |
| 2nd pers. pl. | بخريد | *bexarid* | ⎬ We may buy, etc. |
| 3rd pers. pl. | بخرند | *bexarand* | ⎭ |

The verb بودن *budan* 'to be' does not take ﺑ be-.

The 1st and 3rd pers. sing. and plural of the Subjunctive Present may be used as a Jussive, e.g.

بخرد *bexarad*, Let him buy.

(*e*) The Imperative Singular is formed by the addition of the prefix ﺑ be- to the Present Stem. The plural takes the personal ending ﯿﺪ -*id*, e.g.

بخر *bexar*, Buy (sing.).

بخريد *bexarid*, Buy (pl.).

In compound verbs the prefix ﺑ be- is often omitted, in which case the Imperative Singular is identical with the Present Stem.

The verb بودن *budan* 'to be' does not take ﺑ be-.

2. If the verb has an initial آ *a*, *alef* followed by ى *i*, or *alef* with a short vowel, it follows in the Present the rules given in Lesson III, para. 4 (*c*) concerning the prefixed ﻣﻰ *mi*- of the Imperfect, e.g.

مياورم *miavaram*, I am bringing (from آوردن *avardan* 'to bring').

مى ايستم *miistam*, I am standing (from ايستادن *istadan* 'to stand', Present Stem ايست *ist*).

ميفتم *mioftam*, I am falling (from افتادن *oftadan* 'to fall', Present Stem افت *oft*).

If the verb has an initial آ *a*, a ى *y* is inserted after the prefix ﺑ be- and the *alef* loses its *madde*, e.g.

بيا *beya*, Come (from آمدن *amadan* 'to come', Present Stem آ *a*)

If the verb has an initial *alef* with a short vowel, a ی *y* is inserted after the prefix ِ *be-* and the initial *alef* is dropped, e.g.

بیفتم    beyoftam, I may fall.

If the verb has an initial *alef* followed by ی *i*, the initial *alef* is retained after the prefix ِ *be-*, e.g.

با یستم    beistam, I may stand.

3. If the Present Stem ends in ا *a* or و *u*, a ی *y* is inserted after the final vowel of the Present Stem before the endings of the Present Participle and Noun of the Agent and the personal endings of the 1st pers. sing. and the 3rd pers. sing. and pl. A *hamʒe* is inserted before the personal ending in the 2nd pers. sing. and pl. and the 1st pers. pl. and marks the transition from the final long vowel of the stem to the long vowel of the personal ending. It will not be represented in the transcription. E.g.

شایان   *fayan*, brilliant, fitting, proper (from the defective verb شا یستن *fayestan* 'to be fitting').

گوینده   *guyande*, speaker (from گفتن *goftan* 'to say').

| | | | |
|---|---|---|---|
| 1st pers. sing. | میکویم | *miguyam* | ⎫ |
| 2nd pers. sing. | میکوئی | *migui* | ⎬ I am saying, etc. |
| 3rd pers. sing. | میکوید | *miguyad* | ⎭ |

| | | | |
|---|---|---|---|
| 1st pers. pl. | میکوئیم | *miguim* | ⎫ |
| 2nd pers. pl. | میکوئید | *miguid* | ⎬ We are saying, etc. |
| 3rd pers. pl. | میکویند | *miguyand* | ⎭ |

| | | | |
|---|---|---|---|
| 1st pers. sing. | میایم | *miayam* | ⎫ |
| 2nd pers. sing. | میائی | *miai* | ⎬ I am coming, etc. |
| 3rd pers. sing. | میاید | *miayad* | ⎭ |

| | | | |
|---|---|---|---|
| 1st pers. pl. | میائیم | *miaim* | ⎫ |
| 2nd pers. pl. | میائید | *miaid* | ⎬ We are coming, etc. |
| 3rd pers. pl. | میایند | *miayand* | ⎭ |

4. If the Present Stem ends in و (*av*), this becomes *ōu* in the Imperative Singular, e.g.

بشنو   *befenōu*, hear (from شنیدن *fenidan* 'to hear', Present Stem شنو *fenav*).

28 [IV, 5–8]

**5.** If the Imperative Singular ends in و *ōu* its prefix in some cases becomes *bo*, e.g.

برو *borōu*, Go (from رفتن *raftan*).

بدو *bodōu*, Run (from دویدن *davidan*).

But

بشنو *befenōu*, Hear (from شنیدن *fenidan*).

بشو *befōu*, Become (from شدن *fodan*).

Note also

بگو *bogu* or *begu*, Say (from گفتن *goftan*).

بگذار *bogoʐar* or *begoʐar*, Place, put (from گذاشتن *goʐaftan*).

**6.** The negative of the forms in para. 1 (*c*), (*d*) and (*e*) above is formed by the addition of the prefix ن *na-*. The prefix ب *be-* drops out if the verb is negative, e.g.

نمیخرم *namixaram*, I am not buying.

نخرم *naxaram*, I may not buy.

نخر *naxar*, Do not buy.

The negative of the Imperative can also be formed by the prefix م *ma-*, e.g.

مخر *maxar*, Do not buy.

This form is literary.

If the verb has an initial آ *a*, *alef* followed by ی *i*, or *alef* with a short vowel, it follows the same rules when the negative prefix is added as those set out in Lesson III, para. 6.

**7.** The verb داشتن *daftan* 'to have, possess' forms its Present without the prefix می *mi-*. In Colloquial Persian داشته باش *dafte baf* and داشته باشید *dafte bafid* are used in place of the Imperative دار *dar* and دارید *darid*.

Certain compounds of داشتن *daftan* form their Present and Imperative in the usual way.

**8.** Stress in the verbal forms given above is carried:

(*a*) On the final syllable in the affirmative except where there is a prefixed می *mi-* or ب *be-*. These prefixes always carry the stress, e.g.

خواهان *xa'han*, desiring.

فروشنده *forufan'de*, seller.

میخرم    'mixaram, I am buying.

بخرم    'bexaram ⎫
خرم    xa'ram ⎭ I may buy.

بخر    'bexar, Buy.

(b) On the negative prefix in the negative, e.g.

نمیخرم    'namixaram, I am not buying.

نخرم    'naxaram, I may not buy.

نخر    'naxar ⎫
مخر    'maxar ⎭ Do not buy.

9. The Possessive Adjectives can be translated by Pronominal Suffixes as well as by the method described in Lesson II, para. 9:

م-    -am, my.
ت-    -at, thy.
ش-    -aʃ, -eʃ, his, her, its.
مان-    -eman, our.
تان-    -etan, your.
شان-    -eʃan, their.

These may be added to Nouns and Adjectives, e.g.

کتابم    ketabam, my book.
اسبتان    asbetan, your horse.

If a Pronominal Suffix is added to a word which is the direct object of the verb را -ra is added after the Pronominal Suffix, e.g.

کتابتانرا بمن بدهید    ketabetanra be man bedehid, Give your book to me.

If the Noun qualified by a possessive adjective is also qualified by an adjective or adjectives, the Pronominal Suffix is added to the final adjective, e.g.

دختر کوچکتان    doxtare kuceketan, your small (younger) daughter.

If the Pronominal Suffix refers to more than one noun and these are joined by a conjunction, the Suffix is added to the final noun only, e.g.

پدر و مادرتان    pedar va madaretan, your father and mother.

10. The Pronominal Suffixes are also added to the simple tenses of the verb and prepositions to denote the personal pronouns in the oblique cases,[1] e.g.    زدمش    *ʒadamaʃ*, I hit him.

من همراهش رفتم    *man hamraheʃ raftam*, I went with him.

كجا ديديدش    *koja dididieʃ*, Where did you see him.

The Pronominal Suffixes are never emphatic, whereas the Personal Pronouns may be.

11. If the word to which a Pronominal Suffix is added ends in ا *a* (except in the case of با *ba* 'with') or و *u*, a ى *y* is inserted between the final vowel and the Pronominal Suffix, e.g.

كتابهايم    *ketabhayam*, my books.

زانويتان    *ʒanuyetan*, your knee.

In Colloquial Persian this ى *y* is frequently omitted, especially before ش *-aʃ, -eʃ*, in which case the vowel of the Pronominal Suffix is elided, e.g.

زانوت    *ʒanut*, thy knee.

كتابهاشان    *ketabhaʃan*, their books.

If the word to which a Pronominal Suffix is added ends in ه *e*, an *alef* is written between the final ه *e* and the singular Pronominal Suffixes, e.g.

بچهاش    *bacceaʃ*, his child.

When a plural Pronominal Suffix is added to a word ending in ه *e*, the *e* of the Pronominal Suffix is elided, e.g.

بچهتان    *baccetan*, your child.

12. The Pronominal Suffixes never carry the stress.

13. If the possessive adjective or personal pronoun refers to the subject of the sentence, the word خود *xod*, خويش *xiʃ*[2] or خويشتن *xiʃtan* must be used in the 3rd pers. sing. in place of او *u*[3]; these can also be used in place of من *man*, and تو *to*. E.g.

كتاب خودرا بمن داد    *ketabe xodra be man dad*, He gave his book to me.

---

[1] If the 3rd pers. sing. Pronominal Suffix is added to the preposition به *be* 'to', the ه of به is written and the word is pronounced *beʃ* or more vulgarly *beheʃ*.

[2] خويش *xiʃ* also means 'relation, relative'.

[3] This rule is not always observed in Colloquial Persian.

('His' refers to the subject of the sentence, 'he', and therefore خود *xod* must be used and not او *u*: كتاب اورا بمن داد *ketabe ura be man dad* would mean 'he gave somebody else's book to me'.)

كتاب خودرا باو دادم    *ketabe xodra be u dadam*, I gave my book to him.

خود *xod* and خویش *xiſ* are interchangeable when used in place of the Possessive Adjectives, but خیش *xiſ* is seldom used in Colloquial Persian. خویشتن *xiſtan* can only refer to rational beings. (See also Lesson VIII, para. 16.)

14. خود *xod* is also used as an emphatic particle meaning 'self'. It precedes the word it emphasizes and takes the *eẕafe*, e.g.

خود او بود    *xode u bud*, It was he himself.

خود آن *xode an* and خود این *xode in* mean 'that very' and 'this very' respectively, e.g.

خود آن مرد بود    *xode an mard bud*, It was that very man.

خود *xod* can also follow the word it emphasizes standing in apposition to it without the *eẕafe*, if this word is the subject of the sentence, e.g.

من خود گفتم    *man xod goftam*, I myself said (so).

This latter construction is less common than the former.

The Pronominal Suffixes can be added to خود *xod* when it is used as an emphatic particle, e.g.

خودت برو    *xodat borou*, Go thyself.

خودشان آمدند    *xodeſan amadand*, They came themselves.

خودم کردم    *xodam kardam*, I did (it) myself.

15. خود *xod* is also used with the Pronominal Suffixes and را *-ra* to form a kind of reflexive, e.g.

خودتانرا گول زدید    *xodetanra gul ẕadid*, You deceived yourselves.

In the 3rd. pers. sing. the Pronominal Suffix can be omitted, e.g.

خودرا گول زد    *xodra gul ẕad*, He deceived himself.

16. خود *xod*, خویش *xiſ* and خویشتن *xiſtan* carry the stress; it falls on the final syllable of خویشتن *xiſtan*.

17. The Demonstrative این *in* 'this' and آن *an* 'that' can be
strengthened by هم *ham*,[1] e.g.

همین هفته    *hamin hafte*, this very week.

همان روز    *haman ruz*, that very day.

Note also the use of همین in the following:

همین یکی ماند    *hamin yaki mand*, Only this one remained.

18. چون *cun* 'like' can be contracted and prefixed to the demonstratives این *in* 'this' and آن *an* 'that', e.g.

چنین    *conin*  }
چنان    *conan*  } such, such a one.

چنین *conin* and چنان *conan* are also used to mean 'thus', 'in such
a manner', e.g.

چنین گفت    *conin goft*, He spoke thus.

چنین *conin* and چنان *conan* can be strengthened by the addition of هم
*ham*, e.g.

همچنین آمد و گفت    *hamconin amad va goft*, He came in this way and
spoke (thus).

19. چند *cand* can also be prefixed to the demonstratives این *in* 'this'
and آن *an* 'that', e.g.

چندین    *candin*, several; so much, so many.

چندان    *candan*, so much, so many.

چندین *candin* is used adjectivally and adverbially; when it is used as
an adjective the noun follows and is put in the singular, e.g.

چندین کتاب بمن داد    *candin ketab beman dad*, He gave several
books to me.

چندان *candan* if used with a negative verb means 'not very', 'not
much', e.g.

چندان خوب نبود    *candan xub nabud*, It was not very good.

20. In those of the forms in paras. 17–19 above of which هم *ham* is
one of the component parts, stress can be carried on هم *ham* or on the
final syllable, e.g.

همان    *'haman* or *ha'man*, that very.

همچنین    *'hamconin* or *hamco'nin*, just such as this, just like this.

---

[1] هم *ham* can also stand alone as an emphatic particle. As an adverb it means 'also'.

The other forms in paras. 18 and 19 above carry the stress on the final syllable, e.g.

چندان   *can'dan,* so much, so many.

چنین   *co'nin,* such, such a one.

21. کسی *kasi,* formed from کس *kas* 'person'[1] by the addition of the Indefinite ی *-i,* and شخصی *ʃaxsi,* formed in the same way from شخص *ʃaxs* 'person'[2], are used to mean 'someone, somebody'. With a negative verb they mean 'no one, nobody'. E.g.

کسی هست   *kasi hast,* Is any one there?

کسی نیست   *kasi nist,* No one is there.

22. هیچ *hic* is an adjective meaning 'any'. It precedes the Noun it qualifies. With a negative verb it means 'none, not any'. E.g.

هیچ نان دارید   *hic nan darid,* Have you any bread?

هیچ نان ندارم   *hic nan nadaram,* I have no bread.

In Colloquial Persian هیچ *hic* 'any' tends to be omitted in the affirmative unless it is emphatic, thus نان دارید *nan darid* 'have you any bread', whereas هیچ نان دارید *hic nan darid* would rather mean 'have you any bread whatsoever?'

A noun qualified by هیچ *hic* 'not any' with a negative verb is always put in the singular, e.g.

هیچ بچه ندارد   *hic bacce nadarad,* He has no children.

هیچ کس *hic kas* means 'anyone'. With a negative verb or in answer to a question it means 'no one'. E.g.

هیچ کس آمد   *hic kas amad,* Has any one come?[3]

هیچ کس   *hic kas,* No one.

هیچ کس آنجا نبود   *hic kas anja nabud,* No one was there.

---

[1] The phrase کس و کار *kas o kar* is also used to mean 'household, retainers', e.g.

از کس و کار او بودند   *az kas o kare u budand,* They were some of his retainers (household).

Note also یکی از کسان او   *yaki az kasane u,* one of his people.

[2] شخص *ʃaxs* is also used as an emphatic particle. It precedes the word it emphasizes and takes the *ezafe,* e.g.

شخص او بود   *ʃaxse u bud,* It was he himself.

[3] For the use of the Preterite where the Perfect is used in English, see Lesson XIII, para. 5 (*h*).

هیچ یك *hic yak* means 'any' referring to more than one. With a negative verb it means 'none'. It is usually followed by از *az*, e.g.

هیچ یك از این کتابهارا ندارم    *hic yak az in ketabhara nadaram*, I have none of these books.

هیچ کدام *hic kodam* is an interrogative pronoun meaning 'any' referring to more than one. With a negative verb it means 'none'. It is usually followed by از *az*, or takes the *ezafe*, e.g.

هیچ کدام از آنهارا دیدید    *hic kodam az anhara didid*, Did you see any of them?

هیچ کدام آنها نرفته اند    *hic kodame anha narafte and*, Have none of them gone?

In Colloquial Persian هیچ کدام *hic kodam* is also used as a pronoun (not as an Interrogative), e.g.

هیچ کدام از این اسبها مال او نیست    *hic kodam az in asbha male u nist*, None of these horses are his.

هیچ *hic* is also used as a noun meaning 'anything'. With a negative verb or in answer to a question it means 'nothing'. E.g.

از او هیچ گرفتید    *az u hic gereftid*, Did you take anything from him?

هیچ نگرفتم    *hic nagereftam*, I took nothing.

هیچ *hic* is sometimes used with an affirmative verb to mean 'nothing', e.g.

این همه هیچ است    *in hame hic ast*, All this is nothing.

هیچ *hic* is also used as an adverb to mean 'ever, at all'. With a negative verb it means 'never', e.g.

آنجا هیچ رفته اید    *anja hic rafte id*, Have you ever gone there?

هیچ نرفته ام    *hic narafte am*, I have never gone there.

هیچ وقت *hic vaqt* means 'ever'. With a negative verb or in answer to a question it means 'never', e.g.

هیچ وقت اورا دیده اید    *hic vaqt ura dide id*, Have you ever seen him?

هیچ وقت اورا ندیده ام    *hic vaqt ura nadide am*, I have never seen him.

هیچ *hic* 'anything' and with a negative verb 'nothing' can be strengthened colloquially by the addition of the Indefinite ی *-i*, e.g.

هیچی نخورد    *hici naxord*, He ate (absolutely) nothing.

23. کسی *kasi*, شخصی *ʃaxsi* and هیچی *hici* carry the stress on the first syllable, since the Indefinite ی *-i* never carries the stress.

In compounds formed with هیچ *hic*, the stress falls on هیچ *hic*, e.g.

هیچ کس   '*hic kas*, no one.

24. The word طور *tour* meaning 'way, manner' is used in the following compounds:

چطور   *ce tour*, how (interrog.).

اینطور   *in tour*, in this way, thus.

آنطور   *an tour*, in that way, thus.

همینطور   *hamin tour*, in this very way.

همانطور   *haman tour*, in that very way.

Stress is carried on the first part of the compound, e.g.

چطور   '*ce tour*, how.

اینطور   '*in tour*, in this way.

طور *tour* takes the Indefinite ی *-i* in the following expressions:

طوری نمیشود   *touri namiʃavad*, It will not matter.

طوری نیست   *touri nist*, It does not matter.

## VOCABULARY

| | | | |
|---|---|---|---|
| کلید | *kelid*, key. | دهن | *dahan*, mouth. |
| قهوه | *qahve*, coffee. | بینی | *bini*, nose. |
| چای | *cai*, tea. | لب | *lab*, lip. |
| گوشت | *guʃt*, meat. | دندان | *dandan*, tooth. |
| بازار | *baɣar*, bazaar. | زبان | *ɣaban*, tongue; language. |
| آب | *ab*, water. | انگشت | *angoʃt*, finger. |
| درخت | *daraxt*, tree. | تن | *tan*, body; person. |
| شاخ | *ʃax*, branch; horn (of animal). | خاك | *xak*, dust, earth. |
| برگ | *barg*, leaf. | فارسی | *farsi*, Persian (the language). |
| گل | *gol*, flower. | ایران | *iran*, Persia. |
| صورت | *surat*, face. | رنگ | *rang*, colour. |
| دست | *dast*, hand. | سیاه / مشکی | *siah* / *meʃki* } black. |
| سر | *sar*, head. | سفید | *sefid*, white. |
| چشم | *caʃm*, eye. | | |

قرمز qermeẓ, red.

زرد ẓard, yellow.

سبز sabẓ, green.

آبی abi, blue.

صورتی surati, pink.

خاکی xaki, khaki.

سرد sard, cold.

گرم garm, warm.

داغ daγ, hot.

جوش juʃ, boiling.

برای baraye, for.

با ba, with.

همراه hamrah, together, together with; if used as a preposition it takes the eẓafe, e.g. همراه او hamrahe u, together with him.

گرفتن (گیر) gereftan (gir), to take.

گذاشتن (گذار) goẓaʃtan (goẓar), to place, put.

شنیدن (شنو) ʃenidan (ʃenav-, ʃenou), to hear, listen.

بر داشتن (بر دار) bar daʃtan (bar dar), to take up, away.

ور داشتن (ور دار) var daʃtan (var dar), to take up, away.

زدن (زن) ẓadan (ẓan), to strike.

گول زدن gul ẓadan, to deceive.

آوردن avardan[1], to bring; the Present Stem is formed regularly آور avar or irregularly آر ar.

بردن (بر) bordan (bar), to carry, take, take away.

خوردن xordan, to eat.

شدن (شو) ʃodan (ʃav-, ʃou), to become.

دویدن davidan (dav-, dou), to run.

## EXERCISE 7

این آب سرد است — آب گرم برای من بیاورید — کجا میروید — کلید در باغرا بمن بدهید — همراه پسر و دختر خویش بشهر رفت — کتابرا روی میز بگذار — بچه‌هارا همراه خود ببر — آن پسر آب میخورد و دختر چای — آن کتاب سیاهرا از روی میز بر دارید و باو بدهید — منزل و باغ خودرا فروخت — چای و قهوه و گوشت در شهر خرید — خود آن مردرا دیروز در شهر دیدم — خودشان رفتند — کسی در باغ نبود — اورا چندان زیاد دوست ندارم — هیچی بمن نگفت — هیچ وقت در ایران نبوده‌ام — همین امروز خواهد آمد

[1] Also pronounced avardan.

## EXERCISE 8

1. He saw the child in the garden.   2. He is writing a letter with my pen.   3. He sold his horse yesterday.   4. They are drinking (eating) tea in my room.   5. I shall go to the town tomorrow.   6. Take this book and give it to that man.   7. The children were running in the garden.   8. He has many horses.   9. This book was expensive.   10. He will sell this to me.   11. The pink flower is bigger than the yellow. 12. The leaves of the tree are green.   13. It was not a very good book. 14. He has no children.   15. I did not see anyone.   16. Have you ever been there?   17. He never told me that.

## LESSON V

**Numerals.** خیلی *xeīli.* بسیار *besyar.* یك *yak.* یکی *yaki.* دیگر *digar.* دیگری *digari.* چند *cand.* چندی *candi.* How to express time. How to express age.

1. The numerals are given in the following table. The ordinals are formed from the cardinals by the addition of م *-om.*[1] Figures are read from left to right.

| CARDINAL | ORDINAL | | |
|---|---|---|---|
| یك *yak, yek*[2] | یکم *yakom, yekom*[2] | ١ | 1 |
| دو *do* | دوم *dovvom;* دویم *doyyom*[2] | ٢ | 2 |
| سه *se* | سوم *sevvom;* سیم *seyyom*[2] | ٣ | 3 |
| چهار *cahar* | چهارم *caharom* | ٤ (۴) | 4 |
| پنج *panj* | پنجم *panjom* | ٥ | 5 |
| شش *ʃeʃ* | ششم *ʃeʃom* | ٦ | 6 |
| هفت *haft* | هفتم *haftom* | ٧ | 7 |
| هشت *haʃt* | هشتم *haʃtom* | ٨ | 8 |
| نه *noh* | نهم *nohom* | ٩ | 9 |
| ده *dah* | دهم *dahom* | ١٠ | 10 |
| یازده *yaʒdah* | یازدهم *yaʒdahom* | ١١ | 11 |

---

[1] The ending م *-om* is also added to چند *cand* 'how many', e.g.

چندم ماه است *candome mah ast,* What day of the month is it?

[2] See below, para. 2.

| CARDINAL | ORDINAL | | |
|---|---|---|---|
| دوازده davaχdah | دوازدهم davaχdahom | ١٢ | 12 |
| سیزده siχdah | سیزدهم siχdahom | ١٣ | 13 |
| چهارده cahardah | چهاردهم cahardahom | ١٤ | 14 |
| پانزده panχdah[1] | پانزدهم panχdahom[1] | ١٥ | 15 |
| شانزده ſanχdah[1] | شانزدهم ſanχdahom[1] | ١٦ | 16 |
| هفده hevdah | هفدهم hevdahom | ١٧ | 17 |
| هیجده hijdah[1] | هیجدهم hijdahom[1] | ١٨ | 18 |
| نوزده nuχdah | نوزدهم nuχdahom | ١٩ | 19 |
| بیست bist | بیستم bistom | ٢٠ | 20 |
| بیست و یك bist o yak[2] | بیست و یکم bist o yakom | ٢١ | 21 |
| بیست و دو bist o do | بیست و دوم bist o dovvom | ٢٢ | 22 |
| بیست و سه bist o se | بیست و سوم bist o sevvom | ٢٣ | 23 |
| بیست و چهار bist o cahar | بیست و چهارم bist o caharom | ٢٤ | 24 |
| بیست و پنج bist o panj | بیست و پنجم bist o panjom | ٢٥ | 25 |
| بیست و شش bist o ſeſ | بیست و ششم bist o ſeſom | ٢٦ | 26 |
| بیست و هفت bist o haft | بیست و هفتم bist o haftom | ٢٧ | 27 |
| بیست و هشت bist o haſt | بیست و هشتم bist o haſtom | ٢٨ | 28 |
| بیست و نه bist o noh | بیست و نهم bist o nohom | ٢٩ | 29 |
| سی si | سی‌ام siom | ٣٠ | 30 |
| چهل cehel | چهلم cehelom | ٤٠ | 40 |
| پنجاه panjah | پنجاهم panjahom | ٥٠ | 50 |
| شصت ſast | شصتم ſastom | ٦٠ | 60 |
| هفتاد haftad | هفتادم haftadom | ٧٠ | 70 |
| هشتاد haſtad | هشتادم haſtadom | ٨٠ | 80 |
| نود navad | نودم navadom | ٩٠ | 90 |
| صد sad | صدم sadom | ١٠٠ | 100 |
| صد و یك sad o yak | صد و یکم sad o yakom | ١٠١ | 101 |
| صد و بیست sad o bist | صد و بیست sad o bist | ١٢١ | 121 |
| و یك o yak | و یکم o yakom | | |
| دویست devist | دویستم devistom | ٢٠٠ | 200 |

[1] See below, para. 2.

[2] This و o 'and' is a survival from the Middle Persian uδ and is not the Arabic و va 'and'. It survives in certain other positions, notably in compounds (see Lesson x). In pronunciation it approximates to o (see Introduction, para. 2); in articulation time it approximates to the group e, a, o rather than to the group i, a, u (see Introduction, para. 2).

| CARDINAL | | ORDINAL | | | |
|---|---|---|---|---|---|
| سیصد | si sad | سیصدم | si sadom | ۳۰۰ | 300 |
| چهار صد | cahar sad | چهار صدم | cahar sadom | ٤۰۰ | 400 |
| پانصد[1] | pansad[1] | پانصدم[1] | pansadom[1] | ۵۰۰ | 500 |
| شش صد | ʃeʃ sad | شش صدم | ʃeʃ sadom | ٦۰۰ | 600 |
| هفت صد | haft sad | هفت صدم | haft sadom | ۷۰۰ | 700 |
| هشت صد | haʃt sad | هشت صدم | haʃt sadom | ۸۰۰ | 800 |
| نه صد | noh sad | نه صدم | noh sadom | ۹۰۰ | 900 |
| هزار | haʒar | هزارم | haʒarom | ۱۰۰۰ | 1,000 |
| هزار و یك | haʒar o yak | هزار و یكم | haʒar o yakom | ۱۰۰۱ | 1,001 |
| هزار و بیست | haʒar o bist | هزار و یست و | haʒar o bist o | ۱۰۲۱ | 1,021 |
| و یك | o yak | یكم | yakom | | |
| هزار و صد | haʒar o sad | هزار و صد و | haʒar o sad o | ۱۱۲۱ | 1,121 |
| و بیست و یك | o bist o yak | بیست و یكم | bist o yakom | | |
| دو هزار | do haʒar | دو هزارم | do haʒarom | ۲۰۰۰ | 2,000 |
| ملیون | meliun | | | | 1,000,000 |
| صفر | sefr | | | ۰ | 0 |

2. The Arabic word اول *avval* is usually substituted for the Persian ordinal یكم *yakom*, when this stands alone, e.g.

شب اول    *ʃabe avval*, the first night.

دو *do* 'two' and سه *se* 'three' form their ordinals irregularly, as follows: دوم *dovvom* and سوم *sevvom* respectively. دویم *doyyom* and سیم *seyyom* are alternative forms.

For the pronunciation of دو *do* 'two' and شش *ʃeʃ* 'six' see Introduction, alphabetical table and para. 2 (*b*).

*yek* and *yekom* tend to be used rather than *yak* and *yakom*, and *yeki* rather than *yaki* (see below, paras. 6, 19 and 20).

چهار *cahar*, both standing alone and in compounds, is often contracted into *car*.

The first vowel of پانزده 'fifteen' and شانزده 'sixteen' and پانصد 'five hundred' is pronounced *u* or as a nasalized vowel intermediate between *a* and *o*.

هیجده *hijdah* 'eighteen' is usually pronounced *hejdah* or *heʒdah*.

The *f* of هفده is assimilated to the following *d* and becomes *v*, thus *hevdah*; it is also pronounced *hivdah*.

[1] See below, para. 2.

3. 'Once', 'twice', etc., are translated by the cardinal numbers followed by بار bar, دفعه daf'e or مرتبه martabe, 'time', e.g.

يك دفعه   yak daf'e, once.

صد بار   sad bar, a hundred times.

دو مرتبه   do martabe, twice.

'Twice as much', 'twice as many', etc., are translated by the cardinal number followed by برابر, barabar 'equal', e.g.

دو برابر   do barabar, twice as much.

عده ما چهار برابر شد   eddeye ma cahar barabar ʃod, Our number became four times as many.

4. Multiplicatives are formed by the addition of گانه -gane to the cardinal, e.g.

دوگانه dogane, double.   سه گانه segane, triple.

5. لا la is used to express '-fold', e.g.

دو لا   do la, double (= two-fold).

سه لا   se la, triple (= three-fold).

6. Distributives are formed by repeating the cardinal with or without به be in between, e.g.

سه بسه   se be se, three by three.

يك yak 'one' takes the Indefinite ی -i when used as a distributive, e.g.

يكی يكی   yaki yaki, one by one.

The forms يكايك yakayak and يگان يگان yagan yagan 'one by one' are obsolete.

7. Recurring numerals are expressed as follows:

يك روز در ميان   yak ruz dar mian, (on) alternate days.

شش روز بشش روز   ʃeʃ ruz be ʃeʃ ruz, every six days.

هفت روز يك بار   haft ruz yak bar, once in seven days.

8. Approximate numbers are expressed as follows:

دو سه   do se, two or three.

چهار پنج   cahar panj, four or five.

هفت هشت   haft haʃt seven or eight.

ده دوازده   dah davazdah, ten or twelve.

9. The Arabic forms are often used to express fractions (see Part II, Lesson XXI, para. 7). Fractions are also expressed by the cardinal numbers in apposition, the denominator preceding the numerator, e.g.

سه يك *se yak*, $\frac{1}{3}$;     چهار يك *cahar yak*, $\frac{1}{4}$;

پنج يك *panj yak*, $\frac{1}{5}$;

or by the cardinal of the numerator preceding the ordinal of the denominator, e.g.

سه پنجم *se panjom*, $\frac{3}{5}$.

نيم *nim* means 'half'. In combinations such as 'one and a half', etc., نيم *nim* 'half' follows the noun qualified by the numeral, e.g.

يك ساعت و نيم     *yak sa'at o nim*, one hour and a half.

شش صفحه و نيم     *ſeſ safhe o nim*, six pages and a half.

ربع *rob'* 'quarter' takes a similar construction, e.g.

پنج صفحه و ربع     *panj safhe o rob'*, five pages and a quarter.

10. Percentage is expressed as follows:

صدی ده     *sadi dah*, 10%.

ده در صد     *dah dar sad*, 10%.

11. اند *and* is used to express 'odd' with numbers above nineteen, e.g.

بيست و اند     *bist o and*, twenty odd.

12. Arithmetical operations are performed as follows:
Multiplication:

دو دو تا ميشود چهار تا     *do do ta miſavad cahar ta*, $2 \times 2 = 4$

Division:

دوازده تقسيم بر سه ميشود چهار     *davaʒdah taqsim bar se miſavad cahar*, $12 \div 3 = 4$.

Addition:

شش باضافه شش مساوی است با دوازده     *ſeſ be eʒafeye ſeſ mosavist ba davaʒdah*, $6 + 6 = 12$.

Subtraction:

نه منهای[1] پنج مساوی است با چهار     *noh menhaye[1] panj mosavist ba cahar*, $9 - 5 = 4$.

---

[1] منها *menha* is compounded of the Arabic preposition من *men* 'from' and the 3rd pers. fem. sing. Pronominal Suffix ها *-ha*. For its pronunciation see Introduction, Part II, para. 12.

13. The cardinal numbers precede the noun they qualify, which is put in the singular, e.g.

دو رأس اسب   *do ra's¹ asb*, two horses.

صد نفر   *sad nafar*, a hundred persons.

A Noun qualified by a cardinal does not take را -ra when it is the direct object of the verb, unless it is qualified by some such word as این *in* 'this' or آن *an* 'that', e.g.

دو جلد کتاب خرید   *do jeld¹ ketab xarid*, He bought two books.

آن دو کتابرا خرید   *an do ketabra xarid*, He bought those two books.

14. The ordinals are used as adjectives and follow the noun they qualify, e.g.

کتاب سومرا بمن بدهید   *ketabe sevvomra be man bedehid*, Give me the third book.

نخست *naxost* and نخستین *naxostin* are also used as the ordinal of 'one', but cannot be used to form the ordinals of compound numerals. They precede the noun they qualify, e.g.

نخستین بار   *naxostin bar*, the first time.

An adjectival form of the ordinal ending in ـین -in, which also precedes the noun it qualifies without the *ezafe*, is sometimes found, e.g.

یك صد و هشتمین روز   *yak sad o haftomin ruz*, the hundred and eighth day.

15. صد *sad* 'hundred' and هزار *hazar* 'thousand' when used indefinitely can take the plural ending ها *ha-*. They precede the noun they qualify, which is put in the singular, e.g.

صدها کتاب   *sadha ketab*, hundreds of books.

هزارها گل   *hazarha gol*, thousands of flowers.

هزاران هزار   *hazaran* is also used referring to rational beings. هزاران هزار *hazaran hazar* means 'thousands upon thousands' (referring to rational beings).

¹ See para. 16 below.

Similar constructions are:

سالهای سال   salhaye sal, many long years.

قرنهای قرن   qarnhaye qarn, many long centuries.

16. Certain words are used with cardinals as classifiers, except when referring to units of time. These words are placed between the cardinal and the word qualified by the cardinal. Among them are:

(a) نفر nafar (= person) used for persons,[1] e.g.

سه نفر زن آمدند   se nafar ʒan amadand, Three women came.

یك نفر yak nafar means 'a certain person, someone'.

(b) رأس ra's (= head in Arabic) for horses and cattle, e.g.

صد رأس گاو دارد   sad ra's gav darad, He has a hundred head of oxen.

(c) عدد adad (= number) for small articles, e.g.

پنج عدد مداد بمن داد   panj adad medad be man dad, He gave me five pencils.

(d) جلد jeld (= volume) for books, e.g.

چهار جلد کتاب خرید   cahar jeld ketab xarid, He bought four books.

(e) دست dast (= hand) for clothes, furniture, etc., e.g.

یك دست لباس خرید   yak dast lebas xarid, He bought a suit of clothes.

(f) باب bab (= door in Arabic) for houses, e.g.

دو باب خانه دارد   do bab xane darad, He has two houses.

(g) دانه dane (= grain) for eggs and small articles, e.g.

ده دانه تخم مرغ آورد   dah dane toxme morʒ avard, He brought ten (hen's) eggs.

(h) تا ta is used in Colloquial Persian for almost anything but is seldom written (although it has the sanction of early classical usage).

[1] نفر nafar is also used for camels.

(*i*) The following are also used:

دستگاه    *dastgah* for clocks, furniture and machinery, etc.

قبضه    *qabʒe* for swords and rifles, etc.

عراده    *arrade* for guns, cannons, etc.

فروند    *farvand* and قطعه *qat'e* for ships.

زنجیر    *ʒanjir* for elephants.

قطار    *qetar* and مهار *mehar* for camels.

پارچه    *parce* for villages.

تن    *tan* for persons.

In certain cases where some sort of classifier is contained in the phrase qualified by a numeral an additional classifying word is not added after یك *yak* 'one' and is optional after other numerals,[1] e.g.

یك فنجان چای    *yak fenjan cāi*, a (one) cup of tea.

یك لیوان آب    *yak livan ab*, a (one) glass of water.

17. Real estate is divided into six units known as دانگ *dang*[2], e.g.

شش دانگ خانه مال اوست    *ʃeʃ dange xane male ust*, Six *dangs* of the house belong to him (i.e. he is the sole owner of the house).

دو دانگ ده مال اوست    *do dange deh male ust*, Two *dangs* of the village belong to him (i.e. one-third of the village is his).

18. خیلی *xeili* and بسیار *besyar* mean 'very' (see Lesson III, para. 20) and also 'many'. They precede the noun they qualify, which is put in the singular, e.g.

خیلی اسب دارد    *xeili asb darad*, He has many horses.

بسیار *besyar* can also follow the noun it qualifies, in which case the latter is put in the plural, e.g.

اسبهای بسیار دارد    *asbhaye besyar darad*, He has many horses.

<hr>

[1] See also Lesson XII, para. 2 (*f*).

[2] دانگ *dang* can be applied to certain other objects as well, e.g. آواز شش دانگ *avaʒe ʃeʃ dang*, a good (and loud) voice; شش دانگ جهان *ʃeʃ dange jahan*, the whole world. See also Lesson XIV, para. 2 (*b*).

19. يك *yak* 'one' is sometimes used with a noun to which the Indefinite ى *-i* has been added. Its addition does not materially alter the meaning, e.g.

مردى *mardi* or يك مردى *yak mardi*, a man,

but يك مرد *yak mard*, one man.

20. The Indefinite ى *-i* can be added to يك *yak* to mean 'one', e.g.

يكى بمن بدهيد *yaki be man bedehid*, Give me one.

'One of' is rendered by يكى از *yaki az*, e.g.

يكى از آن كتابهارا بمن بدهيد *yaki az an ketabhara be man bedehid*, Give me one of those books.

21. ديگر *digar* 'other' is used as an adjective, e.g.

اسب ديگر *asbe digar*, the other horse.

اسب ديگرى *asbe digari*, another horse.

With the Indefinite ى *-i* added to it, it is used as an Indefinite Pronoun meaning 'another', e.g.

ديگرى آمد *digari amad*, another came.

يكى ديگر *yaki digar* also means 'another', e.g.

يكى ديگر بمن بدهيد *yaki digar be man bedehid*, Give me another.

يك ديگر *yak digar* and هم ديگر *ham digar* both mean 'each other', e.g.

از يك ديگر جدا شدند *az yak digar joda fodand*, They separated from each other.

از هم ديگر خدا حافظى كردند *az ham digar xoda hafezi kardand*, They said good-bye to each other.

ديگر *digar* also means 'next',[1] e.g.

دفعه ديگر *daf'eye digar*, next time.

روز ديگر *ruze digar*, the next day.

Used as an adverb ديگر *digar* means 'further, in addition, again', e.g.

ديگر چه ميخواهيد *digar ce mixahid*, What further do you want, What else do you want?

ديگر نيامد *digar nayamad*, He did not come again.

(See also Lesson XIV, para. 3.)

---

[1] In Classical Persian ديگر *digar* also means 'second', e.g. بار ديگر *bare digar*, the second time; نماز ديگر *namaze digar* means 'the afternoon prayer'.

22. چند *cand* 'some, several, a few' usually precedes the noun it qualifies, which is put in the singular, e.g.

چند نفر آمدند   *cand nafar amadand*, A few persons came.

If it follows the noun, the Indefinite ی *-i* must be added to the Noun, e.g.

سالی چند گذشت   *sali cand goẕaſt*, A few years passed.

چند *cand* is also used as an interrogative meaning 'how much, how many, how long', e.g.

چند نفر بودند   *cand nafar budand*, How many people were there?

آنرا چند خریدید   *anra cand xaridid*, How much did you buy that for?

تا چند صبر کنم   *ta cand sabr konam*, (Until) how long shall I wait?[1]

چند *cand* used as a noun with the Indefinite ی *-i* means 'some time, a little while', e.g.

چندی ماند و رفت   *candi mand o raſt*, He stayed a little while and (then) went.

چند *cand* and چندی *candi* 'a little while' can be preceded by یك *yak*, e.g.

یك چندی آنجا بودم   *yak candi anja budam*, I was there for a little while.

یك چند صبر کنید   *yak cand sabr konid*, Wait just a little longer.

23. Time of day is expressed by the cardinal number following the word ساعت *sa'at* 'hour', which takes the *eẕafe*, e.g.

ساعت ده   *sa'ate dah*, ten o'clock.

'Half an hour' is نیم ساعت *nim sa'at*.
'Quarter of an hour' is ربع ساعت *rob' sa'at*.
Half hours are expressed as follows:

ده و نیم   *dah o nim*
نیم ساعت از ده گذشته   *nim sa'at aẕ dah goẕaſte*   } 10.30.
نیم ساعت به یازده مانده   *nim sa'at be yaẕdah mande*

Quarter hours are expressed as follows:

ده و ربع   *dah o rob'*
یك ربع از ده گذشته   *yak rob' aẕ dah goẕaſte*   } 10.15.
ده ربع بالا   *dah rob' bala*

---

[1] See Lesson XIII, para. 11 (j), for this use of the Subjunctive.

یازده ربع کم    *yaӡdah robʻ kam*   ⎫
یك ربع بیازده مانده    *yak robʻ be yaӡdah mande* ⎬ 10.45

'Minute' is دقیقه *daqiqe*. Minutes are expressed as follows:

پنج دقیقه از ده گذشته    *panj daqiqe aӡ dah goӡaſte* ⎫
ده و پنج دقیقه    *dah o panj daqiqe* ⎬ 10.5.

پنج دقیقه بیازده مانده    *panj daqiqe be yaӡdah mande* ⎫
یازده پنج دقیقه کم    *yaӡdah panj daqiqe kam* ⎬ 10.55.

24. 'Midday' and 'midnight' are ظهر *ӡohr* and نصف شب *nesfe ſab* respectively, and are used in place of دوازده *davaӡdah* 'twelve'. The construction with و *o* 'and' to express half hours and quarters is not used with ظهر *ӡohr* or نصف شب *nesfe ſab*; one of the other forms must be used, e.g.

نیم ساعت از ظهر گذشته    *nim saʻat aӡ ӡohr goӡaſte*, 12.30 p.m.

یك ربع بظهر مانده    *yak robʻ be ӡohr mande*, 11.45 a.m.

سه ربع از نصف شب گذشته    *se robʻ aӡ nesfe ſab goӡaſte*, 12.45 a.m.

نیم ساعت بنصف شب مانده    *nim saʻat be nesfe ſab mande*, 11.30 p.m.

a.m. is پیش از ظهر *piſ aӡ ӡohr.*
p.m. is بعد از ظهر *baʻd aӡ ӡohr.*

صبح *sobh* means 'morning', عصر *asr* 'afternoon' and شب *ſab* 'evening' or 'night'; سحر *sahar* is the period from midnight to dawn and is used especially for the period just before dawn; آفتاب نزده *aftab naӡade* means 'before sunrise'; سفیده صبح *sefideye sobh* 'the early dawn'.

25. In country districts time is sometimes reckoned with reference to three points, sunrise, sunset and midday, e.g.

چند از روز بالا آمده    *cand aӡ ruӡ bala amade*, How long (is) it after daybreak?

چند بظهر مانده    *cand be ӡohr mande*, How long remains till midday?

چند بغروب مانده    *cand be ɣorub mande*, How long remains till sunset?

دو ساعت از غروب گذشته    *do saʻat aӡ ɣorub goӡaſte*, two hours after sunset.

26. The week is reckoned from Saturday. The days of the week are as follows:

شنبه    *ʃambe*, Saturday.

یکشنبه    *yak ʃambe*, Sunday.

دو شنبه    *do ʃambe*, Monday.

سه شنبه    *se ʃambe*, Tuesday.

چهار شنبه    *cahar ʃambe*, Wednesday.

پنج شنبه    *panj ʃambe*, Thursday.

جمعه    *jomʻe*, Friday.

The following forms generally refer to the latter part of the day:

شب یکشنبه    *ʃabe yak ʃambe*, Saturday.

شب دو شنبه    *ʃabe do ʃambe*, Sunday.

شب سه شنبه    *ʃabe se ʃambe*, Monday.

شب چهار شنبه    *ʃabe cahar ʃambe*, Tuesday.

شب پنج شنبه    *ʃabe panj ʃambe*, Wednesday.

شب جمعه    *ʃabe jomʻe*, Thursday.

شب شنبه    *ʃabe ʃambe*, Friday.

To express the morning, etc., of a certain day, the time of day is put in apposition to the day, e.g.

دو شنبه صبح    *do ʃambe sobh*, Monday morning.

چهار شنبه شب    *cahar ʃambe ʃab*, Wednesday evening.

جمعه شب    *jomʻe ʃab*, Friday evening.

صبح *sobh* 'morning' and عصر *asr* 'afternoon' can instead precede the day of the week, in which case they take an *eʒafe*, e.g.

صبح چهار شنبه    *sobhe cahar ʃambe*, Wednesday morning.

عصر شب جمعه    *asre ʃabe jomʻe*, Thursday afternoon.

27. Expressions of 'time at' or 'time in' do not require a preposition, e.g.

صبح آمد    *sobh amad*, He came in the morning.

ساعت ده رفت    *saʻate dah raft*, He went at ten o'clock.

جمعه آمد    *jomʻe amad*, He came on Friday.

روزی *ruzi* and یك روزی *yak ruzi* mean 'one day'. عصری *asri* may mean 'in the afternoon' (if a single occurrence) or 'in the afternoons' (habitually); similarly ظهری *zohri* 'at midday' may be used for a single or for a habitual action. صبحی *sobhi*, شبی *ʃabi* and غروبی *ɣorubi* 'in the morning', 'in the evening' and 'at sunset' respectively usually signify habitual actions.

28. سال *sal* 'year' and ماه *mah* 'month' can form plurals سالیان *salian* and ماهیان *mahian* respectively when used indefinitely, e.g.

سالیان دراز   *saliane daraz*, (for) long years.

These forms are rare.

29. 'Ago' is expressed by پیش *piʃ* following the noun, which takes the *ezafe*, e.g.

یك هفته پیش بشهر رفت   *yak hafteye piʃ be ʃahr raft*, He went to the town a week ago.

Note also

بعد از یك هفته خواهد آمد   *ba'd az yak hafte xahad amad*, He will come in a week's time.

تا یك شنبه بر میگردد   *ta yak ʃambe bar migardad*, He will return by Sunday.

30. Age is expressed by the verb داشتن *daʃtan* 'to have' together with the number of years or by the verb بودن *budan* 'to be' with سن *senn* 'age' and the number, e.g.

چند سال دارد   *cand sal darad*  ⎫
سن او چقدر است   *senne u ce qadr ast*  ⎬ How old is he?

بیست سال دارد   *bist sal darad*  ⎫ He is twenty years
سن او بیست سال است   *senne u bist sal ast*  ⎭ old.

The following expressions should also be noted:

سال بیستش تمام شد   *sale bisteʃ tamam ʃod*, His twentieth year is completed, i.e. he is twenty years old.

تو بیست میرود   *tu[1] bist miravad*, He is entering his twentieth year, i.e. he is nineteen years old.

جوان بیست و چند ساله بود   *javane bist o cand salei bud*, He was a young man of twenty odd years.

---

[1] In this phrase تو *tu* is usually used without the *ezafe*.

## VOCABULARY

| | |
|---|---|
| هوا | *hava*, weather. |
| آب و هوا | *ab o hava*, climate. |
| بهار | *bahar*, spring. |
| تابستان | *tabestan*, summer. |
| پائيز | *paiz*, autumn. |
| زمستان | *zamestan*, winter. |
| آفتاب | *aftab*, sun. |
| ستاره | *setare*, star. |
| آسمان | *asman*, sky. |
| ماه | *mah*, moon, month. |
| طلوع | *tolu'*, rising; طلوع آفتاب *tolu'e aftab*, sunrise; طلوع كردن *tolu' k.*, to rise (the sun, etc.). |
| غروب | *yorub*, sunset; غروب كردن *yorub k.*, to set. |
| شب | *ſab*, night, evening. |
| امشب | *emſab*, to-night. |
| ديشب | *diſab*, last night. |
| پريشب | *pariſab*, the night before last. |
| صبح | *sobh*, morning. |
| عصر | *asr*, afternoon. |
| صبحانه | *sobhane*, breakfast. |
| عصرانه | *asrane*, afternoon tea. |
| ناهار | *nahar*, *nahar*, lunch. |
| ناشتائى | *naſtai*, breakfast. |
| شام | *ſam*, supper. |
| هفته | *hafte*, week. |
| سال | *sal*, year. |
| امسال | *emsal*, this year. |
| پارسال | *parsal*, last year. |

| | |
|---|---|
| پيرارسال | *pirarsal*, the year before last. |
| نصف | *nesf*, half; نصف شب *nesfe ſab*, midnight. |
| ساعت | *sa'at*, hour; timepiece. |
| دقيقه | *daqiqe*, minute. |
| ربع | *rob'*, quarter. |
| نيم | *nim*, half. |
| عمر | *omr*, life. |
| سن | *senn*, age (of persons). |
| قيمت | *qeimat*, value, price. |
| قدر | *qadr*, amount; چقدر *ce qadr*, how much. |
| زمان | *zaman*, time, season. |
| آينده | *ayande*, future, coming; دفعه آينده *daf'eye ayande*, the coming time, i.e. next time. |
| ليوان | *livan*, glass, tumbler. |
| فنجان | *fenjan*, cup. |
| حاضر | *hazer*, present, ready; حاضر كردن *hazer k.*, to make or get ready. |
| جدا | *joda*, separate; جدا شدن *joda ſ.*, to separate (intrans.); جدا كردن *joda k.*, to separate (trans.). |
| بالا | *bala*, high; up. |
| بيدار | *bidar*, awake; بيدار شدن *bidar ſ.*, to wake, wake up (intrans.); بيدار كردن *bidar k.*, to wake (trans.). |

بلند *boland*, tall; high; بلند
شدن *boland ʃ.*, to get
up, rise; بلند کردن rise;
*boland k.*, to raise.

وقت *vaqt*, time; چند وقت *cand
vaqt*, how long.

دراز *daraz*, long.

نان *nan*, bread.

صفحه *safhe*, page (of book,
etc.).

پول *pul*, money.

خانه *xane*, house.

تخم *toxm*, egg, seed; تخم مرغ
*toxme morɣ*, hen's
egg.

خروس *xorus*, cock.

جوجه *juje*, chicken.

یخ *yax*, ice; یخ بستن *yax
bastan*, to freeze (in-
trans.) (بستن *bastan*
'to bind, tie', Present
Stem بند *band*).

فردا *farda*, to-morrow.

پسفردا *pasfarda*, the day after
to-morrow.

باز *baz*, open; باز کردن *baz
k.*, to open (trans.).

دیگر *digar*, other; again;
further.

چند *cand*, some, a few; how
much, how many,
how long.

پس *pas*, then, after (adv.);
پس از *pas az*, after
(prep.).

بعد *ba'd*, then, after (adv.);
بعد از *ba'd az*, after
(prep.).

پیش *piʃ*, before (adv.); *piʃ(e)*
(prep.), in front of;
in the presence of;
پیش از *piʃ az* (prep.,
time), before.

جلو *jelōu*, in front, forward;
*jelōu(e)* (prep.) in
front of; fast (of a
watch).

عقب *aqab*, behind; when used
as a prep. it takes the
*ezafe*; slow (of a watch).

تا *ta*, until.

هر *har*, every.

چون *cun*, when; since; like.

فقط *faqat*, only.

آواز *avaz*, voice, sound.

جهان *jahan*, world.

گذشتن *gozaʃtan* (*gozar*), to
(گذر) pass (intrans.); گذشته
*gozaʃte*, past; دفعه
گذشته *daf'eye gozaʃte*,
the last, i.e. the pre-
ceding, time.

ارزیدن *arzidan*, to be worth.

صبر کردن *sabr k.*, to wait.

دانستن *danestan* (*dan*), to
(دان) know (of things).

برگشتن *bar gaʃtan* (*bar gard*), to
(بر گرد) return (intrans.).

خوابیدن *xabidan*, to sleep; to go
to bed.

خدا حافظی *xoda hafeʒi k.*, to say good-bye خدا حافظ كردن (*xoda hafeʒ* means [may] God [be your] protector).

پرسيدن *porsidan*, to ask (a question).

شناختن *ʃenaxtan* (*ʃenas*), to recognize, know (a person) (شناس).

بر خاستن *bar xastan* (*bar xiʒ*), to rise (بر خيز).

ماندن *mandan*, to remain.

## EXERCISE 9

پارسال چند وقت آنجا بوديد — پارسال شش ماه ماندم ولی امسال فقط پنج ماه ميمانم — روز چهار شنبه گذشته پنج جلد كتاب خريد — پسفردا پيش از ظهر بشهر ميرويم — ساعت ده صبح راه افتاد — زمستان پيرارسال خيلی سرد بود — دو دانگ اين خانه مال برادر من است و يك دانگش مال هر يكی از خواهرهايم — يكی يكی جلو آمدند — اين منزل اطاقهای زياد دارد — اسب ديگری برای من حاضر كنيد — شب جمعه پيش او بوديم — چند نفر آنجا بودند ولی هيچ يكی از آنهارا نميشناختم — اين كتاب هيچی نمی‌ارزد — ساعت شما نيم ساعت عقب است — تا دو بعد از ظهر برای شما صبر كردم — سه روز پيش آمد و بعد از سه روز ديگر خواهد رفت — در شهر از يك ديگر جدا شدند — بعد از چند دقيقه بر گشت — ده دانه تخم مرغ برای من آورد

## EXERCISE 10

1. The woman came back at noon with her two daughters. 2. He went to bed early last night. 3. We started before sunrise. 4. Wait for me until 10 o'clock. 5. His elder son is nine years old and his younger son seven years old. 6. Give me one of those pencils. 7. After an hour and a half we returned home. 8. He bought a suit of clothes the day before yesterday. 9. Your garden is bigger than our garden. 10. My watch is a quarter of an hour fast. 11. Next week the sun will rise at 5.30 and set at 6.45. 12. We got up early yesterday.

## LESSON VI

The Passive Voice. توانستن *tavanestan.* خواستن *xastan.* گذاشتن *gozaſtan.* بایستن *bayestan.* شایستن *ſayestan.* Impersonal Verbs. The Use of the Subjunctive after تا *ta* and که *ke.*

1. The Passive Voice is formed with the Auxiliary Verb شدن *ſodan* 'to become' (Present Stem شو *ſav-, ſou*) and the Past Participle of the main verb:

| | | |
|---|---|---|
| Infinitive | کشته شدن | *koſte ſodan,* to be killed. |
| Past Participle | کشته شده | *koſte ſode.* |
| Preterite | کشته شدم | *koſte ſodam,* etc. |
| Imperfect | کشته میشدم | *koſte miſodam,* etc. |
| Perfect | کشته شدهام | *koſte ſode am,* etc. |
| Pluperfect | کشته شده بودم | *koſte ſode budam,* etc. |
| Future | کشته خواهم شد | *koſte xaham ſod,* etc. |
| Present | کشته میشوم | *koſte miſavam,* etc. |
| Imperative | کشته شو | *koſte ſou,*[1] etc. |
| Subjunctive Present | کشته بشوم | *koſte beſavam,*[1] etc. |
| Subjunctive Past | کشته شده باشم | *koſte ſode baſam,* etc. |

2. The negative is formed by adding نه *na-* to the auxiliary شدن *ſodan* in the usual way, e.g.

کشته نشدم  *koſte naſodam,* I was not killed.

کشته نشدهام  *koſte naſode am,* I have not been killed.

کشته نخواهم شد  *koſte naxaham ſod,* I shall not be killed.

3. Stress in the affirmative is carried on the final syllable of the main verb, e.g.

کشته شدم  *koſ'te ſodam,* I was killed.

کشته خواهم شد  *koſ'te xaham ſod,* I shall be killed.

In the negative it is carried on the negative prefix, e.g.

کشته نمیشوم  *koſte 'namiſavam,* I shall not be killed.

کشته نشدم  *koſte 'naſodam,* I was not killed.

---

[1] There is a tendency to omit the prefix به *be-* in the Imperative and the Subjunctive Present of the Passive Voice.

4. The Verbs گشتن *gaʃtan* (Present Stem گرد *gard*)[1] and گردیدن
*gardidan*[2] 'to become' can be used in place of شدن *ʃodan* to form the
Passive Voice.

5. The Passive Voice is not used in Persian if the Active Voice can
be used. Thus 'I was hit by him' must be translated as 'he hit me'.

6. The Passive Voice can in some cases be expressed by the 3rd pers. pl.
of the Active Voice. Certain verbs take this construction in preference
to the Passive construction with شدن *ʃodan*, e.g.

> اورا زدند    *ura ʒadand*, He was hit (they hit him).
>
> گفتند    *goftand*, It was said (they said).

7. In addition to the auxiliary verbs بودن *budan* 'to be' and شدن *ʃodan*
'to become', the following auxiliaries are in common use:

> توانستن    *tavanestan* (Present Stem توان *tavan*) to be able.[3]
>
> خواستن    *xastan* (Present Stem خواه *xah*), to want.[4]

Both are normally followed by the Subjunctive Present,[5] e.g.

> میتوانم بروم    *mitavanam beravam*, I can go.
>
> نتوانستم بروم    *natavanestam beravam*, I could not go.
>
> خواهم توانست بروم    *xaham tavanest beravam*, I shall be able to go.
>
> میخواهم بروم    *mixaham beravam*, I want to go.
>
> میخواستم بروم    *mixastam beravam*, I wanted to go.

8. خواستن *xastan* is sometimes used to mean 'to be on the point of
doing something', e.g.

> میخواست بمیرد    *mixast bemirad*, He was about to die.

---

[1] گشتن *gaʃtan* is also used standing alone to mean 'to go for a walk', 'to search (for)', e.g.
   توی شهر گشتیم    *tuye ʃahr gaʃtim*, We walked about in the town.
   عقب او گشتم    *aqabe u gaʃtam*, I went to look for him.
[2] گردیدن *gardidan* standing alone means 'to go round', 'revolve'.
[3] The obsolete verb یارستن *yarastan* 'to be able' was used in Classical Persian in the
same way as توانستن *tavanestan*.
[4] خواستن *xastan* as a transitive verb means 'to send for, summon, desire'.
[5] Note, however, نمیتواند رفته باشد *namitavanad rafte baʃad*, he cannot have gone.

9. گذاشتن *goẕaʃtan* (Present Stem گذار *goẕar*) meaning 'to allow' is followed by the Subjunctive Present with or without که *ke*, e.g.

نگذاشت که بروم     *nagoẕaʃt ke beravam*, He did not allow me to go.

10. The defective verb بایستن *bayestan* is used as an auxiliary and is followed by the Subjunctive. The only forms in common use are the 3rd pers. sing. باید *bayad* 'ought, must', بایست *bayest* and میبایست *mibayest*, 'ought to have'. A form میباید *mibayad* 'must' is occasionally found in place of باید *bayad*.

| | | |
|---|---|---|
| 1st pers. sing. | باید بروم *bayad beravam* | I must go, ought to |
| 2nd pers. sing. | باید بروی *bayad beravi* | go, etc. |
| 3rd pers. sing. | باید برود *bayad beravad* | |

| | | |
|---|---|---|
| 1st pers. pl. | باید برویم *bayad beravim* | We must go, ought |
| 2nd pers. pl. | باید بروید *bayad beravid* | to go, etc. |
| 3rd pers. pl. | باید بروند *bayad beravand* | |

| | | |
|---|---|---|
| 1st pers. sing. | بایست رفته باشم *bayest rafte baʃam* | I must have gone, |
| 2nd pers. sing. | بایست رفته باشی *bayest rafte baʃi* | ought to have |
| 3rd pers. sing. | بایست رفته باشد *bayest rafte baʃad* | gone, etc. |

| | | |
|---|---|---|
| 1st pers. pl. | بایست رفته باشیم *bayest rafte baʃim* | We must have |
| 2nd pers. pl. | بایست رفته باشید *bayest rafte baʃid* | gone, ought to |
| 3rd pers. pl. | بایست رفته باشند *bayest rafte baʃand* | have gone, etc. |

باید *bayad* is also used with the Subjunctive Past and has the same meaning as بایست *bayest* followed by the Subjunctive Past. میبایست *mibayest* is sometimes used in place of بایست *bayest*.[1]

11. The only forms of the defective verb شایستن *ʃayestan* in use are the Participles شایان *ʃayan* 'fitting, splendid, brilliant', شایسته *ʃayeste* 'fitting, proper' and شاید *ʃayad*. The latter means 'perhaps'. When referring to the present it is followed by the Indicative Present, but when referring to the future or past by the Subjunctive:[2]

| | | |
|---|---|---|
| 1st pers. sing. | شاید بروم *ʃayad beravam* | |
| 2nd pers. sing. | شاید بروی *ʃayad beravi* | Perhaps I shall go, etc. |
| 3rd pers. sing. | شاید برود *ʃayad beravad* | |

[1] See also Lesson XII, paras. 1 (*b*), and 3, and Lesson XIII, paras. 1 (*e*), 5 (*h*), 11 (*g*), and 12 (*d* and *f*).

[2] See also Lesson VII, para. 5 (*b*), Lesson XII, para. 3, and Lesson XIII, para. 6 (*a*).

| 1st pers. pl. | شاید برویم | ʃayad beravim | ⎫ |
|---|---|---|---|
| 2nd pers. pl. | شاید بروید | ʃayad beravid | ⎬ Perhaps we shall go, etc. |
| 3rd pers. pl. | شاید بروند | ʃayad beravand | ⎭ |

| 1st pers. sing. | شاید رفته باشم | ʃayad rafte baʃam | ⎫ |
|---|---|---|---|
| 2nd pers. sing. | شاید رفته باشی | ʃayad rafte baʃi | ⎬ Perhaps I have gone, etc. |
| 3rd pers. sing. | شاید رفته باشد | ʃayad rafte baʃad | ⎭ |

| 1st pers. pl. | شاید رفته باشیم | ʃayad rafte baʃim | ⎫ |
|---|---|---|---|
| 2nd pers. pl. | شاید رفته باشید | ʃayad rafte baʃid | ⎬ Perhaps we have gone, etc. |
| 3rd pers. pl. | شاید رفته باشند | ʃayad rafte baʃand | ⎭ |

In the case of بودن budan 'to be', the Preterite is used after شاید referring to past time, e.g.

شاید آنجا بود   ʃayad anja bud, perhaps he was there.

12. The 3rd pers. sing. of بایستن bayestan and شدن ʃodan, and of the Subjunctive and Indicative Present of توانستن tavanestan can be used impersonally, in which case they are followed by the Short Infinitive. If توانستن tavanestan is used impersonally the forms بتوان betavan and میتوان mitavan are used in the Subjunctive Present and the Indicative Present respectively, e.g.

اینرا میتوان کرد   inra mitavan kard, One can do this.

باید رفت   bayad raft, One must go.

شدن ʃodan used impersonally means 'to be possible', e.g.

میشود رفت   miʃavad raft, It is possible to go.

13. The 3rd pers. sing. pres. of the obsolete verb مانستن manestan 'to resemble' is used in Colloquial Persian to mean 'it seems', e.g.

اینطور میماند   in tour mimanad, It seems (to be) thus.

14. The negative prefix نه na- is added to the auxiliaries خواستن xastan, بایستن bayestan, and توانستن tavanestan (and not to the main verb) if the proposition is negative, e.g.

نباید بروید   nabayad beravid, You must not go.

نمیتواند بماند   namitavanad bemanad, He cannot stay.

نمیخواست بگوید   namixast beguyad, He did not want to say.

A similar construction is used with توانستن tavanestan, بایستن bayestan and شدن ʃodan when these are used impersonally, e.g.

نباید رفت   *nabayad raft*, One must not go.

نمیشود کرد   *namifavad kard*, It is impossible to do (this).

نمیتوان کرد   *namitavan kard*, One cannot do (this).

15. In the case of شاید *fayad* the negative prefix is added to the main Verb, e.g.

شاید نروم   *fayad naravam*, Perhaps I shall not go.

16. In Classical Persian the 2nd pers. sing. is sometimes used impersonally, e.g.

تو گفتی   *to gofti* = One would have said.

گوئی   *gui* = One would say.

17. The Subjunctive Present is used after certain conjunctions. Among them are:

(a) که *ke* and تا *ta* introducing a final clause, e.g.

اینرا باو دادم که بمنزل ببرد   *inra be u dadam ke be manzel bebarad*, I gave him this to take to the house.

کتابرا بمن داد تا مرا کمك کند   *ketabra be man dad ta mara komak konad*, He gave me the book to help me.

اینرا باو گفتم تا زودتر برود   *inra be u goftam ta zudtar beravad*, I told him this in order that he should go earlier.

اورا بشهر فرستادند که نان بخرد   *ura be fahr ferestadand ke nan bexarad*, They sent him to the town to buy (some) bread.

In the above examples تا *ta* and که *ke* are interchangeable.

تا *ta* is used in Persian to express consequence where 'and' is used in English, e.g.

اینرا بکن تا پولت بدهم   *inra bekon ta pulet bedeham*, Do this and I will give you (some) money.

(b) تا *ta* 'by the time that' referring to future time, e.g.

تا بشهر برسید خسته میشوید   *ta be fahr berasid xaste mifavid*, You will be tired by the time you reach the town.

تا شما بیائید رفته‌ام   *ta foma beyaid rafte am*, By the time you come I shall have gone.

(c) تا *ta* 'until' referring to future time, usually with نه *na*, e.g.

تا اينرا نخوانم باور نميكنم    *ta inra naxanam bavar namikonam*, I shall not believe this until I read it.

Note however that the نه *na* is by usage omitted in such sentences as the following:

تا شما بيائيد صبر ميكنم    *ta foma beyaid sabr mikonam*, I will wait until you come.

(See also Lesson XIII, paras. 11 and 18.)

Temporal Clauses introduced by تا *ta* usually precede the principal sentence.

18. The Subjunctive is also used in substantive clauses implying intention or determination, with or without كه *ke*, e.g.

مصمم شد كه به برادر خود بنويسد    *mosammam fod ke be baradare xod benevisad*, He determined to write to his brother.

## VOCABULARY

دروغ *doruy*, lie; دروغ گفتن *doruy goftan*, to lie.

خسته *xaste*, tired; خسته شدن *xaste f.*, to be tired.

مصمم *mosammam*, decided, determined upon; مصمم شدن *mosammam f.*, to be determined, decided upon.

خراب *xarab*, destroyed; broken, out of order; bad (of food, etc.).

درست *dorost*, right; in order.

تشنه *tefne*, thirsty.

تشنگى *tefnegi*, thirst.

گرسنه *gorosne*, hungry.

گرسنگى *gorosnegi*, hunger.

برف *barf*, snow; برف آمدن *barf amadan* (باريدن) (*baridan*), to snow.

باران *baran*, rain; باران آمدن *baran amadan* to rain.

بارندگى *barandegi*, rain.

باريدن *baridan*, to rain.

رعد *ra'd*, thunder.

برق *barq*, lightning; electricity.

تگرگ *tegarg*, hail.

توفان *tufan*, storm.

باد *bad*, wind.

موسم *mousem*, season (of year, etc.).

شديد *fadid*, severe; strict.

| | |
|---|---|
| قوه *qovve*, power; قوه برق *qovveye barq*, electric power. | تاجر *tajer*, merchant. |
| | دكان *dokkan*, shop. |
| تولید *tōulid*, production; تولید كردن *tōulid k.*, to produce. | قند *qand*, lump sugar. |
| | ماشین آلات *maʃinalat*, machinery. |
| سطح *sath*, standard, level (noun). | مملكت *mamlekat*, country. |
| | دنیا *donya*, world. |
| زندگی *ʒendegi*, life; سطح زندگی *sathe ʒendegi*, standard of life. | عبارت بودن (از) *ebarat b. (aʒ)*, to consist (of). |
| | صنعت *san'at*, industry. |
| گندم *gandom*, wheat. | صنعتی *san'ati*, industrial. |
| جو *jōu*, barley. | زراعت *ʒera'at*, agriculture. |
| پشم *paʃm*, wool. | زراعتی *ʒera'ati*, agricultural. |
| پنبه *pambe*, cotton. | مواد *mavadd*, materials; مواد اولیه *mavadde avvaliye*, raw materials. |
| قماش *qomaʃ*, cotton piece goods. | جنس *jens*, kind, sort. |
| صادرات *saderat*, exports. | اجناس *ajnas* (broken plural of جنس),¹ kinds, sorts; goods. |
| واردات *varedat*, imports. | كارخانه *karxane*, factory. |
| صادر كردن *sader k.*, to export; to issue. | زیرا (كه) *ʒira (ke)*, because. |
| وارد كردن *vared k.*, to import; وارد شدن *vared ʃ.*, to be imported; to enter, come in. | با وجودیكه *ba vojudike*, با اینكه *ba inke*, in spite of the fact that, notwithstanding. |
| خشك *xoʃk*, dry; خشك بار *xoʃke bar*, dried fruits. | باور كردن *bavar k.*, to believe. |
| خشكی *xoʃki*, dryness, dry land; از راه خشكی *aʒ rahe xoʃki*, by land. | زیاد كردن *ʒiad k.*, to increase (trans.). |
| | كم كردن *kam k.*, to decrease (trans.). |
| تجارت *tejarat*, trade. | مردن (میر) *mordan (mir)*, to die. |
| تجارت خانه *tejaratxane*, trading house, firm. | تهران *tehran*, Tehran. |
| | تا *ta*, as long as (with Indic.). |
| تجارتی *tejarati*, commercial. | خواندن *xundan*, to read. |

¹ For Broken Plurals see Part II, Lesson xx. The use of broken plurals, while not obligatory, is customary with many Arabic words.

## EXERCISE 11

شاید فردا بیاید — سال آینده میخواهم بتهران بروم — امروز نمیتواند بیاید
ولی شاید فردا بتواند بیاید — تا اینرا نبینم باور نمیکنم — میخواست این باغرا
بفروشد ولی نشد — صبر میکنیم تا بیائید — فردا آفتاب نزده باید راه بیفتیم —
پس از چهار روز دیگر میخواهد برود — پریروز سه نفر مرد در شهر کشته
شدند — امسال باران خیلی کم آمده است — روز دو شنبه دو سه ساعت در
شهر گشتیم — نمیتوانم صبر کنم تا بیاید — ساعت شما باید خراب باشد زیراکه
نیم ساعت عقب است — با اینکه میخواستم اورا ببینم نمیتوانستم صبر کنم تا
بیاید — ساعتهای کاررا زیاد کردند تا قوه تولید کارخانه بیشتر شود — صادرات
این مملکت بیشتر مواد زراعتی است تا صنعتی — صادرات این مملکت عبارت
است از گندم و پشم و خشکبار و وارداتش بیشتر عبارت است از قند و چای و
قماش و ماشین آلات

## EXERCISE 12a

1. As long as the children are here you must stay. 2. In spite of the fact that he wanted to go, he was unable to do so. 3. It is impossible to go. 4. He ought to have gone yesterday. 5. She must go to see her children the day after tomorrow. 6. I shall not come unless you write to me. 7. He was summoned by his father. 8. He could not come earlier than this. 9. He must have gone before us. 10. We ought to have gone the day before yesterday. 11. He wanted to write to his brother. 12. It will be night by the time you arrive home. 13. There was a severe storm yesterday. 14. I gave him my book to read. 15. He wants to see you.

## EXERCISE 12b

1. The exports of this country consist of agricultural goods. 2. The standard of living of the country must be raised. 3. I must go now because it is late. 4. The production of this factory has decreased. 5. Although we had (ate) breakfast very late, I am hungry. 6. Although he was tired, he remained in the town with his brother until after midnight. 7. It rained a great deal yesterday and there was a severe storm in the early morning. 8. The merchant opened a business in the town; he wants to import industrial goods and to export dried fruits and wool.

9. There was nobody in the room when I came in.  10. I have never seen him but I should like to know him.  11. Perhaps he has gone; he was getting (himself) ready half an hour ago.  12. Last summer I used to go for a walk every day.  13. I shall not allow you to go. 14. It is impossible to read this.  15. Where were you going this morning?

## LESSON VII

### Adverbs.[1] Conditional Sentences. The Causative.

1. There are no formally distinct adverbs in Persian but certain words correspond in use to the English adverb. These are mainly nouns, or words which were formerly used as nouns, and nouns combined with prepositions. Many adjectives are also used as adverbs.

| | |
|---|---|
| آری | *ari,* yes (this is often pronounced *are*).[2] |
| نه | *na,* no (not normally used alone in polite speech). |
| نخیر | *naxeir,* no. |
| چرا | *cera,* why; yes. |
| هم | *ham,* also (used also as an emphatic particle, see note to Lesson IV, para. 17). |
| با هم | *ba ham,* together. |
| نیز | *niz,* also. |
| خیلی | *xeili* |
| بسیار | *besyar* } very.[3] |
| تنها | *tanha,* alone. |
| چند | *cand,* how much. |
| چندین | *candin* |
| چندان | *candan* } so much; (with negative verb) not very. |
| زیاد | *ziad,* much, too; (with negative verb) not very, not much. |
| اکنون | *aknun,* now. |
| هرگز | *hargez,* ever; (with negative verb) never. |

---

[1] See also Part II, Lesson XXI, paras. 16–18.

[2] بله *bale* is more frequently used for 'yes' in polite conversation.

[3] See also Lesson V, para. 18.

همیشه *hamiſe* ⎱ always.
هـمواره *hamvare* ⎰

فرو *foru* ⎱ down.
فرود *forud* ⎰

بس *bas*, very (used to intensify Adjectives), e.g.

مقامی بس ارجمند دارد *maqami bas arjmand darad*, He has a very exalted position.

و بس *va bas* means 'nothing more, only', e.g.

این کاررا کردم و بس *in karra kardam va bas*, I did this and nothing more.[1]

هنوز *hanuʒ*, still, yet; (with negative verb) not yet.

چه *ce*, how, e.g.

چه خوش گفت فردوسی *ce xoſ goft ferdóusi*, How well spoke Ferdousi.

بارها *barha*, often (from بار *bar* 'time').

اینجا *inja*, here.

آنجا *anja*, there.

کجا *koja*, where (interrog.).

اینطور *in tóur*, thus, in this way.

آنطور *an tóur*, thus, in that way.

چطور *ce tóur*, how.

اینگونه *ingune*, thus, in this way.

آنگونه *angune*, thus, in that way.

چگونه *cegune*, how.

آنگاه *angah*, then.

گاهی *gahi*, sometimes.

گه گاهی *gah gahi*, sometimes, from time to time.

گه بگاه *gah be gah*, from time to time.

ناگاه *nagah*, suddenly.

بخودی خود *be xodiye xod*, involuntarily.

---

[1] بس *bas* used as a noun means 'enough', e.g.

باو بس دادید *be u bas dadid*, You gave him enough.

کابیش‌ *kamabiʃ*, بیش و کم *kam o biʃ*, more or less.

(آئینه) هر آینه *har ayene (aine)*, in any case; assuredly.

روی هم رفته *ruye ham rafte*, altogether, on the whole.

دست کم *daste kam*, at least.

گویا *guya*,[1] apparently, perhaps, e.g.

گویا این مال شماست *guya in male ʃomast*, It seems this is yours.

بالا *bala*, above.[2]

پائین *pain*, below.[3]

کم *kam*, seldom.

دور *dur*, far.

تند *tond*, quickly.

خوب *xub*, well.

سخت *saxt*, strictly, severely; very (used to intensify an adjective), e.g.

سخت مریض است *saxt mariz ast*, He is very ill.

پر *por*, very (used to intensify an adjective), e.g.

این پر گران است *in por geran ast*, This is very expensive.

پیوسته *peivaste*, continually.[4]

Adjectives formed by the suffixes ه *-e*, ینه *-ine* and انه *-ane* are frequently used as adverbs, e.g.

هر ساله *har sale*, annually (every year).

پنجروزه *panjruze*, in or for five days.

روزینه *ruzine*, daily.[5]

عاقلانه *aqelane*, intelligently, wisely.

---

[1] This is apparently a verbal adjective, see Lesson x, para. 6 (a).

[2] Used as an adjective بالا *bala* means 'upper', e.g.

طبقه بالا *tabaqeye bala*, the upper storey.

[3] Used as an adjective پائین *pain* means 'lower', e.g.

طبقه پائین *tabaqeye pain*, the lower storey.

[4] پیوسته *peivaste* is the past participle of پیوستن *peivastan* 'to join'.

[5] The modern usage is روزانه *ruzane*.

Many abstract nouns (see Lesson x, para. 1) are combined with the preposition بِ *be* and used as adverbs, e.g.

بآسانی   *be asani*, easily (from آسانی *asani*, ease).

بخوبی   *be xubi*, well (from خوبی *xubi*, goodness).

2. 'As (in the capacity of)' is expressed by بعنوان *be envan* with the *ezafe*, e.g.

بعنوان نماینده دولت آمد   *be envane namayandeye doulat amad*, He came as the government's representative.

'As...as possible' is rendered by هر چه *har ce* with the comparative adjective, e.g.

هر چه زودتر   *har ce zudtar*, as quickly as possible.

هر چه تمامتر   *har ce tamamtar*, as completely as possible.

هر چه تمامتر *har ce tamamtar* is also used as follows:

با خوشحالی هر چه تمامتر   *ba xoshaliye har ce tamamtar*, with the greatest possible happiness.

3. Stress in the forms given in para. 1 above is carried on the final syllable in the majority of cases.

The following carry the stress on the initial syllable:

آره   *are*, yes.

چرا   *cera*, why?

گاهی   *gahi*, sometimes.

هر آینه (آئینه)   *har ayene (aine)*, in any case.

In compounds formed with طور *tour* and گونه *gune* the stress is carried on the first component, e.g.

چطور   '*ce tour*, how.

آنگونه   '*angune*, thus.

The following carry the stress on the initial or final syllable:

نخیر   *naxeir*, no.

خیلی   *xeili*, very.

کجا   *koja*, where?

4. Adverbs or adverbial phrases denoting time normally precede other adverbs or adverbial phrases. Adverbs or adverbial phrases of manner usually precede those of place, e.g.

ديروز ساعت ده با اسب بشهر آمد    *diruz sa'ate dah ba asb be fahr amad,*
Yesterday at ten o'clock he came on horseback to the town.

5. Conditional Sentences are introduced by اگر *agar* 'if'. The protasis normally precedes the apodosis.

(*a*) Possible Conditions. (i) Possible Conditions which refer to the future take the present or future in the apodosis and the Subjunctive Present in the protasis, e.g.

اگر بروید من هم ميروم    *agar beravid man ham miravam,* If you go, I shall go also.

If the action in the 'if clause' is a single action and precedes the action in the main clause, the preterite can be used in the 'if clause', e.g.

اگر آمد باو بگوئيد    *agar amad be u beguid,* If he comes tell him.

See also Lesson XIII, paras. 5 (*c*), 5 (*e*) and 9 (*e*).

(ii) Possible conditions which refer to the present in the protasis, i.e. to an action which may be actually taking place, or to a state which may be actually in existence, take the Indicative Present in the protasis and the Indicative Present or Future in the apodosis, e.g.

اگر کتاب خودرا ميـخوانـد چيزی باو    *agar ketabe xodra mixanad cizi be*
نخواهم گفت    *u naxaham goft,* If he is reading his book I shall not say anything to him.

If, however, the verb بودن *budan* is used in the protasis of a conditional sentence of this type, it is usual to use the Subjunctive Present, e.g.

اگر مريض باشد نخواهد آمد    *agar mariz bafad naxahad amad,* If he is ill he will not come.

(iii) Possible Conditions referring to past time in the protasis and present or future in the apodosis take the Subjunctive Past in the protasis and the present or future in the apodosis, e.g.

اگر نرفته باشد باو ميکويم    *agar narafte bafad be u miguyam,* If he has not gone I will tell him.

اگر اورا دیده باشید کافیست — *agar ura dide baſid kafist,* If you have seen him it is enough.

اگر کتابرا گم کرده باشید یکی دیگر میخرم — *agar ketabra gom karde baſid yaki digar mixaram,* If you have lost the book I will buy another.

(*b*) Impossible Conditions, whether relating to the past or present, take the Imperfect in both parts, e.g.

اگر میتوانستم میامدم — *agar mitavanestam miamadam,* I would have come if I could; if I could come I would (but I cannot).

اگر زودتر میرفتید میرسیدید — *agar ʒudtar miraftid mirasidid,* If you had gone earlier you would have arrived (in time).

اگر جوان بودم ١ میرفتم — *agar javan budam miraftam,* If I had been young I would have gone; I would go if I was young (but I am not).

The Pluperfect can be used in either or both parts instead of the Imperfect in Impossible Conditions relating to the past, e.g.

اگر تفنگ داشت ٢ مرا کشته بود — *agar tofang daſt mara koſte bud,* If he had had a gun he would have killed me.

اگر ارزان بود ٢ خریده بودم — *agar arʒan bud xaride budam,* If it had been cheap I would have bought it.

اگر پائیز میامدید هنوز نرفته بودیم — *agar paiʒ miamadid hanuʒ narafte budim,* If you had come in the autumn we would still have been there (we should not yet have gone).

If شاید *ſayad* 'perhaps' is introduced into the main sentence, the tense is not affected, e.g.

اگر آنجا میرفتید شاید اورا میدیدید — *agar anja miraftid ſayad ura mididid,* If you had gone there, perhaps you would have seen him.

See also Lesson XIII, para. 27.

---

١ بودن *budan* does not take می *mi-* in the Imperfect, see Lesson III, para. 8.

٢ داشتن *daſtan* does not take می *mi-* in the Imperfect, see Lesson III, para. 7.

6. 'But if not', 'or else', 'otherwise' are rendered by و اگر نه *va agar na* or و الا *va ella*, e.g.

اگر ممکن باشد میروم و اگر نه اینجا میمانم

*agar momken baſad miravam va agar na inja mimanam*,
If it is possible I shall go, but if not I shall stay here.

باید اینرا بخورید و الا گرسنه میمانید

*bayad inra bexorid va ella gorosne mimanid*,
You must eat this or else you will be (remain) hungry.

7. چنانچه *conance* is also used as a conditional conjunction, e.g.

چنانچه مایل باشید میتوانید بیائید    *conance mayel baſid mitavanid be-yaid*, If you care (to come) you can come.

چنانچه جویای حال ما باشید بد نیستیم    *conance juyaye hale ma baſid bad nistim*, If you want to know how we are (are inquiring of our state), we are well.

چنانچه کاری ندارید با ما بیائید    *conance kari nadarid ba ma beyaid*, If you have no work, come with us.

هرگاه *hargah* 'whenever' is also used as a conditional conjunction = 'if', e.g.

هرگاه اورا دیدید سلام مرا برسانید    *hargah ura didid salame mara berasanid*, If (whenever) you see him remember me (to him).

هرگاه مسافرت کنید یادی از ما بکنید    *hargah mosaferat konid yadi aʒ ma bekonid*, If (whenever) you go on a journey, think of us.

که *ke* is also used occasionally to mean 'if' when referring to the future and is followed by the Indicative Present, e.g.

این پولرا که باو میدهیم از دستمان میرود    *in pulra ke be u midehim aʒ dasteman miravad*, If we give him this money it will be lost to us.

8. The infinitive of the Causative is formed by the addition of انیـدن -anidan or اندن -andan to the present stem of the verb, e.g.

رسانیـدن rasanidan, رسـاندن rasandan, to cause to arrive, transmit (from رسیدن rasidan 'to arrive').

جوشانیدن jušanidan, جوشاندن jušandan to boil (trans.) (from جوشیدن jušidan to boil (intrans.)).

In Colloquial Persian the causative in اندن -andan tends to be used rather than the form in انیدن -anidan. نشستن nešastan 'to sit down' forms its causative irregularly thus: نشاندن nešandan 'to cause to sit down, to seat'.

Verbs the Present Stem of which ends in ان an, such as ماندن mandan 'to remain', cannot form a Causative.

9. Possibility is expressed by such expressions as ممکن است momken ast 'it is possible', or احتمال دارد ehtemal darad 'it is probable'. 'May' is normally translated by ممکن است momken ast followed by the Subjunctive Present with or without که ke.

## VOCABULARY

فکر fekr, thinking, thought; فکر کردن fekr k., to think.

سر وقت sare vaqt, on time, punctually.

وقتیکه vaqtike, when.

درس dars, lesson; درس خـواندن dars xandan, to take a lesson, have lessons, study.

حال hal, state, condition.

مسافرت mosaferat, journey.

کشتی kašti, ship; با کشتی ba kašti, by ship.

اقامت eqamat, residence, sojourn.

پایتخت païtaxt, capital city.

طبقه tabaqe, class (of people, etc.); storey (of building).

مقام maqam, place; rank, position.

کوه kuh, mountain.

رودخانه rudxane, river.

دریا darya, sea.

قصبه qasabe, small town.

ممکن momken, possible.

قدری qadri, a little.

ارجمند arjmand, exalted, high.

طولانی tulani, long, lengthy.

مختصر moxtasar, brief.

مدید madid, lengthy (of time).

قشنگ qašang, beautiful.

خوش    *xoʃ*, happy

خوشی    *xoʃi*, happiness.

آسان    *asan*, easy.

آسانی    *asani*, ease.

تفنگ    *tofang*, gun, rifle.

تمام    *tamam*, whole, complete; تمام کردن *tamam k.*, to complete, finish.

لازم    *laʒem*, necessary; لازم داشتن *laʒem daʃtan*, to need.

مدرسه    *madrase*, school.

قد    *qadd*, stature.

بلند قد    *boland qadd*, tall (of person).

کوتاه قد    *kutah qadd*, short (of person).

مؤدب    *mo'addab*, polite.

روان    *ravan*, flowing, fluent.

تنبل    *tambal*, lazy.

تنبلی    *tambali*, laziness; تنبلی کردن *tambali k.*, to be lazy.

حالا    *hala*, now.

هرگاه    *hargah*, whenever.

هرجا    *harja*, wherever, everywhere.

هم    *ham*, also.

اگرچه    *agarce*, although.

نشستن (نشین)    *neʃastan (neʃin)*, to sit.

نشان    *neʃan*, sign, badge; نشان دادن *neʃan dadan*, to show.

کم    *gom*, lost; گم کردن *gom k.*, to lose.

سعی    *saī*, effort; سعی کردن *saī k.*, to try, strive.[1]

سلام    *salam*, greeting.

یاد    *yad*, memory, mind.

حرف زدن    *harf ʒadan*, to speak.

## EXERCISE 13

پایتخت این مملکت شهر بزرگی است — اگر خواهر مرا دیدید این نامه را باو بدهید — اگر زودتر میامدید شما را آنجا میبردم — وقتیکه همراه خواهر و برادر خود بشهر میرفت ما را دید — ایران کوههای زیاد دارد — با سعی هر چه تمامتر درس میخواند — اگر زودتر راه افتاده بودیم این قدر دیر نمیرسیدیم — امسال باران هنوز نیامده است — شاید رفته باشد — اینرا باید از خواهر خودتان بپرسید — اگر منزل باشد از او میپرسم — باید آمده باشد — اگر فردا هوا خوب باشد بشهر میرویم — اگر این کتابرا خوانده باشید دیگر لازم ندارید — این پسر پیوسته درس میخواند همیشه زود در مدرسه حاضر میشود بسیار خوب درس میخواند و هرگز تنبلی نمیکند بیشتر کار میکند و کمتر حرف میزند با همه مؤدب است و همواره سعی میکند درس خود را خوب روان کند

---

[1] See Introduction, Alphabetical Table, under ع.

## EXERCISE 14*a*

1. If you go into the town buy me a little tea and coffee. 2. If your brother goes home he will take you with him. 3. It would have been better if you had gone last week. 4. They went to Persia by sea but they returned by land. 5. If I go tomorrow will you come with me? 6. There are many small towns and villages in this country. 7. If it is cold tonight it may freeze. 8. If it snows heavily the road may be closed. 9. This is worth at least twenty *rials*. 10. We go every year to the capital. 11. When I saw him he was walking quickly in the garden. 12. If you had come a fortnight ago the summer would not yet have been over.

## EXERCISE 14*b*

1. He did not allow us to go together. 2. I said this to him and nothing more. 3. Altogether it was not a bad book. 4. He suddenly got up and went out of the room. 5. He is given a certain amount of money every week. 6. We used to go to the town every year and stay there two months. 7. Persia consists chiefly of mountain and desert. 8. There are two hundred and fifty children in the school and all of them are under fifteen years of age. 9. I will come with you so that you do not get lost. 10. Let us sit down here because I am tired. 11. If you want to arrive punctually you had better go now (it is better that you go now). 12. You must go or you will be late.

## LESSON VIII

Conjunctions.[1] Relative Clauses. هر *har.* چنانکه *conanke* and چنینکه *coninke.* چنانچه *conance* and چنینچه *conince.* Indefinite Nouns and Pronouns.

1. Conjunctions can be divided into two main classes: co-ordinating conjunctions and subordinating conjunctions.

(*a*) Co-ordinating Conjunctions, e.g.

آیا...یا *aya...ya,* whether...or (interrog.).

چه...چه *ce...ce*
خواه...خواه *xah...xah*  } whether...or.

[1] See also Part II, Lesson XXI, paras. 19–21.

هم(و)...هم    *ham...(va) ham*, both...and.

نه(و)...نه    *na...(va) na*, neither...nor.

¹ مگر    *magar*, but (used with a negative question expecting the answer 'yes' or with an affirmative question expecting the answer 'no'), e.ʒ.

مگر اینطور نیست    *magar in tōur nist*, But is it not so?

مگر نرفتید    *magar naraftid*, But did you not go?

مگر آنجا بودید    *magar anja budid*, But were you there?

(*b*) Subordinating Conjunctions. These can be subdivided into

    (i) Adversative, e.g.

        مبادا (که)    *mabada (ke)*, lest.

    (ii) Conditional, e.g.

        اگر    *agar*, if.

        هرگه    *hargah*, if.

        که    *ke*, if.

        چنانچه    *conance*, if.

        مگر (اینکه)    *magar (inkc)*, unless.

        بدون اینکه    *bedune inke*, unless (without this that)

        تا    *ta*, unless.

    (iii) Concessive, e.g.

    با اینکه (آنکه)    *ba inke (anke)*, in spite of the fact that, notwithstanding that.

    هرچند( که)    *har cand (ke)*, even if, however much, although.

    چنانچه    *conance*, as, lest.

    چندانکه    *candanke*, notwithstanding that.

    اگرچه    *agarce*, although, even if.

If a concessive clause is introduced by اگرچه *agarce* the main clause is sometimes introduced by some such word as ولی *vali* 'but' or باز *baʒ* 'still', or with a negative verb by هنوز *hanuʒ*, e.g.

---

¹ In Classical Persian مگر *magar* is also used in story-telling='now, now it happened that'.

اگرچه مدتی با او زندگی کرده‌ام هنوز اورا نمیشناسم

*agarce moddati ba u ʒendegi karde am hanuʒ ura namiʃenasam,*

Although I lived with him for a (long) time, I do not know him.

اگرچه دیر وقت بود باز بمنزل برگشتیم

*agarce dir vaqt bud baʒ be manʒel bar gaʃtim,*

Although it was late we returned home.

(iv) Causal, e.g.

چون (که)   *cun (ke)*  ⎫
چه   *ce*   ⎪
زیرا (که)   *ʒira (ke)* ⎬ because.
از اینکه   *aʒ inke*   ⎪
که   *ke*   ⎭

(v) Final, e.g.

که   *ke,* that, in order that.

تا   *ta*   ⎫
تا اینکه   *ta inke* ⎭ in order that.

(vi) Consecutive, e.g.

آنقدر...که   *an qadr...ke* ⎫
چنان...که   *conan...ke* ⎭ so...that, e.g.

اوقاتش چنان تلخ شد که نتوانست حرف بزند

*ōuqateʃ conan talx ʃod ke natavanest harf beʒanad,*

He was so angry he could not speak.

از بس که   *aʒ bas ke,* so long, so much...that, e.g.

از بس که گفتم خسته شدم   *aʒ bas ke goftam xaste ʃodam,* I have
said (it) so much that I am tired.

از بس که نشستم خوابم میبرد   *aʒ bas ke neʃastam xabam mibarad,*
I have sat so long I am sleepy.

(vii) Temporal, e.g.

تا   *ta,* as long as, until, by the time that, since, as
soon as.

تا اینکه (آنکه)   *ta inke (anke),* as long as, by the time that; until.

چون   *cun,* when.

از موقعیکه   *aʒ mōuqe'ike,* since (from the time that).

پس از آنکه (اینکه)   *pas aʒ anke (inke)*, after.

پیش از آنکه (اینکه)   *piſ aʒ anke (inke)*, before.

هرگاه   *hargah*, whenever.

هیینکه   *haminke*, as soon as.

که   *ke*, when.

وقتیکه   *vaqtike*, when.

موقعیکه   *mōuqe'ike*, when, as.

The subject of the temporal clause precedes که *ke* 'when', e.g.

زمستان که میشود میرویم   *ʒamestan ke miſavad miravim*, When
it is winter we will go.

(viii) Comparative, e.g.

که *ke*, than, e.g.

بقدریکه *be qadrike*, as much as, e.g.

بقدریکه شما خوانده‌اید من نخوانده‌ام   *be qadrike ſoma xande id man
naxande am*, I have not read as
much as you.

اینقدر (آنقدر)...که *in qadr (an qadr)...ke*, as much...as, e.g.

هیچ وقت اینقدر حرف نمیزد که امشب حرف زد

*hic vaqt in qadr harf namiʒad ke emſab harf ʒad*,
He never used to speak as much as he spoke to-night.

2. Final Conjunctions take the Subjunctive Present (see Lesson VI,
para. 17 (a). تا *ta* 'by the time that' and تا *ta* 'until' referring to future
time also take the Subjunctive Present (see Lesson VI, para. 17 (b) and (c)).

مبادا (که) *mabada (ke)* 'lest' takes the subjunctive, e.g.

ترسیدم مبادا فراموش کرده باشید   *tarsidam mabada faramuſ karde baſid*,
I feared (lest) you had forgotten.

میترسم مبادا فراموش بکند   *mitarsam mabada faramuſ bekonad*,
I fear (lest) he may forget.

مگر اینکه *magar inke* 'unless' and بدون اینکه *bedune inke* 'unless'
also take the Subjunctive except in impossible conditions when they are followed by the Imperfect or
Pluperfect.

نمیایم مگر اینکه   *namiayam magar inke be man benevisid*, I shall not come
بمن بنویسید   unless you write to me.

پیش از آنکه (اینکه) *piʃ aʒ anke (inke)* 'before' takes the Subjunctive Present even when referring to time past, e.g.

پیش از آنکه اورا ببیم کاغذرا نوشتم     *piʃ aʒ anke ura bebinam kaɣaʒra neveʃtam*, I wrote the letter before I saw him.

بجای اینکه *bejaye inke* 'instead of (this that)', its synonym در عوض اینکه *dar avaʒe inke,* and جز اینکه *joʒ inke* and غیر از اینکه *ɣeir aʒ inke* 'except' are also followed by Present Subjunctive.

Other conjunctions, except Conditional Conjunctions,[1] are followed by the Indicative or Subjunctive according to whether the statement is one of fact or contains an element of doubt. Thus خواه...خواه *xah... xah* 'whether...or' referring to the future takes the Subjunctive, e.g.

خواه بیاید خواه نیاید میروم     *xah beyayad xah nayayad miravam*, Whether he comes or not I shall go.

Clauses introduced by Conditional, Concessive, Consecutive or Temporal Conjunctions normally precede the principal sentence. Clauses introduced by Adversative, Causal (except از اینکه *aʒ inke*) and Final Conjunctions follow the principal sentence.

3. Stress falls on the initial syllable of the following conjunctions:

        مگر     *magar,* but, unless.
        هرچند (که)     *har cand (ke),* even if.
        مبادا (که)     *mabada (ke),* lest.
        هرگه     *hargah,* whenever.
        اگرچه     *agarce,* although.
        چون (که)     *cun (ke)*
        زیرا (که)     *ʒira (ke)* } because.
        چرا (که)     *cera (ke)*
        همینکه     *haminke,* as soon as.
        چندانکه     *candanke,* not withstanding that.

In the case of اگر *agar* 'if' it falls on the initial or final syllable.
In the following it falls on the initial syllable or on این *in* or آن *an*:

        با اینکه (آنکه)     *ba inke (anke),* notwithstanding.
        تا اینکه (آنکه)     *ta inke (anke),* until, etc.

_____
[1] See Lesson VII, paras. 5–7 above.

پیش از آنکه (اینکه) *piʃ aẓ anke (inke)*, before.

پس از آنکه (اینکه) *pas aẓ anke (inke)*, after.

In از بس که *aẓ bas ke* 'so long' stress falls on بس *bas*.

4. تا *ta* is also used to mean 'let us see, behold, beware, namely' and is usually followed by the Subjunctive Present. This use of تا *ta* is common in Classical Persian especially in poetry, e.g.

بین تا چه بازی کند روزگار

*bebin ta ce baẓi konad ruẓgar,*

See (let us see) what tricks time will play.

عمر گرانمایه در این صرف شد ٭ تا چه خورم صیف و چه پوشم شتا

*omre geranmaye dar in sarf ʃod ta ce xoram seif o ce puʃam ʃeta,*

(My) precious life was spent in this, namely (in thinking) what shall I eat in summer and what shall I wear in winter.

ای که شخص منت حقیر نمود ٭ تا درشتی هنر نپنداری

*ei ke ʃaxse manat haqir namud ta doroʃti honar napandari,*

O thou to whom my person appeared contemptible, beware lest thou consider size (largeness) virtue.

5. Relative Clauses are introduced by the Relative Pronoun که *ke* 'who, which'. ی *-i* is added to the antecedent if definite unless this is a proper noun, a personal pronoun, a singular demonstrative pronoun,[1] a word doing duty for a pronoun,[2] a word to which a pronominal suffix has been added, a plural which is not particularized, or a noun used generically (see para. 12 below), e.g.

مردیکه آنجا بود کتابرا بمن داد *mardi ke anja bud ketabra beman dad,* The man who was there gave me the book.

If the antecedent is qualified by an adjective or adjectives these with the antecedent are regarded as a syntactical whole and the Relative ی *-i* is added to the final qualifying word, e.g.

دختر کوچکیکه پیش شما بود کی بود *doxtare kuceki ke piʃe ʃoma bud ki bud,* Who was the small girl who was with you?

[1] See below, para. 13.
[2] E.g. بنده *bande* 'slave', which is used for the Personal Pronoun 1st pers. sing. (see Lesson XIV, para. 1 (a) below).

If the word to which the Relative ی -i is added ends in ا a, و u, or ه e
it follows the same rules when the Relative ی -i is added as when the
Indefinite ی -i is added, see Lesson I, para. 2.

6. If the antecedent is definite and the direct object of the verb of the
principal sentence, and the relative pronoun is the subject of the relative
clause, the use of را -ra is optional. The Demonstrative Pronoun آن *an*
frequently qualifies the antecedent, e.g.

آن زنیرا که دیروز آمد دیدم      *an ʒanira ke diruʒ amad didam*, I saw
                                                     the woman who came yesterday,

or      آن زنیکه دیروز آمد دیدم      *an ʒani ke diruʒ amad didam.*

7. If the antecedent is definite and the subject of the principal sentence
and the relative pronoun is the direct object in the relative clause, the
antecedent can take را -ra; this, again, is optional, e.g.

زنیرا که دیدید اینجاست      *ʒanira ke didid injast*, The woman
                                                       whom you saw is here,

or      زنی که دیدید اینجاست      *ʒani ke didid injast.*

کتابیرا که بمن دادید گم شده است      *ketabira ke be man dadid gom ſode
                                                    ast*, The book which you gave
                                                    me is lost,

or   کتابی که بمن دادید گم شده است      *ketabi ke be man dadid gom ſode ast.*

8. If the relative pronoun is the indirect object of the relative clause
or governed by a preposition, a pronoun or pronominal suffix must be
used in the relative clause in addition to the Relative که *ke*, e.g.

مردهائیکه کتابهارا بآنها داده بودید رفتند      *mardhai ke ketabhara be anha
                                                           dade budid raftand*, The
                                                           men to whom you gave
                                                           the books went.

این همان مردیست که اسبی از او خریدم      *in haman mardist ke asbi aʒ u
                                                           xaridam*, This is the (same)
                                                           man from whom I bought
                                                           a horse.

این همان شخصی‌است که دیروز برادر شما با      *in haman ſaxsist ke diruʒ bar-
او بود                                                          adare ſoma ba u bud*, This
                                                           is the same person with
                                                           whom your brother was
                                                           yesterday.

9. If the antecedent is the predicate of the principal sentence, the verb of the principal sentence precedes the Relative که *ke* (see the last two examples in para. 8 above).

10. Since ی *-i* is added to the antecedent where this is definite, it follows that there will be a confusion between a definite antecedent followed by the Relative که *ke* and an indefinite antecedent to which the Indefinite ی *-i* has been already added, and that therefore پسریکه *pesari ke...* may mean 'the boy who' or 'a boy who'.

11. A distinction is made between 'descriptive' and 'restrictive' relative clauses. The latter type is closely linked to the antecedent in thought, whereas the former, while in a formal sense a dependent clause, does not limit the application of the antecedent, so that it is logically an independent proposition. In a 'descriptive' relative clause the relative pronoun که *ke* only is used, e.g.

مؤلف که نویسنده خوبی‌است این سبکرا اختیار کرده‌است

*mo'allef ke nevisandeye xubist in sabkra exteyar karde ast,*

The author, who is a good writer, has chosen this style.

12. If the antecedent is a plural which refers to a class or group as a whole, the Relative ی *-i* is not added to the antecedent, e.g.

باعتماد حسن ظن سیاستمداران جهان که در حل اینگونه مسائل تجربه زیاد
دارند موضوعرا مطرح میکنیم

*be e'temade hosne ẓanne siasatmadarane jahan ke dar halle ingune masa'el tajrebeye ẓiad darand mouẓu'ra matrah mikonim.*

Trusting in the good-will of the statesmen of the world, who have (had) much experience in solving such problems, we are bringing up the matter.

If the Relative ی *-i* were added to the antecedent in the above example, the meaning would be '...to those of the statesmen of the world who have...'.

Similarly if the antecedent is an abstract noun used generically, it does not take the Relative ی *-i*, e.g.

عقل که انسان بدان بر حیوان برتری دارد نعمت بزرگیست

*aql ke ensan bedan bar heivan bartari darad ne'mate boẓorgist.*

Reason, by which man has superiority over animals, is a great gift.

When not used generically abstract nouns take the Relative ی -i unless they end in ی -i, in which case the Relative ی -i is not added, e.g.

عقلیکه دارید ناقص است *aqli ke darid naqes ast,* Your reason (the reason which you have) is defective.

مهربانیرا¹ که بمن نشان دادید فراموش نمیکنم *mehrabanira ke be man neʃan dadid faramuʃ namikonam,* I shall not forget the kindness which you showed me.

13. The Relative ی -i is sometimes added to the Demonstrative Pronouns آنها *anha* 'those' and اینها *inha* 'these', e.g.

آنهائیکه آنجا بودند رفتند *anhai ke anja budand raftand,* Those who were there went.

Other Pronouns do not take the Relative ی -i, e.g.

شما که آنجا بودید بما بگوئید چه دیدید *ʃoma ke anja budid be ma beguid ce didid,* You, who were there, tell us what you saw.

In Colloquial Persian the Relative ی -i can be added to the personal pronouns; thus in the preceding example it would be possible to say شمائی که *ʃomai ke...* instead of شما که *ʃoma ke.*

In Colloquial Persian, also, the plural termination ها -ha can be added to the 1st and 2nd pers. pl. of the personal pronouns with the Relative ی -i to single out a group, e.g.

شماهائی که آنجا بودید چه دیدید *ʃomahai ke anja budid ce didid,* Those of you who were there, what did you see?

14. After آن *an* 'that' and این *in* 'this' چه *ce* is used as a Relative Pronoun, e.g.

از آنچه گفته شد معلوم میشود *az ance gofte ʃod maʿlum miʃavad,* It is (will be) evident from what has been said.

15. The Relative ی -i and the Relative Pronouns که *ke* and چه *ce* do not carry the stress.

¹ مهربانی *mehrabani,* kindness.

16. خود *xod*, خویش *xiſ* and خویشتن *xiſtan* used in a relative clause refer to the subject of that clause and not to the subject of the principal sentence, e.g.

حسین نامه‌ای بمن داد که علی به پدر خود نوشته بود

*hosein namei be man dad ke ali be pedare xod neveſte bud.*

Hosein gave me a letter which Ali had written to his (Ali's) father.

حسین نامه‌ای بمن داد که علی به پدرش نوشته بود

*hosein namei be man dad ke ali be pedaraſ neveſte bud.*

Hosein gave me a letter which Ali had written to his (Hosein's) father.

17. هر *har* 'every' is a distributive adjective which precedes the noun it qualifies. Prefixed to چه *ce*, که *ke* and کدام *kodam*, it means 'whatever', 'whoever' and 'whichever' respectively, e.g.

هرکه میخواهد بیاید زود بیاید　*har ke mixahad beyayad ʒud beyayad,* Whoever wants to come must be quick (let him be quick).

هرکدام از شما حاضر است برود　*har kodam aʒ ſoma haʒer ast beravad,* Whichever of you is ready can go (let him go).

هرچه کرد نتوانست دررا باز کند　*har ce kard natavanest darra baʒ konad,* Whatever he did he could not open the door.

هرچه *har ce* also means 'however much', e.g.

هرچه گشتم اورا پیدا نکردم　*har ce gaſtam ura peida nakardam,* However much I looked I did not find him.

هرکس *har kas* means 'anyone', e.g.

هر کسی که بیاید اورا بنشانید　*har kasi ke beyayad ura beneſanid,* Make whoever comes sit down.

هرکسیکه اینرا میداند بگوید　*har kasi ke inra midanad beguyad,* Let anyone who knows this speak.

هر دو *har do* means 'both', e.g.

هر دوشان رفتند　*har doeſan raftand,* They both went.

هر سه *har se*, هر چهار *har cahar*, etc., mean 'all three', 'all four', etc.

18. The Relative Pronoun که *ke* is suffixed to the Demonstratives چنان *conan* and چنین *conin* to mean 'just as, in the same way that, in this way that'.

---

**80**       **[VIII, 19–20**

19. چه *ce* is suffixed to چنان *conan* to mean 'just as, in the same way that, in case'.

20. There are a number of indefinite nouns, pronouns and adjectives in use. Among them are the following:

(a) همه *hame* 'all', e.g.

همه رفتند    *hame raftand*, All went.

همه شما بیائید    *hameye ʃoma beyaid*, All of you come.

همه‌کس *hame kas* means 'everyone'.

If the Pronominal Suffix for the 3rd pers. sing. is added to همه *hame* the *e* of *hame* is elided, e.g.

باغ همه‌اش سبز بود    *baɣ hamaʃ sabz bud*, The whole garden was green (the garden, the whole of it, was green).

(b) تمام *tamam* 'the whole, whole, complete', e.g.

تمام روز در شهر بود    *tamame ruz dar ʃahr bud*, He was the whole day in the town.

آنرا تمام خورد    *anra tamam xord*, He ate it all (wholly).

با خوشی تمام بیرون رفت    *ba xoʃiye tamam birun raft*, He went out completely happy (with complete happiness).

(c) سائر *sa'er* (also written سایر and pronounced *sayer*) 'the rest', e.g.

سائر کتابهارا فروخت    *sa'ere ketabhara foruxt*, He sold the rest of the books.

(d) فلان *folan* means 'such a one, such and such, so-and-so' and is used as a noun or adjective, e.g.

فلان کس آمد    *folan kas amad*, Such and such a person came.

The Indefinite ی *-i* can be added to فلان *folan* when it is used as a noun, e.g.

فلانی آمد    *folani amad*, So-and-so came.

(e) بعضی *ba'zi* means 'some'. It precedes the noun it qualifies, which is put in the plural, and does not take the *ezafe*, e.g.

بعضی کتابها    *ba'zi ketabha*, some books.

در بعضی جاها    *dar ba'zi jaha*, in some places.

It is also used as a noun, e.g.

بعضی رفتند بعضی ماندند    *ba'zi raftand ba'zi mandand*, Some went (and) some remained.

When used as a noun بعضی *ba'ʒi* takes از *aʒ* rather than the *eʒafe*, e.g.

بعضی از شما    *ba'ʒi aʒ ʃoma*, some of you.

بعضی از آنها    *ba'ʒi aʒ anha*, some of them.

بعضی از برادران او    *ba'ʒi aʒ baradarane u*, some of his brothers.

In Colloquial Persian the plural termination ها *-ha* is often added to بعضی *ba'ʒi* when it is used as a noun, e.g.

بعضیها آنجا هستند    *ba'ʒiha anja hastand*, Some are there.

(*f*) برخی *barxi* 'some' is used in the same way as بعضی *ba'ʒi* above, but it does not take the plural termination ها *-ha*.

(*g*) اندك *andak* means 'a little, few'. It usually precedes the word it qualifies, e.g.

اندك فرصت بمن بدهید    *andak forsat be man bedehid*, Give me a little (short) respite.

It can be strengthened by the addition of the Indefinite ی *-i*, e.g.

اندکی فکر کرد    *andaki fekr kard*, He thought a little.

(*h*) بس *bas* means 'many a'. It precedes the noun it qualifies, which is put in the singular, e.g.

بس جان بلب آمد    *bas jan be lab amad*, Many a soul has passed away.

The Indefinite ی *-i* is added to بس *bas* to mean 'many a'. The following noun is put in the plural, e.g.

بسی مردم    *basi mardom*⎫
بسی اشخاص   *basi aʃxas*⎭ many people.

بسی *basi* is also used to mean 'a long while'.

(*i*) The Indefinite ی *-i* is added to بسیار *besyar* to mean 'many'. It is used as a noun and followed by از *aʒ*, e.g.

بسیاری از مردم میگویند    *besyari aʒ mardom miguyand*, Many people say.

(*j*) یك خرده *yak xorde* means 'a little', e.g.

یك خرده آب بمن بدهید    *yak xorde ab be man bedehid*, Give me a little water.

(*k*) جزئی *joʒ'i* (from جزء *joʒ'* 'part, portion') also means 'a little', e.g.

جزئی کسالت دارد    *joʒ'i kesalat darad*, He is slightly indisposed.

## VOCABULARY

شمال *femal, famal*, north (subs.).

جنوب *jonub*, south (subs.).

مغرب *mayreb*, west (subs.).

مشرق *mafreq*, east (subs.)

عید *id*, festival, feast-day; عید گرفتن *id gereftan*, to celebrate a festival.

علم *elm*, knowledge.

عیب *eib*, fault.

هنر *honar*, skill; knowledge.

فائده *fa'ede*, benefit.

اندیشه *andife*, thought.

فرق *farq*, difference; فرق کردن *farq k.*, to make a difference.

نوروز *nouruz*, New Year's day (1st Farvardin, which coincides with 20th, 21st or 22nd March).

ییلاق *yeilaq*, summer quarters, hill station.

قشلاق *qeflaq*, winter quarters (of a tribe).

مدت *moddat*, period (length of time).

جان *jan*, soul.

جنگ *jang*, war.

صلح *solh*, peace.

ریال *rial*, a unit of currency.

شماره *fomare*, number.

مردم *mardom*, people.

روزنامه *ruzname*, newspaper.

مبلغ *mablay*, sum (of money).

حساب *hesab*, account, bill.

بانک *bank*, bank.

نشانی *nefani*, address.

دفتر *daftar*, office; exercise book.

درد *dard*, pain; بدرد خوردن *be dard xordan*, to be useful; بدرد من نمیخورد *be darde man namixorad*, it is no use to me.

ملایم *molayem*, soft.

معتدل *mo'tadel*, moderate.

تاریک *tarik*, dark.

تاریکی *tariki*, darkness.

روشن *roufan*, light, clear.

روشنائی *roufanai*, light, clearness.

ملی *melli*, national, popular.

منتشر *montafer*, published; منتشر کردن *montafer k.*, to publish.

دریافت *daryaft*, receipt (of something).

مرتب *morattab*, orderly, regular.

تحویل *tahvil*, handing over, transfer; تحویل کردن *tahvil k.*, to hand over.

کامل *kamel*, complete, full, perfect.

اتفاق *ettefaq*, happening; اتفاق افتادن *ettefaq oftadan*, to happen, take place.

وزیدن *vazidan* to blow (wind, etc.).

مهربان *mehraban*, kind.

مهربانی *mehrabani*, kindness.

فراموش کردن *faramuʃ kardan*, to forget.

معلوم *maʿlum*, evident, known.

ناقص *naqes*, defective.

پشیمان *paʃiman*, regretful.

آخر *axer*, end; last; finally.

اختیار *exteyar*, freedom of choice.

حرف *harf*, word, speech.

عمل *amal*, action, practice.

مایل بودن *mayel budan*, to desire, be inclined (to).

فرستادن (فرست) *ferestadan* (*ferest*), to send.

اعتماد *eʿtemad*, confidence; reliance (on).

انسان *ensan*, mankind, man (used generically).

تجربه *tajrebe*, experience.

حسن *hosn*, beauty, goodness; حسن ظن *hosne zann*, good-will.

حل *hall*, solving, solution.

مسئله *masʿale*, problem (pl. مسائل *masaʿel*).

حیوان *heivan*, animal (pl. حیوانات *heivanat*).[1]

سیاست *siasat*, policy; politics; diplomacy.

سیاستمدار *siasatmadar*, statesman.

سبك *sabk*, style.

زیان *zian*, loss, injury; زیان دیدن *zian didan*, to suffer loss.

نصیحت *nasihat* } advice.
اندرز *andarz* }

خیر *xeir*, good (noun); خواه خیر *xeirxah*, well-wisher.

وصول *vosul*, arrival, arriving.

عقل *aql*, reason, intelligence.

مطرح کردن *matrah kardan*, to bring up, discuss, debate.

موضوع *mouzuʿ*, subject, matter.

بر حذر بودن *bar hazar b.*, to be beware.

مراجعت *morajeʿat*, return; مراجعت کردن *morajeʿat k.*, to return.

آموختن (آموز) *amuxtan* (*amuz*), to learn; teach.

پذیرفتن (پذیر) *paziroftan* (*pazir*), to accept; to entertain.

عاید گردیدن *ayed gardidan*, to accrue.

کسالت *kesalat*, indisposition.

---

[1] This is an Arabic sound feminine plural (see Part II, Lesson xix).

## EXERCISE 15

آن کتابهائیکه دیروز خریدید بمن نشان بدهید — پسریکه بمنزل ما آمد برادر
آن دختر است — هرکسی که میخواهد بیاید باید زود بیـایـد — بچههائیکه
همراه او بودند کوچك بودند — آنچهرا که گفته شد شنید¹ — عیـد نوروز کـه در
اول بهار اتفاق میافتد بزرگترین عید ملی ایران است — بعضی روزها در تابستان
هوا بسیارگرم میشود — بهارکه میشود بیشتر مردم بییلاق میروند — کسانیکه
مایل بدریافت مرتب روزنامه باشند² میتوانند مبلغ یك صد و هشتاد ریال برای
مـدت یك سال و یك صد ریال برای شش ماه بحساب روزنامه ببانك ملی تحویل
کنند و نشانی کامل خودرا بدفتر روزنامه بنویسند تا هر روزه یك شماره مرتب
فرستاده شود — هرکه عیب دیگران با تو گوید از او بر حذر باش که عیب ترا
نیز بدیگران گوید — تا توانید علم و هنر آموزید که فائده آن بشما عاید گردد —
بسیار فرق باشد از حرف تا عمل — تا مراجعت کنید درسرما حاضر خواهم کرد —
چه بگوید چه نگـویـد این کاررا خواهم کرد — چه کردید که اینگونه پشیمان
شدید — اندرز خیرخواهانرا بپذیرید چه هرکه نصیحت نشنود زیان بیند

## EXERCISE 16

1. This is the man who was here yesterday. 2. He waited for the man whom I had seen in the garden. 3. Perhaps the boy who was in the garden opened the door so that his sister might go in. 4. Last night it was dark when I returned home. 5. He could not come because he was ill. 6. The boy cannot come until his father returns. 7. Notwithstanding the fact that we went early it was dark by the time that we arrived at the town. 8. He thought for a little and then answered. 9. When we arrived everyone (all) had gone. 10. You are so late I feared you had forgotten. 11. Write the letter before you go. 12. I did not stay long (much) after you went home. 13. There is no point in your coming unless you want to come (it has no benefit that you should come unless...). 14. Whenever I go there I want to stay (there).

¹ آنچه *ance* cannot be divided by را *ra*. If را *ra* is used که *ke* must usually be added.
² See Lesson XIII, para. 10 for the use of the General Present.

### EXERCISE 17

1. I saw him yesterday after I had seen you.　2. As soon as it rained we returned.　3. I wanted to buy the rest of the books.　4. At (the time of the) New Year, which is the biggest festival of the year in Persia, the people go to see each other and celebrate the holiday for at least five days.　5. If you wish to receive the newspaper regularly you must send 250 rials to the office of the newspaper.　6. If you rely upon their good-will you will be disappointed.　7. If you are unable to come it does not matter.　8. If I knew the solution of this problem I would tell you.　9. He feared that his mother was ill.　10. If you go to Tehran write a letter to me.　11. If he has not gone I will tell him.　12. He forgot to tell you.　13. I should like to come with you to Persia, because I have never been there.　14. In my opinion, it would be better if we discussed the matter now.　15. Whether you go or not makes no difference.　16. This book will be useful to you.

## LESSON IX

### Compound Verbs

1. Compound verbs are formed by a simple verb combined with a noun, adjective, adverb or prepositional phrase. The following simple verbs are commonly used to form compounds: (کن ) کردن *kardan* (*kon*) 'to do, make', (نما) نمودن *namudan* (*nama*) 'to show', (دار) داشتن *daſtan* (*dar*) 'to have, possess', (ده) دادن *dadan* (*deh*) 'to give', (زن) زدن *zadan* (*zan*) 'to strike', (شو) شدن *ſodan* (*ſav-, ſou*) 'to become', (گرد) گشتن *gaſtan* (*gard*) 'to become', خوردن *xordan* 'to eat', (آ) آمدن *amadan* (*a*) 'to come', کشیدن *kaſidan* 'to pull, draw', (افت) افتادن *oftadan* (*oft*) 'to fall', (گیر) گرفتن *gereftan* (*gir*) 'to take', (یاب) یافتن *yaftan* (*yab*) 'to find' and (بر) بردن *bordan* (*bar*) 'to take, carry'.

　شدن *ſodan* and گشتن *gaſtan*, while interchangeable when used to form the Passive Voice (see Lesson VI, para. 4), are not in all cases interchangeable when used to form compound verbs. نمودن *namudan* can usually be substituted for کردن *kardan*.

　　(*a*) Compound verbs formed by a simple verb[1] and a noun, e.g.
(دادن) گوش کردن *guſ kardan* (*dadan*), to listen.

---

[1] For the Present Stems of Irregular Verbs see Appendix L.

گردش کردن  gardef kardan, to go for a walk.

دست دادن  dast dadan, to shake hands.

چانه زدن  cane ʒadan, to bargain (over a price, etc.).

آتش زدن  atef ʒadan, to set fire to.

آتش گرفتن  atef gereftan, to catch fire.

آتش کردن  atef kardan, to start (an engine, trans.).

کشتی گرفتن  kofti gereftan, to wrestle.

پاس دادن  pas dadan, to keep watch (sentry-go).

سپری شدن  separi fodan, to disappear, come to an end.

سوگند خوردن  sŏugand xordan, to swear, take an oath.

زمین خوردن  ʒamin xordan, to fall down (usually of persons).

سر آمدن  sar amadan, to overflow, boil over; fall due.

بار آمدن  bar amadan, to be trained, brought up.

رنج کشیدن (بردن)  ranj kafidan (bordan), to suffer, take trouble.

سر کشیدن  sar kafidan, to drink to the dregs; to revolt, turn aside; to oversee.

راه افتادن  rah oftadan, to set out, start (on a journey).

رخت بستن  raxt bastan, to set off on a journey, pack; to die.

یخ بستن  yax bastan, to freeze (intrans.).

نام گذاشتن  nam goʒaftan, to give a name to (someone).

نماز گذاشتن  namaʒ goʒaftan, to perform one's prayers, to pray.

Many verbs are formed with a Verbal Noun and a simple verb such as کردن kardan. The tendency in Modern Persian is to use such compounds rather than the simple verb, e.g.

وادار کردن  vadar k. 'to persuade, oblige' rather than وا داشتن va daftan.

کوشش کردن  kufef kardan, 'to try, strive' rather than کوشیدن kufidan.

(b) Compound verbs formed by a simple verb and an adjective, e.g.

باز کردن  baʒ kardan, to open.

پیدا کردن  pēida kardan, to find.

جوش آمدن     *juʃ amadan*, to boil (intrans.).

پسند آمدن     *pasand amadan*, to be agreeable.

دور افتادن     *dur oftadan*, to be separated.

بلند کردن     *boland kardan*, to raise, lift; to steal (colloq.).

(c) Compound verbs formed by a simple verb and a preposition or adverb equivalent:

باز *baʒ*, again, back, e.g.

باز آمدن     *baʒ amadan*, to come again.

باز داشتن     *baʒ daʃtan*, to restrain, intern, detain.

وا *va* (used only in compounds), back, again, e.g.

وا داشتن     *va daʃtan*, to restrain; persuade, oblige (someone to do something).

وا زدن     *va ʒadan*, to reject, refuse.

واگذاشتن     *va goʒaʃtan*, to leave, abandon; cede, make over.

بر *bar*, on, up, off, e.g.

بر آمدن     *bar amadan*, to be accomplished; to rise, swell.

بر آوردن     *bar avardan*, to fulfil, accomplish, estimate.

بر آشفتن     *bar aʃoftan*, to disturb, agitate.

بر افراشتن     *bar afraʃtan*, to raise up.

بر انداختن     *bar andaxtan*, to overthrow.

بر انگیختن     *bar angixtan*, to stir up, excite.

بر خاستن     *bar xastan*, to rise, get up.

بر خوردن (به)     *bar xordan (be)*, to meet (fortuitously); to offend.

بر داشتن     *bar daʃtan*, to take up, off, remove; کلاه بر داشتن *kolah bar daʃtan*, to swindle; محصول بر داشتن *mahsul bar daʃtan*, to collect the crops, harvest.

بر کندن     *bar kandan*, to take off (clothes); to uproot.

بر گزیدن     *bar goʒidan*, to choose, select.

بر گشتن     *bar gaʃtan*, to return.

ور *var*, away, off, up (used only in compounds), e.g.

ور آمدن     *var amadan*, to rise (bread, etc.).

ور رفتن     *var raftan*, to fiddle, fidget.

پیش *piʃ*, before, forward, e.g.

پیش آمدن    *piʃ amadan*, to occur, happen.

پیش افتادن    *piʃ oftadan*, to come to the fore, take the lead.

پیش کشیدن    *piʃ kaʃidan*, to bring forward.

پیش بردن    *piʃ bordan*, to win, gain the upper hand.

در *dar*, in; also conveys a sense of completion. E.g.

در آمدن    *dar amadan*, to come out (in Modern Persian); to go in, to come out (in Classical Persian).

در آموختن    *dar amuxtan*, to learn thoroughly.

در آوردن    *dar avardan*, to bring in, out, take out; to learn.

در رسیدن    *dar rasidan*, to overtake, come upon.

در رفتن    *dar raftan*, to flee, slip away; to go off (a gun, etc.).

در گذشتن    *dar goɀaʃtan*, to die; to pass over, forgive.

در گرفتن    *dar gereftan*, to catch (a fire, etc.); to 'catch on'.

در ماندن    *dar mandan*, to become helpless, distressed, destitute; to be tired out.

در کردن    *dar kardan*, to let off (a gun, etc.).

فرا *fara*, behind, back, again; the addition of فرا *fara* makes the verb emphatic.[1] E.g.

فرا آمدن    *fara amadan*, to come.

فرا رفتن    *fara raftan*, to go.

فرا افکندن    *fara afkandan*, to throw.

فرا گرفتن    *fara gereftan*, to learn (well).

فرو *foru*, فرود *forud* down; فرو *foru* is also used to make the verb emphatic. E.g.

فرود آمدن    *forud amadan*, to alight, come down.

فرو بردن    *foru bordan*, to swallow; to immerse.

---

[1] فرا *fara* is used to form compound verbs in Classical rather than Modern Persian. فراز *faraɀ*, up, again, under, back, is similarly used in Classical Persian to emphasize the verb, e.g.

فراز آمدن    *faraɀ amadan*, to approach, enter.
فراز دادن    *faraɀ dadan*, to give back.
فراز آوردن    *faraɀ avardan*, to obtain.

فرو رفتن *foru raftan*  
فرو شدن *foru ſodan* } to sink, go under.

فرو نشستن *foru neſastan,* to subside (a rebellion, etc.); to sit down.

فرو ایستادن *foru istadan,* to stop (rain, etc.).

(*d*) Compound verbs formed by a simple verb and a prepositional phrase, e.g.

بجا آوردن *be ja avardan,* to perform, accomplish.

در صدد بر آمدن *dar sadad bar amadan,* to intend (to do something).

بكار بردن *be kar bordan,* to make use of.

بسر بردن *be sar bordan,* to spend, pass (time).

بسر آمدن *be sar amadan,* to fall due.

از دست دادن *aʒ dast dadan,* to give up, lose.

از بین رفتن *aʒ bein raftan,* to disappear, be lost.

سر بسر گذاشتن *sar be sar goʒaſtan,* to tease.

بشمار رفتن *be ſomar raftan,* to be considered, reckoned as.

در بر گرفتن *dar bar gereſtan,* to embrace.

در میان نهادن *dar mian nehadan,* to lay before (someone, something), discuss.

(*e*) Compound verbs formed by a simple verb and the present stem or some part of another verb, e.g.

گیر کردن *gir kardan,* to get stuck.

گیر آوردن *gir avardan,* to get, obtain (possession of something).

نیست و نابود کردن *nist o nabud kardan,* to destroy utterly.

2. Compound verbs are also formed by a simple verb combined with an Arabic participle, noun or adjective:[1]

(*a*) With an Arabic Noun, e.g.

فكر کردن *fekr kardan,* to think.

حرکت کردن *harakat kardan,* to set out, start.

صبر کردن *sabr kardan,* to wait, have patience.

---

[1] For Arabic forms see Part II.

قناعت کردن  *qana'at kardan*, to be contented, satisfied (with), make do (with).

تعلیم کردن  *ta'lim kardan*, to teach.

مطالعه کردن  *motale'e kardan*, to study, read.

غارت کردن  *ɣarat kardan*, to plunder.

تعجب کردن  *ta'ajjob kardan*, to be surprised.

التفات کردن  *eltefat kardan*, to pay attention.

دوام کردن  *davam kardan*, to be durable.

نقش بستن  *naqʃ bastan*, to stamp (cloth, etc.).

فائده بردن (از)  *fa'ede bordan (aʒ)*, to benefit (from).

حمله بردن (به)  *hamle bordan (be)*, to attack.

اتفاق افتادن  *ettefaq oftadan*, to happen, occur.

ارسال داشتن  *ersal daʃtan*, to send.

امکان داشتن  *emkan daʃtan*, to be possible.

جرأت داشتن  *jor'at daʃtan*, to dare.

شهرت داشتن  *ʃohrat daʃtan*, to be famous.

حرف زدن  *harf ʒadan*, to talk.

قدم زدن  *qadam ʒadan*, to walk (up and down).

صدا زدن  *sada ʒadan*, to call.

طعنه زدن  *ta'ne ʒadan*, to make insulting insinuations.

شعله زدن  *ʃo'le ʒadan*, to be in flames.

نسبت دادن (به)  *nesbat dadan (be)*, to attribute (to).

خبر کردن (دادن)  *xabar kardan (dadan)*, to inform, notify.

عذر خواستن  *oʒr xastan*, to ask pardon.

مصلحت دیدن  *maslahat didan*, to consider expedient.

طول کشیدن  *tul kaʃidan*, to last (of time).

انس گرفتن  *ons gereftan*, to become fond of.

قرار گرفتن  *qarar gereftan*, to become established, settled; to be calmed, consoled.

تصمیم گرفتن  *tasmim gereftan*, to decide.

عیب گرفتن  *eib gereftan*, to find fault.

تغافل ورزیدن  *taɣafol varʒidan*, to show neglect.

وفات یافتن  *vafat yaftan*, to die.

تأسف خوردن   *ta'assof xordan*, to regret.

سفره انداختن   *sofre andaxtan*, to lay the table.

ادامه پیدا کردن   *edame peida kardan*, to continue (intrans.).

(b) With an Arabic Participle, e.g.

منکوب کردن   *mankub kardan*, to conquer.

مغلوب کردن   *maγlub kardan*, to defeat.

منصرف کردن   *monsaref kardan*, to dissuade.

متحیر کردن   *motahaiyer kardan*, to surprise, astonish.

غالب آمدن (بر)   *γaleb amadan (bar)*, to conquer.

(c) With an Arabic Adjective, e.g.

اسیر گرفتن (کردن)   *asir gereftan (kardan)*, to take prisoner.

مریض شدن   *mariz ʃodan*, to be, become ill.

سوار کردن   *savar kardan*, to take on board, to put on a horse, etc.

(d) With an Arabic Noun combined with a preposition, e.g.

باتمام رساندن   *be etmam rasandan*, to finish, bring to an end.

بوجود آوردن   *be vojud avardan*, to bring into existence.

بخاطر آوردن   *be xater avardan*, to bring to mind, recall.

بغارت بردن   *be γarat bordan*, to carry off as plunder.

بهدر رفتن   *be hadar raftan*, to be wasted, go to waste.

3. Compound verbs, with certain exceptions, form their passive in the usual way with شدن *ʃodan*, e.g.

بر انداخته شدن   *bar andaxte ʃodan*, to be overthrown.

بر گزیده شدن   *bar goɀide ʃodan*, to be chosen.

(a) If a compound verb formed with کردن *kardan* is transitive شدن *ʃodan* replaces کردن in the Passive Voice, e.g.

اعلام کردن   *e'lam kardan*, to announce.

اعلام شدن   *e'lam ʃodan*, to be announced.

راضی کردن   *raɀi kardan*, to satisfy, secure the agreement of (someone).

راضی شدن   *raɀi ʃodan*, to be satisfied.

اسیر کردن   *asir kardan*, to take prisoner.

اسیر شدن   *asir ʃodan*, to be taken prisoner.

(b) Some compound verbs formed with زدن ẓadan change this into خوردن xordan in the Passive Voice, e.g.

گول زدن   gul ẓadan, to deceive.

گول خوردن   gul xordan, to be deceived.

بهم زدن   be ham ẓadan, to disturb, break up, dissolve (a meeting, etc.).

بهم خوردن   be ham xordan, to be broken up, dissolved.

مجلس بهم خورد   majles be ham xord, The meeting (assembly) broke up.

Note also the colloquial phrase (used only of persons)

میانشان بهم خورد   mianefan be ham xord, Relations between them were broken off, they quarrelled.

(c) Some compound verbs formed with دادن dadan also change this into خوردن xordan in the Passive Voice, e.g.

شکست دادن   fekast dadan, to defeat.

شکست خوردن   fekast xordan, to be defeated.

(d) Some compound verbs formed with دادن dadan change this into یافتن yaftan in the Passive Voice, e.g.

پرورش دادن   parvaref dadan, to educate, bring up.

پرورش یافتن   parvaref yaftan, to be educated.

انجام دادن   anjam dadan, to accomplish.

انجام یافتن   anjam yaftan, to be accomplished.

(e) ارسال داشتن ersal daftan 'to send' becomes ارسال شدن ersal fodan in the Passive Voice.

4. The verbal prefixes are affixed in the normal way to the verbal part of a compound, e.g.

بر میگردم   bar migardam, I will return.

فکر نمیکنم   fekr namikonam, I do not think.

Compound verbs formed with بر bar, باز baẓ, وا va, ور var or در dar and a simple verb omit the verbal prefix بِ be, e.g.

بر گرد   bar gard, Return.

5. The Pronominal Suffixes are added to the non-verbal part of the verb, e.g.

بیرونش کردم     *biruneʃ kardam*, I turned him out.

بهمش زد     *be hameʃ ʒad*, He broke it up.

خبرشان کرد     *xabareʃan kard*, He informed them.

برش گرداندم     *bareʃ gardandam*, I caused him to return, turned him back.

Not only are the Pronominal Suffixes interposed between the verbal and the non-verbal parts of the compound, but, if the compound is formed by a simple verb and a noun or participle, other words and phrases can be so interposed with the *eʒafe*, e.g.

جرأت این کاررا نداشت     *jor'ate in karra nadaʃt*, He did not dare do this (work).

سوار کشتی شد     *savare kaʃti ʃod*, He went on board the ship.

6. Stress in compound verbs falls:

(a) In the affirmative on the final syllable of the non-verbal part of the compound, e.g.

پرورش یافت     *parva'reʃ yaft*, He was educated.

پیدا میکند     *peï'da mikonad*, He will find.

بر میگردیم     *'bar migardim*, We shall return.

بکار خواهد برد     *be 'kar xahad bord*, He will use (it).

حرکت کرده است     *hara'kat karde ast*, He has set out.

راضی شد     *ra'ʒi ʃod*, He was satisfied.

بوجود آورد     *be vo'jud avard*, He created.

(b) In the negative on the negative prefix. A secondary stress may also be carried on the final syllable of the non-verbal part of the compound, e.g.

بر نمیگردیم     *bar 'namigardim* or *'bar 'namigardim*, We shall not return.

حرکت نکرده است     *harakat 'nakarde ast* or *hara'kat 'nakarde ast*, He has not set out.

7. Secondary verbs are in some cases formed from the Present Stem of irregular verbs, e.g.

کوبیدن     *kubidan* 'to pound' from کوفتن *kuftan* (کوب *kub*).

تابیدن     *tabidan* 'to twist, shine' from تافتن *taftan* (تاب *tab*).

## Vocabulary

استیلا estila, conquest.

مغول moɣul, moɣol, Mongol.

دوره doure, period.

تاریخ tarix, history; تاریخی tarixi, historical.

امیر تیمور گورکان amir teimur gurakan, Tamerlane.

واقعه vaqe'e, event, happening (pl. وقایع vaqaye').

قبل از qabl aʒ, before.

صفویه safaviye, the Safavid Dynasty (which ruled in Persia A.D. 1502–1736).

صفوی safavi, Safavid.

نوبه noube, turn.

باعث ba'es, cause.

قتل qatl, murder, killing.

غارت ɣarat, plunder.

خونریزی xunriʒi, bloodshed.

خرابی xarabi, ruin, devastation.

بیشمار bifomar, innumerable.

کشور kefvar, country.

اسلامی eslami, Islamic.

عموماً omuman, in general.

خصوصاً xosusan, in particular.

حمله hamle, attack (pl. حملات hamalat).

صدمه sadame, injury, blow; صدمه دیدن sadame didan, to suffer injury.

پرتگاه partgah, precipice.

انحطاط enhetat, decay, decline.

عجیب ajib, strange, wonderful.

قوس qous, arc.

نزولی noʒuli, descending.

پیمودن peimudan (peima), to measure, tread. (پیما)

تنزل tanaʒʒol, decline.

کمک komak, help; کمک کردن komak k., to help.

ترقی taraqqi, progress.

بر رو(ی) bar ru(ye), on.

گذشته از goʒafte aʒ, apart from.

خرافات xorafat, superstition(s).

وهم vahm, vanity, fancy (pl. اوهام ouham).

ترک tork, Turk; Turkish (adj.).

نتیجه natije, result.

تعصب ta'assob, fanaticism.

جاهلانه jahelane, ignorant.

مرکز markaʒ, centre.

تمدن tamaddon, civilization.

اروپا orupa, Europe.

غربی ɣarbi, western.

امریکا amrika, America.

مانع mane', impediment, obstacle (pl. موانع mavane').

داخل daxel, inner, inside; داخل شدن daxel f., to enter.

داخلی daxeli, internal, interior.

¹ See Part II, Lesson XXI, for the formation of Arabic Adverbs.

رابطه *rabete*, connexion, relation (pl. روابط *ravabet*).

خارج *xarej*, abroad, outside.

خارجه *xareje*, abroad, a foreign country.

سهولت *sohulat*, ease; بسهولت *be sohulat*, easily, with ease.

اخذ کردن *axz kardan*, to take.

مانند *manand*, like; it is followed by the noun it governs and takes the *ezafe*.

ممالك *mamalek*, pl. of مملکت *mamlekat*, country.

قدم *qadam*, step; قدم بر داشتن *qadam bar daftan*, to advance, progress.

استیلای مغول در ایران [1]

دوره دویست ساله تاریخی مغول و استیلای امیر تیمور گورکان و وقایع دیگریکه قبل از صفویه در ایران اتفاق افتاد هریك بنوبه خود باعث قتل و غارت و خونریزی و خرابیهای بیشمار در کشورهای اسلامی عمومًا و کشور ایران خصوصًا گردید ایران از همه بیشتر در این حملات صدمه دید و در پرتگاه انحطاط عجیب افتاده [1] قوس نزولیرا میپیمود و چیز دیگری که بانحطاط و تنزل ایران کمک میکرد و روز بروز درهای ترقیرا بر روی آن میبست گذشته از خرافات و اوهامیکه از استیلای مغول و ترکان نتیجه شده بود تعصب جاهلانه مردم و قرار گرفتن مرکز [2] تمدن در اروپای غربی و امریکا بود و ایران با موانع داخلی که برای روابط با خارج داشت دیگر نمیتوانست از اروپا بسهولت اخذ تمدن کند یا مانند آن ممالك در راه ترقی قدم بر دارد

[1] اقتباس از تاریخ ایران از مغول تا افشاریه تألیف رضا پازوکی

## EXERCISE 18

1. In winter when it is cold it freezes. 2. Yesterday morning we went for a walk outside the town. 3. What we said offended them. 4. Before you return you must listen to what I have (want) to say. 5. He has not yet come out of his room. 6. It is a long time since he died. 7. This book is attributed to him. 8. He determined to go to Persia. 9. He died twenty years ago. 10. I was reading a book when he came in. 11. He was defeated. 12. The village was plundered. 13. We considered it expedient to go because it was late and we wanted

[1] For this use of the Past Participle see Lesson XIII, para. 2 (c).

[2] For this use of the Infinitive see Lesson XIII, para. 1 (a).

to reach home before it got dark. **14.** The Mongol invasion, which took place in the thirteenth century, caused much damage to Persia and it was many years before the country recovered from the devastation caused by the Mongols; many centres of learning and civilization were destroyed and thousands of people were killed.

## LESSON X

**Word Formation. Abstract Nouns. Verbal Nouns. Nominal Suffixes. Diminutives. Adjectival Suffixes. Compound Nouns. Compound Adjectives.**

**1.** Abstract Nouns are formed by the suffix ی -*i*, e.g.

خوبی    *xubi*, goodness (from خوب *xub* 'good').

مردی    *mardi*, manliness, generosity (from مرد *mard* 'man').

درشتی    *dorofti*, thickness (from درشت *doroft* 'thick').

If the Abstract ی -*i* is added to a word ending in ا *a* or و *u*, a *hamʒe* over a bearer is prefixed to it. This marks the transition from one vowel to another and is not represented in the transcription, e.g.

دانائی    *danai*, wisdom (from دانا *dana* 'wise').

خوشروئی    *xofrui*, beauty (from خوشرو *xofru* 'beautiful').

If the Abstract ی -*i* is added to a word ending in ه -*e*, the latter is changed into ک *g*, e.g.

خستگی    *xastegi*, fatigue (from خسته *xaste* 'tired').

شایستگی    *fayestegi*, fitness, worthiness (from شایسته *fayeste* 'worthy fitting').

زندگی    *ʒendegi*, life (from زنده *ʒende* 'alive').

بچگی    *baccegi*, childhood (from بچه *bacce* 'child').

**2.** The Abstract ی -*i* carries the stress, which distinguishes it from the Indefinite ی -*i* and the Relative ی -*i*.

**3.** Verbal Nouns are formed by the addition of ش -*ef*,[1] اک -*ak*, or ه -*e* to the Present Stem, e.g.

فرمایش    *farmayef*, command (from فرمودن *farmudan* 'to command').

سوزش    *suʒef*, burning (from سوختن *suxtan* 'to burn').

---

[1] If the present Stem of the verb to which ش -*ef* is added ends in ا *a* or و *u* a ی *y* is inserted between the final vowel and the suffix ش -*ef*.

گردش    gardeʃ, a walk, turn, excursion (from گشتن gaʃtan 'to go for a walk').

کوشش    kuʃeʃ, effort (from کوشیدن kuʃidan 'to strive').

پوشاك    puʃak, clothing (from پوشیدن puʃidan 'to wear').

خوراك    xorak, food (from خوردن xordan 'to eat').

شماره    ʃomare, number (from شمردن ʃomordan 'to count').

خنده    xande, laugh (from خندیدن xandidan 'to laugh').

شپره    ʃappare, bat (=شب پر ʃab pare from شب ʃab 'night' and پریدن paridan 'to fly, jump, flit').

ناله    nale, whine, wail, complaint (from نالیدن nalidan 'to whine', etc.).

A Verbal Noun is also formed, but less commonly, in ن -n, e.g.

فرمان    farman, order (from فرمودن farmudan 'to order').

پیمان    peīman, measure (from پیمودن peīmudan 'to measure').

A form in ار -ar which originally expressed 'the agent', is used as a Verbal Noun, e.g.

رفتار    raftar, conduct (from رفتن raftan 'to go').

گفتار    goftar, speech, talk (from گفتن goftan 'to say').

گرفتار    gereftar (used as an adj.), being overtaken by, suffering from (from گرفتن gereftan 'to take').

کردار    kerdar, action (from کردن kardan 'to do' with modification of the stem vowel).

خریدار    xaridar, purchaser, buyer (from خریدن xaridan 'to buy').

In the last example the original force of the suffix has been retained. Some verbs do not form verbal nouns.

4. The following suffixes are used to form nouns:

(a) ا -a and نا -na added to adjectives, e.g.

گرما    garma, warmth (from گرم garm 'warm').

پهنا    pahna, width, breadth (from پهن pahn 'wide').

تنگنا    tangna, ravine (from تنگ tang 'narrow').

(b) ه -e added to nouns and numerals, e.g.

نیمه    nime, half (from نیم nim 'half').

کینه    kine, vengeance (from کین kin 'vengeance').

چشمه *cašme*, spring, river-source (from چشم *cašm* 'eye').

پنجه *panje*, claw (from پنج *panj* 'five').

دسته *daste*, handle (from دست *dast* 'hand').

دهکده *dehkade*, small village (from ده *deh* 'village' and کد *kad* 'house, household', the latter used only in compounds).

آتشکده *ateškade*, fire-temple (from آتش *ateš* 'fire' and کد *kad*, see above).

(c) بان *-ban*, وان *-van* 'keeper', e.g.

باغبان *bayban*, gardener (from باغ *bay* 'garden').

دربان *darban*, gate-keeper, door-keeper (from در *dar* 'door').

پاسبان *pasban*, policeman, watchman (from پاس *pas* 'watch').

شتربان (شتروان) *šotorban* (*šotorvan*), camel-driver (from شتر *šotor* 'camel').

وان *-van* is seldom used in Colloquial Persian.

(d) بد *-bod* 'lord, master', e.g.

سپهبد *sepahbod*, lieutenant-general (from سپه *sepah* 'army').

(e) کار *-kar*, گار *-gar*, گر *-gar* 'agent' or 'worker in', e.g.

گناهکار *gonahkar*, sinner (from گناه *gonah* 'sin').

خدمتکار *xedmatkar*, servant (from خدمت *xedmat* 'service').

آفریدگار *afaridegar*, the Creator (from آفریدن *afaridan* 'to create').

یادگار *yadgar*, memorial (from یاد *yad* 'memory').

روزگار *ruzgar*, time (from روز *ruz* 'day').

آموزگار *amuzgar*, teacher (from آموختن *amuxtan* 'to teach').

زرگر *zargar*, goldsmith (from زر *zar* 'gold').

آهنگر *ahangar*, ironsmith (from آهن *ahan* 'iron').

توانگر *tavangar*, a powerful person (from توانستن *tavanestan* 'to be able').

دادگر *dadgar*, a just person (from داد *dad* 'justice').

(f) دان *-dan* 'receptacle', e.g.

قلمدان *qalamdan*, pencase (from قلم *qalam* 'pen').

قنددان *qanddan*, sugar-bowl (from قند *qand* 'lump sugar').

(g) ستان- -estan, -stan 'place of', e.g.

هندوستان  hendustan, India (from هندو hendu 'Hindu').

گلستان  golestan, rose-garden (from گل gol 'rose, flower').

(h) لاخ -lax, سار- -sar, زار- -ʒar, بار- -bar, شن- -ʃan 'place abounding in', e.g.

سنگلاخ  sanglax ⎫
سنگسار  sangsar ⎬ stony place (from سنگ sang 'stone').

گلزار  golʒar ⎫
گلشن  golʃan ⎬ flower-bed (from گل gol 'flower, rose').

رودبار  rudbar, place abounding in rivers or streams (from رود rud 'river, stream').

کارزار  karʒar, battle, battlefield (from کار kar in its obsolete meaning of 'army' or 'group of people moving about').

مرغزار  marɣʒar, water-meadow (from مرغ marɣ 'a kind of grass').

چنزار  camanʒar, meadow (from چمن caman 'turf').

(i) ان -an[1]

(1) names of places, e.g.

توران  turan, Turania (from تور Tur).

بیابان  biaban, desert (from بی‌آب bi ab 'without water').

(2) patronymics, e.g.

بابکان  babakan, son of Babak.

(j) گان -gan 'origin, relation, similarity', e.g.

گروگان  gerōugan, hostage (from گرو gerōu 'pledge').

(k) چی -ci, جی -ji 'agent', e.g.

درشکه‌چی  doroʃkeci, cabman (from درشکه doroʃke 'cab'). This suffix is derived from Turkish.

(l) اباد -abad 'place of abode', used in place-names, e.g.

خرماباد  xorramabad, Khorramabad (from خرم xorram 'happiness, gladness').

اسداباد  asadabad, Asadabad (from اسد asad 'lion').

---

[1] If the word to which ان -an is added ends in ا a or و u a ی y is inserted between the final vowel and the suffix.

5. Diminutives are formed by the addition of one of the following suffixes: ك‍ -ak, ه‍ -e, كه‍ -eke, چه‍ -ce, يچه‍ -ice or و -u.

The diminutive suffixes when applied to rational beings denote also affection or contempt, e.g.

دخترك‍  *doxtarak*
دختره‍  *doxtare* } little girl.

مردكه‍  *mardeke*, little man, manikin.

پسرو  *pesaru*, little boy.

يارو  *yaru*, fellow (used in a derogatory sense from يار *yar* 'helper, friend').

باغچه‍  *bayce*, little garden.

دريچه‍  *darice*, little door.

Less commonly used are the diminutive suffixes يجه‍ -*ije*, يزه‍ -*iẓe*, and يژه‍ -*iʒe*.

6. There are a variety of adjectival suffixes. Among them are:

(*a*) ١ -*a*, added to the Present Stem of verbs, used to form verbal adjectives, e.g.

دانا  *dana*, wise (from دانستن *danestan* 'to know').

توانا  *tavana*, powerful (from توانستن *tavanestan* 'to be able').

زيبا  *ẓiba*, comely (from the obsolete verb زيبيدن *ẓibidan* 'to be comely').

(*b*) مند -*mand*, 'possessed of', e.g.

خردمند  *xeradmand*, wise (from خرد *xerad* 'wisdom').

ثروتمند  *servatmand*, rich (from ثروت *servat* 'wealth').

گله‍مند  *gelemand*, complaining (from گله‍ *gele* 'complaint').

(*c*) ور -*var*, اور -*avar* 'characterized by', e.g.

شعله‍ور  *ʃoʻlevar*, blazing, flaming (from شعله‍ *ʃoʻle* 'flame').

نامور  *namvar*, famous, illustrious (from نام *nam* 'name').

دلاور  *delavar*, courageous (from دل *del* 'heart, stomach').

The form جانور *janevar*, originally adjectival meaning 'having a soul' (جان *jan*), is now used as a noun meaning 'animal'.

(d) وار -*var*, 'fit for, characterized by', e.g.

شاهوار   *ʃahvar*, fit for a king (from شاه *ʃah* 'king').

دیوانه‌وار   *divanevar*, like a madman (from دیوانه *divane* 'mad').

بزرگوار   *boʒorgvar*, great, worthy of a great man (from بزرگ *boʒorg* 'great').

(e) وش -*vaʃ*, مان -*man*, سا- اسا -*sa*, -*asa*, سار- سان -*sar*, -*san* 'like', e.g.

ماهوش   *mahvaʃ*, like the moon (from ماه *mah* 'moon').

پریوش   *parivaʃ*, like a fairy (from پری *pari* 'fairy').

شادمان   *ʃadman*, happy (from شاد *ʃad* 'happy').

فیلسا   *filsa*  
فیل‌آسا   *filasa*  } like an elephant (from فیل *fil* 'elephant').

شرمسار   *ʃarmsar*, ashamed (from شرم *ʃarm* 'shame').

گرگسان   *gorgsan*, like a wolf (from گرگ *gorg* 'wolf').

یکسان   *yaksan*, equal, like (from یك *yak* 'one').

(f) ـن -*in*, ینه -*ine*, added to a 'material' to express the meaning 'made of' the substance, e.g.

زرین   *ʒarrin*,[1] made of gold (from زر *ʒar* 'gold').

پشمینه[2]   *paʃmine*, woollen (from پشم *paʃm* 'wool').

دیرینه   *dirine*, ancient (from دیر *dir* 'late').

(g) ـن -*in*, added to certain numerals and prepositions to form adjectives denoting time or place, e.g.

برین   *barin*, upper (from بر *bar* 'on').

پسین   *pasin*, posterior (of time; from پس *pas* 'after').

اولین   *avvalin*, first (from اول *avval* 'first').

نخستین   *naxostin*, first (from نخست *naxost* 'first').

آخرین   *axerin*, last (from آخر *axer* 'last').

(h) گین -*gin*, ناك -*nak* 'full of', e.g.

غمگین   *ʒamgin*, sorrowful (from غم *ʒam* 'grief').

سهمگین   *sahmgin*, dreadful (from سهم *sahm* 'terror, dread').

دردناك   *dardnak*, painful (from درد *dard* 'pain').

---

[1] The doubling of the *r* would appear to be irregular.

[2] پشمی *paʃmi* is more commonly used to mean 'woollen'.

(i) یار -yar, e.g.

هوشیار   *hufyar*, intelligent (from هوش *huf* 'intelligence').

بختیار   *baxtyar*, fortunate (from بخت *baxt* 'fortune, luck').

(j) ی -i 'belonging to', e.g.

دهاتی   *dehati*, belonging to the country, a countryman (from دهات *dehat* 'country').

شهری   *fahri*, belonging to the town, townsman (from شهر *fahr* 'town').

شیرازی   *firazi*, belonging to Shiraz, a native of Shiraz.

If this ی -i is added to certain Persian words ending in the 'silent' *h*, the latter is changed into گ, e.g.

خانگی   *xanegi*, belonging to the house (from خانه *xane* 'house').
But

سرمئ   *sormei*, dark blue (from سرمه *sorme* 'collyrium').

The adjectival ی -i carries the stress like the Abstract ی -i (see para. 2 above) and is thereby distinguished from the Indefinite ی -i and the Relative ی -i.

The Arabic termination ـیّ -iyon, which forms Relative Adjectives (see Part II, Lesson XVI, para. 18), becomes ی -i in Persian, e.g.

مصری   *mesri*, Egyptian, an Egyptian (from مصر *mesr* 'Egypt').

(k) ه -e, added to compounds, e.g.

چکاره   *ce kare*, belonging to what profession.

7. Compound nouns are formed in a variety of ways, e.g.

(a) By a qualifying noun with a noun, e.g.

مهمانخانه   *mehmanxane*, hotel (مهمان *mehman* 'guest'; خانه *xane* 'house').

سربازخانه   *sarbazxane*, barracks (سرباز *sarbaz* 'soldier'; خانه *xane* 'house').

پالایشگاه   *palayefgah*, refinery (پالایش *palayef* 'refining'; گاه *gah* 'place').

(b) By two nouns placed in apposition, e.g.

پدر زن   *pedarzan*, father-in-law (of the husband) (پدر *pedar* 'father'; زن *zan* 'woman, wife').

دختر عمو  *doxtaramu*, cousin (daughter of a paternal uncle)
(دختر *doxtar*, 'girl, daughter'; عمو *amu* 'paternal
uncle').

صاحب خانه  *sahebxane*, landlord, owner or master of the house
(صاحب *saheb* 'master, owner'; خانه *xane* 'house').

میراب  *mirab*, an official in charge of the distribution of
water (میر *mir* a title; آب *ab* 'water').

(c) By two nouns with the *ezafe*, e.g.

تخت خواب  *taxte xab*, bed (تخت *taxt* 'wooden platform or
seat' خواب *xab*, 'sleep').

(d) By two nouns joined by و *o* 'and',[1] e.g.

آب و هوا  *ab o hava*, climate (آب *ab* 'water'; هوا *hava* 'air').

(e) By a noun and an adjective, e.g.

نوروز  *nōuruz*, New Year (نو *nōu* new; روز *ruz* 'day').

(f) By a noun and the Present Stem of a verb, e.g.

سرباز  *sarbaz* soldier (سر *sar* 'head'; باختن *baxtan* 'to lose').

پیغامبر  *pēiyambar*, messenger (پیغام *pēiyam* 'message'; بردن
*bordan* 'to carry').

(g) By the Short Infinitive of two verbs united by و *o* 'and',[1] e.g.

آمد و شد  *amad o fod*, traffic, coming and going (آمدن *amadan*
'to come'; شدن *fodan* in its obsolete meaning
'to go').

(h) By the Present Stem and Short Infinitive of a verb with or
without و *o* 'and', e.g.

گفتگو  *goftogu, goftegu*, or گفت‌وگو *goftogu*, conversation, discussion (from گفتن *goftan* 'to say').

جستجو  *jostoju, josteju*, or جست‌وجو *jostoju*, search, seeking (from
*jostan* 'to seek').

(i) By the Present Stem of two verbs united by و *o* 'and', e.g.

گیرودار  *girodar*, struggle (گرفتن *gereftan* 'to take'; داشتن
*daftan* 'to have, hold').

---

[1] See above, p. 38, footnote 2, for this و.

(*j*) By a noun and a Past Participle, e.g.

شاهزاده‎ *ʃahzade*, prince (شاه‎ *ʃah* 'king'; زائیدن‎ *zaidan* 'to give birth to'; زاده‎ being a contracted form of زائیده‎).

(*k*) By a word used as an adverb and the Present Stem of a verb, e.g.

پیشکش‎ *piʃkaʃ*, present (from an inferior to a superior) (پیش‎ *piʃ* 'forward'; کشیدن‎ *kaʃidan* 'to pull, draw').

پس انداز‎ *pasandaz*, savings (پس‎ *pas* 'behind'; انداختن‎ *andaxtan* 'to throw').

(*l*) By an adjective and the Present Stem of a verb, e.g.

نو آموز‎ *nouamuz*, beginner (نو‎ *nou* 'new'; آموختن‎ *amuxtan* 'to learn, teach').

(*m*) By two nouns united by a preposition, e.g.

اعتماد بنفس‎ *e'temad be nafs*, self-reliance (اعتماد‎ *e'temad* 'reliance'; نفس‎ *nafs* 'self').

The plural of compound nouns is formed by adding the plural termination to the last part of the compound, e.g.

مهمانخانه‌ها‎ *mehmanxaneha*, hotels.

8. Compound adjectives are formed by

(*a*) Two nouns in juxtaposition, e.g.

سنگدل‎ *sangdel*, stony-hearted (سنگ‎ *sang* 'stone'; دل‎ *del*, 'heart, stomach').

(*b*) An adjective and a noun, e.g.

خوش اخلاق‎ *xoʃaxlaq*, good-natured (خوش‎ *xoʃ* 'pleasant, happy'; اخلاق‎ *axlaq* 'morals, ethics, character').

بزرگمنش‎ *bozorgmaneʃ*, magnanimous (بزرگ‎ *bozorg* 'big'; the obsolete word منش‎ *maneʃ* 'thinking').

(*c*) A noun and the Present Stem of a verb, e.g.

سرافراز‎ *sarafraz*, exalted, honoured (سر‎ *sar* 'head'; افراشتن‎ *afraʃtan* 'to raise, exalt').

کامیاب‎ *kamyab*, successful, prosperous (کام‎ *kam* 'desire'; یافتن‎ *yaftan* 'to obtain').

(d) A noun and a Past Participle, e.g.

جهانديده jahandide, experienced, widely travelled (جهان jahan 'world'; ديدن didan 'to see').

(e) An adjective and the Present Stem of a verb, e.g.

تيزرو tiȝrou, fleet (of foot), speedy (تيز tiȝ 'sharp, quick'; رفتن raftan 'to go').

(f) A noun and a preposition, e.g.

باصفا basafa, pleasant, agreeable (با ba 'with'; صفا safa 'purity').

بى صفا bisafa, unpleasant, disagreeable (بى bi 'without').

بافهم bafahm, intelligent (فهم fahm 'understanding').

بى فهم bifahm, unintelligent, stupid.

بى كس bikas, friendless, forlorn (كس kas 'person'; بى bi 'without').

زبردست ȝabardast, skilful, quick, able (دست dast 'hand'; زبر ȝabar 'above').

برقرار bar qarar, settled, fixed, established (بر bar 'on'; قرار qarar 'settling, establishing').

خانه بدوش xane be duʃ, nomadic (خانه xane 'house'; دوش duʃ 'shoulder, back').

(g) Two nouns united by ا a, e.g.

برابر barabar, equal, opposite (بر bar 'breast').

9. Compound Adjectives form their comparative by the addition of تر -tar or with بيشتر biʃtar, e.g.

$$\left.\begin{array}{l}\text{باصفاتر} \quad basafatar \\ \text{بيشتر با صفا} \quad biʃtar\ basafa\end{array}\right\} \text{pleasanter.}$$

The superlative is formed in the usual way by the addition of ترين -tarin, e.g.

باصفاترين basafatarin, pleasantest.

Forms compounded with بى bi- do not logically admit of a comparative or superlative.

10. The particle هم *ham* 'like' is used to form compound nouns and adjectives, e.g.

همشهری   *hamfahri*, fellow-townsman.

هماهنگ   *hamahang*, harmonious (آهنگ *ahang* 'melody').

همعقیده   *hamaqide*, having the same opinion (عقیده *aqide* 'opinion, belief').

11. Adjectival compounds are formed with کم *kam* 'little, less', e.g.

کم‌بضاعت   *kambaʒa'at*, of little wealth (بضاعت *baʒa'at* 'merchandise, goods').

کم‌زور   *kamʒur*, weak (زور *ʒur* 'power, strength').

12. The negative particle نا *-na* is used to form compound adjectives and nouns, e.g.

نادان   *nadan*, ignorant
نادانی   *nadani*, ignorance } (دانستن *danestan* 'to know').

ناهموار   *nahamvar*, uneven (هموار *hamvar* 'even').

حق‌ناشناس   *haqqnafenas*, ungrateful (حق *haqq* 'right'; شناختن *fenaxtan* 'to know, recognize').

ناکس   *nakas*, an ignoble, mean person (کس *kas* 'person').

نامرد   *namard*, an ignoble, mean person (مرد *mard* 'man').

تغییر ناپذیر   *taɣyirnapaʒir*, unchangeable (تغییر *taɣyir* 'change'; پذیرفتن *paʒiroftan* 'to accept').

نارو   *narōu*, treacherous (of a person) (رفتن *raftan* 'to go').

The Imperative affirmative followed by the imperative negative is also used to form compounds, e.g.

کشمکش   *kefmakef*, struggle (کشیدن *kafidan* 'to pull').

13. The particle غیر *ɣeir* 'other' ('un-') is used to form compounds. It takes the *eʒafe*, e.g.

غیر رسمی   *ɣeire rasmi*, unofficial (رسمی *rasmi* 'official').

غیر قابل تحمل   *ɣeire qabele tahammol*, insupportable (قابل *qabel* 'worthy, able'; تحمل *tahammol* 'patience, endurance').

14. خود *xod* 'self' is also used to form compounds, e.g.

خودداری    *xoddari*, restraint, self-control (داشتن *daſtan* 'to have, hold').

خودپسند    *xodpasand*, conceited (پسند *pasand* 'pleasant, agreeable').

از خود گذشتگی    *az xod goʒaſtegi*, self-sacrifice (گذشتن *goʒaſtan* 'to pass by').

بی‌خود    *bixod*, in vain (بی *bi* 'without').

15. A rhyming compound is formed, the second part of which is a meaningless word beginning with م *m-* or occasionally with پ *p* and rhyming with the first part of the compound. Such compounds are frequently used in Colloquial Persian, e.g.

بچه مچه    *bacce macce* or بچه مچه‌ها *bacce macceha*, children.

پول مول    *pul mul*, money.

قاطی پاتی    *qati pati*, mixed.

This type of compound sometimes gives a plural sense as in the first example above. It is also occasionally found in the literary language, e.g.

تار و مار    *tar o mar*, destroyed, scattered.

16. Stress on compound nouns and adjectives is carried on the final syllable, e.g.

اعتماد بنفس    *e'temad be 'nafs*, self-reliance.

سرافراز    *saraf'raʒ*, exalted, honoured.

خانه بدوش    *xane be 'duſ*, nomadic.

پیغامبر    *peīʒam'bar*, messenger.

سربازخانه    *sarbaʒxa'ne*, barracks.

## VOCABULARY

شاه    Shah Tahmasp (reigned
طهماسب    A.D. 1524–76).
انگلیسی    *englisi*, English.
انگلستان    *englestan*, England.
انتنی جنکینسن    Antony Jenkinson.

طرف    *taraf*, side; از طرف *az taraf(e)*, on behalf of;
طرفین    *tarafein*,[1] two parties, sides.
ملکه    *maleke*, queen.

[1] For the Arabic dual see Part II, Lesson XIX.

الیزابت Elizabeth.

هجری *hejri*, belonging to the Hejri era (see Appendix III).

سفارت *sefarat*, embassy, mission.

روانه گردیدن *ravane g.*, to set out for.

مزبور *mazbur*, mentioned, aforesaid.

جهت *jehat*, side; reason; *jehat(e)*, for.

پادشاه *padefah*, king, ruler.

دایر بر *da'er bar*, depending on, relating to.

ایجاد *ijad*, creation.

دوستی *dusti*, friendship.

حفظ *hefz*, preservation.

مصالح *masaleh* (pl. of مصلحت *maslahat*), interests.

انسانیت *ensaniyat*, humanity, humanitarianism.

منفعت *manfa'at*, benefit (pl. منافع *manafe'*).

ذو الحجة *zol-hejja*,[1] the twelfth month of the Muslim lunar year.

قزوین Qazvin.

آداب *adab* (pl. of ادب *adab*), customs, habits.

رسم *rasm*, custom (pl. رسوم *rosum*).

آشنا *afna*, acquainted with.

دولت *doulat*, government, state; دولت متبوع *doulate matbu'* sovereign government (i.e. government to which one is subject).

عهد نامه *ahdname*, treaty, agreement.

منعقد کردن *mon'aqed k.*, to conclude.

ناچار *nacar*, having no remedy.

روسیه *rusiye*, Russia.

بدون *bedun(e)*, without.

حصول *hosul*, acquisition, obtaining.

هیئت *hei'at*, commission, body, group.

جانب *janeb*, side; چ از جانب *az janeb(e)*, on behalf of.

شرکت *ferkat*, company; participation.

مسکو *moskou*, Moscow.

نسبت به *nesbat be*, with regard to, towards.

اجازه *ejaze*, permission.

تجار *tojjar* (pl. of تاجر *tajer*), merchants.

آزاد *azad*, free.

آزادی *azadi*, freedom.

جستن *jostan* (*ju*), to seek; (جو) find.

شوهر *fouhar*, husband.

روابط ایران و اروپا[1]

در زمان شاه طهماسب یك نفر انگلیسی بنام انتنی جنكینسن از طرف ملكه انگلستان الیزابت در سال ۹۶۹ هجری بعنوان سفارت روانه ایران گردید و نامۀ از طرف ملكه مزبور جهت شاه طهماسب اول پادشاه صفوی آورد دایر بر ایجاد روابط دوستی و حفظ مصالح انسانیت و منافع طرفین نماینده مزبور در ماه ذوالحجة سال ۹۶۹ بقزوین پایتخت شاه طهماسب آمد ولی چون با آداب و رسوم ایران آشنا نبود نتوانست جهت دولت متبوع خود عهدنامه تجارتی منعقد نماید ناچار برگشت بار دیگر همین نماینده در سال ۹۷۰ از طرف دولت روسیه بایران آمد ولی این دفعه هم بدون حصول نتیجه مراجعت نمود در سال ۹۷۲ هیئتی دیگر[2] از جانب شركت مسكو بایران آمد و شاه هم نسبت باین هیئت بمهربانی رفتار نمود اجازه دادكه تجار انگلیسی و روسی بآزادی در ایران تجارت و مسافرت نمایند

## EXERCISE 19

1. He has news of his sister.  2. It is a very long time since I have been to (in) England.  3. It was impossible to stay any longer.  4. The man to whom you were speaking this morning is a fellow-townsman of mine.  5. He showed great self-reliance.  6. He brought up his son well.  7. We live the whole year in the country.  8. He would like to live outside the town.  9. I am of the same opinion as you.  10. We decided to stay here because it was pleasanter.  11. He intended to set out for India last week.  12. If he goes by sea his journey will last three weeks.  13. She likes her father-in-law better than her mother-in-law.  14. I tried to come earlier but although I intended to set out at ten o'clock it was eleven before I was ready to start, and as a result it was late when I arrived and you had gone home.  15. Commercial relations between Persia and Europe began in Safavid times. Many envoys came from Europe to Persia and sought to make trade agreements on behalf of their governments with the Persian government and to establish friendly relations. Some of them were successful; others returned to Europe without achieving their object.

اقتباس از تاریخ ایران از مغول تا افشاریه تالیف رضا پازوكی[1]

[1] See Lesson XII, para. 1 (a) (iii) for the addition of the Indefinite ی -*i* to the noun instead of to the qualifying adjective.

# LESSON XI

## Prepositions[1]

1. Prepositions can be divided into two classes: those which take the *eẓafe* and those which do not.[2]

2. Prepositions which do not take the *eẓafe* include the following:

(a) از *aẓ* (from, in, by, through, over, of, than, made of, among, by way of, because, out of, belonging to) denotes direction from, deprivation or liberation; it denotes the material anything is made of; it is used in partitive expressions and to express comparison.

| | |
|---|---|
| از رفتن صرف نظر میکنم | *aẓ raftan sarfe naẓar mikonam*, I shall refrain from (give up) going. |
| از این استفاده کرد | *aẓ in estefade kard*, He benefited from this. |
| از وزارت معزول شد | *aẓ veẓarat ma'ẓul ſod*, He was dismissed from the post of minister (lit. from the ministry). |
| از خونریزی باید جلوگیری کرد | *aẓ xunriẓi bayad jelõugiri kard*, Bloodshed must be prevented. |
| از او اطمینان دارم | *aẓ u etminan daram*, I have confidence in him. |
| از شهر عبور کردیم | *aẓ ſahr obur kardim*, We passed through the town. |
| از دریافت کاغذتان مسرور گشتم | *aẓ daryafte kaɣaẓetan masrur gaſtam*, I was made happy by the receipt of your letter. |
| از فیض دیدار شما محروم ماندم | *aẓ fēiẓe didare ſoma mahrum mandam*, I was deprived of the pleasure of seeing you. |
| از او خبر ندارم | *aẓ u xabar nadaram*, I have no news of him. |

[1] See also Part II, Lesson XXI, paras. 14 and 15.

[2] The examples given in the following paras. are intended to serve as an indication of the use of the prepositions in Persian and should not be regarded as exhaustive.

این منزل عبارت است از پنج عدد اطاق　　*in manzel ebarat ast az panj adad otaq*, This house consists of five rooms.

این بچه از آن بچه بزرگتر است　　*in bacce az an bacce bozorgtar ast*, This child is bigger than that child.

دور باغ دیواری از خشت[1] کشیدند　　*doure baɣ divāri az xeʃt kaʃidand*, They made a brick wall round the garden.

سعدی از شعرای معروف ایران است　　*saʿdi az ʃoʿaraye maʿrufe iran ast*, Saʿdi is among the famous poets of Iran.

این از عجائب دنیاست　　*in az ajaʿebe donyast*, This is among the wonders of the world.

اینرا از دلتنگی گفت　　*inra az deltangi goft*, He said this out of sadness.

این کتاب از آن من است　　*in ketab az ane man ast*, This book is one of my books.

The following verbs take از *az*:

استدعا کردن　　*estedʿa k.*, to ask, beseech (someone).

استفاده کردن　　*estefade k.*, to benefit (from).

استمداد کردن　　*estemdad k.*, to ask help (of).

اطمینان داشتن　　*etminan d.*
اعتماد داشتن　　*eʿtemad d.* } to have confidence (in).

آمدن　　*amadan*, to come (from).

باز داشتن　　*baz d.*, to restrain (from).

بر داشتن　　*bar d.*, to lift, raise, take away (from).

برکنار رفتن　　*bar kenar raftan*, to go aside, withdraw (from).

بهره بردن　　*bahre bordan*, to benefit (from).

پذیرائی کردن　　*pazirai k.*, to entertain (someone).

پرسیدن　　*porsidan*, to ask (someone).

پرهیز کردن　　*parhiz k.*, to refrain (from).

ترسیدن　　*tarsidan*, to fear.

تعریف کردن　　*taʿrif k.*, to describe, praise.

---

[1] خشت *xeʃt*, a sun-baked brick.

جلوگیری کردن   *jelōugiri k.*, to prevent.

خبر داشتن   *xabar d.*, to have news (of).

دوری جستن   *duri jostan*, to avoid (someone).

رد شدن   *radd ʃ.*, to pass (by), overtake.

سؤال کردن   *so'al k.*, to ask (someone).

صرف نظر کردن   *sarfe naẕar kardan*, to refrain (from).

عبارت بودن   *ebarat b.*, to consist (of, in).

عبور کردن / گذشتن   *obur k.* / *goẕaʃtan*} to pass (through, by).

محروم بودن (ماندن)   *mahrum b. (mandan)*, to be deprived of.

مستفیض گشتن   *mostafiẕ g.*, to derive benefit (from).

مسرور گشتن   *masrur g.*, to be made happy (by).

معذرت خواستن   *ma'ẕarat xastan*, to ask pardon (from someone).

معزول کردن   *ma'ẕul k.*, to dismiss (from).

The following compounds of از are also used:

غیر از   *yeir aẕ*, other than.

بعد از   *ba'd aẕ*} after. / پس از   *pas aẕ*}

قبل از   *qabl aẕ*} before (time). / پیش از   *piʃ aẕ*}

بیرون از   *birun aẕ*} outside. / خارج از   *xarej aẕ*}

(b) با *ba* (with, on the responsibility of, to) denotes association with or opposition to.

با او مشورت کردم   *ba u maʃvarat kardam*, I consulted him.

با او آشنا نیستم   *ba u aʃna nistam*, I am not acquainted with him.

با ما بد است   *ba ma bad ast*, He is on bad terms with us, dislikes us.

تصویب آن با هیئت مدیره است   *tasvibe an ba heï'ate modire ast*, Its ratification is the responsibility of the executive committee.

The following verbs take با *ba*:

| | | |
|---|---|---|
| ارتباط داشتن | *ertebat d.*, | to have connexions or relations (with). |
| ازدواج کردن | *ezdevaj k.*, | to marry. |
| آشنا بودن | *afna b.*, | to be acquainted (with a person). |
| بد بودن | *bad b.*, | to be on bad terms (with). |
| حرف زدن | *harf zadan*, | to talk (with), speak (to). |
| خوب بودن | *xub b.*, | to be on good terms (with). |
| صحبت کردن | *sohbat k.*, | to talk (with), speak (to). |
| مخالف بودن | *moxalef b.*, | to be opposed (to). |
| مشورت کردن | *mafvarat k.*, | to consult (with). |

(*c*) بر *bar* (on, upon, over, about, for, from, of, with, up to = the responsibility of) is used to denote position in a figurative sense or otherwise.

| | |
|---|---|
| بر دشمنان تاختند | *bar dofmanan taxtand*, They attacked the enemy. |
| بر آنها مستولی گشت | *bar anha mostouli gaft*, He gained dominion over them (overcame them). |
| بر این حادثه تأسف خورد | *bar in hadese ta'assof xord*, He was sorry about this happening. |
| بر مردمان عاقل واضح است | *bar mardomane aqel vazeh ast*, It is clear to wise persons. |
| بر من پوشیده نیست | *bar man pufide nist*, It is not hidden from me. |
| این بر صحت گفته شما دلالت میکند | *in bar sehhate gofteye foma dalalat mikonad*, This is proof of the rightness of what you said. |
| بر مردم است که اورا مجازات کنند | *bar mardom ast ke ura mojazat konand*, It is up to the people to punish him. |
| بر این کار کمر بست | *bar in kar kamar bast*, He girt up his loins to do this work. |
| پیشنهاد شما مبنی بر سوء تفاهم است | *pifnehade foma mabni bar su'e tafahom ast*, Your proposal is based upon a misunderstanding. |

The following verbs take بر *bar*[1]:

| | |
|---|---|
| اعتماد کردن | *e'temad k.*, to rely (upon). |
| افزودن | *afʒudan*, to increase. |
| بر خوردن | *bar xordan*, to meet (with). |
| پوشیده بودن | *puʃide b.*, to be hidden (from). |
| تاختن | *taxtan*, to attack. |
| تأسف خوردن | *ta'assof xordan*, to regret, be sorry (about). |
| حمله کردن | *hamle k.*, to attack. |
| چیره گردیدن | *cire g.*, to obtain dominion (over). |
| دلالت کردن | *dalalat k.*, to be or give proof (of). |
| رحمت کردن | *rahmat k.*, to have mercy (upon). |
| روا بودن | *rava b.*, to be permissible (for). |
| ریختن (ریز) | *rixtan (riʒ)*, to pour (over); rush (upon), fall (upon). |
| شایسته بودن | *ʃayeste b.*, to be fitting (for). |
| غالب آمدن | *ɣaleb amadan*, to conquer, overcome. |
| فرمانروائی کردن | *farmanravai k.*, to rule (over a country, etc.). |
| کمر بستن | *kamar bastan*, to gird up one's loins (to do something). |
| مبنی بودن | *mabni b.*, to be based (upon). |
| مستولی گشتن | *mostōuli g.*, to gain dominion (over), overcome. |
| واضح بودن | *vaʒeh b.*, to be clear (to someone). |

(*d*) برای *baraye* and its compound از برای *aʒ baraye*, for,[2] e.g.

اینرا برای شما خریدم     *inra baraye ʃoma xaridam*, I bought this for you.

(*e*) به *be* (to, in, into, at, with, on, upon, of, for, from, as) is used in a wide variety of contexts. It covers motion towards in a figurative sense or otherwise. It shows the relation of an action or state to the limits of space, time or condition. It expresses result, degree, amount and possession. It is also used to form adverbs and in oaths.

اینرا بمن داد     *inra be man dad*, He gave this to me.

بما خوش گذشت     *be ma xoʃ goʒaʃt*, We enjoyed ourselves.

---

[1] It will be seen that many verbs admit of a choice between بر *bar* and به *be*.
[2] The ی of برای *baraye* was probably originally an *eʒafe*.

به این امر رسیدگی کنید   *be in amr rasidegi konid*, Look into this matter.

باو کمك کردند   *be u komak kardand*, They helped him.

باو متوسل شدند   *be u motavassel fodand*, They had recourse to him.

باطاق وارد شد   *be otaq vared fod*, He entered the room.

بشما شباهت دارد   *be foma fabahat darad*, He resembles you.

مطلب باینجا کشید   *matlab be inja kafid*, The matter reached this point (here).

بوزارت جنگ منتقل شد   *be veӡarate jang montaqel fod*, He was transferred to the ministry of war.

باین اعتراض کرد   *be in e'teraӡ kard*, He protested at this.

راجع باین باو اعتراض کردم   *raje' be in be u e'teraӡ kardam*, I protested about this to him.

بشهر رسید   *be fahr rasid*, He reached (arrived at) the town.

این بمن مربوط نیست   *in be man marbut nist*, This does not concern me.

در راه باو بر خوردیم   *dar rah be u bar xordim*, We met him on the way.

این کار باو بر خورد   *in kar be u bar xord*, This affair offended him.

بسرما خوردگی مبتلا شد   *be sarmaxordegi mobtala fod*, He was afflicted with a chill.

باین واقعه واقف بود   *be in vaqe'e vaqef bud*, He was aware of this happening.

معروف است بولخرجی   *ma'ruf ast be velxarji*, He is known for (his) extravagance.

اینرا بدو ریال میفروشد   *inra be do rial miforufad*, He will sell this for two *rials*.

بعضویت هیئت انتخاب شد   *be oӡviyate hei'at entexab fod*, He was chosen as a member of the commission (committee).

باین باغ طمع دارد   *be in baɣ tama' darad*, He covets this garden.

بما تعدی کرد   *be ma ta'addi kard*, He oppressed us.

باین قایل نیستم   *be in qayel nistam,* I do not admit (accept) this.

این رنگ بآن میخورد   *in rang be an mixorad,* This colour matches that.

این لباس بشما میاید   *in lebas be ʃoma miayad,* This costume suits you.

این هوا بمن میسازد   *in hava be man misaʒad,* This climate suits me.

بفارسی   *be farsi,* in Persian.

بنظر من   *be naʒare man,* in my view.

بعقیده من   *be aqideye man,* in my opinion.

بهر حال   *be har hal* ⎫
بهر صورت   *be har surat* ⎭ in any case.

بهمان حال   *be haman hal,* in the same condition.

باشتباه   *be eʃtebah,* in error.

بقول آنها   *be qoule anha,* in their words, according to them.

شمشیر بدست   *ʃamʃir be dast,* sword in hand.

بمرور زمان   *be morure ʒaman,* in the course of time, with the passing of time.

باین سبب   *be in sabab,* for this reason.

بخدا   *be xoda,* by God.

The following verbs take به *be:*[1]

احتیاج داشتن   *ehteyaj d.,* to be in need (of).

ارسال داشتن   *ersal d.,* to send (to).

اعتراض کردن   *e'teraʒ k.,* to protest (to a person), object (to a thing).

اعتماد کردن   *e'temad k.,* to rely (upon).

انتخاب کردن   *entexab k.,* to choose (as).

ایمان آوردن (داشتن)   *iman avardan (d.),* to believe (in).

بر خوردن   *bar xordan,* to meet, offend.

بسته بودن   *baste b.,* to be dependent (upon something).

تعدی کردن   *ta'addi k.,* to oppress.

[1] It will be seen that many verbs admit of a choice between بر *bar* and به *be.*

| | |
|---|---|
| تمايل داشتن | *tamayol d.*, to be inclined (to). |
| حاجت داشتن | *hajat d.*, to be in need (of). |
| خوش گذشتن | *xoʃ goɣaʃtan* (used impersonally), to be enjoyed (by), pass pleasantly. |
| دادن | *dadan*, to give (to). |
| در گذشتن (بمرض) | *dar goɣaʃtan* (*be maraɣ*), to die (of an illness). |
| دعوت کردن | *da'vat k.*, to invite (to). |
| ربط داشتن | *rabt d.*, to be concerned (with). |
| رسيدن | *rasidan*, to reach, arrive (at). |
| رسيدگى کردن | *rasidegi k.*, to investigate, inquire (into). |
| ساختن | *saxtan*, to suit. |
| سبقت جستن | *sabqat jostan*, to outstrip, outrun. |
| شباهت داشتن | *ʃabahat d.* ⎫ |
| شبيه بودن | *ʃabih b.* ⎭ to resemble. |
| طعنه زدن | *ta'ne ɣadan*, to make insulting insinuations. |
| طمع داشتن | *tama' d.*, to covet. |
| فروختن | *foruxtan*, to sell (for a price, to a person). |
| قايل بودن | *qayel b.*, to admit, accept, affirm. |
| کشيدن | *kaʃidan*, to lead (to), reach, result (in). |
| کمك کردن | *komak k.*, to help. |
| گفتن | *goftan*, to say (to). |
| مأمور کردن | *ma'mur k.*, to appoint (as). |
| مايل بودن | *mayel b.*, to be inclined (to). |
| مبادرت کردن (ورزيدن) | *mobaderat k.* (*varɣidan*), to hasten (to do something). |
| مبتلا شدن | *mobtala ʃ.*, to be afflicted (with). |
| متوسل شدن | *motavassel ʃ.*, to have recourse (to). |
| مربوط بودن | *marbut b.*, to be connected (with). |
| مساعدت کردن | *mosa'edat k.*, to help. |
| مشروط بودن | *maʃrut b.*, to be conditional (upon). |
| معترض شدن | *mo'tareɣ ʃ.*, to protest (at), object (to something) |
| معروفيت داشتن | *ma'rufiat d.* ⎫ |
| معروف بودن | *ma'ruf b.* ⎭ to be famous (for). |

منتقل شدن *montaqel ʃ.*, to be transferred (to).

نیاز داشتن *niaʒ d.*, to be in need (of).

واقف بودن *vaqef b.*, to be aware (of).

Certain verbs are followed by the preposition به *be* and the Infinitive. Among them are:

بنا کردن *bana kardan*, to begin (to).

پرداختن *pardaxtan*, to set to work (to).

مشغول شدن *maʃγul ʃ.*, to become engaged (in), busy (with). شروع کردن شروع کرد بحرف زدن *ʃoruʿ k.*, to begin (to), e.g. *ʃoruʿ kard be harf ʒadan*, he began to speak.

(f) بی *bi*, without.

(g) تا *ta*, up to, to, e.g.

تا شهر رفتیم *ta ʃahr raftim*, We went to (as far as) the town.

از زمین تا آسمان فرق دارد *aʒ ʒamin ta asman farq darad*, It is as different as chalk from cheese (from the earth to the sky).

تا یک ساعت دیگر بر میگردیم *ta yak saʿate digar bar migardim*, We will return in an hour's time.

(h) جز *joʒ* and its compound بجز *bejoʒ*, except.

(i) در¹ *dar* (in, into, at, as, by), shows the relation of an action or state to the limits of space or time in a figurative sense or otherwise. It is also used to express area.

در اطاق نشسته بودیم *dar otaq neʃaste budim*, We were sitting in the room.

در این فکر بودم *dar in fekr budam*, I was thinking of this.

در عین حال *dar eine hal*, at the same time.

در نتیجه *dar natije*, as a result.

شش گز در چهار *ʃeʃ gaʒ dar cahar*, six gaʒ by four.

(j) مگر *magar*, except.

¹ In Classical Persian اندر *andar* 'in, into' is used as a preposition and also as a postposition, e.g. بشهر اندر *be ʃahr andar* in (into) the town.

3. Prepositions taking the *eẓafe*, which are derived from primitive adverbs (originally nouns) and nouns, include the following:

بدون     *bedun*, without.

برابر     *barabar*, opposite.

بهر     *bahr* and its compound از بهر *aẓ bahr*, for.

بیرون     *birun*, outside.

پائین     *pain*, below.

پس     *pas* and its compound در پس *dar pas*, behind.

پشت     *poft* and its compounds در پشت *dar poft*, behind and از پشت *aẓ poft*, from behind.

پیش     *pif* and its compound در پیش *dar pif* (in front of, before, with) are used to denote position and association with, e.g.

> پیش او و درس میخوانم     *pife u dars mixanam*, I have lessons with him (i.e. from him).

> کتاب پیش شماست     *ketab pife fomast*, The book is with you.

> اورا پیش وزیر بردند     *ura pife vaẓir bordand*, They took him before the minister.

جلو     *jelou*, in front of.

دم     *dam*, at, on the edge of, e.g.

> دم در ایستاد     *dame dar istad*, He stood at the door.

دنبال     *dombal*, behind, after, e.g.

> دنبال او گشتیم     *dombale u gaftim*, We went after him (to look for him).

زیر     *ẓir* and its compound در زیر *dar ẓir*, under.

سر     *sar*, at, on, over, e.g.

> سر میز مینشستیم     *sare miẓ minefastim*, We were sitting at table.

> سر این اشتباه کردند     *sare in eftebah kardand*, They made a mistake over this.

And its compounds:

بر سر     *bar sar*, on.

از سر     *aẓ sar*, from, on, off.

پشت سر   *poſte sar*, after, behind, e.g.

پشت سر شما میامد   *poſte sare ſoma miamad*, He was coming (along) behind you.

کنار   *kenar* and its compound بر کنار *bar kenar*, beside.

گرد   *gerd*, round, around.

لب   *lab*, on the edge of, e.g.

لب دریا   *labe darya*, on the seashore.

میان   *mian*, between, and its compounds:

در میان   *dar mian*, among; between.

از میان   *aʒ mian*, from among.

نزد   *naʒd*, in front of, beside, with, next, and its compounds:

در نزد   *dar naʒd*, near, beside.

از نزد   *aʒ naʒd*, from, before.

نزدیك   *naʒdik*, near.

همراه   *hamrah*, together, along with.

بالا   *bala* (with the *eʒafe* بالای *balaye*), above.

پا   *pa* (with the *eʒafe* پای *paye*), at the foot of.

پهلو   *pahlu* (with the *eʒafe* پهلوی *pahluye*), beside, by the side of.

پی   *pēi* (with the *eʒafe* پی *pēiye*), after, in pursuit of, and its compounds:

در پی   *dar pēi*, after; in continuation of.

از پی   *aʒ pēi*, after.

تو   *tu* (with the *eʒafe* توی *tuye*), in, into.

جا   *ja* (with the *eʒafe* جای *jaye*) and its compound:

بجا   *beja*, instead of, in place of.

رو   *ru* (with the *eʒafe* روی *ruye*), on; and its compounds:

از رو   *aʒ ru*, from upon, off.

رو برو   *ru be ru*, opposite.

سو   *su* (with the *eʒafe* سوی *suye*), towards; and its compounds:

از سو   *aʒ su*, from the direction of.

بسو   *be su*, towards.

در باره   *dar bare* (with the *eʒafe*, *dar bareye*), about, concerning.

# VOCABULARY

شرلی Sherley.

رابرت Robert.

میلاد *milad*, birth.

میلادی *miladi*, A.D.

قمری *qamari*, lunar.

مطابق *motabeq*, equal to, coinciding with.

اتحاد *ettehad*, union, unity.

ضد *ʒedd(e)*, بر ضد *bar ʒedd(e)*, against.

عثمانی *osmani*, Ottoman.

تحصیل *tahsil*, acquisition; تحصیل کردن *tahsil k.*, to acquire, study.

امتیاز *emteyaʒ*, concession (pl. امتیازات *emteyaʒat*).

همراهان *hamrahan*, companions.

عده *edde*, number.

نظام *neʒam*, order; military affairs.

نظامی *neʒami*, military; a military man.

توپ *tup*, cannon.

توپچی *tupci*, artillery-man.

وضع *vaʒ'*, situation, condition.

آگاهی *agahi d.*, to be informed, aware of.

هلند Holland.

اسپانیا *espania*, Spain.

اواخر *avaxer* (pl. of آخر *axer*) = towards the end of (month, year, century, etc.).

قرن *qarn*, century.

شرکت *ʃerkat jostan*, to participate in.

موقع *mōuqe'*, time, situation; موقعیکه *mōuqe'ike*, when.

عباس Abbas.

خراسان *xorasan*, Khurasan, a province in N.E. Persia.

دفع *daf'*, repelling (noun).

فتنه *fetne*, sedition, rebellion.

تاتار *tatar*, Tartar.

ورود *vorud*, arrival.

پیغام *pēiɣam*, message.

فرنگی *farangi*, European.

مایحتاج *ma yahtaj* (Arabic for 'what is needed'), needs, necessities.

نوکر *nōukar*, servant.

امثال آن *amsale an*, such like (the likes of that).

مهیا *mohāiya*, prepared, provided.

بر خلاف *bar xelaf(e)*, contrary to.

خطر *xatar*, danger.

پست *past*, mean (adj.).

ملازمان *molaʒeman*, attendants, retinue.

بریدن *boridan*, to cut (off).

تنگدستی *tangdasti*, being in difficulties, straits.

نعمت *ne'mat*, bounty.

دریغ داشتن *dariɣ d.*, to grudge.
هنگام *hengam*, time.
گریختن *gorixtan* (*goriɀ*), to flee
(گریز) from.
دربار *darbar*, court.
وزارت *veɀarat*, ministry.
وزارت *veɀarate kefvar*, the
کشور Ministry of the In-
terior.
پل *pol*, bridge.
امر *amr* (pl. امـور *omur*),
matter, affair.
موجب *mōujeb*, cause.
پیشرفت *pifraft*, advance, progress.
کاهل *kahel*, lazy, negligent,
slow.

محتاج *mohtaj*, needing, in need
of.
عزت *eɀɀat*, honour.
مذلت *maɀallat*, meanness, ignominy.
نرم *narm*, soft.
دلیر *dalir*, brave, audacious.
سیر *sir*, satiated.
بشر *bafar*, man, humanity.
گشودن *gofudan* (*gofa*), to
(گشا) open.
آزمودن *aɀmudan* (*aɀma*), to try,
(آزما) test.
امید *omid*, hope.
زشت *ɀeft*, ugly.
معذور *ma'ɀur*, excused.
شر *farr*, evil.

## آمدن برادران شرلی بایران[1]

شرلیها دو برادر بودند بنام انتنی و رابرت کـه در ۱۵۹۷ میلادی مطابق با
۱۰۰۷ هجری قمری با بیست و پنج نفر انگلیسی جهت اتحاد با ممالک اروپا بر ضد
دولت عثمانی و تحصیل امتیازات برای تجار انگلیسی از خاک عثمانی و مغرب ایران
خودرا بقزوین رساندند (و از همراهان آنها عده نظامی و توپچی بودند کـه بوضع
نظام اروپا بخوبی آگاهی داشته و خود انتنی شرلی هم خدمت سربازیرا انجام داده
و در جنگهای هلند و اسپانیا در اواخر قرن شانزدهم میلادی شرکت جسته بود)
در این موقع شاه عباس در خراسان مشغول دفع فتنه تاتارها بود چون خبر ورود
نمایندگان انگلیسی بشاه رسید پیغام داد کـه بایـد از مهمانان فرنگی ما پذیرائی
کامل شود و ما یحتاج آنان از اسب و نوکر و امثال آن مهیا باشد و هرکس بر
خلاف این فرمان رفتار کند جانش در خطر خواهد بود و هرگاه کسی بیشترین
ملازمان ایشان بدرفتاری نماید سرش بریده خواهد شد (نا تمام)

[1] See p. 95, footnote 1.

EXERCISE 20

دوستی مردمرا ` بدو چیز توان شناخت یکی آنکه چون دوسترا تنگدستی رسد نعمت از او دریغ ندارند و دیگر آنکه هنگام تنگدستی از او نگریزند—این مسافرت بما بسیار خوش گذشت—پاسبان شروع کرد برسیدگی کردن باین موضوع—از وزارت جنگ بوزارت کشور منتقل شد—برادر کوچك شما بیشتر بمادرتان شباهت دارد تا بپدرتان—سر این کار میانشان بهم خورد—اگرچه حق با شماست با وجود این باید از او معذرت بخواهید—این امر با آن امر هیچ ربطی ندارد—دیروز پیش یکی از دوستان شما بودم و خیلی از شما تعریف کرد—پس از آنکه از پل عبور کردم بعده زیادی از مردم بر خوردم—ازکاهلی و تن آسانی دوری کنید چه مردم کاهل و تن آسان محتاج این و آنند— توانگری بهنراست نه بمال و بزرگی بعقل است نه بسال—بگفته خود کار کن تا بگفته تو کار کنند—مردمرا بلباس نتوان شناخت—مردن بعزت به از زندگانی بمذلت—بر دوستی پادشاهان اعتماد نشاید کرد `—نه چندان نرمی کن که بر تو دلیر شوند و نه چندان درشتی که از تو سیر گردند—آنکه بشر است هرگز زبان بشر نگشاید—تا کسیرا بارها نیازمائید بر وی اعتماد نکنید—بامید هزار دوست یك دشمن مکن—هرگه کسی از تو زشت گوید ویرا معذورتر از آن کس دان که آن سخن را بتو رساند

EXERCISE 21

1. He came with me to the town and there we separated. 2. He did not return home because he feared his father. 3. He was sent as his country's representative to England. 4. The army attacked the enemy and defeated them. 5. If he had been there we would have asked him. 6. After he had conquered his enemies he ruled over the whole of the country. 7. He sought to avoid us. 8. We besought him to remain. 9. His possessions consist of three houses and two gardens. 10. We consulted together and decided to go. 11. He began to laugh. 12. In my opinion it would be better if you refrained from writing this letter. 13. Among the early English travellers who came to Persia were two brothers, named Sherley; they came to the court of Shah Abbas in the hope of obtaining trade concessions. They stayed a number of years in Persia and entered the service of Shah Abbas. One of them had some knowledge of military affairs, having taken part in several wars in Europe.

` See Lesson XII, para. 3. ` *Ibid.*

## LESSON XII

The various uses of ی -i. The use of the *ezafe*. The omission
of the *ezafe*. The use of را -ra. The use of the plural in ان -an.
The agreement of nouns of multitude and collective nouns with
the verb. Nouns used generically. The Vocative. The use of
the comparative degree of adjectives. Repetition. و 'and'.

1. It will be useful here to recapitulate the various uses of ی -i and to
add some remarks concerning them.

  (a) Nominal.

  (i) The Adjectival ی -i = belonging to,[1] e.g.

       یزدی   *yazdi*, a native of Yazd, belonging to Yazd.

       وطنی   *vatani*, native, home-made (= made in Persia; from
       وطن *vatan* 'homeland').

The following relative adjectives should be noted:

       ساوجی   *saveji*, a man of ساوه Save.

       رازی   *razi*, a man of ری Rei.

       مروزی   *marvazi*, a man of مرو Marv.

       آوجی   *avaji*, a man of آوه Ave.

       دهلوی   *dehlavi*, a man of دهلی Delhi.

       سگزی   *sagzi*, a man of Sistan (Segestan).

The Adjectival ی -i is not usually added to the name of the tribes, e.g.

       نادر شاه افشار   *nader šah affar*[2], Nader Shah, the Afshar,
but it is added to the names of dynasties, e.g.

       یعقوب بن لیث صفاری   *ya'qub ebne leise saffari*, Ya'qub son of Leis,
       the Saffarid.

The Adjectival ی -i when added to the Infinitive gives the meaning
'fit for, worthy of', e.g.

       خوردنی   *xordani*, fit to eat, edible.

       خواندنی   *xandani*, readable, interesting (to read).

       دیدنی   *didani*, worth seeing.

---

[1] = The Middle Persian *-ik* > *iy*.
[2] For the omission of the *ezafe* see para. 2 (ƒ) below.

This ی -i is also added to the Infinitive to form a kind of present participle referring to future time, e.g.

در تهران ماندنی نیستم   dar tehran mandani nistam, I am not staying in Tehran.

رفتنی هستم   raftani hastam, I am going.

The Adjectival ی -i is capable of wide extension and can be added to almost any word or combination of words, e.g.

اتومبیل چهار نفری   otomobile cahar nafari, a four-seater car.

خانه دو طبقه   xaneye do tabaqei, a two storeyed-house.

(ii) The Abstract ی -i,[1] e.g.

مهربانی   mehrabani, kindness (from مهربان mehraban 'kind').

تاریکی   tariki, darkness (from تاریك tarik 'dark').

(iii) The Indefinite ی -i (=one),[2] e.g.

مردی   mardi, a (one) man.

The Indefinite ی -i is also capable of extension:
It is used to form adverb equivalents, e.g.

هفته چند   haftei cand, a few weeks.

سالی دو   sali do, (for) about two years.[3]

Added to صد sad 'hundred' it is used to express percentages, e.g.

صدی سه   sadi se, 3%.

The Indefinite ی -i is also used to emphasize the noun or the quality expressed by the noun or the adjective qualifying the noun, e.g.

بلائی‌است   balaist, It is a (great) calamity.

مردی‌است   mardist, He is a (fine) man.

مرد خوبی‌است   marde xubist, He is a (very) good man.

چنین ملت بزرگی   conin mellate bozorgi, such a great people.

---

[1] — The Middle Persian -ih.

[2] — The Middle Persian ē, ēv <Old Persian aiva.

[3] A more usual way to express 'about' is to use در حدود dar hodud(e) or تقریباً taqriban, e.g. در حدود دو سال dar hodude do sal, or تقریباً دو سال taqriban do sal, about two years.

Used in this way the Indefinite ی -*i* can be added to a plural noun or adjective qualifying a plural noun, e.g.

تلفات بسیاری دادند  *talafate besyari dadand*, They suffered (very) many losses.

خانمهای خوبی هستند  *xanomhaye xubi hastand*, They are (very) good women.

The ی -*i* added to قدر *qadr*, اندك *andak*, کم *kam* and چند *cand* emphasizes the idea of indefiniteness, e.g.

قدری  *qadri* ⎫
کمی  *kami* ⎬ (just) a little.
اندکی  *andaki* ⎭

The Indefinite ی -*i* is sometimes added to a plural noun to particularize it, e.g.

ملاحظاتی راجع بادبیات در دوره مشروطیت

*molahezati*[1] *raje' be adabiyat dar doureye mafrutiyat,*

some (a few) observations on literature during the period of the Constitution.

With a negative verb the Indefinite ی -*i* conveys the idea of 'none whatever, no special, not very', e.g.

چندان دوام و ثباتی ندارد  *candan davam va sabati nadarad*, It is not very firmly established (it has not much permanence or stability).

تعصبی ندارد  *ta'assobi nadarad*, He has no fanaticism (whatever).

کاری ندارم  *kari nadaram*, I have no (special) work.

The Indefinite ی -*i* used in this way can be further strengthened by the addition of هیچ *hic* 'none' which precedes the noun it governs, e.g.

هیچ عیبی ندارد  *hic ēibi nadarad*, It has no fault (whatever).

The Indefinite ی -*i* is added to plural nouns qualified by چه *ce* 'what sort of', e.g.

چه کسانی هستند  *ce kasani hastand*, What sort of people are they?

---

[1] Sound feminine plural of ملاحظه *molaheze* (see Part II, Lesson XIX, para. 7).

The Indefinite ی -i is also used to convey the idea of 'totality', e.g.

بهم بر مکن تا توانی دلی  *  که آهی جهانی بهم بر کند

*beham bar makon ta tavani deli ke ahi jahani beham bar konad.*

Do not disturb a (single) heart as long as you can (avoid it), because a (single) sigh (to God) destroys a (whole) world.

In Lesson III, para. 13, it was stated that the noun and its attributes were regarded as a syntactical whole and the Indefinite ی -i was added to the final qualifying word. For the sake of variety, the Indefinite ی -i is sometimes added to the noun instead of to the adjective, in which case the *eẓafe* is omitted, e.g.

مردی خوب  *mardi xub*, a good man.

تنی چند  *tani cand*, a few persons.

If two nouns, both indefinite, are united by a preposition, only the first takes the Indefinite ی -i, e.g.

سربازی با پاسبان در خیابان ایستاده بود  *sarbaẓi ba pasban dar xiaban istade bud*, A soldier was standing in the street with a policeman.

مردی با بچه در باغ نشسته بود  *mardi ba bacce dar baɣ nefaste bud*, A man was sitting in the garden with a child.

If the intention is to refer to an article in general terms, rather than to differentiate or to particularize it, the Indefinite ی -i is not used, e.g.

کاغذ مینویسد  *kaɣaẓ minevisad*, He is writing a letter.[1]

کتاب میخواند  *ketab mixanad*, He is reading a book.

مداد خرید  *medad xarid*, He bought a pencil.

اطاق پنجره دارد  *otaq panjare darad*, The room has a window (windows).

سیب میخورد  *sib mixorad*, He is eating an apple.

---

[1] = 'he is "letter-writing"', or 'he is writing letters'; کاغذی مینویسد *kaɣaẓi minevisad* would mean 'he is writing some letter or other' and کاغذرا مینویسد *kaɣaẓra minevisad* 'he is writing the letter'.

Similarly, if a noun is used generically it does not take the Indefinite ی -*i*, e.g.

هنوز وزیر نشده‌است    *hanuʒ vaʒir naʃode ast*, He has not yet become a minister.

هنوز مرد نشده‌است    *hanuʒ mard naʃode ast*, He has not yet reached his majority (become a man).

Compare the above with the following:

مردی مثل شما این کاررا نمیکند    *mardi mesle ʃoma in karra namikonad*, A man like you would not do this.

(iv) The Relative ی -*i*,[1] e.g.

مردیکه...    *mardike*, the (this) man who....

(i) and (ii) carry the stress; (iii) and (iv) are unstressed. Formerly (iii) and (iv) were pronounced *e*.

(*b*) Verbal.

(i) The Personal Ending for the 2nd pers. sing., e.g.

میکنی    *mikoni*, Thou dost.

(ii) The Conditional or Continuous ی -*i* which is added to the Preterite, except in the 2nd pers. sing., to form a Conditional Past and an Imperfect, e.g.

گفتی    *gofti*, He would have said, used to say, was saying.

کردمی    *kardami*, I would have done, used to do, was doing.

The Conditional or Continuous ی -*i* is not used in Modern Persian apart from the form بایستی *bayesti*, which is occasionally found, e.g.

سلطان احمد شبی که صبح آن بایستی بجانب کرمان حرکت کند گفت...

*soltan ahmad ʃabi ke sobhe an bayesti be janebe kerman harakat konad goft....*

Soltan Ahmad on the evening before he was to have set out for Kerman said....

**2.** The principal uses of the *eʒafe* have already been given. These are recapitulated below together with certain other uses of the *eʒafe*.[2]

---

[1] = The Pahlavi *i* (*iy*).

[2] Persian grammarians enumerate several different kinds of *eʒafe*. These are covered by, although they do not coincide exactly with, the uses of the *eʒafe* in para. 2 above.

(a) The 'possessive' *ezafe* (to express the genitive), e.g.

    کتاب پسر    *ketabe pesar*, the boy's book.

    در باغ    *dare bay*, the door of the garden.

(b) The 'qualifying' or 'adjectival' *ezafe*, e.g.

    مرد خوب    *marde xub*, the good man.

    بچه کوچك    *bacceye kucek*, the small child.

(c) The 'prepositional' *ezafe*, e.g.

    سر میز    *sare miz*, at table.

    پشت خانه    *poste xane*, behind the house.

(d) The *ezafe* of 'sonship', e.g.

    رستم زال    *rostame zal*, Rustam son of Zal.

(e) The *ezafe* used to express distance from, e.g.

    ده فرسخی اصفهان    *dah farsaxiye esfahan*, ten *farsaxs* distant from Isfahan (being a distance of ten *farsaxs* from Isfahan).

(f) The *ezafe* is used in many cases in Persian where in English two nouns are used in apposition, e.g.

    یعقوب پیغمبر    *ya'qube peiyambar*, Jacob, the prophet.

    رود نیل    *rude nil*, the River Nile.

    محمد خان تاجر    *mohammad xane tajer*, Mohammad Khan, the merchant.

Various words meaning 'kind, sort' do not take the *ezafe*. Among them are: نوع *noū'*, طور *toūr*, جور *jur*, and قبیل *qabil*, e.g.

    این نوع خانه    *in noū' xane*, this kind of house.

    این قبیل اشخاص[1]    *in qabil afxas*, people of this kind.

    این طور رفتار    *in toūr raftar*, this kind of conduct.

The Personal Pronouns, with the exception of من *man* 'I', do not take the *ezafe* and must be used in apposition, e.g.

    بیچاره شما باید بمانید    *bicare foma bayad bemanid*, You, unfortunate one, must remain.

    من بدبخت نرفتم    *mane badbaxt naraftam*, I, unfortunate one, did not go.

---

[1] Plural of شخص *faxs*.

همه *hame* 'all' when it means an aggregate without regard to the component parts is used without the *ezafe*, e.g.

همه راه در این فکر بود    *hame rah dar in fekr bud*, He was thinking of this the whole way.

همه شب بیدار بود    *hame ʃab bidar bud*, He was awake the whole night.

مایل نیستم این همه زحمت بکشید    *mayel nistam in hame zahmat bekaʃid*, I do not want you to take all this trouble.

There is no *ezafe* after weights and measures, e.g.

دو متر گودی    *do metr goudi*, two metres deep.

سه سنگ آب    *se sang ab*, three *sangs* of water.

یك چارك گوشت    *yak carak guʃt*, one *carak* of meat.

Similarly

یك لیوان آب    *yak livan ab*, a glass of water.

یك فنجان چای    *yak fenjan cāi*, a cup of tea.

The *ezafe* is not used between a proper name and the titles following it, the two being placed in apposition to each other, e.g.

جناب آقای بهمن نخست وزیر    *janabe aqaye bahman naxost vazir*, H. E. Bahman, the Prime Minister.

It has been seen above that when the Indefinite ی *-i* is added to the noun instead of the following qualifying word the *ezafe* falls out. This also happens if the word order is inverted and the adjective precedes the noun it qualifies, e.g.

خوب خانه خرید    *xub xanei xarid*, He bought a good house.

Inversion takes place with the words عجب *ajab* 'strange, wonderful' and مرحوم *marhum* 'late, deceased'. The former does not take the *ezafe* whereas the latter does, e.g.

عجب کتابی است    *ajab ketabist*, It is a strange book.

این شهر عجب هوای خوبی دارد    *in ʃahr ajab havaye xubi darad*, This town has a wonderful climate.

مرحوم پدرم    *marhume pedaram*, my late father.

3. In Lesson I, para. 6, the use of را *-ra* to mark the definite direct object was described. را *-ra* is also used to express the dative, e.g.

اورا دو پسر بود    *ura do pesar bud*, He had two sons (to him
were two sons).

شاه وزیررا خلعت داد    *ʃah vaʒirra xel'at dad*, The Shah gave the
minister a robe of honour.

را -*ra* cannot be used to mark both the definite direct object and the
indirect object in the same sentence: either the latter must be preceded
by به *be* 'to' or the را -*ra* must be omitted after the definite direct object.
The use of را -*ra* to express the dative is a classical rather than a modern
usage.

A similar construction is found with certain intransitive verbs in
both Classical and Modern Persian, e.g.

این کتاب مرا پسند آمد    *in ketab mara pasand amad*, I liked this book
(this book came pleasantly to me).

بایستن *bayestan* and شایستن *ʃayestan* are used impersonally with را -*ra*
to mean 'it behoves, it is fitting', etc.[1] This construction is classical
rather than modern, e.g.

پادشاهرا باید...    *padeʃahra bayad*, It behoves the king to....

شمارا شاید...    *ʃomara ʃayad*..., It befits you to....

If an adjective or participle used as an adjective is placed in apposition
to a noun which is indefinite, the latter, if the object of the verb, takes
را -*ra*, e.g.

ظالمیرا خفته دیدم    *ʒalemira xofte didam*, I saw a (certain) tyrant
asleep.

سربازیرا در راه کشته دیدم    *sarbaʒira dar rah koʃte didam*, I saw on the
road a soldier [who had been] killed.[2]

In Colloquial Persian a certain latitude prevails in the use of را -*ra*,
e.g.

کدام کتابرا میخواهید    *kodam ketabra mixahid*, Which book do you
want?

رفت کتابیرا بخرد    *raft ketabira bexarad*, He went to buy a book.

---

[1] When used thus شاید *ʃayad* takes the negative prefix whereas شاید *ʃayad* 'perhaps'
does not, e.g.

نشاید این کاررا کرد    *naʃayad in karra kard*, It is not fitting to do such a work.

[2] سربازی کشته در راه دیدم    *sarbaʒi koʃte dar rah didam* would be a more usual
construction.

The use of را -ra in such a construction gives the force of 'a certain' to the Indefinite ی -i and sometimes implies that the sentence is incomplete, some phrase such as که لازم داشت ke lazem daſt being perhaps in the speaker's mind in the second of the above examples.

Compare also:

یکی بمن بدهید *yaki beman bedehid*, Give me one.

And

یکیرا بمن بدهید *yakira beman bedehid*, Give me (one of them).

In certain cases را -ra is added to an indefinite noun for the sake of clarity, e.g.

شنیدم گوسفندیرا بزرگی رهانید *ſonidam gusfandira boʒorgi rahanid*, I have heard that a certain great man set free a sheep.

The words فلان *folan* 'a certain', فلانی *folani* 'so-and-so', همه *hame* 'all', سائر *sa'er* 'other, the rest', تمام *tamam* 'all, the whole', هر یکی *har yaki* 'each one', هردو *har do* 'both', etc., are considered definite and take را -ra.

را -ra is also used in Classical Persian, though not commonly, to form combinations corresponding to an adverbial phrase in English, e.g.

قضارا *qaʒara*, by chance.

خدارا *xodara*, for God's sake.

The expression ترا بخدا *tora bexoda* is used between intimate friends to express surprise or to emphasize something.

In Classical Persian the particle مر *mar* is sometimes found preceding a noun or pronoun followed by را -ra, e.g.

پادشاه مر عامه را بار دادی[1] *padeſah mar ammera bar dadi*, The king used to hold a court for the common people.

4. Two nouns are frequently used in Persian where an adjective and a noun or an adverb and an adjective are used in English, e.g.

کمال امتنانرا دارم *kamale emtenanra daram*, I am extremely grateful (have the perfection of gratitude).

در نهایت سختی زندگی میکند *dar nehayate saxti ʒendegi mikonad*, He lives in great hardship (in the extremity of difficulty).

با نهایت خوشحالی *ba nehayate xoſhali*, with great (the limit of) happiness.

---

[1] See above, para. 1 (b) (ii) for the Continuous Past in ی -i.

5. Adjectives used as nouns denoting rational beings take the plural in ان -*an*, e.g.

بزرگان  *boẕorgan*, the great.

حسودان  *hasudan*, the envious.

Relative Adjectives ending in ی -*i*, however, normally form a plural in ها -*ha*.

Certain words denoting irrational beings or inanimate objects also sometimes form a plural in ان -*an*. Among them are:

| | | | |
|---|---|---|---|
| لب | *lab*, lip. | بازو | *baẕu*, forearm. |
| چشم | *cafm*, eye. | گناه | *gonah*, sin. |
| درخت | *daraxt*, tree. | سخن | *soxan*, word. |
| آهو | *ahu*, gazelle. | ستاره | *setare*, star.[1] |

سرها *sarha* means 'heads'; سران *saran* means 'leaders', e.g.

سران لشکر  *sarane lafkar*, army leaders.

نیا *nia* 'ancestor' and پله *pelle* 'stair' form their plurals نیاکان *niakan* and پلکان *pellekan* respectively.

Words of foreign origin, even if they denote rational beings, do not usually take the plural in ان -*an*, thus خانمها *xanomha*, ladies, انگلیسها *englisha*, the English, but فرانسویان *faransavian*, the French.

6. Nouns of Multitude denoting rational beings are followed by the singular or the plural according to whether the idea of unity or plurality is uppermost in the speaker's mind, e.g.

قشون حمله کرد  *qofun hamle kard*, The army attacked.

جمعیتی بزرگ در میدان جمع شد  *jam'iyati boẕorg dar meidan jam' fod*, A large crowd assembled in the square.

عده متفرق شدند و عده ماندند  *eddei motafarriq fodand va eddei mandand*, A number dispersed and a number remained (behind).

جمعیت ما از صد نفر تشکیل میشود  *jam'iyate ma aẕ sad nafar tafkil mifavad*, Our group (society) is composed of one hundred persons.

مردم *mardom* 'people' always takes a plural verb, e.g.

مردم جمع شدند  *mardom jam' fodand*, The people assembled.

---

[1] Plural ستارگان *setaregan*.

7. Certain collective nouns take a plural termination when it is intended to signify diversity or variety, e.g.

ایران میوه‌های خوب دارد — *iran mivehaye xub darad*, Persia has good fruit (of different kinds).

شرابهای فرانسه معروف است — *ʃarabhaye faranse maʿruf ast*, The wine (i.e. the different wines) of France is famous.

انگورهای آذربایجان شیرین است — *angurhaye aʒarbāijan ʃirin ast*, The grapes (i.e. the different kinds of grapes) of Azerbaijan are sweet.

8. Nouns denoting rational beings, when used generically, are usually put in the plural, e.g.

ایرانیها طبع شعر دارند — *iraniha tabʿe ʃeʿr darand*, The Persian is poetical.

زنهای دهاتی زیاد کار میکنند — *ʒanhaye dehati ʒiad kar mikonand*, The country-woman works hard (much).

Nouns denoting irrational beings and inanimate objects, when used generically, are put in the singular, e.g.

سگ تازی برای شکار خوب است — *sage taʒi baraye ʃekar xub ast*, Salukis are good for hunting.

خربوزه در گرگاب خوب بعمل میاید — *xarbuʒe dar gorgab xub be amal miayad*, Melons grow well in Gorgab.[1]

If a noun used generically forms the predicate it is put in the singular even if the subject of the sentence is plural, e.g.

ما همه بنده خدا ایم — *ma hame bandeye xoda im*, We are all servants of God.

این مردها حیوان اند — *in mardha hēivan and*, These men are (like) animals.

آنها دشمن ما هستند — *anha doʃmane ma hastand*, They are our enemies.

If a noun used generically follows another noun which takes the *eʒafe* it is put in the plural, e.g.

[1] A village near Isfahan.

این کار کار بچه‌هاست    *in kar kare baccehast,* This work is
the work of a child.

این مناسب حال بزرگان نیست    *in monasebe hale boʒorgan nist,* This
is not in keeping with the dignity
of the great.

مردی با لباس درویشان وارد شهر شد    *mardi ba lebase darviʃan varede ʃahr
ʃod,* A man in darvish's clothes
entered the town.

9. If a series of nouns are united to each other by و *va, o,* the plural
termination can be omitted, e.g.

وزیر و وکیل و صاحب منصب و آخوند همه حاضر بودند

*vaʒir o vakil o saheb mansab o axund hame haʒer budand,*
Ministers, deputies, officers and mullas, all were present.

بزرگ و کوچک همه آمدند

*boʒorg va kucek hame amadand,*
Great and small, all came.

گاو و گوسفند و الاغ و اسب در چمن بود

*gav o gusfand o olaɣ o asb dar caman bud,*
Cows, sheep, asses, and horses were in the meadow.

قلم و مداد و کتاب بین بچه‌ها تقسیم کرد

*qalam o medad o ketab bēine bacceha taqsim kard,*
He distributed pens, pencils and books among the children.

در باغ ما گیلاس و انگور و انجیر خوب پیدا میشود

*dar baɣe ma gilas o angur o anjire xub pēida miʃavad,*
In our garden good cherries, grapes and figs are to be had (found).

10. In certain cases a noun which is logically plural is nevertheless put
in the singular, e.g.

روی دوش همه بارهای سنگین بود    *ruye duʃe hame barhaye sangin bud,*
Heavy loads were on the back(s)
of all.

تغییر عقیده دادند    *taɣyire aqide dadand,* They changed
their minds.

کاغذ مبادله کردیم    *kaɣaʒ mobadele kardim,* We ex-
changed letters.

**11.** The vocative is expressed by the particle ای *ei* or (when addressing God or one of the Imams, etc.) یا *ya* preceding the noun or pronoun, e.g.

ای پادشاه    *ei padefah,* O king!

...ای تو که    *ei to ke...,* O thou, who....

**12.** An ا *-a* can be added to nouns and adjectives to form an interjection, e.g.

خداوندا    *xodavanda,* O God!

خوشا بحال شما    *xofa be hale foma,* O happy your state!

خوشا شیراز    *xofa firaʒ,* O happy Shiraz!

If the noun to which this 'interjectory' *alef* is added ends in ا *a* or و *u*, a ی *y* is inserted between the final vowel and the 'interjectory' ا *-a*, e.g.

خدایا    *xodaya,* O God!

Personal Pronouns, with the exception of من *man* 'I', do not take the 'interjectory' ا *-a.*

**13.** Certain nouns are used as adjectives, e.g.

این خانه بسیار راحت است    *in xane besyar rahat ast,* This house is very comfortable (راحت =ease, comfort).

**14.** The comparative degree of adjectives is sometimes used in Persian where the superlative is used in English, e.g.

بهر شهریکه نزدیکتر است بروید    *be har fahri ke naʒdiktar ast beravid,* Go to the nearest town.

The comparative ending is also added to certain nouns, e.g.

این طرفتر بنشینید    *in taraftar benefinid,* Sit nearer this way (side).

A phrase such as 'he got better and better' is rendered

روز بروز بهتر میشد    *ruʒ be ruʒ behtar mifod,*

or

هی بهتر میشد    *hei behtar mifod.*

(See also Lesson XIII, para. 24.)
    'The sooner the better' is translated

هر چه زودتر بهتر    *har ce ʒudtar behtar.*

هر قدر *har qadr* can be used instead of هر چه *har ce*, e.g.

هر قدر برودخانه نزدیکتر میشوید زمین حاصلخیزتر است

*har qadr be rudxane naẓdiktar miſavid ẓamin haselxiẓtar ast,*

The nearer you get to the river the more fertile the land.

'How much the more' and 'how much the less' are rendered as follows:

اگر آن وقت از او بدتان میامد بطریق اولی[1] باید حالا از او نفرت
داشته باشید

*agar an vaqt aẓ u badetan miamad be tariqe ūla bayad hala aẓ u nefrat daſte baſid,*

If you disliked him then, how much the more must you dislike him now.

اگر این کتابرا دوست دارید چقدر باید آن یکیرا دوست داشته باشید[2]

*agar in ketabra dust darid ce qadr bayad an yakira dust daſte baſid,*

If you like this book, how much the more must you like that one.

باو نمیشود اعتماد کرد تا چه رسد ببرادرش

*be u namiſavad e'temad kard ta ce rasad be baradaraſ,*

One cannot trust him, much less his brother.

15. In Classical Persian the absolute use of the comparative and superlative is sometimes found, e.g.

قشنگترین  *qaſangtarin*, most beautiful (=very beautiful).

قشنگتر  *qaſangtar*, more beautiful (=very beautiful).

16. Comparison can be expressed by که *ke*, e.g.

مردنت به که مردم آزاری[3]  *mordanat beh ke mardom aẓari,* Thy death is better than oppression of the people (it is better that thou shouldst die, than that thou shouldst oppress the people).

This usage is classical rather than modern.

For other methods of expressing comparison see Lesson III, para. 17.

[1] اولی *ūla* is the elative of اول *avval*; see Part II, Lesson XVI, para. 16.
[2] For the use of the Subjunctive Past of داشتن *daſtan* see Lesson XIII, para. 12 (*h*).
[3] From آزردن *aẓordan* 'to oppress'.

17. Many adjectives can be used as nouns. Their use as nouns, however, tends to be more common in the plural than the singular. The use of the plural termination ان‎ -*an* with adjectives used as nouns denoting rational beings has already been noted (see above para. 5).

18. In Persian two nouns or two adjectives with the same or similar meanings are often used together, e.g.

گریه و زاری‎    *gerie o ɤari*, weeping and wailing.

تك و تنها‎    *tak o tanha*, single and alone.

تر و تازه‎    *tar o taɤe*, moist and fresh.

خوش و خرم‎    *xoʃ o xorram*, happy and cheerful.

Such combinations are not considered bad style.

19. Repetition of a word indicates:

(*a*) Intensity, e.g.

تند تند بيا‎    *tond tond beya*, Come very quickly.

زار زار گریه میکرد‎    *ɤar ɤar gerye mikard*, She was weeping bitterly.

This is also the case where an adjective is repeated with the copula و‎ *o*, or with the *eɤafe*, e.g.

تند و تند آمدم‎    *tond o tond amadam*, I came very quickly.

خطرناك خطرناك‎    *xatarnake xatarnak*, very dangerous.

(*b*) Continuation, e.g.

یواش یواش میامد‎    *yavaʃ yavaʃ miamad*, He was coming along slowly.

باران نم نم میامد‎    *baran nam nam miamad*, It kept on drizzling.

(*c*) Grouping, e.g.

کبکها دسته دسته بلند شدند‎    *kabkha daste daste boland ʃodand*, The partridges rose in coveys.

(See also Lesson XIII, para. 3 (*b*) below)

20. و‎ 'and' is derived from two different sources: namely و‎ = *va* from the Arabic and و‎ = *o* from Middle Persian (see p. 38, n. 2). The latter form, in addition to its use in compound numerals and in certain com-

pounds (see Lesson X) tends to be used rather than و = va when it connects words or phrases commonly associated together, e.g.

روز و شب   *ruẓ o ʃab*, day and night.

In rapid speech it tends to be used in other contexts also, and in poetry it may be necessitated by the scansion.

و 'and' is used

(*a*) As a copulative, e.g.

آمد و از ما خدا حافظی کرد   *amad va aẓ ma xoda hafeẓi kard*, He came and said good-bye to us.

If a noun is qualified by several adjectives these may be united by و instead of the *eẓafe*, e.g.

آدم هوشیار و لایق و صبوری بود   *adame huʃyar va layeq va saburi bud*, He was an intelligent, worthy and very patient man,

instead of

آدم هوشیار لایق صبوری بود   *adame huʃyare layeqe saburi bud*.

(*b*) To introduce a qualifying phrase, e.g.

سر میز نشسته بود و قلمی بدستش بود   *sare miẓ neʃaste bud va qalami be dasteʃ bud*, He was sitting at the table with a pen in his hand.

(*c*) To mean 'is equal to, accompanied by, is the same as', e.g.

پیری و صد عیب   *piri o sad ɛ̄ib*, Old age is accompanied by a hundred defects.

(*d*) To mean 'or', e.g.

گل همین پنج روز و شش باشد   *gol hamin panj ruẓ o ʃeʃ baʃad*, A flower lasts but five or six days.

(*e*) To indicate association, e.g.

من و شراب خوردن چه حرفها میزنید   *man o ʃarab xordan ce harfha miẓanid*, I—drink wine? What are you saying?

تابستان آینده ما و اصفهان   *tabestane ayande ma o esfahan*, Next summer Isfahan for us.

This و is frequently used in poetry, e.g.

كه گر جستم از دست این تیر زن  *  من و کنج ویرانه پیر زن

*ke gar jastam aʒ daste in tir ʒan man o konje vēiraneye pir ʒan,*

... saying if I escape the hand of this archer, I will be content with
a corner of the old woman's ruined hut.

چو فردا برآید بلند آفتاب  *  من و گرز و میدان و افراسیاب

*co¹ farda bar ayad boland aftab man o gorʒ o mēidan o afrasiab,*

When tomorrow the sun mounts high (in the heavens) there will
I be with my club in the battlefield with Afrasiab.

## VOCABULARY

بقیه *baqiye*, remainder.

ترتیب *tartib*, arrangement, arranging.

حکمران *hokmran*, governor.

قسم *qesm*, kind, sort.

وسایل *vasayel* (pl. of وسیله *vasile*), means.

استراحت *esterahat*, rest, repose.

جماعت *jama'at*, group, body, company (of people).

ساختن (ساز) *saxtan* (*saʒ*), to make.

فراهم *faraham*, available.

حاکم *hakem*, governor.

ناظر *naʒer*, overseer, bailiff; a kind of inspector.

استقبال *esteqbal*, going out to give a ceremonial welcome (to someone).

بوسیدن *busidan*, to kiss; روبوسی *rubusi*, kissing on the face.

احترام *ehteram*, respect, honour.

تحف *tohaf* (pl. of تحفه *tohfe*), presents.

هدایا *hadaya* (pl. of هدیه *hadiye*), presents.

لگام *legam*, bridle.

قاطر *qater*, mule.

بخشیدن *baxʃidan*, to bestow, give.

سپس *sepas*, then.

ملاطفت *molatefat*, showing favour, kindness.

خدمتگذار *xedmatgoʒar*, servant, retainer.

صمیمی *samimi*, sincere.

صداقت *sadaqat*, sincerity, faithfulness.

صمیمیت *samimiyat*, sincerity.

معتقد *mo'taqed*, having faith (in), believing (in), convinced (of).

دستیاری *dastyari*, help.

¹ چو *co* is a contraction of چون *cun* used in poetry.

الله وردی خان Allahverdi Khan (one of Shah Abbas' military leaders).

سپهسالار sepahsalar, army commander.

فنون fonun (pl. of فن fann), art.

رنج ranj, trouble, vexation; رنج بردن ranj bordan, to suffer trouble, vexation.

سپاه sepah, army.

سپاهی sepahi, soldier.

تهیه tahie, preparing, making ready.

پیشنهاد pišnehad, proposal.

سفیر safir, ambassador, envoy, plenipotentiary.

سلاطین salatin (pl. of سلطان soltan), rulers, sultans.

متحد mottahed, united.

متملق motamalleq, a flatterer.

فریفتن (فریب) fariftan (farib), to deceive.

پشیمانی / ندامت pašimani / nedamat, regret.

گزیدن gazidan, to bite, sting.

قفا qafa, nape of the neck; در قفا dar qafa, behind.

وجه vajh, way, manner.

نیک nik, good.

نام nam, name.

برتری bartari, superiority.

مژده mozde, good news.

انوشیروان عادل anuširavane adel, Anushiravan the Just (the Sasanian ruler who reigned A.D. 531–78).

خدایتعالیٰ xodaye ta'ala, God most high[1].

عدو adu, enemy.

حکایت hekayat, story.

متفرق کردن motafarreq k., to disperse (trans.).

آمدن برادران شرلی بایران

(بقیه از درس پیش)

با این ترتیب حکمران قزوین از او پذیرائی شایان نمود و همه قسم وسایل استراحت آن جماعترا فراهم ساخت تا آنکه خبر ورود شاه بنزدیکی قزوین بشهر رسید و برادران شرلی و همراهانشان بهمراهی ناظر و حاکم قزوین باستقبال شاه رفتند و شاه هم با آن دو برادر روبوسی کرده با احترام تمام از آنها پذیرائی نمود و تحف و هدایای زیاد (۱٤٠ اسب با لگام زرین و ۱۰۰ قاطر و ۱۰۰ شتر و مقدار زیادی پول) بآنها و همراهانشان بخشید سپس با آن جماعت بپایتخت (اصفهان) رفت و ششماه در آن شهر از آنها پذیرائی کرد و بقدری نسبت بآنها ملاطفت

---

[1] تعالیٰ ta'ala is an Arabic verbal form ( =he is exalted) used here as an adjective.

نمود که خودشانرا از خدمتگذاران صمیمی شاه عباس دانستند و انتنی هم در مدت اقامت در اصفهان شاهرا بصداقت و صمیمیت خـود معتقد ساخت و بدستیاری الله وردیخان سپهسالار ایران در آموختن فنون جنگی ایران رنـج بسیار برد و ایرانیان فنون جنگرا از شرلی آموختند و سپاهیان مرتب و ۵۰۰ عراده توپ و ۲۰,۰۰۰ تـفـنـك تـهـیـه كـردنـد سپس انتنی بشاه عباس پیشنهاد کرد که سفیری بدربار سلاطین اروپا فرستد و با ایشان بر ضد دولت عثمانی متحد شود

(نا تمام)

## EXERCISE 22

بسخنان دروغ مـتـمـلقان فـریـفـتـه نشوید و از شنیدن آنها بر حذر باشید تـا پشیمانی نبرید و انگشت ندامت بدندان نگزید — هرکـه در قفای دیگران بد گوید بهیچ وجه دوستیرا نشاید — هرکهرا در زندگانی کار نیك نباشد پس از مردن نام نیك نباشد — مردمانرا برتری بر جانوران برفتار نیك است و كردار خوب — کسی مـژده پیش انوشیروان عـادل بردکه شنیدم فلان دشمنرا خدای تعالی بر داشت گفت هـیـچ شنیدی که مرا خواهد گذاشت

مرا بمرگ عدو جای شادمانی نیست ٭ که زندگانی ما نیز جاودانی نیست

## EXERCISE 23

1. He has gone into the bazaar to buy a book. 2. After he had been two years in the army he became an officer. 3. This story is worth hearing. 4. I do not care for this kind of book. 5. Many kinds of fruit grow in Persia. 6. The people began to assemble in the square; men, women and children were there and did not disperse until after sunset. 7. The women were carrying their children on their backs. 8. The book is both interesting and well written. 9. I am going and nobody can prevent me. 10. It has not done me much good nor any one else either (it had not much benefit for me...). 11. Facilities for rest are available for all the workmen by day and by night. 12. I never spoke or wrote to him. 13. Either he or I must go. 14. He cannot have gone out else he would have told me.

# LESSON XIII

The use of the tenses. The Negative. Impersonal Constructions.
Continuous Tenses formed with داشتن *daʃtan*. The particle هی
*hēi*. Certain Classical usages.

1. (a) The Infinitive and Short Infinitive are used as nouns, e.g.

دانا شدن توانا شدن است   *dana ʃodan tavana ʃodan ast,* To be
learned is to be powerful.

گفتن این صلاح نیست   *goftane in salah nist,* It is not expedient to say this.

پیشرفت او شایان تحسین است   *piʃrafte u ʃayane tahsin ast,* his progress is praiseworthy.

(b) The Infinitive is used to express purpose or finality with the
preposition به *be,* e.g.

بدیدن برادر خود رفت   *be didane baradare xod raft,* He went to
see his brother.

شروع کرد بنوشتن   *ʃoru' kard be neveʃtan,* He began to write.

بخواندن پرداخت   *be xandan pardaxt,* He set to work to read.

If the subordinate verb is a compound verb one part of which is
a noun the verbal part can sometimes be omitted, e.g.

شروع کرد بگریه   *ʃoru' kard be gerie* (for گریه کردن *gerie kardan*), He
began to weep.

شروع کرد بفرار   *ʃoru' kard be farar* (for فرار کردن *farar kardan*),
He began to flee.

But

شروع کردند بجمع شدن   *ʃoru' kardand be jam' ʃodan,* They began to
assemble.

(c) The Short Infinitive is used after impersonal verbs (see Lesson VI,
para. 12), e.g. میشود کرد *miʃavad kard,* It can be done.

(d) In Classical Persian the Infinitive is sometimes used in final
clauses where in Modern Persian the Subjunctive would be used, e.g.

لقمان گفت دریغ باشد کلمه حکمت با ایشان گفتن
*loqman goft dariɣ baʃad kalameye hekmat ba iʃan goftan,*
Loqman said it would be a pity to waste on them (to say to
them) words of wisdom.

مصلحت نـدیـدم از این بیـش ریش درونشرا بملامت خراشیدن و
نمك پاشیدن

*maslehat nadidam aʒ in biſ riſe daruneſra be malamat xaraſidan va namak paſidan,*

I did not consider it expedient to rub (scratch) his inner wound more than this by reproach or (and) to sprinkle salt upon it.

(*e*) In Classical Persian the Infinitive is sometimes used with the auxiliaries توانستن *tavanestan* 'to be able', خواستن *xastan* 'to want', and بایستن *bayestan* and شایستن *ſayestan* used impersonally. E.g.

بقیه عمررا از عهده شکر آن بیرون آمدن نتوانم

*baqiyeye omrra aʒ ohdeye ſokre an birun amadan natavanam,*

For the rest of (my) life I shall not be able to pay the debt of gratitude I owe for that.

(*f*) In Classical Persian the Infinitive is sometimes used with a preposition to express the passive, e.g.

پادشاه همه‌را بکشتن اشارت فرمود¹ *padeſah hamera be koſtan eſarat farmud,* The king gave a sign for them all to be killed.

2. The Past Participle, apart from its use in conjugating the verb, is used

(*a*) As an adjective, e.g.

آماده باشید *amade baſid,* Be prepared.

The negative of the Past Participle when it is used as an adjective or a noun (see immediately below) is نا *na-*, e.g.

ناگفته نماند *nagofte namanad,* Let it not remain unsaid.

(*b*) As a noun, e.g.

گفته مرا شنید *gofteye mara ſenid,* He heard what I said.

The Past Participle is widely used as a noun in the plural referring to human beings, but less frequently in the singular, e.g.

بازداشت شدگان *baʒdaſt ſodegan,* the internees.

کشتگان *koſtegan,* the killed.

¹ See Lesson XIV, para. 1 (*c*) for this use of فرمودن (فرما) *farmudan (farma).*

(c) In apposition in the event of the subject of two co-ordinate sentences being the same and the action of the former of the two preceding the latter, e.g.

نامه شما رسیده خوانده شد    *nameye ʃoma raside xande ʃod,* Your letter has been received and read.

If the tenses of the verbs of two or more co-ordinate sentences are the same and their actions concurrent, the Past Participle followed by و *va* can be used in all but the final sentence, provided the subjects are the same.

3. The Present Participle is used:

(a) As an adjective, e.g.

خواهان سلامتی شما هستم    *xahane salamatiye ʃoma hastam, I* am desirous of your well-being (health).

(b) As an adverb, in which case it is usually repeated, e.g.

دوان دوان جلو آمد    *davan davan jelou amad,* He came forward running.

4. The Noun of the Agent, formed by the addition of نده -*ande* to the Present Stem, is also sometimes used as an adjective, e.g.

درخشنده    *daraxʃande,* shining (from درخشیدن *daraxʃidan* 'to shine').

مرد بخشنده    *marde baxʃandei,* a liberal man (from بخشیدن *baxʃidan* 'to give, bestow').

5. The Preterite is used:

(a) For a single definite action in the past, e.g.

دیروز رفت    *diruʒ raft,* He went yesterday.

(b) For an action just performed, e.g.

اورا الآن دیدم    *ura al'an didam,* I saw him just now.

(c) For the anterior of two possible future actions, e.g.

انگلستان که رفتید نامه بمن بنویسید
*englestan ke raftid namei be man benevisid,*
When you go to England, write a letter to me.

This use is comparable with its use in Present and Future conditions (see Lesson VII, para. 5 (a) above).

(*d*) For an action about to be completed, e.g.

آمدم   *amadam*= I am coming (in answer to a question or implied question such as 'are you coming?' or a command such as 'hurry up').

رفتم   *raftam*= I am going.

(*e*) In one or both parts of a conditional sentence to denote a foregone conclusion, e.g.

اگر رفتی بردی اگر خفتی مردی   *agar rafti bordi agar xofti mordi*, If you go you win, if you sleep you die.

(*f*) In narrating past events that closely follow one another where the Pluperfect would be used in English, e.g.

وتیکه حرف خودرا تمام کرد جواب دادم
*vaqtike harfe xodra tamam kard javab dadam*,
When he had finished what he had to say, I answered.

(*g*) With certain compound verbs formed with شدن *fodan*, indicating a state which began in the past and continues into the present, or a state which has just come to pass, e.g.

حاضر شدم   *hazer fodam*= I am ready.

تشنه شدم   *tefne fodam*= I am thirsty.

پشیمان شدم   *pafiman fodam*= I am sorry (repentant).

خسته شدم   *xaste fodam*= I am tired.

In certain contexts the Preterite of such verbs can refer to the past, e.g.

دیروز گرسنه شدم   *diruz gorosne fodam*, Yesterday I was hungry.

(*h*) In sentences such as the following where the Perfect or Present is used in English:

کتابمرا فراموش کردم   *ketabamra faramuf kardam*, I have forgotten my book.

زود آمدید   *zud amadid*, You are early.

دیر کردید   *dir kardid*, You are late.

جستمش   *jostamef*, I have found it.

In Colloquial Persian the Preterite بایست *bayest* is sometimes used with a present meaning, e.g.

بایست رفت   *bayest raft*= It is time to go.

6. The Imperfect is used:

(a) For a continuous action in the past, e.g.

نامهٔ مینوشت    *namei mineveʃt*, He was writing a letter.

باران میامد    *baran miamad*, It was raining.

وقتیکه مرا صدا زد کتاب میخواندم    *vaqtike mara sada ʒad ketab mixandam*, When he called me I was reading a book.

میخواستم از شما بپرسم    *mixastam aʒ ʃoma beporsam*, I wanted to ask you.

میخواست برود    *mixast beravad*, He wanted to go.

شاید آنها هم دلشان میخواست وسایل راحتی مرا داشتند    *ʃayad anha ham deleʃan mixast vasaʿele rahatiye mara daʃtand*, Perhaps they also wished they had the facilities for comfort I had.[1]

(b) For habitual action in the past, e.g.

هر سال آنجا میرفتم    *har sal anja miraftam*, Every year I went there.

(c) For an impossible action or state referring to the past or present (see also Impossible Conditions, Lesson VII, para. 5 (b) above), e.g.

اگر میدانست میگفت    *agar midanest migoft*, If he had known he would have said;

and in unfulfilled wishes (see below, para. 16).

(d) Sometimes with the force of 'to be about to', e.g.

طیاره بر زمین فرود میامد که آتش گرفت

*taiyare bar ʒamin forud miamad ke ateʃ gereft*,
The aeroplane was about to land when it caught fire.

The Imperfect of خواستن *xastan* is sometimes used as a kind of auxiliary with this meaning, e.g.

میخواست بنشیند که صداش کردند    *mixast beneʃinad ke sadaʃ kardand*, He was about to sit down when they called him.

---

[1] In this example شاید *ʃayad* does not affect the tense of the main verb. See also para. 12 (e) below.

(e) In the case of خواستن *xastan*, sometimes in Colloquial Persian in place of the Present, e.g.

کجا میخواستید بروید *koja mixastid beravid* = Where do you want to go?

(f) With the force of 'to begin to', e.g.

در اثنای این حال تشنگی بر ملك مستولی شد مركب هر طرف میتاخت

*dar asnaye in hal tefnegi bar malek mostōuli fod markab har taraf mitaxt,*
Meanwhile thirst overcame the king; he began to gallop his horse in every direction.

This usage is literary and is more common in Classical than in Modern Persian.

### 7. The Perfect is used:

(a) For an action in the past the results of which continue to be effective or apparent after the action itself, e.g.

کتاب گم شده است *ketab gom fode ast,* The book is lost (i.e. has been lost and is still lost).

شاه عباس این كاروانسرا را بنا كرده است *fah abbas in karevansarara bana karde ast,* Shah Abbas built this caravanserai.

The Perfect is thus used when referring to the sayings or writings of famous men (on the assumption that these are still effective and have lived on), e.g.

سعدی گفته است... *sa'di gofte ast,* Sa'di said....

(b) To refer to some indefinite time in the past, e.g.

زمانی این سخنرا شنیده‌ام *famani in soxanra fenide am,* I heard these words at some time or other.

تشخیص داده ایم كه لازم میباشد *tafxis dade im ke lazem mibafad,* We decided (at some indefinite time in the past) that it was necessary.

(c) To refer to the future in the main clause after a temporal clause introduced by تا *ta* 'by the time that', e.g.

تا منزل بر گردید تمام پولتانرا خرج كرده اید

*ta manzel bar gardid tamame puletanra xarj karde id,*
By the time you return home you will have spent all your money.

(*d*) Occasionally with a prefixed می *mi-*, e.g.

كتابهای تاریخ در هر دوره بساده‌ترین طریق نوشته میشده است

*ketabhaye tarix dar har doūre be sadetarin tariq neveſte miſode ast,*

Histories, in every period, were written in the simplest style.

8. The Pluperfect is used:

(*a*) To describe the anterior of two actions or states in the past which do not follow one another immediately, e.g.

وقتیکه رسید رفته بودند  *vaqtike rasid rafte budand,* When he arrived they had gone.

نامه‌ٔ که نوشته بودید خواندم  *namei ke neveſte budid xandam,* I read the letter which you wrote (had written).

(*b*) In one or both parts of an impossible condition referring to the past (see Lesson VII, para. 5 (*b*) above), e.g.

اگر میدانستم گفته بودم  *agar midanestam gofte budam,* If I had known, I would have said (so).

(*c*) To describe unfulfilled wishes in the past (see below, para. 16).

9. The Present is used:

(*a*) For a state or action taking place in the present, e.g.

كاغذ مینویسد  *kaɣaz minevisad,* He is writing a letter.

باران میاید  *baran miayad,* It is raining.

(*b*) For an action or state beginning in the past and continuing in the present, e.g.

چند وقت است که اینجا هستید  *cand vaqt ast ke inja hastid,* How long have you been here?

دو سال است که در ایران هستم  *do sal ast ke dar iran hastam,* I have been two years in Persia (and am still there).

از دیروز تا حالا مشغول این کار است  *az diruz ta hala maſɣule in kar ast,* He has been busy with this work (affair) ever since yesterday.

چکار میکنید  *ce kar mikonid,* What are you doing, what have you been doing?

(c) For something said by a well-known person in the past, e.g.

نویسندگان معروف میگویند...    *nevisandegane ma'ruf miguyand*...,

Famous writers say....

It is more usual in such cases to use the Perfect (see para. 7 (a) above).

(d) For the Future, e.g.

فردا باو میگویم    *farda be u miguyam*, I will tell him to-morrow.

In compound verbs formed with شدن *šodan* of the type mentioned in para. 5 (g) above, the present usually has a future meaning, e.g.

خسته میشوید    *xaste mišavid*, You will be tired.

(e) In certain cases after اگر *agar* 'if', e.g.

بروید و ببینید احمد درس خودرا میخواند یا نه اگر میخواند خوب
است و اگر نمیخواند تنبیهش بکنید

*beravid va bebinid ahmad darse xodra mixanad ya na agar
mixanad xub ast va agar namixanad tambiheš bekonid,*

Go and see if Ahmad is doing his lessons or not. If he is
doing them it is well, but if not punish him.

It should be noted that there is a tendency in Colloquial Persian to substitute the present indicative for the present subjunctive in the protasis of Possible Conditions referring to future time.

10. The General Present (see Lesson IV, para. 1 (c) above) is used for general statements relating to the present or future, e.g.

در آنچه گویم یا نویسم خدا داند که تعصبی ندارم

*dar ance guyam ya nevisam xoda danad ke ta'assobi nadaram,*

I have no fanaticism—God knows—in whatever I say or write.

هرجا سهوی بینند و خطائی نگرند بگویند

*har ja sahvi binand va xatai negarand, beguyand,*

Wherever they see a mistake or perceive an error, let them say (so).

هر که شاه آن کند که او گوید * حیف باشد که جز نکو¹ گوید

*har ke šah an konad ke u guyad heif bašad ke joz neku guyad,*

It is a pity that anyone whose word the king follows should say anything but (what is) good.

¹ For نیکو *niku* 'good'.

In the case of بودن *budan* the general present is frequently used, e.g.

تهران که پایتخت ایران باشد شهر بزرگی‌است

*tehran ke pāitaxte iran bafad fahre boʒorgist,*

Tehran, which is the capital of Persia, is a large town.

11. The Subjunctive Present is used:

(a) In a subordinate clause to express a state or action about which there is an element of doubt, e.g.

ممکن است که بیاید   *momken ast ke beyayad,* It is possible that he may come.

(b) To express purpose, with or without که *ke,* e.g.

خواهش میکنم درخواست مرا قبول کنید

*xahef mikonam darxaste mara qabul konid,*

I ask you to agree to (accept) my request.

تصمیم گرفتند که بروند

*tasmim gereftand ke beravand,*

They decided to go.

(c) After final conjunctions, e.g.

اینرا پنهان کرد تا کسی پیدا نکند

*inra panhan kard ta kasi pēida nakonad,*

He hid this so that no one would find it.

تا نشان سم اسبت گم کنند * ترکانا نعلرا وارونه زن

*ta nefane some asbat gom konand torkomana na'lra varune ʒan,*

O Turkoman, put the horseshoe on back to front so that the print of thy horse's hoof will be lost!

این کاررا حالا بکنید تا زودتر تمام شود

*in karra hala bekonid ta ʒudtar tamam favad,*

Do this now so that it will be finished sooner.

In Classical Persian تا *ta* as a final conjunction can be followed by the Indicative to indicate that the action depending upon the main verb has been performed, e.g.

باو فرمود تا رفت   *be u farmud ta raft,* He ordered him to go (and he went).

(d) After تا *ta* 'by the time that, until' in general statements and when referring to the present or future: e.g.

تا بيائيد تاريك خواهد شد

*ta beyaid tarik xahad ʃod,*

By the time you come it will be dark.

تا اينرا نخوانيد نميفهميد

*ta inra naxanid namifahmid,*

You will not understand this until you read it.

(e) In general relative clauses, e.g.

هر وقتيكه آنرا بخوانم ياد شما ميفتم

*har vaqtike anra bexanam be yade ʃoma mioftam,*

Whenever I read that I think of you.

(f) After the verbs توانستن *tavanestan* 'to be able' and خواستن *xastan* 'to want' (see Lesson VI, para. 7), e.g.

نتوانست بيايد *natavanest beyayad,* He could not come.

ميتوانيد آنرا باز كنيد *mitavanid anra baʒ konid,* Can you open that?

ميخواست برود *mixast beravad,* He wanted to go.

ميخواهند شمارا ببينند *mixahand ʃomara bebinand,* They want to see you.

(g) After بايد *bayad* 'must, ought' referring to the present or future, e.g.

بايد برويم *bayad beravim,* We must go.

(h) After شايد *ʃayad* 'perhaps' referring to the present or future, e.g.

شايد اينجا باشد *ʃayad inja baʃad,* Perhaps he is here.

شايد بيايد *ʃayad beyayad,* Perhaps he will come.

(i) In Conditional Clauses (see Lesson VII, para. 5 (a) above), e.g.

اگر وقت بكنيم بگردش ميرويم *agar vaqt bekonim be gardeʃ miravim,* If we have time, we will go for a walk.

(j) To refer to the 'future with doubt' in the 1st pers. sing., e.g.

بروم يا نروم *beravam ya naravam,* Shall I go or not?

چه بگويم *ce beguyam,* What shall I say?

(k) As a Jussive in the 1st and 3rd pers. sing. and pl., e.g.
برویم *beravim*, Let us go.

(l) After پیش از آنکه *piʃ aʒ anke* and قبل از آنکه *qabl aʒ anke*, 'before', بجای اینکه *be jaye inke* and در عوض اینکه *dar avaʒe inke*, 'instead of (this that)', and جز اینکه *joʒ inke* and غیر از اینکه *ɣeir aʒ inke*, 'except'.

12. The Subjunctive Past is used:

(a) To refer to an action or state in the past about which there is an element of doubt, e.g.

گمان میبرم که رفته باشد  *gaman mibaram ke rafte baʃad*, I think he may have gone.

(b) To describe the anterior of two future actions or states, e.g.

تا دکتر برسد مریض مرده باشد  *ta doktor berasad mariʒ morde baʃad*, By the time the doctor arrives the sick man will have died.

This usage is classical, the Perfect being used rather than the Subjunctive Past in modern usage.

(c) To refer to an action presumed to have been already performed, or a state presumed to be in existence, e.g.

میترسم تمام شده باشد  *mitarsam tamam ʃode baʃad*, I fear it will have finished.

تصور میکنم تا حالا رسیده باشد  *tasavvor mikonam ta hala raside baʃad*, I think he will have arrived by now.

(d) After باید *bayad* and بایست *bayest* 'ought, must', referring to past time, e.g.

باید (بایست) رفته باشد  *bayad (bayest) rafte baʃad*, He must have gone.

(e) After شاید *ʃayad* 'perhaps', referring to past time unless the action or state referred to is continuous (see para. 6 (a) above) or forms the apodosis of an impossible condition in the past (see Lesson VII, para. 5 (b) above). E.g.

شاید اینرا خوانده باشید  *ʃayad inra xande baʃid*, Perhaps you have read this.

(*f*) After میبایست *mibayest* 'ought to have', e.g.

میبایست دیده باشید     *mibayest dide baʃid*, You ought to have seen (this).

میبایست این کتابرا خوانده باشد    *mibayest in ketabra xande baʃad*, He ought to have read this book.

(*g*) In conditional clauses (see Lesson VII, para. 5 (*a*, iii above), e.g.

اگر کرده باشد چه خواهید کرد   *agar karde baʃad ce xahid kard*, If he has done (it), what will you do?

(*h*) In the case of the verb داشتن *daʃtan* 'to have' for the Subjunctive Present, e.g.

باید خیلی حوصله داشته باشید   *bayad xeili hŏusele daʃte baʃid*, You must have great patience.

هر چیزیکه میل داشته باشید تهیه میکنم   *har ciẕi ke meil daʃte baʃid tahie mikonam*, I will obtain (prepare) whatever you want.

13. The Future is used:

(*a*) To refer to a future action or state, e.g.

فردا خواهد رفت   *farda xahad raft*, He will go to-morrow.

(*b*) To indicate certainty, e.g.

این علی خواهد بود   *in ali xahad bud*= This must be 'Ali (said in reply to some such remark as کسی در میزند *kasi dar miẕanad* 'someone is knocking at the door').

14. The Imperative is used:

To express a command, e.g.

برو. *borŏu*, go.

15. A form in اد -*ad* (3rd pers. sing.) has a precative sense. It is the sole surviving form of the old Optative.

The prefix بـ *be-* is often added to it, e.g.

برساد *berasad*, May he arrive.

The negative is formed by the prefix مـ *ma-*, e.g.

مکناد *makonad*, May he not do.

This form is seldom, if ever, used in Colloquial Persian.

The precative of بودن *budən* is باد *bad*. (که) مبادا *mabada* (*ke*) used as a conjunction (=lest) is the negative precative to which the interjectory *alef* has been added (see Lesson XII, para. 12). It is also used in the phrase روز مبادا *ruʒe mabada*=a rainy day, or (in Classical Persian) the day of judgement.

16. Wishes are expressed by کاشکه *kaʃke* or کاشکی *kaʃki* 'would that' followed by the Subjunctive Present, e.g.

کاشکی بیاید  *kaʃki beyayad*, Would that he would come.

The tense in unfulfilled wishes is the Imperfect or the Pluperfect, e.g.

کاشکی میامد (آمده بود)  *kaʃki miamad* (*amade bud*), Would that he had come.

17. After verbs of saying, thinking, knowing, seeing, etc., the tense of the verb is normally that of direct speech, but the pronoun is not necessarily that of direct speech. The particle که *ke* 'that' sometimes follows the main verb. E.g.

بمن گفت که نمیایم  *be man goft ke namiayam*⎫ He told me that he
بمن گفت که نمیاید  *be man goft ke namiayad*⎭ was not coming.

گفت که اسبها حاضرند  *goft ke asbha haʒer and*, He said the horses were ready.

باو گفتم که نمیایم  *be u goftam ke namiayam*, I told him I was not coming.

دیدیم که اینجا هستند  *didim ke inja hastand*, We saw they were here.

فکر کرد که این آسان است  *fekr kard ke in asan ast*, He thought this was easy.

افسوس میخورم که چرا آمدم  *afsus mixoram ke cera amadam*, I regret that I came.

پرسید کسی منزل هست  *porsid kasi manʒel hast*, He asked if anyone was at home.

از ما پرسیدند که کیستیم  *aʒ ma porsidand ke kistim*, They asked us who we were.

پیغام داد که فردا میایم  *peiʸam dad ke farda miayam*, He sent a message to say he would come the next day.

فکر نمیکردم که خواهد آمد  *fekr namikardam ke xahad amad*, I did not think that he would come.

Indirect Speech is occasionally used. The last example could thus be rendered:

فكر نميكردم كه بيايد ‎*fekr namikardam ke beyayad.*

قول دادن ‎*qoul dadan* and ‎وعده كردن ‎*va'de kardan* 'to promise' are usually followed by a final clause with the Subjunctive Present, e.g.

وعده كرد كه بيايد ‎*va'de kard ke beyayad*, He promised to come.

كه ‎*ke* can sometimes be translated by 'saying', e.g.

مدبران ممالك آن طرف در دفع مضرت ايشان مشورت كردند كه اين طايفه گر۱ هم بر اين نسق روزگارى مداومت نمايند مقاومت ايشان ممتنع گردد

*modabberane mamaleke an taraf dar daf'e mazarrate ifan mafvarat kardand ke in tayefe gar ham bar in nasaq ruzgari modavamat namayand moqavamate ifan momtane' gardad,*

The statesmen of the kingdoms of that region consulted together concerning the repelling of their evil, saying 'if this group (tribe) continues in this way for any (length of) time, it will be impossible to resist them'.

18. Although تا ‎*ta* as a temporal conjunction is capable of five distinct meanings, careful observation of the tenses employed both in the تا ‎*ta* clause and in the main clause will show that in Modern Persian no ambiguity arises, e.g.

(i) 'as long as'

تا باران ميايد بيرون نميرويم

*ta baran miayad birun namiravim,*

As long as it rains we shall not go out.

تا مدرسه ميرفتم چيزى ياد نميگرفتم

*ta madrase miraftam cizi yad namigereftam,*

As long as I went to school I learnt nothing.

تا ميتوانيد آنرا تحمل كنيد

*ta mitavanid anra tahammol konid,*

Bear it as long as you can.

(ii) 'by the time that'

تا برسيد دير ميشود

*ta berasid dir mifavad,*

It will be late by the time you arrive.

---

۱ For اگر ‎*agar.*

تا دکتر رسید مریض مرده بود

*ta doktor rasid mariҳ morde bud,*

By the time the doctor arrived the sick man was dead.

تا برسید ما رفته ایم

*ta berasid ma rafte im,*

We shall have gone by the time you arrive.

تا سایه‌ور درختی گردد نهالکی \* بنگر که چند آب[1] در آید بجویبار

*ta sayevar daraxti gardad nehalaki benegar ke cand ab dar ayad be juubar,*

By the time (before) a small sapling becomes a shady tree, see how many times water flows along the stream.

بپایان تا رسد یکشمع صد پروانه میسوزد

*be payan ta rasad yak ʃamʻ sad parvane misuҳad,*

A hundred moths will be burnt by the time (before) a candle burns out.

(iii) 'as soon as'

تا بشهر رسیدید[2] بمن خبر بدهید

*ta be ʃahr rasidid be man xabar bedehid,*

Let me know as soon as you reach the town.

تا مارا صدا کنید بر میگردیم

*ta mara sada konid bar migardim,*

We will return as soon as you call us.

تا منزل بر گشتم کاغذرا نوشتم

*ta manҳel bar gaʃtam kaɣaҳra neveʃtam,*

I wrote the letter as soon as I returned home.

(iv) 'until'

تا آنرا نشنوم باور نمیکنم

*ta anra naʃenavam bavar namikonam,*

I shall not believe it until I hear (it).

تا اورا ندیدم نمیدانستم که اینجاست

*ta ura nadidam namidanestam ke injast,*

I did not know he was here until I saw him.

---

[1] آب *ab* 'water' also means water allowed to flow along an irrigation channel for a specific period of time.

[2] For the use of the Preterite to refer to the Future see above para. 5 (c).

من و برادرم تا زن نگرفته بودیم همیشه زیر یك سقف خوابیده و تا
پانزده بیست سال قبل با یکدیگر در زندگی شریك بودیم

*man o baradaram ta ʒan nagerefte budim hamiʃe ʒire yak saqf xabide va ta panʒdah bist sal qabl ba yak digar dar ʒendegi ʃarik budim,*

My brother and I until (before) we married always slept under one roof, and until fifteen or twenty years ago we shared a common life.

(v) 'since'

تا بانگلستان رفته است از او خبری ندارم

*ta be englestan rafte ast aʒ u xabari nadaram,*

I have no news of him since he went to England.

It should be noted that (*a*) تا *ta* in the sense of 'until' normally requires نه *na* in the تا *ta* clause though usage sanctions such a phrase as تا بیایم صبر کنید *ta beyayam sabr konid* 'wait until I come', and (*b*) تا *ta* as a final conjunction 'in order that' is distinguished from the temporal تا *ta* by the fact that it follows the main clause.[1]

Classical usage with the temporal تا *ta* differs somewhat from modern usage. The Present Subjunctive is used after تا *ta* in the sense of both 'as long as' and 'as soon as' referring to the present and future and in general statements, e.g.

تا صلح توان کرد در جنگ مکوب

*ta solh tavan kard dare jang makub,*

As long as peace can be achieved, do not knock on the door of war.

مرا تا جان بود امید باشد  *  که روزی جفت من خورشید باشد

*mara ta jan bovad omid baʃad ke ruʒi jofte man xorʃid baʃad,*

As long as I am alive I have hope that one day my consort may be the sun.

If تا *ta* 'by the time that' refers to the future the Subjunctive Past is used in the main clause, e.g.

---

[1] In colloquial usage, however, emphasis may require the clause introduced by the temporal تا *ta* to follow the main clause, e.g.

صبر کنید تا بیایم   *sabr konid ta beyayam*, Wait until I come (where the emphasis is on 'wait').

تا تریاق از عراق آرند مار گزیده مرده باشد

*ta taryaq aҙ eraq arand mar gaҙide morde baſad,*

By the time they bring the antidote from Iraq the person bitten by
the snake will have died.

In modern usage also if the verb of the clause introduced by تا *ta* 'as long
as' is بودن *budan* 'to be' and refers to the present or future the Present
Subjunctive is used, e.g.

تا دولتها اینطور باشند اوضاع خوب نمیشود

*ta doulatha in tōur baſand ōuҙa' xub namiſavad,*

As long as the governments are like this conditions will not
improve.

19. The use of a negative verb with هیچ *hic* and هرگز *hargeҙ* has already
been mentioned (see Lesson IV, para. 22 and Lesson VII, para. 1, respectively) and the use of the double negative with تا *ta* 'until' (see
Lesson VI, para. 17 (*c*) above).

Certain verbs of prohibition require a negative in the subordinate
clause, e.g.

منع کردم که آنجا نرود      *man' kardam ke anja naravad,* I forbade him
to go there.

But

ممنوع بود که کسی آنجا برود      *mamnu' bud ke kasi anja beravad,* It was
forbidden for anyone to go there.

The word قدغن *qadaɣan* 'forbidden' requires a negative verb, e.g.

ضمناً قدغن شد که دیگر بخانه مادرم نروم

*ҙemnan qadaɣan ſod ke digar be xaneye madaram naravam,*

Meanwhile it was forbidden for me to go any more to my mother's
house.

The Arabic forms اصلاً¹ *aslan* and ابداً¹ *abadan* are used with a negative verb to mean 'not at all' and 'never', e.g.

ابداً آنجا نبودم      *abadan anja nabudam,* I was never there.

اصلاً نمیخواهم      *aslan namixaham,* I do not want (it) at all.

The use of the negative in the following idioms should be noted:

از باغ بیرون نیامده بود که مرا دید      *aҙ baɣ birun nayamade bud ke mara*
*did,* He had barely come out of
the garden when he saw me.

¹ See Part II, Lesson XXI, para. 16 (*b*) for Arabic Nouns in the accusative used as adverbs.

آفتاب نزده راه افتادیم *aftab naʒade rah oftadim*, We set off before sunrise (the sun not having risen).

بمیدان نرسیده کوچه آخر دست راست *be mēidan naraside kuceye axer daste rast*, the last street on the right before reaching the square (not having arrived at the square).

20. Certain verbs, notably آمدن *amadan* 'to come' and افتادن *oftadan* 'to fall' are used impersonally with or without a preposition governing the logical subject, e.g.

یادم آمد *yadam amad*, I remembered (it came to my mind).

یادش رفت *yadeʃ raft*, He forgot (it went from his mind).

گیرش نیامد *gireʃ nayamad*, He did not obtain (it).

پسندشان نیامد *pasandeʃan nayamad*, They did not like (it).

خوشم آمد *xoʃam amad*, I was pleased (at it).

بما خوش گذشت *be ma xoʃ goʒaʃt*, We enjoyed ourselves.

21. داشتن *daʃtan* is used impersonally in the following constructions:

عیب ندارد *ēib nadarad*
ضرر ندارد *ʒarar nadarad* } It does not matter.

احتمال دارد *ehtemal darad*, It is probable.[1]

چاره ندارد *care nadarad*, It cannot be helped (there is no remedy).

22. خواستن *xastan* is sometimes equivalent to 'to need, to make necessary', e.g.

این کار وقت میخواهد *in kar vaqt mixahad*, This affair needs time.

23. In Modern Persian the continuous past and continuous present can be expressed by the Imperfect of داشتن *daʃtan* together with the Imperfect of the main verb and by the Present of داشتن *daʃtan* together with the Present of the main verb respectively, e.g.

داشتم مینوشتم *daʃtam mineveʃtam*, I was in the act of writing.

دارم مینویسم *daram minevisam*, I am in the act of writing.

---

[1] Also احتمال کلی (تام) دارد *ehtemale kolli (tamm) darad*, it is very probable, there is every probability.

24. The Particle هی *heī* is also used to express repeated action, e.g.

هی میگفت   *heī migoft*, He kept on saying.

هی میگوید   *heī miguyad*, He keeps on saying.

25. In Classical Persian the Habitual Past is sometimes rendered by the prefix همی *hami-* in place of می *mi-*, e.g.

همیکردم   *hamikardam*, I was doing, used to do, etc.,

or by the suffix ی *-i* added to the Preterite, e.g.

کردمی   *kardami*, I was doing, used to do, etc.

This latter form is defective and is only used in the 1st pers. sing. and the 3rd pers. sing. and pl.

26. In Classical Persian a prefix ﺑ *be-* is sometimes added to the Preterite to give a sense of completion or finality, e.g.

برفت   *beraft*, he went.

بکفت   *begoft*, he said.

27. In Classical Persian a Conditional Past was formed by adding ی *-i* to the Imperfect or Preterite and a Conditional Present by adding ی *-i* to the Subjunctive Present. These tenses, like the Habitual Past with suffix *-i* (see above, para. 25), are defective, e.g.

تا بدانستمی ز¹ دشمن دوست   *   زندگانی دو بار بایستی

*ta bedanestami ʒe doſman dust ʒendegani do bar bayesti,*

Life would be needed twice over to know friend from foe.

گر آنها که میگفتمی کردمی   *   نکو سیرت و پارسا بودمی

*gar anha ke migoſtami kardami neku sirat o parsa budami,*

If I had done those things which I used to say, I would have been of good character and pious.

درخت اگر متحرك شدی ز جای بجای   *   نه جور اره کشیدی و نی جفای تبر

*daraxt agar motaharrek ſodi ʒe jāi be jāi na joūre arre kaſidi o neī jafaye tabar,*

If a tree could move from place to place it would not suffer the tyranny of the saw and the oppression of the axe.

¹ For ز ا *aʒ*.

اگر مملکترا زبان باشدی    *    از این دیو و ددها فغان باشدی

*agar mamlekatra ʒaban baʃadi aʒ in div o dadha feyan baʃadi,*

If the kingdom had a tongue it would cry out against these demons and wild beasts.

**28.** In early Classical Persian a passive construction is found with the verb آمدن *amadan* 'to come', e.g.

ذکر هر یکی مختصر کرده آید    *ʒekre har yaki moxtasar karde ayad,* Mention of each one will be made briefly.

**29.** If two or more co-ordinate clauses follow each other, where the same auxiliary verb is used to conjugate the verb, it can be omitted from all but the first or final clause, e.g.

طایفه دزدان عرب بر سر کوه نشسته بودند و منفذ کاروان بسته و رعیت
بلدان از مکاید¹ ایشان مرعوب و لشکر سلطان مغلوب بحکم آنکه
ملاذی منیع از قله کوهی بدست آورده بودند

*tayefeye doʒdane arab bar sare kuh neʃaste budand va manfaʒe karavan baste va ra'iyate boldan aʒ makayede iʃan mar'ub va laʃkare soltan maylub be hokme anke malaʒi mani' aʒ qolleye kuhi bedast avarde budand,*

A group (tribe) of Arab thieves had established themselves (were sitting) on the top of a mountain and closed the caravan route and the peasants of (these) regions were terrified by their tricks and the sultan's army was defeated by virtue of this that they (the thieves) had obtained possession of an impregnable refuge on the summit of a mountain (where بودند *budand* has been omitted after بسته, مرعوب and مغلوب).

Similarly the verbal part of a compound verb in the first of two or more co-ordinate clauses may be omitted, e.g.

متمنی‌است مبلغ صد ریال بحساب روزنامه ببانک تحویل و نشانی کامل
بنویسید تا روزنامه مرتب فرستاده شود

*motamannist mablaye sad rial be hesabe ruʒname be bank tahvil va neʃaniye kamel benevisid ta ruʒname morattab ferestade ʃavad,*

It is requested that you should transfer the sum of 100 rs. to the newspaper's account at the bank and write your full address so that the paper may be sent to you regularly (where دهید *dehid* has been omitted after تحویل).

¹ Plural of مکیده *makide* 'trick, stratagem'.

## VOCABULARY

ولايات velayat (pl. of ولايت), provinces.

آغاز aɣaȥ, beginning.

تسليم taslim, surrender; تسليم كردن taslim k., to surrender.

سفرا sofara (pl. of سفير safir), envoys plenipotentiary.

عيسوى isavi, Christian.

مذهب maȥhab, religion.

جمله jomle, collection; sentence; از آن جمله aȥ an jomle, among them.

بحر bahr, sea; بحر خزر bahre xaȥar, the Caspian Sea.

ابيض abyaȥ, white.

آلمان alman, Germany.

ايطاليا italia, Italy.

بر عليه bar aleih(e), against.

افتتاح eftetah, opening.

ابريشم abrifom, silk.

تقديم taqdim, offering; تقديم كردن taqdim k., to offer.

ما بين ma bein(e), between.

نفاق nefaq, quarrel, dispute.

بروز boruȥ, appearance; بروز كردن boruȥ k., to appear, break out.

نواختن (نواز) navaxtan (navaȥ), to cherish, favour, patronize.

واقع vaqe', situated; happening, occurring.

عزم aȥm, determination; صاحب عزم saheb aȥm, determined (the owner of determination).

محبت mohabbat, love.

جلب jalb, attracting; جلب كردن jalb k., to attract.

مأموريت ma'muriyat, office, charge.

مجروح majruh, wounded.

سردار sardar, leader.

هراس haras, fear.

بيانات bayanat (pl. of بيان bayan), explanations, expositions.

اظهار eȥhar, expressing; expression, manifestation; اظهار داشتن eȥhar d., to express.

بدواً badvan, at first.

تشجيع tafji', encouraging, encouragement; تشجيع كردن tafji' k., to encourage.

عازم aȥem, setting out (for).

بالاخره belaxere, at last, finally (see Part II, Lesson XXI, para. 16 (c)).

حسين على بك بيات Hosein Ali Bak Bayat.

بعدها ba'dha, afterwards.

| | | | |
|---|---|---|---|
| دهقان | dehqan, small landowner; peasant. | تدبیر | tadbir, counsel, plan, administration. |
| شکر | fokr, thanks. | نگریستن (نگر) | negaristan (negar), to look, see. |
| خرده گرفتن | xorde gereftan, to criticize, belittle. | جسارت | jesarat, boldness. |
| کدو | kadu, marrow. | پوزش | puʒef, forgiveness. |
| بوته | bote,¹ shrub. | استغفار | esteyfar, asking pardon. |
| نازك | naʒok, thin, delicate. | فرصت | forsat, chance, opportunity; فرصترا غنیمت شمردن forsatra ɣanimat fomordan, to seize a chance (esteem the chance booty). |
| بلوط | balut, sweet chestnut; acorn. | | |
| خالق | xaleq, creator. | | |
| مخلوقات | maxluqat, pl. of مخلوق maxluq 'what is created'. | دلتنگ | deltang, distressed, sad; دل ما برای شما تنگ شد dele ma baraye foma tang fod, we miss you. |
| خلاف | xelaf(e), contrary to. | | |
| فراز | faraʒ, top. | | |
| دماغ | demaɣ, brain; damaɣ, nose. | تکذیب | takʒib, denial; تکذیب کردن takʒib k., to deny. |
| جاری | jari, flowing. | | |
| ضعف | ʒa'f, weakness. | رستن (رو) | rostan (ru), to grow (of things). |
| رأی | ra'i, rāi, judgement, opinion. | تنبیه | tambih, punishment; تنبیه کردن tambih k., to punish. |
| سستی | sosti, looseness, slackness, weakness. | | |

آمدن برادران شرلی بایران (بقیه از درس پیش)

شاه که در این زمان میخواست با دولت عثمانی از در جنگ در آید و ولایاتیراکه در آغاز پادشاهی خود بآن دولت تسلیم کرده بود باز گیرد باین ترتیب سفرائی² بدربار تمام پادشاهان عیسوی مذهب اروپا فرستاد از آن جمله انتنی شرلیرا بهمراهی حسینعلی بك بیات باروپا جهت نمایندگی روانه کرد و آنها هم از راه بحر خزر و مسکو و دریای اییض و دریای شمال و آلمان بایطالیا وارد

---

¹ This word is pronounced *bote* not *bute* (see Introduction to Part I, Alphabetical Table).

² Note the use of ى -*i* with the plural (see Lesson XII, para. 1 (a) (iii) above).

شدند و در تمام ممالك بین راه نامه‌های دوستانه شاه عباس دایر بر اتحاد با ایران بر علیه عثمانی و افتتاح روابط تجارتی برای فروش ابریشم ایرانرا با هدایائیکه شاه داده بود تقدیم کردند و در ایطالیا مابین حسینعلی بك بیات و انتنی شرلی نفاق بروز كرد و انتنی از او جدا شده باسپانیا رفت و دیگر بایران بر نگشت اما رابرت شرلی برادر انتنی که در خدمت شاه عباس مانده بود مورد نوازش واقع گشت¹ و چون از آمدن انتنی خبری نشده شاه عباس نسبت باو بی‌لطف گشت ولی رابرت شرلی چون جوانی صاحب عزم و نیکو رفتار بود باز محبت شاهرا نسبت بخود جلب كرد اولین مأموریتی که از طرف شاه عباس برابرت شرلی داده شد انتخاب او بریاست دسته‌ از سپاه و فرستادن وی بجنگ با عثمانی بود و همچنین در جنگهائیکه شاه عباس در سالهای ۱۰۱۳ و ۱۰۱٤ هجری با عثمانی کرد شرکت نمود و سه مرتبه مجروح شد و در جنگ عده زیادی از سپاه عثمانیرا كشته و سرداران آنهارا اسیر گرفت و در یك جنگ كه با عثمانیها روبرو شد پس از مرتب كردن سپاه خود چون دید سربازانش از زیادی عدد دشمن در هراسند رو بدیشان کرده بیاناتی اظهار داشت سپس خود بدوا بطرف دشمن حمله برد و سپاهیانش هم تشجیع شده باین ترتیب عثمانیهارا شکست داده مورد نوازش شاه عباس واقع گشت و بعدها از طرف شاه عباس در ۱۰۱٦ هجری (۱٦۰۸ میلادی) از اصفهان عازم اروپا شد و پس از مسافرت طولانی و انجام مأموریت خویش در سال ۱۰۲۰ هجری بانگلستان رفت و بالاخره پس از هشت سال مسافرت در سال ۱۰۲٤ بایران برگشت        (پایان)

## EXERCISE 24

دهقانی ناشکر بر خدای تعالی خرده میگرفت که چرا كدوی بزرگرا بر بوته نازكی سبز نموده و بلوط کوچکرا بر درختی بلند رویانیده است من اگر خالق مخلوقات بودم بر خلاف این كار میکردم دهقان در این اندیشه بود که بلوطی از فراز درخت چنان بر دماغش خورد که خون جاری شد دهقان با خود گفت ضعف رأی و سستی تدبیر من بنگر اگر این بلوط كدو میشد مرا کشته بود پس از جسارت خویش پوزش خواست و استغفار كرد

---

¹ Literally 'he became situated (in) the place of favour'. مورد *moured*, originally drinking-place, is used in Persian in certain stereotyped phrases to mean 'place, site' in general.

## EXERCISE 25

1. I do not understand how it occurred.   2. Not even his enemies were unkind to him, let alone his friends.   3. The house is uninhabitable in summer let alone in winter.   4. Seize the chance, else you will regret it.   5. I miss him, yet I am glad he went (although I miss him...).   6. He is always ill; nevertheless he is always cheerful.   7. He is living in great hardship; meanwhile his brother on the contrary is living in the greatest comfort.   8. The factory caught fire last night; it was completely destroyed and on that account many workmen will be unemployed.   9. The work had to be done; accordingly we did it.   10. There was no one there so I went away.   11. It is best that he should go.   12. His best friends will not deny that he was in error.   13. My only terror is that my father should follow (come after) me.   14. It is probable that he will come to-day.   15. It is not known which road he took (by which road he went).   16. It is immaterial whether he comes or goes.   17. Such books as this and such men as he are rare.

## LESSON XIV

**Polite Conversation. Some discrepancies between the spoken and the written word. دیگر *digar* and که *ke*.**

1. Politeness requires the use of certain honorifics and phrases in formal conversation.

(a) Personal Pronouns. The 1st pers. sing. من *man* is sparingly used. بنده *bande* (lit. 'slave') is used in place of من *man* 'I' if the speaker wishes to indicate humility towards a person of equal or higher rank. بنده منزل *bande manzel* means 'my house'. Politeness does not require that mention of oneself should be made last if more than one pronoun is used, or a noun or nouns and the pronoun. The 1st pers. usually comes first, e.g.

من و شما   *man o foma*, you and I.

من و برادرم   *man o baradaram*, my brother and I.

The use of the 3rd pers. pl. for the 3rd pers. sing. is common when reference is being made to a person of equal or superior rank.[1]

---

[1] It is probably due to this custom that آنها *anha* has come to be used in Modern Persian for the 3rd pers. pl. of the Personal Pronoun ایشان *ifan*.

The 2nd pers. sing. is used only to children, intimate friends and servants.

سرکار *sarkar* is often used in place of شما *foma* in referring to an equal or superior.

(*b*) Formerly many honorific titles were in use and strict rules governed their employment. Most of these have fallen into disuse. The only officially recognized honorific title is جناب *janab*, which is accorded to ministers and high officials, e.g.

جناب نخست وزير   *janabe naxost vaʒir*, H.E. the Prime Minister.

The term جناب عالی *janabe ali* or حضرت عالی *haʒrate ali* is sometimes used to address a person of superior (or equal) rank.

The Shah is referred to as اعلیحضرت *a'la haʒrat*[1] and the Queen as علیا حضرت *olia haʒrat*.

(*c*) When referring to what a person of equal or higher rank has said it is customary to use the verb فرمودن *farmudan* 'to command' rather than گفتن *goftan* 'to say', e.g.

چه فرمودید   *ce farmudid*, What did you say?

فرمودن *farmudan* is substituted for کردن *kardan* and certain other verbs used to form compound verbs when reference is to a person of equal or higher rank, e.g.

خواهش میکنم وقترا تعیین بفرمائید   *xahef mikonam vaqtra ta'yin be-farmaid*, Please (I request you) appoint the time.

نامه‌را که مرقوم فرموده بودید رسید   *nameira ke marqum farmude budid rasid*, The letter you wrote arrived.

فرمایش داشتن *farmayef daftan* is similarly used for 'to want, desire', e.g.

چه فرمایش دارید (داشتید)   *ce farmayef darid (daftid)*, What do you want?

or

چه فرمایشی دارید (داشتید)   *ce farmayefi darid (daftid)*.

When referring to oneself, if speaking to a person of equal or higher rank, it is customary to use the verb عرض کردن *arʒ kardan* 'to make a petition' instead of گفتن, e.g.

...عرض کردم   *arʒ kardam*, I said....

---

[1] Usually pronounced *ala haʒrat*.

عرض میشود *arҳ miʃavad* is similarly prefixed to an expression of opinion or statement.

The following compounds are used when reference is to a person of equal or higher rank. They must never be used when referring to oneself:

تشریف داشتن *taʃrif daʃtan*, to be in, be present.

تشریف بردن *taʃrif bordan*, to go, depart.

تشریف آوردن *taʃrif avardan*, to come, arrive.

E.g.

آقا تشریف دارند *aqa taʃrif darand*, Is (your) master in?

فردا تشریف میاورند *farda taʃrif miavarand*, He (they) will come to-morrow.

بشهر تشریف بردند *be ʃahr taʃrif bordand*, He has (they have) gone to the town.

When accepting an invitation on one's own behalf from a person of equal or higher rank or arranging to call upon such a person, the verb شرفیاب شدن *ʃarafyab ʃodan* 'to become a recipient of honour' is used or خدمت رسیدن *xedmat rasidan* 'to arrive at the service of', e.g.

فردا شرفیاب میشوم *farda ʃarafyab miʃavam*, I will come to-morrow.

خدمت شما میرسم *xedmate ʃoma mirasam*, I will come to see you.

These expressions must not be used when referring to anyone other than oneself.

خدمت *xedmat* is also used in place of به *be* 'to' and پیش *piʃ* = with, and درخدمت *dar xedmat* = با *ba* 'with', when referring to a person of equal or superior rank, e.g.

خدمت شما عرض میکنم *xedmate ʃoma arҳ mikonam*, I will tell you.

خدمت وزیر بودم *xedmate vaҳir budam*, I was with the minister.

در خدمت ایشان باصفهان رفتم *dar xedmate iʃan be esfahan raftam*, I went with him to Isfahan.

مرحمت کردن *marhamat kardan* is used in place of دادن *dadan* 'to give' when reference is to a person of equal or higher rank. It must never be used with reference to oneself.

کتابرا مرحمت کنید *ketabra marhamat konid*, Give (me) the book.

ملتفت شدن *moltafet ʃodan* is used rather than فهمیدن *fahmidan* for 'to understand'.

(*d*) The most usual formula of greeting is سلام علیکم *salam aleikom* 'peace be upon you', which is repeated in answer by the person to whom the greeting is given.

احوال شما چطور است *ahvale ʃoma ce tour ast* 'how are you' is a common formula used when inquiring after someone's health. شریف *ʃarif* 'noble, noble person' can be substituted for شما *ʃoma* and مزاج *meʒaj* 'disposition', وجود *vojud* 'existence', or حال *hal* 'state' for احوال *ahval*. The answer to such an inquiry is الحمد لله *al hamdo lellah* 'Praise be to God'.

صبح شما بخیر *sobhe ʃoma be xeir* '(may) your morning (be) good' is an alternative greeting which can be used in the morning. عاقبت شما بخیر *aqebate ʃoma be xeir* '(may) your end (be) good' is sometimes said in reply to this.

On a feast-day or holiday, such as New Year's Day, the usual greeting is عید شما مبارك *ide ʃoma mobarak* 'may your feast be blessed'.

(*e*) The phrase خوش آمدید *xoʃ amadid* 'welcome' is used to welcome someone to one's house. If a long time has elapsed since the previous visit of the visitor the phrase چه عجب *ce ajab* 'what a wonder (that you have at last honoured me)' is sometimes used. The phrase عجب بجمال شما *ajab be jamale ʃoma* 'the marvel is at your kindness' may be said in reply.

(*f*) A variety of expressions are used on taking leave. On wishing to terminate a meeting or visit it is customary to ask one's host's permission to leave by some such phrase as مرخص میفرمائید *moraxxas mifarmaid*, or اجازه میفرمائید *ejaʒe mifarmaid* 'do you give me permission to depart' or by indicating that one has troubled one's host long enough by a phrase such as زحمت کم کنم *ʒahmat kam konam* 'let me make the trouble (given by me) less'.

If one's host then deprecates such an intention by saying زود است *ʒud ast*, it is customary to stay a few more minutes and then once more ask permission to depart. As a guest leaves he can say زحمت دادم *ʒahmat dadam* 'I have given (you) trouble' to which his host replies زحمت کشیدید *ʒahmat kaʃidid* 'you have taken trouble (in coming)'; if one's host says first زحمت کشیدید *ʒahmat kaʃidid* the answer is زحمت دادم *ʒahmat dadam*. As the guest departs the host may say to him, if he (the guest) is of equal or higher rank, مشرف فرمودید *moʃarraf farmudid* 'you have conferred honour (on me).'

On parting from someone it is usual to use some phrase such as التفات شما زیاد *eltefate ʃoma ʒiad* 'your favour (was) great', لطف شما زیاد *lotfe ʃoma ʒiad*, لطف فرمودید *lotf farmudid* 'you have conferred honour on me', لطف عالی کم نشود *lotfe ali kam naʃavad* 'may the high favour not grow less', or سايه شما كم نشود *sayeye ʃoma kam naʃavad* 'may your shadow never grow less'. مبارك *mobarak* can be substituted for شما *ʃoma* in the last phrase but is more formal.

خدا حافظ *xoda hafeʒ* or خدا حافظ شما *xoda hafeʒe ʃoma* 'may God be your protector' is also used, especially when the person to whom it is said is going on a journey. The answer to this is بامان خدا *be amane xoda* 'in the protection of God'.

شب بشما خوش *ʃab be ʃoma xoʃ* or شب بخير *ʃab be xeir* 'good-night' is used, but not widely.

(g) بفرمائيد *befarmaid* is used for 'please do, please come in, please sit down', etc.

(h) چه عرض كنم *ce arʒ konam* is an expression used when the speaker does not know the answer to a question or wishes to give a non-committal reply.

(i) بى زحمت *bi ʒahmat* 'without trouble' is an expression prefixed to a request asking someone to do something, e.g.

بى زحمت اينجا تشريف بياوريد *bi ʒahmat inja taʃrif beyavarid*, Please come here.

بى زحمت آنرا بمن بدهيد *bi ʒahmat anra be man bedehid*, Please give that to me.

(j) دست شما درد نكند *daste ʃoma dard nakonad* 'may your hand not pain you' is said to someone who has, for example, fetched something or done something for one involving some degree, however slight, of physical effort. In answer to this is sometimes heard

سر شما درد نكند *sare ʃoma dard nakonad* 'may your head not pain you'.

(k) چشم *caʃm* '(upon my) eye' is said in answer to a request or command and signifies an intention to comply with the request.

(l) 'Excuse me (= forgive me)' is translated by ببخشيد *bebaxʃid*, to which the answer خدا ببخشد *xoda bebaxʃad* 'may God forgive (you)' is sometimes given.

(m) 'Please (= I pray you)' can be translated by خواهش ميكنم *xaheʃ mikonam* 'I request (you)' or استدعا ميكنم *ested'a mikonam* 'I beseech (you)'.

(n) اختيار داريد *exteyar darid* 'you have the choice (= you are free to make such a statement, but...)' is said by way of remonstrance or protest at a remark.

(*o*) The phrase ان شاء الله *en ʃa allah* 'if God wills' is often prefixed
to an expression of an intended action or of hope concerning some future
state or action. It is also used alone to mean 'yes' or 'I hope so' in
answer to a question regarding one's intentions or some future possibility,[1] e.g.

فردا تشریف میاورید   *farda taʃrif miavarid*, Are you coming to-
morrow?

ان شاء الله   *en ʃa allah*, I hope so.

(*p*) It is customary to prefix the phrase ما شاء الله *ma ʃa allah*
'what God wills' to an expression of praise of anyone's belongings, etc.,
or of some action, in order to avert the evil eye, popularly supposed to
be stimulated by praise to fall upon an object or person, e.g.

ما شاء الله پسر خوبیست   *ma ʃa allah pesare xubist*, He is a good
boy.

ما شاء الله خوب درس میخواند   *ma ʃa allah xub dars mixanad*, He studies,
learns his lessons, well.

(*q*) The phrase خدا نکند *xoda nakonad* 'may God not do (it)' is
customarily prefixed to mention of the possible occurrence of some
undesirable event, e.g.

خدا نکند مریض بشوید...   *xoda nakonad mariʒ beʃavid*, If, God forbid,
you should fall ill....

(*r*) چشم ما روشن *caʃme ma roῦʃan* 'our eye (is) bright' is an expression used to express pleasure on seeing someone who has been
absent for a time, for example, on a journey. The use of the plural arises
from a belief or assumption that the speaker, as an individual, is too
insignificant to express pleasure on his own behalf alone. A similar idea
lies behind the use of the plural in the phrase همیشه دعاگو هستیم *hamiʃe
do'agu hastim* 'we are always praying (for you)' sometimes said in reply
to a question from a person of equal or higher rank such as چکار میکنید
*ce kar mikonid* 'what have you been (are) you doing?'

(*s*) تبریک گفتن *tabrik goftan* and تسلیت گفتن *tasliat goftan* mean 'to
offer congratulations' and 'to offer condolences' respectively. عرض کردن
*arʒ kardan* may be substituted for گفتن *goftan*.

---

[1] This phrase is also used when the speaker has little or no intention of performing the
action referred to.

(t) زیارت کردن ‌ *ɀiarat kardan* 'to make a pilgrimage' is used for 'to visit' (an equal or person of higher rank), e.g.

میل دارم سرکاررا زیارت کنم *mēil daram sarkarra ɀiarat konam*, I should like to visit you.

(u) زیارت رفتن *ɀiarat raftan* means 'to go on a pilgrimage'. مشرف شدن *moʃarraf ʃodan* 'to be the recipient of honour' means to have performed a pilgrimage, i.e. to have visited a shrine and carried out the necessary rites. On meeting someone on the road returning, or who has returned, from a pilgrimage the phrase زیارت قبول *ɀiarat qabul* '(may your) pilgrimage (be) acceptable' is used, to which the answer is خدا حافظ شما *xoda hafeɀe ʃoma* '(may) God (be) your protector'.[1] On meeting someone who is going to perform a pilgrimage the phrase التماس دعا *eltemase do'a* '(I) beseech (your) prayer' may be said, to which the reply is محتاج دعا *mohtaje do'a* '(I) need (your) prayer'.

2. In the Introduction the vowel system and its relation to the written word was described. Although this relation is remarkably constant certain discrepancies are found. Some of these have already been noted in the Introduction and in Lesson v, para. 2. Certain other tendencies in Colloquial Persian should be noted:

(a) ا *a* followed by ن *n* tends to become *u*, e.g.

    نان   *nan* 'bread' becomes *nun*.

    آن   *an* 'that, it' becomes *un*.

(b) In certain words ا *a* followed by ن *n* tends to become a relatively short vowel intermediate between *a* and *o*.[2] It has this quality in the word خانم *xanom* 'lady' (see also Lesson v, para. 2) and دانگ *dang* (see Lesson v, para. 17). This 'shortened' *a* is frequently nasalized.

In certain Turkish words the written ا has a similar quality, even when not followed by ن *n*, e.g. the first *a* of باطلاق *batlaq* 'swamp'.

را *-ra* sometimes becomes *-ro*, the *o* of *-ro* being somewhat prolonged, and approximating to *ōu*.

(c) است *ast* 'is' is often replaced by *e*, e.g. خوب است *xub ast* 'it is good' becomes *xub e*.

(d) Certain verbs, notably دادن *dadan* 'to give' and گفتن *goftan* 'to say' and گذاشتن *goɀaʃtan* 'to place, put, allow', tend to contract, the

---

[1] جای شما خالی *jaye ʃoma xali* 'your place (was) empty' is also said.
[2] This modified *a* is also used in the recitation of poetry.

*eh, u(y)* and *go* respectively of tenses formed from the Present Stem being elided, e.g.

میدهم     *mideham* 'I give' becomes *midam.*

میگویم     *miguyam* 'I say' becomes *migam.*

میگوئید     *miguid* 'you say' becomes *migid.*

میگذارید.     *migoẓarid* 'you put', etc., becomes *miẓarid.*

(e) Instances of vowel harmony have already been given, namely in the case of the Imperatives of certain verbs, the Present Stem of which ends in *ōu* (see Lesson IV, para. 5). The *a* of the Present Stem of رفتن *raftan* 'to go' and شدن *ſodan* 'to become' when followed by the Personal endings ی *-i,* ایم *-im* and اید *-id* tends to become *e,* e.g.

میرویم     *miravim* 'we are going' becomes *mirevim.*

The verbal prefix *na* when followed by *mi* tends to become *ne,* e.g.

نمیکنم     *nemikonam* rather than *namikonam.*

هیچ کس     tends to become *hic kes* rather than *hic kas.*

3. The words دیگر *digar* (sometimes pronounced *dige*) and که *ke* are used in Colloquial Persian as catchwords with no specific meaning. دیگر. *digar* sometimes adds a slight degree of finality to the sentence; it may also convey a slight suggestion of protest that the person addressed should not be aware of, or should not believe, the statement made by the speaker, e.g.

منزل بودم دیگر     *manẓel budam digar,* I *was* at home.

منزل نبودم دیگر     *manẓel nabudam digar,* I was *not* at home.

نرفتم که     *naraftam ke,* I did not go.

او که مرد     *u ke mord,* he, he's dead.

4. In Colloquial Persian there is a tendency to add the Pronominal Suffix ش *-eſ* (-*aſ*) to the 3rd pers. sing. of intransitive verbs, especially when this is composed of one syllable[1], e.g.

بودش     *budeſ,* he was (there).

نیستش     *nisteſ,* he is not there.

مردش     *mordeſ,* he died.

رفتش     *rafteſ,* he went.

[1] This usage is occasionally found in Classical Persian also.

## Vocabulary

کمپانی kompani, Company.

هند hend, India.

شرقی ʃarqi, east (adj.).

شاه صفی Shah Safi (ruled Persia A.D. 1629–42).

جانشین janeʃin, successor.

حقوق hoquq (pl. of حق haqq), rights.

شعبان ʃaʿban, the 8th month of the hejri year (see Appendix III).

مساعدت mosaʿedat, help.

اتباع atbaʿ (pl. of تابع tabeʿ), subjects.

مودت movaddat, friendship.

اساسا asasan, essentially.

قسمت qesmat, portion, part.

مهم mohemm, important.

توسعه tõuseʿe, extension, expansion; توسعه یافتن tõuseʿe yaftan, to be extended, expanded, to spread.

رقابت reqabat, rivalry.

تأسیس taʿsis, founding; تأسیس کردن taʿsis k., to found.

همایونی homayuni, blessed, august.

عمومی omumi, general.

عفو afv, pardon; عفو عمومی afve omumi, general amnesty.

ستاد setad, military staff.

ارتش arteʃ, army; ستاد کل ارتش setade kolle arteʃ, the General Staff.

لشکر laʃkar, army; division (of an army).

فرماندهی farmandehi, command (of an army, etc.).

عشایر aʃayer, tribes.

کلیه kolliye, all, the totality.

رئیس raʿis, head, chief, director; (pl. رؤسا roʿasa).

ایلات ilat (pl. of ایل il), tribes.

ابلاغ eblaɣ k., to send, convey, کردن notify.

اطلاع ettelaʿ, information.

بقرار be qarar(e), according to.

ضمن ʒemn(e), in the course of, while.

اسلحه aslehe, arms, firearms.

مسلح mosallah, armed.

بشرط آنکه be ʃarte anke, on condition that.

پروانه parvane, licence, permit.

مخصوص maxsus, special.

علاوه بر alave bar, in addition to.

اطمینان etminan, assurance, confidence.

دشت daʃt, plain, field, steppe.

تماشا tamaʃa, sight, spectacle; تماشا کردن tamaʃa k., to watch, look at.

باك bak, fear.

| | |
|---|---|
| تنبلى | *tambali*, laziness. |
| محكم | *mohkam*, firm, strong. |
| مقصود | *maqsud*, aim, object. |
| حدت | *heddat*, vehemence, force. |
| قرنطينه | *qarantine*, quarantine. |
| توقف | *tavaqqof*, stopping, delay, pause. |
| مسافر | *mosafer*, traveller (pl. مسافرين *mosaferin*). |
| قانون | *qanun*, law, rule (pl. قوانين *qavanin*). |
| صرف و نحو | *sarf o nahv*, grammar and syntax. |
| تلخ | *talx*, bitter; اوقات او تلخ شد *ōuqate u talx ſod*, he became angry (lit. his times became bitter). |
| صفت | *sefat*, quality (pl. صفات *sefat*). |
| شك | *ſakk*, doubt. |

| | |
|---|---|
| سوء قصد کردن (بر علیه کسی) | *su'e qasd k.* (*bar aleihe kasi*), to make an attempt on the life (of someone). |
| رایج | *rayej*, current, in use. |
| كفيل | *kafil*, substitute, deputy, acting (for someone else). |
| نائب | *na'eb*, substitute; assistant. |
| وبا | *vaba*, cholera. |
| مختل | *moxtall*, disorganized, confused. |
| بر عكس | *bar aks*, on the contrary. |
| اصطلاح | *estelah*, expression, idiom. |
| عنصر | *onsor*, element (pl. عناصر *anaser*). |
| تن در دادن (به) | *tan dar dadan* (*be*), to submit (to). |
| فاسد | *fased*, corrupt. |

## ایران و انگلیس

بعد از شاه عباس بزرگ در سال ۱۰۳۸ کمپانی تجارتی هند شرق انگلیس فرمان تازه در باب تجارت ابریشم از شاه صفی جانشین وی گرفتند ولی نتوانستند تمام امتیازات و حقوق را که در زمان شاه عباس بزرگ تحصیل کرده بودند بار دیگر بدست آورند و با آنکه از طرف چارلز اول پادشاه انگلیس در ماه شعبان ۱۰۳۹ (۱۶۳۰) نماینده و نامه برای کمک و مساعدت بتجار و اتباع انگلیسی در ایران برای شاه صفی آمد و از طرف پادشاه ایران هم بخوبی این اظهار مودت و دوستی پذیرفته شد ولی در زمان این پادشاه اساساً قسمت مهم تجارت ایران بدست تجار هلندی بود و بار دیگر چارلز اول برای کمک بشرکت هند شرق انگلیس نامهٔ دیگر برای شاه صفی فرستاد و از طرف پادشاه صفوی هم این نامه بخوبی پذیرفته

شـد و نـامه دوستانه هم برای پـادشـاه انگلستان فرسـتاد و بـالاخره در ١٠٥٣
(١٦٤٣) شـرکـت تجارق هند شرق انگلیس برای خود تجارتخانه در بصره تأسیس
کردند در این ضمن روز بروز تجارت هـلـنـدیـهـا در ایران تـوسـعـه مییافت و بـا
انگلیسها برقابت میپرداختند ‌ (ناتمام)

## عفو عمومی عشایر

بنابر پیشنهاد ستاد لشکر جنوب و تصویب اعلیحضرت همایونی فرمـان عـفـو
عمومی نسبت بکلیه عشایر فارس صادر شد و این فرمـان از طـرف فرماندهی لشکر
برؤسای ایلات و عشایر ابلاغ گردیده است بقرار اطلاع از ستاد کل ارتش ضمن
ابلاغ این فرمان اعلام شده است کـه ایلات و عشایر میتوانند اسلحه بـا خود
داشته و مسلح شوند بشرط آنکه پروانه مخصوصی دریافت دارند علاوه بر ابلاغ
عفو عمومی بکلیه عشایر و ایلات از طرف دولت از هر جهت اطمینان داده شده و
آنانرا بکمکهای لازم از طرف دولت امیدوار نموده است

## آرزو

بچه بودم تابستان بییلاق رفته بودیم هر روز عصر بچهها بدنبال گوسفندان از
کـوه میامدند میگفتند نزدیک قله دشت سبزی است آبهای زیاد دارد از آن بالا
شهر و دنیارا میشود تماشا کـرد تا نبینی نمیشود گفت دلم میخواست مـن به
بیپاکی و توانائی آنها بـودم شاید آنهـا هم دلشان میخواست وسایل تنبلی مـرا
داشتند یـك روز بکدخدا گفتم مـن فردا بـا بچهها بدشت میروم تـا آنجا چقدر
راه است خندیده گفت خیلی باید رفت تا آنجا برسی و خیلی خسته میشوی گفتم اگر
دشت پشت این کوه باشد برای مـن دور نیست مگر تا آنجا چقدر راه است گفت
پنج ساعت تمام باید سربالا رفت از ترس دلم فرو ریخت اما کار گذشته بود فردا
با قدمهای محکم با کدخدا و بچهها بطرف مقصود روانه شدم با خود گفتم تـا
جان دارم خستگی نشان نمیدهم هنوز در حدت تصمیم بودم کدخدا گفت رسیدیم
دشت اینجاست از خوشحالی چند قدمی دویده گفتم من حاضرم تا قله بروم اما شما
گفتید پنج ساعت راه است دو ساعت و نیمست کـه حرکت کـردهایم گفت اگر
میگفتم دو ساعت راه است خسته باینجا میرسیدی پنج ساعت گفتم که دو ساعت
راه آسان بیائی

‌• اقتباس از آئینه تألیف محد حجازی

## Exercise 26

1. He often becomes angry; for all that we like him and he has some good qualities.   2. There was no doubt that his life would be aimed at.   3. Whatever he talks about will be interesting.   4. It is immaterial whether he comes himself or he sends a substitute.   5. I always considered him my best friend.   6. The cholera scare has produced (been the cause of) a severe quarantine that has upset all commercial relations, to say nothing of the interruption of passenger traffic.   7. I have not nearly finished my work; on the contrary I have only just begun.   8. The expression is contrary to the rules of grammar; all the same it is part of the common tongue.   9. In every society, however seemingly corrupt, there are those who have not submitted to the evil elements.   10. Since its formation some years ago, this company has made large profits.   11. I wish you had come yesterday; then you would have seen my brother before he set out.

# PART II
# THE ARABIC ELEMENT

# Introduction[1]

1. There is a large Arabic element in Persian. This element is an indispensable part of the spoken and written word. The student will have already come across many Arabic words in the vocabularies—nouns, adjectives, adverbs, prepositions and conjunctions. The Arabic words incorporated into the Persian language have become Persianized. Many of them have acquired a meaning other than their present-day meaning in Arabic-speaking countries or have retained the meaning which they held at the time when they were incorporated into the Persian language. Not only have a large number of Arabic words been incorporated into Persian, but many Arabic phrases also. Persian literature abounds in quotations from Arabic writings, especially from the *Qor'an* and religious works such as the *Nahj ol-Balaghe*.

2. In the following lessons an attempt will be made to describe the formation of the main derivative Arabic forms which are used in Persian. The Arabic language is built up on triliteral and quadriliteral roots, of which the former are the more common. By addition to the root of one or more of the letters ا, ت, س, م, ن, و or ى (known as servile letters) or by altering the vowel pattern the full conjugation of the verb can be formed. The servile letters are also found in their own right, as it were, forming one or more of the letters of the triliteral or quadriliteral root.

3. The letters ت, ث, د, ذ, ر, ز, س, ش, ص, ض, ط, ظ, ل and ن are known as 'sun letters' (اَلْحُرُوفُ ٱلشَّمْسِيَّةُ). When the Arabic definite article ال is prefixed to a word beginning with one of the sun letters, the *l* is assimilated to the sun letter, e.g.

ٱلسُّلْطَان   *as-soltan*, the Sultan.

4. The other letters of the alphabet are known as 'moon letters' (اَلْحُرُوفُ ٱلْقَمَرِيَّةُ) and the *l* of the article is not assimilated to them.

5. The value of the consonants and vowels in Arabic differs from their value in Persian, but Arabic words and phrases, when used in Persian,

[1] In this and the following chapters I am indebted to W. Wright's *Grammar of the Arabic Language* (C.U.P.). The student is advised to consult further this or some other reputable Arabic Grammar.

are usually Persianized and hence no attempt will be made in the following pages to differentiate between Arabic and Persian values (see also para. 12 below). The long vowels *i*, *a*, and *u* are indicated by placing the *kasre*, *fathe* and *ʒamme* before the letters ى, ا, and و respectively; in which case these letters are called 'letters of prolongation' (حُرُوفُ ٱلمَدّ). In some common words *a* is indicated merely by *fathe* or by a stroke written perpendicularly to resemble a small *alef*, e.g. اَللّٰه God, لٰكِن but.

6. ا *alef*, و *vav* and ى *ye* are 'weak letters' (حُرُوفُ ٱلعِلّة) so called because they undergo certain changes according to their phonetic context.

7. *Tanvin* (nunation). At the end of nouns and adjectives when these are indefinite, the vowel signs ُ (*o*) and ِ (*e*) are written double, thus ٌ and ٍ, and pronounced *on* and *en* respectively. The vowel sign َ (*a*) is also written double and pronounced *an*. It then takes an *alef* unless the word ends in ة (*t*)[1] or *hamʒe*, in which case it is written ً and ء respectively. E.g.

وَالِدٌ    *valedon*, father (nom.).

وَالِدٍ    *valeden*, father (gen.).

وَالِدًا   *valedan*, father (acc.).

دَفْعَةً    *daf'atan*, once.

اِبْتِدَاءً  *ebteda'an*, in the beginning.

8. ء *hamʒe* in Arabic is of two kinds; هَمْزَةُ ٱلوَصْل and هَمْزَةُ ٱلقَطْع respectively. The former cannot be dropped, whereas the latter is omitted under certain circumstances.

The following rules govern the writing of the هَمْزَةُ ٱلقَطْع:

(a) At the beginning of a word it is always written with *alef*, e.g.

أَمْر order.    إِبِل camel.    أُفُق horizon.

In Persian the sign ء in an initial position is omitted: thus امر.

[1] The feminine ending (see Lesson XVI, para. 5 et seq.) is written ة.

(*b*) In a medial position, three cases arise:

(i) *hamẓe* is unvowelled. It is then borne by the letter cognate with the *preceding* vowel, i.e. by ا *alef* if the vowel is *a*, by و *vav* if the vowel is *o*, and by ى *ye* if the vowel is *e* (written without dots).

E.g.   رَأْس head.   مُوْمِن believer.   بِئْر well.

(ii) *hamẓe* is vowelled and follows a *sokun* not marking a long vowel or diphthong. It is then borne by the letter cognate with the *following* vowel, e.g.

مَسْأَلَة question.   مَسْوُول responsible.   مَرْئِى visible.

(iii) *hamẓe* is vowelled and follows a short or a long vowel. If *either* of the vowels is *e* or *i* the bearer is ـئ *ye* without dots; if not, but either is *o* or *u*, the bearer is و *vav*, otherwise the bearer is ا *alef*, unless the first vowel is *a*, when there is no bearer.

E.g.   خَطِيئَة sin.          سُئِل He was asked.

وَسَائِل means.          طَاوُوس peacock.

سُوَال question.          تَأَمُّل thought, consideration.

سَأَل He asked.          قِرَاءَة reading.

For *hamẓe* in a medial position both Arabic and Persian admit deviations from the rule to avoid two consecutive *vavs* or *yes*. For this purpose (i) وُ may change to ـؤ, e.g. مَسْؤُول, and (ii) both وُ and ء may be written without the bearer, either between two letters or above the ligature joining two letters, e.g. رؤوس, heads, مَشِيئَة wish. Two consecutive *alefs* are always so avoided (as in قِرَاءَة, in (iii) above). ا may even be changed to ء when there is no such compulsion, as in مَسْئَلَة (the usual form of the word in Persian). It is improper, though by no means unknown, for *hamẓe* to be written over a letter of prolongation which should follow it, e.g. طَاؤُس (for طَاوُوس). In such cases the long vowel must be retained in pronunciation.

(*c*) In a final position:

Preceded by a *sokun* or a long vowel it has no bearer, e.g.

ضَوْء light, brightness.   شَىْء thing.   سُوء evil.

Otherwise it follows the same rules as the *hamze* in a medial position. In a final position the sign ‒ is often omitted in Persian.

هَمْزَةُ ٱلْوَصْل occurs at the beginning of some words but does not represent an essential part of the word itself. When such a word follows another word the هَمْزَةُ ٱلْوَصْل with its vowel is dropped and the sign ‒ known as وَصْلَة replaces the *hamze*, and the *alef* which supported the *hamze*, while preserved in writing, is not represented in pronunciation, e.g.

عَبْدُ ٱلْقَادِر     Abd ol-Qader (a proper name).

The *hamze* of the definite article ال, the Imperative of the I form of the verb and of the Perfect, Imperative and Verbal Noun of the VII, VIII, IX and X forms of the verb is a هَمْزَةُ ٱلْوَصْل, as also is the *hamze* of the following words:

| | | | |
|---|---|---|---|
| ٱبْن | son. | ٱبْنَة | daughter. |
| ٱثْنَان | two (m.). | ٱثْنَتَان | two (f.). |
| ٱمْرُؤ | man. | ٱمْرَأَة | woman. |

If the word preceding a هَمْزَةُ ٱلْوَصْل does not end in a vowel, the final consonant generally receives a *kasre* (e) except مِن 'from' which takes a *fathe* (a) before the article, e.g.

مِنَ ٱلْوَلَد     from the boy.

The Personal Pronouns هُم 'they', كُم 'you' and أَنْتُم 'ye', the personal ending تُم of the 2nd pers. pl. of the Perfect and the preposition مُذ 'since' take a *zamme* (o) before a هَمْزَةُ ٱلْوَصْل, e.g.

لَعَنَهُمُ ٱللّٰه     may God curse them.

If the word preceding a هَمْزَةُ ٱلْوَصْل ends in ا (*a*) و (*u*) or ى (*i*) the vowels *a*, *u* and *i* become short. In Persian they are pronounced a, o and e respectively, e.g.

أَبُو ٱلْبَشَر     *abol-bašar*, the father of humanity (a proper name).

فِى ٱلْفَوْر     *fel-foŭr*, immediately.

In certain expressions the همزةُ ٱلوَصل is omitted in writing, e.g.

بِسم ٱللهِ (for باسم الله)   in the name of God.

It is also omitted from the word اِبن 'son' when this comes between the name of the son and his father, provided it is not at the beginning of a line, e.g.

زید بن علی   *zeid ebne ali*,[1] Zeid son of Ali,

and from the article ال when this is preceded by ل 'to, for' or the particle

لَ 'verily', e.g.

للرَّجُل   to the man.          لَلحَقّ   verily the truth.

If the noun begins with ل then the ل of the article also falls out, e.g.

لِلَّیلَة   for the night.          لله   to God.

9. In a medial position a *hamze* in Arabic words is pronounced in Persian as a glottal plosive and is represented in the transcription by the sign ', e.g.

رئیس   *ra'is*, chief, director.

Initial or final *hamze* is not represented in the transcription; final *hamze* is not usually pronounced. There are, however, certain exceptions to this rule, among them جزء *joz'* 'part, portion' and سوء *su'* 'evil', the final *hamze* of which is pronounced and therefore represented in the transcription. In words which have, in Arabic, a final *hamze* preceded by an *alef*, the *hamze* being usually omitted in Persian, the *ezafe* when added to such words is written as ی, e.g.

اقتضای وقت   *eqtezaye vaqt*, the exigency of the time.

10. A stroke resembling a *madde* is generally put above abbreviations. The following abbreviations are in common use in Persian:

صَلّی ٱللهُ عَلَیه وَسَلَّم = ص   God bless him and give him peace (used after the name of Muhammad).

عَلَیه ٱلسَّلام = ع   Upon him be peace (used after the names of the prophets).

---

[1] The transcription gives the Persian pronunciation, which differs from Arabic usage.

رَضِيَ ٱللّٰهُ عَنْهُ = رضی    May God be pleased with him (used after the names of the Companions of Muhammad).

رَحِمَهُ ٱللّٰهُ = رح    May God have compassion on him (used after the names of the dead).

11. The Arabic ة is written in Persian ت (*t*) or ه. The tendency is for it to become ت if it occurs in the following forms of the Verbal Noun of the I form: فَعَالِيَة, فِعَالَة, فَعَالَة, فَعُولَة (see Lesson XV, para. 4) or in the Abstract Noun of Quality (see Lesson XVI, para. 13). If it is the feminine ending it is written ه. In pronunciation it falls away and the *fathe* preceding the ة in Arabic is changed in Persian to *e*,[1] thus وَالِدَة 'mother' becomes والده *valede*. The ة of Verbal Nouns of the II and III forms is also usually changed to the 'silent' *h*.

Sometimes both forms are found with a different meaning, e.g.

اراده    *erade*, will.

ارادت    *eradat*, respect for, devotion to (someone).

امنیه    *amniye*, gendarmerie.

امنیت    *amniyat*, security, public order.

12. It was stated above that Arabic words and phrases were usually Persianized when used in Persian. There are a few exceptions. The case of numerals has already been noted (see note to para. 11 above). In the following phrases the Arabic *kasre* preserves its Arabic value, that is it approximates to the vowel in the English word 'bit':

بِسْمِ ٱللّٰه    in the name of God.

اَلْحَمْدُ لِلّٰه    Praise be to God.

مِنْهَا    the formula used to perform subtraction (see above, Lesson V, para. 12).

[1] This does not apply to numerals used in dates. The ة in such cases is preserved in the orthography, but is not pronounced, and the *fathe* or *a* of the Arabic preserved. In the names of the months ذُو ٱلْقَعْدَة and ذُو ٱلْحِجَّة the *fathe* is also preserved.

In the expression عَيْنِهِ (in Persian) 'exactly like', the ʒamme also preserves its Arabic value, that is it approximates to the Persian vowel *u* but its articulation time is less. These differences are not shown in the transcription.

ِيّ in Arabic words is represented in the transcription as *iy*,[1] e.g.

رعيت (for رَعِيَّة)   *ra'iyat*, peasant.

بلديه (for بَلَدِيَّة)   *baladiye*, municipality.

َيّ becomes *aīy*, e.g. مهيّا *mohaīya*, prepared.

ى followed by ا *a* in some Arabic words (notably the Verbal Noun of the VII and VIII form of Hollow Verbs, see Lesson XVIII, para. 4) is represented in the transcription by *ey*, but this *e* approximates to the vowel in the English word 'bit' (and not to the *e* in the English word 'bed'), e.g.

امْتِياز   *emteyaʒ*.

This does not apply to ى followed by ا in Persian words, e.g.

شيرازيان   *firaʒian*, people of Shiraz.


# LESSON XV

## The Triliteral Root.

1. The Arabic verbal root contains three radical letters or four,[2] e.g.

فَعَل   to do (of which the radical letters are ف, ع and ل).

تَرْجَم   to translate (of which the radical letters are ت, ر, ج and م).

2. The triliteral root is the more common of the two. In the 3rd pers. sing. Perfect Active the first and third radicals always have an *a* as their vowel. The medial radical may have *a*, *e* or *o*, e.g.

فَعَل   to do.      حَزِن   to be sad.      حَسُن   to be beautiful.

---

[1] It is thus differentiated from يَة (يه) *ie* in the form تَفْعِله when the third radical is ى.

[2] Arabic dictionaries give the verb under the 3rd pers. sing. masc. of the Perfect Active of the root form. This is given in Arabic-English dictionaries as the infinitive, thus فَعَل 'to do' and تَرْجَم 'to translate'; the real meaning of these forms is 'he did' and 'he translated' respectively. The derived forms must be looked up in Arabic dictionaries under the root form.

3. From the simple or root form are derived fourteen forms. Only nine of these are in common use and only these will be given in this and the following lessons. All ten forms seldom occur in one root. The Arabic dictionaries give only those forms which are in use.

4. The Active and Passive Participles and the Verbal Noun of the Arabic verb are used in Persian. Only these forms together with the 3rd pers. masc. sing. of the Perfect Active will be given in the tables in this and the following lessons.[1] The verb فَعَلَ is commonly used by Arabic grammarians as a paradigm. The derivative forms are formed by the addition of servile letters (see p. 181, para. 2 above), vowel permutations and the doubling of the 2nd and 3rd radical letters, as follows:

| Form | 3rd pers. sing. Perfect Active | Active Participle | Passive Participle |
|---|---|---|---|
| I | فَعَلَ | فَاعِل | مَفْعُول |

E.g.

كَتَبَ he wrote. كاتب scribe. مكتوب written; letter.

There are some forty forms of the Verbal Noun of the root form of the verb. Only those in more frequent use will be given here:

e.g.: فَعْل

فَهْم understanding    from    فَهِم to understand.

e.g.: فَعَل

فَرَح joy    „    فَرِح to be glad.

e.g.: فُعُول

جُلُوس accession    „    جَلَسَ to sit.

e.g.: فُعُولَة [2]

سُهُولَت ease    „    سَهُلَ to be easy.

---

[1] There are a few cases in Persian of other Arabic verbal forms, e.g. يَعْنِي, used in Persian to mean 'namely', is the 3rd pers. sing. of the Imperfect Active of عَنَى 'to mean'. أَعْنِي, also used to mean 'namely', is the 1st pers. sing. of the Imperfect Active of the same verb.

[2] Usually written with ت in Persian.

e.g.: فَعَالَة¹

سَعَادَت   prosperity   from   سَعَد   to be auspicious.

e.g.: فُعْل

شُغْل   occupation   „   شَغَل   to be occupied.

e.g.: فِعْل

قِسْم   part   „   قَسَم   to divide.

e.g.: فِعَال

لِقَاء   meeting   „   لَقِیَ   to meet.

e.g.: فِعَالَة¹

خِلَافَت   caliphate   „   خَلَف   to succeed.

e.g.: فُعَال

سُؤَال   question   „   سَأَل³   to question.

e.g.: فَعَال

خَلَاص   liberation   „   خَلَص   to be freed (from).

e.g.: فَعْلَى

دَعْوَى   claim   „   دَعَا   to call out, etc.

e.g.: فُعْلَان

غُفْرَان   pardon   „   غَفَر   to forgive.

e.g.: فِعْلَان

عِرْفَان   mysticism   „   عَرَف   to know.

e.g.: فَعُول

قَبُول   acceptance   „   قَبِل   to accept.

---

¹ Usually written with ت in Persian.

² For the rules governing the formation of the derived forms of weak verbs see Lesson XVIII.

³ For the rules governing the formation of the derived forms of hamzated verbs see Lesson XVII.

فَعِيل .e.g:

رَحِيل   departure, journey   from   رَحَلَ   to depart (from).

فَعَالِيَة¹ .e.g:

صَلَاحِيَت   competence   „   صَلُحَ   to be honest.

مَفْعَلَة² .e.g:

مَقَالة   treatise   „   قَالَ³   to say.

5. The meanings of the derived forms are modifications of the
meaning of the root form as follows:

II. فَعَّلَ intensive; makes intransitive verbs transitive. E.g. ضَرَبَ to beat,
ضَرَّبَ to beat violently; فَرَقَ to separate (intrans.), فَرَّقَ to disperse
(trans.).

III. فَاعَلَ the relation of the action of I to another person, e.g. قَتَلَ to
kill, قَاتَلَ to fight with.

IV. أَفْعَلَ causative; brings about the condition or action implied in I,
e.g. عَلِمَ to know, أَعْلَمَ to inform (someone of something);
بَلُغَ to be eloquent, أَبْلَغَ to speak eloquently.

V. تَفَعَّلَ Reflexive of II; describes the consequences of II, especially with
reference to oneself, e.g. فَرَّقَ to disperse (trans.), تَفَرَّقَ to be
dispersed; خَوَّفَ to terrify, تَخَوَّفَ to be afraid.

VI. تَفَاعَلَ Reflexive of III; expresses the consequences of III; reciprocal.
E.g. رَامَى to throw (at the same time as another), تَرَامَى to throw
oneself down; خَادَعَ to try to outwit, تَخَادَعَ to pretend to be deceived; قَاتَلَ to fight with, تَقَاتَلَ to fight with one another.

¹ Usually written with ت in Persian.
² Usually written with ه in Persian, the ه being then treated like the 'silent' h.
³ For the rules governing the formation of the derived forms of weak verbs see
Lesson XVIII.

VII. اِنْفَعَل Passive; being affected by I especially from the point of view of the person initiating action for his own ends, e.g. كَسَرَ to break off, اِنْكَسَرَ to be broken; هَزَمَ to put to flight, اِنْهَزَمَ to let oneself be put to flight, to flee.

VIII. اِفْتَعَل Reflexive of I; reciprocal, e.g. ضَرَبَ to beat, اِضْطَرَبَ [1] to move oneself to and fro, to be agitated; قَتَلَ to kill, اِقْتَتَلَ to fight with one another.

IX. اِفْعَلَّ used for colours and physical defects, e.g. اِسْوَدَّ to be black, اِحْوَلَّ to squint.

X. اِسْتَفْعَل Reflexive of IV; desiring, seeking, asking for, considering or thinking a thing possesses the qualities expressed by I, e.g. أَوْجَبَ to make it necessary for others, اِسْتَوْجَبَ to make something necessary for oneself; غَفَرَ to pardon, اِسْتَغْفَرَ to ask pardon, غَاثَ to help, اِسْتَغَاثَ to call for help, حَسُنَ to be comely, اِسْتَحْسَنَ to think beautiful.

6. Arabic Verbal Nouns are abstract and denote the state, action or feeling indicated by the verb.

7. The Active Participle is used as an adjective or noun referring to a continuous action, habitual state or permanent quality, e.g.

عَالِم    learned, a learned man.

مُعَلِّم    teacher.

The tendency in Persian is for the Active Participle of the I form to be used as an adjective in the singular rather than as a noun, but to be widely used as a noun in the plural.

8. The Passive Participle is used as an adjective or noun, e.g.

مَعْلُوم    known.

مَكْتُوب    letter (what is written).

[1] See below, para. 9.

| Form | 3rd pers. sing. Perfect Active | | Active Participle | | Passive Participle | Verbal Noun | |
|---|---|---|---|---|---|---|---|
| II | نَزَّلَ | | مُنَزِّل | | مُنَزَّل | تَنْزِيل or تَنْزِلَة | |
| E.g. | عَلَّمَ | to teach | مُعَلِّم | teacher | | تَعْلِيم | teaching |
| | فَرَّقَ | to separate | مُفَرِّق | discriminative | مُفَرَّق dispersed | تَفْرِيق | separation, disunity |
| III | فَاعَلَ | | مُفَاعِل | | مُفَاعَل | فِعَال or مُفَاعَلَة | |
| E.g. | كَاتَبَ | to correspond | مُكَاتِب | correspondent | | مُكَاتَبَة | correspondence |
| | حَافَظَ | to observe carefully | حَافِظ | guardian | | مُحَافَظَة | preservation, defence |
| | قَاتَلَ | to wage war against | مُقَاتِل | fighter, warrior | | قِتَال | battle |
| IV | أَفْعَلَ | | مُفْعِل | | مُفْعَل | إِفْعَال | |
| E.g. | أَحْسَنَ | to do good | مُحْسِن | beneficent | مُحْسَن | إِحْسَان | beneficence |
| V | تَفَعَّلَ | | مُتَفَعِّل | | مُتَفَعَّل | تَفَعُّل | |
| E.g. | تَكَبَّرَ | to magnify oneself | مُتَكَبِّر | proud | | تَكَبُّر | pride |

| Form | | | | | | |
|---|---|---|---|---|---|---|
| VI | تَفاعَلَ | | تَفاعَلَ | | تَفاعُل | |
| E.g. | تَعاهَدَ | to make a mutual compact | تَعاهَد | contracting party | تَعاهُد | a mutual agreement |
| VII | اِنْفَعَلَ | | يَنْفَعِل | | اِنْفِعال | |
| E.g. | اِنْكَسَرَ | to be broken | مُنْكَسِر | broken | اِنْكِسار | fracture, rupture |
| VIII | اِفْتَعَلَ | | يَفْتَعِل | | اِفْتِعال | |
| E.g. | اِمْتَنَعَ | to be inaccessible | مُمْتَنِع | impossible | اِمْتِناع | abstention |
| IX | اِفْعَلَّ | | | | اِفْعِلال | |
| E.g. | اِحْمَرَّ | to be red | أَحْمَر | red | اِحْمِرار | redness |
| X | اِسْتَفْعَلَ | | يَسْتَفْعِل | | اِسْتِفْعال | |
| E.g. | اِسْتَقْبَلَ | to come forward | مُسْتَقْبِل | one who goes to meet (someone) | مُسْتَقْبَل | future (tense) |
| | | | | | اِسْتِقْبال | going to meet |

Usually written with • in Persian.

² In Persian this usually becomes • and the *fathe* of the ح frequently becomes a *karre*, thus مخالفه *mokhafeqe* but مكاتبه *mokatabe*.

³ The Passive Participle of this form where the latter is Passive in meaning (see above, para. 5) does not occur.

9. The inserted ت of the VIII form undergoes the following changes:

(a) If the first radical of the root is ت this unites with the inserted ت, e.g.

اِتِّبَاع    submission, obedience (from تَبِعَ).

(b) If the first radical is د or ز the inserted ت changes into د which unites with the radical د, e.g.

اِدِّرَاك    attainment (from دَرَكَ).

اِزْدِحَام    crowding (from زَحَمَ).

(c) If the first radical is ذ the inserted ت changes into ذ and unites with the radical ذ, e.g.

اِذِّخَار    hoarding (from ذَخَرَ).

(d) If the first radical is ص, ض or ط the inserted ت is changed into ط, which unites with the radical ط, e.g.

اِطِّلَاع    information (from طَلَعَ).

اِصْطِلَاح    expression (from صَلَحَ).

اِضْطِرَاب    anxiety (from ضَرَبَ).

10. Arabic forms are used in Persian not only standing alone, but also combined with Persian words and particles to form compounds. Many examples of Compound Verbs thus formed have been given in Lesson IX, para. 2. Persian particles and suffixes are also added to Arabic forms to form compounds, e.g.

حاجتمند    *hajatmand*, needy (حاجت need).

شعله‌ور    *ʃoʻlevar*, blazing (شعله flame).

اولین    *avvalin*, first (اول first).

نامعلوم    *namaʻlum*, unknown (معلوم known).

ناصالح    *nasaleh*, dishonest (صالح good, just).

عاقلانه    *aqelane*, wise; wisely (عاقل wise, reasonable).

## ايران و انگليس (بقيه از درس پيش)

در زمان پادشاهی شاه عباس دوم نفوذ انگليسها بمراتب کمتر از سابق گرديد و بر عکس تسلط و نفوذ هلنديها در ايران و خليج فارس زياد ميگشت و بطوری از پيشرفت کار خود در ايران گستاخ شده بودند کـه حتی بـا کشتيهای جنگ خود در بصره دار التجارههای انگليسيرا ويران کردند ولی بعدا در نتيجه جنگی که در اروپا ميان دو دولت فوق الذکر روی داد روابط تجارتی ايشان در هندوستان و ايران مختل شد و دولت ايران هم از موقع استفاده کرده از نفوذ و امتيازات آن دو دولت در ايران کاست از آنجمله از ادای مـبـلـغـی کـه هر سـالـه از بـابـت در آمدهای گمرکی بندر عباس بانگليسها داده ميشد خودداری کرد و شرکت هند شرقی هم بپادشاه انگلستان کـه در آنزمان چارلز دوم بود بود توسل جست و او در سال ١٠٨١ بشاه سليمان[٤] در اين باب نـامـه نوشت و تـا اواخر قرن دوازدهم هجری نفوذ هلنديها در خليج بمراتب بيشتر از انگليسها بـود ولی در اواخر اين قرن بعضی حـوادث تـازه کـه در اروپا اتفاق افتاد مايه ضعف هلنديها گرديد و در همين موقع هم بواسطه اختلافاتيکه در ميان شرکای هنـد شرقی روی داد دولت انگليس در سال ١١٢٠ هجری (١٧٠٨ ميلادی) تمام شرکتهای قديمرا با يکديگر متحد نموده شرکتی بزرگ بنام شرکت تجار انگليسی برای تجارت هند شرقی تأسيس کرد و ضمنا پادشاه انگلستان هم رؤسای شرکترا بمقامات قنسولی و سفارت در دربار پادشاهان هندوستان گماشت و نفوذ آنان افزون گشت    پايان

## طهران

طـهـران هنـوز ببزرگی امـروزه نـشـده بـود و بيشتر خيابانهائی کـه اکنـون هرکس از اهالی شهر اسم آنرا ميداند و مـايـه جلال پايتخت شده بوجود نيامده بود هنوز در دروازههارا موقع اذان غروب ميبستند عبور و مرور از داخل بخارج و در خود شهر از اول شب قطع ميشد زمستانها که آفتاب زودتر غروب ميکرد در دروازههارا هم زودتر ميبستند در اين اوقات بود که يکی از سفرا تا صبح بيرون دروازه ماند و در ميان چارواداران بيتوته کرد همين اوقات بودکه در چند قدمی دروازهها دزدان برای چند تومان مردمرا سر ميبريدند

٤ Shah Soleiman ruled from A.H. 1077 to 1105.

### Exercise 27

1. The Prime Minister was both detested and despised. 2. He has treated me badly and yet I wish to do him justice. 3. He has an enemy, namely his own brother. 4. A great deal of the forest of the west is Crown land, and to prevent it from being wasted the government has decreed that no one can cut down the trees without permission. 5. He said 'All that I have is at your disposal'. 6. It was that which killed him. 7. He always does that which the hour demands, not that which he would like to do. 8. I have made such alterations as occurred to me. 9. He is the same man that we met yesterday. 10. That is the reason why he cannot succeed. 11. I know that he has come. 12. I feared that it might anger him. 13. Take the money, there is no saying but you will need it. 14. No one doubts that he will be successful.

## LESSON XVI

### The Declension of Nouns. The Gender of Nouns. The Noun of Place. The Noun of Instrument. Abstract Nouns. Diminutives. Adjectives.

1. Arabic has three cases, nominative, genitive and accusative. If the noun is not defined by the definite article الـ the case endings are generally ´ *on*, ‿ *en* and ‗ *an*, e.g.

Nom. وَالِدٌ  
Gen. وَالِدٍ } father.  
Acc. وَالِدًا

For certain classes of nouns, known as diptotes, the accusative ending is used also for the genitive when the noun is indefinite.

2. If the noun is defined by the definite article the case endings for all nouns are ´ *o*, ‿ *e* and ‗ *a*, e.g.

Nom. اَلْوَالِدُ  
Gen. اَلْوَالِدِ  
Acc. اَلْوَالِدَ

3. If a word is in the construct state[1] and definite it does not take the article, e.g.

صاحبُ ٱلْبَيْت    the owner of the house.

حُبُّ ٱلْوَطَنِ    patriotism (love of the country).

4. In Persian the case endings fall away when a word stands alone, but in phrases such as those given in para. 3 above, which are used in Persian as compounds, the nominative ending of the first part is retained, thus

وَالِدٌ    father (nom.) becomes in Persian والد *valed.*

حُبُّ ٱلْوَطَنِ    patriotism becomes in Persian حبّ الوطن *hobb ol-vatan.*

5. Arabic has two genders: masculine and feminine. Most masculine words can be made feminine by the addition of ة, e.g.

وَالِدٌ    father.

وَالِدَةٌ    mother (in Persian والده *valede*).

6. Many words singular in form have a collective meaning in Arabic. To indicate a single object the feminine ending ة is added, e.g.

شَجَر    tree (trees in general).

شَجَرَة    a tree.

7. Words denoting males and ending in ة are masculine, e.g.

خَلِيفَة    caliph (in Persian خليفه *xalife*).

8. Adjectives qualifying a feminine noun or pronoun also take the feminine ending ة unless they have special feminine forms (see below),[2] e.g.

كَبِيرٌ    great (m.).

كَبِيرَةٌ    great (f.) (in Persian كبيره *kabire*).

---

[1] I.e. in the form of the substantive used when standing before another having an attributive (or genitive) relation to it.

[2] In Arabic certain adjectives which refer only to women do not take the feminine ending. This rule is not always observed in Persian e.g. حامِل 'pregnant' becomes in Persian حامله *hamele.*

9. Broken plurals (see Lesson XX) are feminine [1] and therefore take a feminine adjective. This agreement is sometimes preserved in Persian, e.g.

امور مهمه    *omure mohemme*, important matters (امور being the broken plural of امر *amr*).

10. A Noun of Place is formed on the measure مَفْعَل, مَفْعِل, or مَفْعَلَة, e.g.

مَقْصَد    destination.

مَسْجِد    mosque.

مَدْرَسَة    school (in Persian مدرسه *madrase*).[2]

مَقْبَرَة    cemetery (in Persian مقبره *maqbere*).

Nouns of Place from the derived forms of the Triliteral Verb are identical in form with the Passive Participle.

11. A noun denoting the Instrument is formed on the measure مِفْعَال, مِفْعَل or مِفْعَلَة, e.g.

مِفْتَاح    key.

مِبْضَع    lancet.

مِشْرَبَة    copper bowl used in the *hammam* (in Persian مشربه and pronounced *meʃrabe* or *maʃrabe*).

12. Nouns denoting professions and trades are formed on the measure فَعَّال, e.g.

نَجَّار    carpenter.

خَبَّاز    baker.

13. Abstract Nouns of Quality are formed by adding the feminine termination ة to Relative Adjectives (see below, para. 18). This becomes ت or the 'silent' *h* in Persian.

---

[1] Certain other classes of words are feminine in Arabic, but since they are not so regarded in Persian they will not be mentioned here.

[2] مدرسه is usually pronounced *madrese* in Persian.

This form is used to denote the abstract idea of the thing as distinguished from the concrete thing itself; and also to represent the thing or things signified by the primitive noun as a whole or totality, e.g.

إِنْسَانِيَّة  humanity (in Persian انسانیت *ensaniyat*; إِنْسَان human being).

نَصْرَانِيَّة  what constitutes being a Christian (in Persian نصرانیت *nasraniyat*; نَصْرَانِى a Christian).

This termination is occasionally added to Persian nouns, e.g.

خریت  *xariyat* stupidity (from خر *xar* ass, donkey).

This form is also occasionally used in Persian to denote a dynasty; in this case the ة becomes the 'silent' *h*, e.g.

قاجاریه  *qajariye*, the Qajar Dynasty.

صفویه  *safaviye*, the Safavid Dynasty.

14. Diminutives are formed on the measure فُعَيْل, e.g.

طُفَيْل  a little child (from طِفْل child).[1]

حُسَيْن  Hosein (diminutive of Hasan).

If the noun has a feminine ending this is attached to the diminutive, e.g.

قُلَيْعَة  a small fortress (from قَلْعَة).

15. Adjectives are formed on a variety of measures. Among them are:

(a) فَعِيل e.g.

شَرِيف  noble.            مَرِيض  sick.

When derived from transitive verbs this form has a passive meaning, e.g.

أَسِير  captive.

(b) فَعْلَان, fem. فَعْلَى, e.g.

سَكْرَان  drunk (m.); سَكْرَى (f.).

(c) فَعْل e.g.

صَعْب  difficult.

[1] طُفَيْل *tofeil* is used in Persian to mean 'parasite'.

(d) فَعَل .e.g

حَسَن  beautiful.

(e) the following forms intensive in meaning:

فُعُول .e.g

صَبُور  (very) patient (in Persian usually pronounced *sabur*).

جَهُول  (very) ignorant (in Persian usually pronounced *jahul*).

فَعَّال .e.g

عَلَّام  very learned.          فَعَّال  very active.

فَعِيل .e.g

صَدِّيق  very sincere.

فُعُّول .e.g

قُدُّوس  very holy.

16. The Elative is formed on the measure أَفْعَل, fem. فُعْلَى,[1] e.g.

اَكْبَر  greater, greatest (m.) (from كَبِير great).

كُبْرَى  greater, greatest (f.).

The Arabic elative is used in Persian as an adjective and follows the noun it qualifies, e.g.

پسر ارشد  *pesare arſad*, the eldest son.

It can also be used as a noun, e.g.

اشرف انبیا  *aſrafe ambia*, the most illustrious of prophets.

The elative اعلى *a'la* is also used to mean 'excellent, first-rate' as well as 'the highest', e.g.

کشمش اعلى در ایران پیدا میشود  *keſmeſe a'la dar iran peida miſavad*, Excellent raisins are found in Persia.

---

[1] The Persian comparative and superlative endings are sometimes added to an Arabic elative, e.g. اوَّلَى (from اوَّل 'first') and اوَّلَى تر ‎ *aulatar*, better, superior.

17. Adjectives denoting a colour or physical defect are also formed on the measure أَفْعَل. The feminine is formed on the measure فَعْلَاء; the alternate form فُعْلَى is rare, e.g.

أَصْفَر   yellow (m.).                صَفْرَاء  (f.).

18. Relative Adjectives are formed by the addition of ى to the noun. In Arabic this ى has a *taſdid*, but in Persian it becomes *i*, e.g.

دِمَشْقِى   an inhabitant of Damascus or person born in Damascus

(دِمَشْق).

Certain nouns to which this ى is added undergo various changes:

(a) The feminine ending ة is omitted, e.g.

حَقِيقِى   real, true (from حَقِيقَة truth, reality).

طَبِيعِى   natural (from طَبِيعَة nature).

صِنَاعِى   industrial (from صِنَاعَة industry).

(b) The feminine termination ى (or ا) of the form فُعْلَى is omitted or changed into و, e.g.

دُنْيَوِى   worldly (from دُنْيَا = world, fem. of the elative أَدْنَى lower, lowest).

(c) The termination ة falls away if the word ends in ية, e.g.

إِسْكَنْدَرِى   a native of Alexandria (from إِسْكَنْدَرِيَّة).

(d) If the final radical is a ى, و or *alef hamꝫe*, this is changed into و, e.g.

مَعْنَوِى   spiritual (from مَعْنَى meaning).

عَلَوِى   an Alid (from عَلِى Ali).

سَمَاوِى   heavenly (from سَمَاء heaven).

(e) If the noun contains more than four letters (radicals together with servile letters), the final being ى, the latter is omitted, e.g.

مُصْطَفَى   pertaining to the chosen (from مُصْطَفَى chosen).

(ƒ) Certain words such as اَب 'father' and اَخ brother are defective, having lost the final weak radical. In the adjectival form this reappears as و, e.g.

اَبَوی   paternal.[1]                  اَخَوی   fraternal.[2]

Cf. also لُغَوی   dialectical (from لُغَة, Pers. لغت word, dialect).

19. Certain nouns form relative adjectives in ‍انی, e.g.

جِسْمانی   bodily, corporeal (from جِسْم body).

رُوْحانی   spiritual (from رُوح spirit).[3]

برنامه دولت

برنامه دولت که در مجلس شورای ملی مورد مذاکره قرار گرفت از این قرار است — (۱) در سیاست خارجی دولت با رعایت کامل مصالح کشور مقتضی میداند با دولتهائیکه منافع ایران با منافع آنها ارتباط دارد همکاری نزدیك داشته باشد — (۲) اصلاح و رفع نقصهای قوانین دادگستری برای تکمیل امنیت قضائی و نیز تجدید نظر در قوانین دیگریکه با مقتضیات امروز وفق نمیدهد — (۳) تجدید نظر در سازمان قوای تأمینیه و تکمیل وسائل امنیت — (٤) اهتمام مخصوصی در تأمین خواروبار لازم برای کشور — (٥) تجدید نظر در قوانین استخدام کارمندان دولت — (٦) اصلاح در امور اقتصادی و مالی کشور از قبیل تعدیل مالیاتها برای تخفیف تحمیلات مالیاتی و جلوگیری از هزینههائیکه مقتضای اوضاع کنونی کشور نیست در موقع تهیه بودجه سال آینده تجدید نظر در مقررات بازرگانی و الغای انحصارهای غیر ضروری که تاکنون ملغی نشده است و اهتمام در پائین آوردن قیمت زندگی — (۷) توجه مخصوص بپیشرفت کار کشاورزی و بهبود زندگی کشاورزان و توسعه امور آبیاری منع تدریجی کشت و استعمال تریاك تجدید نظر در قوانین عمران و اجرای برنامه کشاورزی — (۸) ترقی و تکمیل صنایع بقدر امکان با تمایل باین که کارخانهها بدست افراد شرکتهای غیر دولتی اداره شود و اهتمام در بهبود زندگی کارگران — (۹) تکمیل

[1] Used in Persian to mean 'father'.        [2] Used in Persian to mean 'brother'.
[3] Also pronounced *rūhānī* in Persian.

راه‌ها و راه‌آهن در حدود استطاعت کشور— (۱۰) اصلاح قانون تقسیمات کشور
و توجه باینکه اهالی در اداره امور محلی خود شرکت داشته باشند —
(۱۱) تکمیل و ترقی تأسیسات فرهنگی و اهتمام در اصلاح اخلاق عمومی —
(۱۲) توسعه سازمان بهداری و توجه مخصوص بهداشت عمومی

## آمیزش زبانها[۱]

در عالم هیچ زبانی نیست که بتواند از آمیختگی با زبان دیگر خود را برکنار
دارد مگر زبان مردمی که هرگز با مردم دیگر آمیزش نکنند و این نیز محال است
چه بوسیله تجارت و سفر و معاشرت و حتی بوسیله شنیدن افسانه‌ها و روایات ملل
دیگر لغاتی از آن مردم در این مردم نفوذ میکند و همه زبانهای عالم از این رو
دارای لغتهای دخیل است باید دید از آمیختن زبانی با زبان دیگر چه نتایجی
حاصل می‌شود آمیختن زبانها بر چند قسم است یکی اینکه زبانی هر چه را ندارد
بالطبع از همسایه یا جای دورتر بستاند و ملایم بلهجه و سلیقه خویش نماید
یعنی آن لغت را فرو برده و نشخوار کرده و قابل هضم سازد و از حالات و
اختصاصات اصلی آنرا بیندازد و حتی بمیل خود آنرا گاهی قلب کند گاهی
تصحیف کند گاهی مفهوم آنرا تغییر دهد اگر جامد است مشتق کند و اگر
مشتق است جامد کند الی آخر چنانکه عربان بلغات بیگانه همین کار را کرده و
میکنند و ماهم با برخی از لغات عربی و لغات ترکی و فرنگی این عمل را نموده‌ایم ولی
این کار در میان ما عمومیت نداشته است

[۱] سبک شناسی تألیف محمد تقی بهار (ملک الشعرا)

## EXERCISE 28

1. What changes we make in our plans will be announced later.
2. The enemy devastated the country as they retreated. 3. You ought
to have told me instead of I you. 4. The more money he makes the
more he wants. 5. So long as the nation retains its vigour its language
never grows old. 6. I doubt whether he was there. 7. I do not know
whether he (his condition) is better or worse. 8. I asked him whether he
would come himself or send a substitute. 9. Little did she foresee what
a difference this would make. 10. I insist upon it that he should go.
11. I came as soon as I heard of it. 12. I shall come as soon as ever I can.
13. When your work is done let me know. 14. I shall be ready by the
time you get back.

## LESSON XVII

### Doubled Verbs. Hamzated Verbs.

1. In Lesson XV an example of the 'sound' Triliteral Verb was given. Certain additional rules have to be borne in mind in the formation of the derived forms of 'doubled' verbs, i.e. verbs whose second and third radical is the same, 'hamzated' verbs, i.e. verbs one of whose radicals is a *ham₂e*, and 'weak' verbs, i.e. verbs one of whose radicals is و or ي.

2. The following rules will enable the reader to find the Verbal Nouns and Participles of 'doubled' verbs and their derived forms.

(*a*) If the first and third radicals are vowelled, the second radical rejects its vowel (unless it is itself doubled), unites with the third and forms a doubled letter.

(*b*) If the first radical is vowelless and the third vowelled, the second radical gives up its vowel to the first, combines with the third and forms a doubled letter.

(*c*) When the second radical is separated from the third by a long vowel no contraction takes place.

مَدَّ to stretch out

| Form | 3rd pers. sing. masc. Perfect Active | Active Participle | Passive Participle | Verbal Noun |
|---|---|---|---|---|
| I | مَدَّ | مَادّ | مَمْدُود | مَدّ |
| II | مَدَّد | مُمَدِّد | مُمَدَّد | تَمْدِيد |
| III | مَادّ | مُمَادّ | مُمَادّ | مِدَاد |
| IV | أَمَدّ | مُمِدّ | مُمَدّ | إِمْدَاد |
| V | تَمَدَّد | مُتَمَدِّد | مُتَمَدَّد | تَمَدُّد |
| VI | تَمَادّ | مُتَمَادّ | مُتَمَادّ | (تَمَادّ or) تَمَادُد |
| VII | إِنْفَلّ¹ | منفَلّ | | إِنْفِلَال |
| VIII | إِمْتَدّ | ممتَدّ | | إِمْتِدَاد |
| IX | Seldom occurs | — | — | — |
| X | إِسْتَمَدّ | مُسْتَمِدّ | مُسْتَمَدّ | إِسْتِمْدَاد |

¹ إِنْفَلّ to be notched (a sword), broken (a tooth). The VII form of مَدَّ does not occur.

3. The following rules, in conjunction with those given in the Introduction to Part II for the writing of *hamẓe*, will enable the reader to form
the Verbal Nouns and Participles of 'hamzated' verbs and their derived
forms. It should be remembered that the *hamẓe* is a consonant and like
other consonants may be vowelled or vowelless.

(*a*) If a *hamẓe* with *a* is prefixed, as in the IV form, to the first
radical and this is a *hamẓe*, the two come together and are written آ.

(*b*) If a *hamẓe* with *e* or *o* is prefixed to the first radical and this is
a *hamẓe*, the *hamẓe* of the radical is changed to ى (*i*) or و (*u*) respectively.
Exceptionally the VIII form of أَخَذَ 'to take' is اتَّخَذَ.

(*c*) The Verbal Noun of the II form is formed on the measure تَفْعِلَة
if the third radical is a *hamẓe*.

| Form | 3rd pers. sing. masc. Perfect Active | Active Participle | Passive Participle | Verbal Noun |
|------|------|------|------|------|
| I | أَسَرَ[1] | آسِر | مَأْسُور | أَسْر |
| II | أَثَّرَ[2] | مُؤَثِّر | مُؤَثَّر | تَأْثِير |
| III | آثَرَ | مُوَائِر | مُوَائَر | إِثَار |
| IV | آثَرَ | مُؤْثِر | مُؤْثَر | إِيثَار |
| V | تَأَثَّر | مُتَأَثِّر | مُتَأَثَّر | تَأَثُّر |
| VI | تَآثَرَ (or تَوَائَر) | مُتَآثِر | مُتَآثَر | تَآثُر (or تَوَائُر). |
| VII | Does not occur | — | — | — |
| VIII | ايْتَثَر | مُوتَثِر | مُوتَثَر | ايتَثَار |
| IX | Does not occur | — | — | — |
| X | اسْتَأْثَر | مُسْتَأْثِر | مُسْتَأْثَر | اسْتِئْثَار |

[1] أَسَرَ to take captive, bind.          [2] أَثَرَ to leave a trace.

| Form | 3rd pers. sing. masc. Perfect Active | Active Participle | Passive Participle | Verbal Noun |
|------|------|------|------|------|
| I | سَأَلَ¹ | سَائِل | مَسْؤُول | سُؤَال |
| II | لَأَّمَ² | مُلَئِّم | مُلَأَّم | تَلْئِيم |
| III | لَاءَمَ | مُلَائِم | مُلَاءَم | مُلَاءَمَة |
| IV | أَلْأَمَ | مُلْئِم | مُلْأَم | إِلْآم |
| V | تَلَأَّم | مُتَلَئِّم | مُتَلَأَّم | تَلَؤُّم |
| VI | تَلَاءَم | مُتَلَائِم | مُتَلَاءَم | تَلَاؤُم |
| VII | اِنْجَأَث³ | مُنْجَئِث | مُنْجَأَث | اِنْجِئَاث |
| VIII | اِلْتَأَم | مُلْتَئِم | مُلْتَأَم | اِلْتِئَام |
| IX | Does not occur | — | — | — |
| X | اِسْتَلْأَم | مُسْتَلْئِم | مُسْتَلْأَم | اِسْتِلْآم |
| I | دَنُوَ⁶, خَطِئَ⁵, بَرَأَ⁴ | بَارِئ | مَبْرُوء | بُرْء |
| II | بَرَّأَ | مُبَرِّئ | مُبَرَّأ | تَبْرِئَة |
| III | بَارَأَ | مُبَارِئ | مُبَارَأ | مُبَارَأَة |
| IV | أَبْرَأَ | مُبْرِئ | مُبْرَأ | إِبْرَاء |
| V | تَبَرَّأَ | مُتَبَرِّئ | مُتَبَرَّأ | تَبَرُّؤ |

¹ سَأَلَ to ask.

² لَأَّمَ to dress (a wound); to solder.

³ اِنْجَأَث to be split (a tree).

⁴ بَرَأَ to create.

⁵ خَطِئَ to fail, make a mistake.

⁶ دَنُوَ to be mean.

| Form | 3rd pers. sing. masc. Perfect Active | Active Participle | Passive Participle | Verbal Noun |
|---|---|---|---|---|
| VI | تَبَارَأَ | مُتَبَارِئ | مُتَبَارَأ | تَبَارُؤ |
| VII | اِنْسَبَأَ[1] | مُنْسَبِئ | مُنْسَبَأ | اِنْسِبَاء |
| VIII | اِهْتَنَأَ[2] | مُهْتَنِئ | مُهْتَنَأ | اِهْتِنَاء |
| IX | Does not occur | — | — | — |
| X | اِسْتَبْرَأَ | مُسْتَبْرِئ | مُسْتَبْرَأ | اِسْتِبْرَاء |

## بهداری راه آهن

در کارهای ساختمانی مانند هر نوع کار بزرگ و کوچک دیگر بهداشت و تندرستی کارگران را از آغاز باید مورد توجه قرار داد هی از آزمایشهای بسیار دانسته‌اند چنانچه تمام اسباب و افزار کار فراهم گردد ولی مهندس و استاد و ناظر و سر عمله و عمله ناتوان و رنجور باشند کاری از پیش نمیرود از همین جهت در پیشرفتهای ساختمانی مسئله بهداشت کارگران یکی از عوامل مؤثر کار بشمار میاید سازمانهای بزرگ ساختمانی که در شهر بکار مشغولند شاید چندان نیازمند بنگاه‌های بهداری نباشند چه بنگاه‌های بهداری شهرداریها و غیره مراقب تندرستی مردم شهرنشین میباشند ولی کارگرانیکه در راه‌ها و نقاط دور از آبادی براه سازی مشغولند بدوا و درمان دسترسی ندارند باین جهت چنانچه در بهداشت این قبیل کارگران اندکی مسامحه شود پیشرفت کارها از نظم بیرون شده و تندرستی هزاران تن بمخاطره خواهد افتاد اداره بهداری ساختمان راه آهن که برای آسایش کارگران راه آهن تأسیس شده ضامن تندرستی آنهاست سازمان این اداره در تمام راه‌ها بلستیاری شعب مخصوصی که برای حفظ تندرستی کارگران دارد از سه راه اقدام مینماید (۱) تدابیر احتیاطی برای جلوگیری از سرایت بیماریهای مسری (۲) مداوای کارگران بیمار (۳) کمک بآسیب دیدگان چون مقاطعه کاران ساختمانی بنابر مفاد تعهدات خود موظفند خانه و آب مشروب و خواربار کارگران را مطابق اصول بهداشت آماده سازند اداره بهداری برای حفظ کارگران از بیماریهای

[1] اِنْسَبَأَ to be flayed.　　　[2] اِهْتَنَأَ to administer carefully.

واگیری انجام شدن تعهداترا مراقبت نموده و بوسیله مأمورین و بازرسهای فنی رسیدگی لازم و بموقع بعمل میاورد بعلاوه هنگام ضرورت بکارگرانیکه در نزدیکی نقاط بیماریهای مسری مشغول کار هستند مایه ضد بیماری تلقیح نموده و بوسیله پخش کننده در تهیه موجبات تندرستی آنان اقدام مینماید

## علم ادب ۱

موضوع علم ادب کلام منظوم و منثور و بعبارت دیگر سخنان پیوسته و پراکنده است که در این علم از آنها بحث کنند غرض از علم ادب آن است که سخنان پیوسته و پراکنده در هر رشته که باشد با رعایت اصول فصاحت و بلاغت انشاء شده و مطابق روش سخنسنجان و دانشمندان ترکیب یابد و پایه نثر و نظم دبیر یا شاعر بجائی رسد که عقلرا از آن لذت و اهتزاز دست دهد و دلرا فرح و گشایش حاصل گردد فائده علم ادب آن است که مردرا از لغزش نادانی نگاه دارد و درشتی طبیعترا هموار سازد و اخلاقرا روشنی و پاکیزگی بخشد و حس فتوت و مردانگیرا بر انگیزد و همت مردرا بسوی کسب افتخار براند و بکارهای نیك و مقاصد بزرگ ارشاد و رهنمونی کند چه مرد ادیب ناگزیر باشد که در آثار بزرگان و استادان و سخنان حکیمان و دانشمندان بر رسی و کنجکاوی فراوان کند و از هر خرمنی خوشهای بر دارد پس از هر سخنی پندی فرا گیرد و از هر نکته سودی بدست آورد و چون چنین کند ناچار از آنچه فرا گرفته است در نفس وی نقشی باز ماند و در خاطر وی نشاط و گشایشی پدیدار گردد و در خویهای وی تهذیب و تأثیری بسزا متمکن شود

۱ آئین نگارش تالیف حسین سمیعی (ادیب السلطنه)

## EXERCISE 29

1. I visit him as often as I can. 2. As he grew richer he grew more ambitious (he had more ambition). 3. In proportion as the writer's aim comes to be the transcribing, not of the world of mere fact, but of his sense of it, he becomes an artist, his work fine art. 4. His efforts were so far successful (successful up to this limit) as they reduced the number of those suffering from infectious diseases. 5. This proposal, so far as it interests the general public, is well known. 6. Run there as fast as you can. 7. He was not so cross as he had the right to be (as was his right). 8. It is better that ten criminals should escape than that one

innocent man should be hanged.   9. She is better than when I last wrote
to you.   10. The English love their liberty even more than their kings.
11. He dared not stir lest he should be seen.   12. Of course, if I were
rich, I would travel.   13. We should have arrived sooner but that we
had a collision.


# LESSON XVIII

### Weak Verbs. Assimilated Verbs. Hollow Verbs. Defective Verbs.

1. 'Weak' verbs can be divided into three classes: 'Assimilated' verbs,
i.e. those the first radical of which is و or ى, 'Hollow' verbs, i.e. those
the second radical of which is و or ى, and 'Defective' verbs, i.e. those
the third radical of which is و or ى.

2. The following changes are undergone by a verb the first radical
of which is و:

(a) If the first radical is vowelless and preceded by e, the و of the
first radical is changed into ى; thus the Verbal Noun of the IV form of
وَجَدَ 'to find' is إيجَاد and the Verbal Noun of the X form of وَجَبَ 'to
become binding, obligatory' is اِسْتِيجَاب.

(b) If the first radical is vowelless and preceded by o, the و of the
first radical is assimilated to the o and becomes u.

(c) In the VIII form the و is assimilated to the inserted ت. The
Verbal Noun of the VIII form of وَصَلَ 'to arrive' is thus اِتِّصَال and the
Active Participle مُتَّصِل.

3. The following changes are undergone by a verb the first radical
of which is ى:

(a) If the first radical is vowelless and follows o, it is changed into u;
thus the Active Participle of the IV form of يَسَرَ 'to become gentle,
tractable' is مُوسِر.

(b) In the VIII form the ى is assimilated to the inserted ت; thus the
Verbal Noun of the VIII form of يَسَرَ is اِتِّسَار and the Active Participle
مُتَّسِر.

4. The 3rd pers. sing. masc. past tense of 'Hollow' verbs is usually written with *alef* as the medial letter. This *alef* may represent a radical و or ي.

(*a*) The forms II, III, V, VI and IX are conjugated like the strong verb. In the remaining forms

(*b*) If the و or ي is vowelled and the first radical is vowelless the vowel of the و or ي is given to the first radical and becomes *a* or *i* respectively.

(*c*) If the first and third radicals are vowelled, the former with an *a*, this with the radical و or ي becomes ا *a*.

(*d*) If the first and third radicals are vowelled, the former with an *o*, this with the radical و or ي becomes ي *i*.

(*e*) The Verbal Nouns of the IV and X forms drop the second radical and add ة after the third radical.

(*f*) In the Active Participle of the I form the و or ي is changed to *hamze*.

(*g*) In the Passive Participle of the I form, if the second radical is و, one of the two و's is usually dropped.

(*h*) In the Passive Participle of the I form, if the second radical is ي, the و is usually dropped.

(*i*) 'Hollow' verbs denoting colours and physical defects retain the و or ي in the IX form.

قَالَ to speak;          سَارَ to go, travel

| Form | 3rd pers. sing. masc. Perfect Active | Active Participle | Passive Participle | Verbal Noun |
|------|------|------|------|------|
| I | سَارَ ;قَالَ | سَائِر ;قَائِل | مَبِيع[1] ;مَقُول | سَيْر ;قَوْل |
| II | سَيَّرَ ;قَوَّلَ | مُسَيِّر ;مُقَوِّل | مُسَيَّر ;مُقَوَّل | تَسْيِير ;تَقْوِيل |
| III | سَايَرَ ;قَاوَلَ | مُسَايِر ;مُقَاوِل | مُسَايَر ;مُقَاوَل | مُسَايَرَة ;مُقَاوَلَة |
| IV | أَقَالَ | مُقِيل | مُقَال | إِقَالَة |
| V | تَسَيَّرَ ;تَقَوَّلَ | مُتَسَيِّر ;مُتَقَوِّل | مُتَسَيَّر ;مُتَقَوَّل | تَسَيُّر ;تَقَوُّل |

[1] بَاعَ to buy.

| Form | 3rd pers. sing. masc. Perfect Active | Active Participle | Passive Participle | Verbal Noun |
|---|---|---|---|---|
| VI | تَسَايَر ; تَقَاوَل | مُتَسَايِر ; مُتَقَاوِل | مُتَسَايَر ; مُتَقَاوَل | تَسَايُر ; تَقَاوُل |
| VII | انْشَالَ [1] | | مُنْشَال | انْشِيَال |
| VIII | اقْتَالَ | | مُقْتَال | اقْتِيَال |
| IX | ابْيَضَّ [3] ; اسْوَدَّ [2] | | | ابْيِضَاض ; اسْوِدَاد |
| X | اسْتَقَامَ [4] | مُسْتَقِيم | مُسْتَقَام | اسْتِقَام |

5. The following rules will enable the reader to find the Verbal Nouns and Participles of 'Defective' verbs and their derived forms. In the Infinitive the final radical is sometimes written ا, which represents an original ى.

(a) If the second and third radicals are vowelled with an *a* and no letter is added after the last radical, this combination is reduced to ا (-*a*).

(b) If the second radical is vowelled with an *e* and the third is ى and vowelled with an *a* and no letter is added after the last radical this combination becomes ـَى.

(c) In the derived forms the third radical of 'Defective' verbs always appears as ى.

(d) In the Active Participles the final ى or ى unites with *tanvin* and is written ـً. If the article precedes the Participle the final radical reappears as ى; this is also the case with the Verbal Nouns of the V and VI forms.

(e) In the Passive Participles the third radical appears as ى and the *tanvin* is written ـً over the medial radical, e.g. مُنْقَضًى *monqaẓan*. In Persian this is written مُنْقَضَى *monqaẓa*, i.e. the form used in Arabic with the article.

(*f*) In the Passive Participle of the I form, if the third radical is ى, the ى of the third radical and the inserted ى coalesce and are written with a *tafdid*.

| | | | |
|---|---|---|---|
| [1] انْشَالَ | to be lifted. | [2] اسْوَدَّ | to be black. |
| [3] ابْيَضَّ | to be white. | [4] اسْتَقَامَ | to be straight; to rise. |

(g) In the Passive Participle of the I form, if the third radical is ى, the و of the Participle form is changed into ى and assimilated to the ى of the radical.

(h) The Verbal Noun of the II form is on the measure تَفْعِلَة.

(i) In the Verbal Nouns of the IV, VII, VIII and X forms, where the third radical follows ١ (a), the ى is changed into a *hamʒe*, which is written without a bearer.

(j) In the Verbal Nouns of the V and VI forms, the final ى is dropped unless the noun is defined by the article.

| Form | 3rd pers. sing. masc. Perfect Active | | Active Participle | Passive Participle | Verbal Noun |
|------|------|------|------|------|------|
| I | نَدَا | to call | نَاد | مَنْدُوّ | نَدْو |
| | رَمَى | to throw | رَام | مَرْمِيّ | رَمْى |
| | رَضِىَ | to be satisfied | رَاضٍ | — | رِضْوَان , رِضاً |
| | | قَضَى to decide | | | |
| II | قَضَّى | | مُقَضٍّ | مُقَضًّى | تَقْضِيَة |
| III | قَاضَى | | مُقَاضٍ | مُقَاضًى | قِضاء , مُقَاضَاة |
| IV | أَقْضَى | | مُقْضٍ | مُقْضًى | إِقْضاء |
| V | تَقَضَّى | | مُتَقَضٍّ | مُتَقَضًّى | تَقَضٍّ |
| VI | تَقَاضَى | | مُتَقَاضٍ | مُتَقَاضًى | تَقَاضٍ |
| VII | إِنْقَضَى | | مُنْقَضٍ | مُنْقَضًى | إِنْقِضاء |
| VIII | إِقْتَضَى | | مُقْتَضٍ | مُقْتَضًى | إِقْتِضاء |
| IX | Wanting | | | | |
| X | إِسْتَقْضَى | | مُسْتَقْضٍ | مُسْتَقْضًى | إِسْتِقْضاء |

6. In Persian the Active Participles and the Verbal Nouns appear in the form which they would have in Arabic if preceded by the article.

7. The final radical of the Verbal Noun of the VI form is usually written ا in Persian, e.g.

تماشا   *tamaʃa* (for تَمَاشِ and اَلتَّمَاشِی) beholding, a spectacle, show.

8. In Persian if the *eʒafe* is added to the Passive Participle of the derived forms of a 'Defective' verb the final ی is changed into ا, e.g.

منتهای کوشش   *montahaye kuʃeʃ*, the utmost effort (for مُنْتَهِی).

## فرهنگ امروز

یکی از مشخصات بر جسته و امتیازهای نمایان فرهنگ امروز وجود آزمایشگاههای مختلف بنگاههای فرهنگیاست در پیش آنچهرا دانشآموزان و دانش جویان رشتههای گوناگون فرا میگرفتند منحصر بهمان نکات و مسائل کتابچههای درسی ویا کتابهای چاپی بود اما اصول و روش فرهنگ امروز با گذشته از این حیث متفاوت و بلکه برتر است که دانشآموزان و دانشجویان آنچهرا در کتابها میخوانند و بذهن میسپارند در آزمایشگاهها طرزکار و روش اعمال آنرا نیز بچشم دیده و میاموزند و این روش تازه راهنمایان اصول آموزش و پرورشرا برآن داشته که حتی در تدریس اصول تاریخ و علم شناسائی ادوار باستانی ملل و اقوام نیز این اصولرا بکار برده و برای اثبات مدعای تاریخی دانشجویانرا بموزهها و خرابههای زیر زمینی بکشانند

## در فن انشاء ¹

اکنون از آنچه بفن انشاء و دبیری اختصاص دارد شمه باز گوئیم و باز نمائیم که انشاء چیست و از آن چه خواهند انشاء در لغت شروع کردن و بوجود آوردنرا گویند و در اصطلاح علمی است که بدان علم راه در یافت معانی و تعبیر از آن معانی بالفاظ و عبارات پسندیده و دلپذیر چنانکه گوارای طبیعت و نزدیک بفهم خواننده و روشن کننده مقصود نویسنده باشد شناخته شود و این فن دبیری بود و دبیر ناچار بفراگرفتن بسی از دانشها نیازمند است و باید که درکار دبیری از فنون گوناگون استفاده کند و یاری جوید چه دبیر سخنسنج همیشه در

¹ آئین نگارش

يك موضوع سخن نراند و بر يك نسق چيز ننويسد بل اختلاف سخن او باندازه
اختلاف مبحث‌ها و موضوعهائى است كه ويرا پيش آيد و ناگزير بايد كه از
هر چيز بهره‌اى بسزا داشته باشد تا بتواند در همه گونه سخنها وارد شود و در
هر باب سخنورى كند نحو صرف منطق معانى بيان بديع تاريخ قصص لغت
امثال اخلاق رجال انساب محاضرات و بسى ديگر از اين گونه دانشها همه از
عوامل علم ادب و بويژه از اسباب و ابزار فن ديرى شمرده شده و دير و نگارنده
از آموختن آنها ناگزير باشد و بى اين دانشها و آگاهيها بهنر نگارش
دست يافته در هر باره كه خواهد چيز نويسد چون غرض من از تمهيد اين
مجموعه گفتگو و بررسى در علم ادب و اصول و فروع آن نيست و تنها ببخشى
از آن كه ديرى و انشاء است ميپردازم در باره دانشهاى نامبرده و ارتباط آنها
با علم ادب وارد شرح و تفصيل نميشوم و از آنچه استادان فن در اين باب
نگاشته اند كه كدام يك از علوم جزو اصول ادب است و كدام يك جزو فروع
و تأثير هر يك از آنها در ادبيات بچه اندازه است و مدخليت كدام بيشتر در
ميگذرم و هيمنقدر ميگويم كه از اين اشارات بخوبى ميتوان درجه ارتباط و
پيوستگى علم ادبرا بتمام معارف بشرى بدست آورد و خدمات بزرگيرا كه
بتمام دانشهاى صورى و معنوى انجام ميدهد معلوم داشت

### EXERCISE 30

1. I have stood it as long as I can; my patience is now exhausted.
2. He spends his money as fast as he gets it.   3. Nothing could be more
distasteful to me than that I should have to go.   4. I do not say that
he has been in any way negligent or that he has been dishonest.   5. He is
speaking so loudly that I hear him even from here.   6. He is so badly
injured that he must die.   7. He is so badly injured he will probably die.
8. He is so badly injured that he may die.   9. The crops failed because
it was a dry year.   10. He cannot be tired since he has walked only
a short way.

# LESSON XIX

## Quadriliteral Verbs. The Dual. The Sound Masculine Plural. The Sound Feminine Plural.

1. Quadriliteral Verbs are formed on the measure فَعْلَلَ, e.g.

تَرْجَمَ   to translate

| 3rd pers. sing. masc. Perfect Active | Active Participle | Passive Participle | Verbal Noun |
|---|---|---|---|
| تَرْجَمَ | مُتَرْجِم | مُتَرْجَم | تَرْجَمَة |

There are three derived forms, of which the following two are more commonly found:

| 3rd pers. sing. masc. Perfect Active | Active Participle | Verbal Noun |
|---|---|---|
| تَسَلْطَنَ to become sultan | مُتَسَلْطِن | تَسَلْطُن |
| اِطْمَأَنَّ to be at rest | مُطْمَئِنّ | اِطْمِئْنَان |

2. Arabic has three numbers: singular, dual and plural.

3. The dual is formed by adding the termination اَن in the nominative and اَيْن in the oblique cases, e.g.

| Nom. | مَلِكَان } two kings. | مَلِكَتَان } two queens. |
|---|---|---|
| Gen. and Acc. | مَلِكَيْن | مَلِكَتَيْن |
| Nom. | كَبِيرَان } great (m.) | كَبِيرَتَان } great (f.). |
| Gen. and Acc. | كَبِيرَيْن | كَبِيرَتَيْن |

The dual is occasionally used in Persian, usually in the oblique cases, e.g.

از طرفين   *az tarafēin*, from both sides.

والدين   *valedēin*, parents.

4. The plural is of two kinds: sound and broken.

5. The sound plural masculine of nouns and adjectives is formed by adding ـُونَ in the nominative and ـِنَ in the oblique cases, e.g.

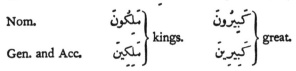

| | | |
|---|---|---|
| Nom. | مَلِكُونَ } kings. | كَبِيرُونَ } great. |
| Gen. and Acc. | مَلِكِينَ | كَبِيرِينَ |

6. The sound plural masculine is used for:

(a) Masculine proper names, except those ending in ة.

(b) Diminutives denoting rational beings.

(c) Participles.

(d) Nouns of the measure فَعَّال (denoting workers in a trade or profession).

(e) Relative Adjectives.

(f) Adjectives of the form أَفْعَل denoting elatives.

7. The sound plural of feminine nouns and adjectives is formed by changing ة[1] into ـَات in the nominative and ـَات in the oblique cases, e.g.

| | | |
|---|---|---|
| Nom. | مَلِكَات } queens. | كَبِيرَات } great. |
| Gen. and Acc. | مَلِكَات | كَبِيرَات |

8. The main types of word for which the sound feminine plural is used are:

(a) Feminine proper names.

(b) Class names ending in ة.

(c) The feminine of adjectives the masculine of which takes the sound masculine plural.

(d) Verbal Nouns of the derived forms.[2]

(e) Diminutives denoting irrational beings and things.

(f) Foreign words.

(g) Certain masculine nouns, e.g.

حَيَوَان animal.          حَيَوَانَات animals.

---

[1] In Persian this may be ت or ه. In either case the plural is ـَات, e.g. ملاحظه *molaheze* 'consideration, view, etc.' pl. ملاحظات *molahezat*.

[2] The Verbal Nouns of the II and IV forms also have Broken Plurals (see Lesson xx).

9. The sound feminine plural is sometimes added to Persian nouns, e.g.

فرمایشات    *farmayefat*, orders, commands.

نگارشات    *negarefat*, writings.

باغات    *bayat*, gardens.

دهات *dehat* (from ده *deh* 'village') is used as a singular to mean 'country (as opposed to town)'.

A plural on the analogy of the sound feminine plural is also sometimes formed from Persian and Arabic words ending in ه -e, this being changed into ج before the termination of the sound feminine plural, e.g.

میوجات    *mivejat*, fruits.

نوشتجات    *nevestejat*, writings.

کارخانجات    *karxanejat*, factories.

روزنامجات    *ruznamejat*, newspapers.

حوالجات    *havalejat*, transfers.

قبالجات    *qabalejat*, title-deeds.

باغ فلاحتی

در دو کیلومتری شهر اهواز در سمت مغرب رود کارون باغ بسیار بزرگی که دارای انواع و اقسام درختهای متناسب با آب و هوای خوزستان است تأسیس و با موتور از کارون برای مشروب ساختن اشجار اقدام بآبیاری آن باغ وسیع نموده‌اند و انواع و اقسام اشجار خرما انار زیتون موز و غیره در آن باغ غرس حتی گیاهها و نهالهای گرمسیری نیز برای نمونه در اراضی زراعتی باغ مزبور کاشته و ملیونها تومان خرج باغ و خرید لوازم و اثاثیه برای کشاورزی و وارد کردن نهال اشجار از خارجه شده است

ملاحظاتی راجع بادبیات در دوره مشروطیت۲

ظهور مشروطیت که فرمان آن در سال ۱۳۲۴ قمری صادر شد نتیجه یك سلسله مقدمات سیاسی و علمی و ادبی بود که شرح و بسط آنرا کتابی جداگانه باید اجمالاً توان گفت که در این دوره ادبیات ایران گذشته از دوام در موضوعات

۲ تاریخ ادبیات ایران تالیف دکتر رضازاده شفق

و طرزهای قدیم تازگیهائی نیز پیدا کرد و ممکن است آنهارا بطریق ذیل تلخیص نمود (۱) زبانهای بیگانه خاصه زبان فرانسوی در ایران که از اوایل دوره قاجاریه شروع بانتشار نموده بود رواج یافت و راه آمدوشد بین ایران و فرنگستان بیشتر از سابق باز شد و تصانیف ادبی آن سرزمین از نظم و نثر و داستان و رمان در این دیار معروف گردید در نتیجه این اختلاط نه تنها عده‌ای از کتب فرنگی بفارسی ترجمه و مقداری لغات فرنگی داخل زبان فارسی شد بلکه برخی نویسندگان جدید در معانی و الفاظ تا حدی سبک و روش و طرز فکر مغرب زمین‌را اقتباس کرده و گاهی در این خط دورتر رفته از شیوه زبان فارسی خارج شدند (۲) از موضوعات تازه‌ای که داخل ادبیات گردید افکار آزادیخواهانه و عقاید اجتماعی و سیاسی و فکر تساوی حقوق سیاسی و مسئله آزادی افکار و حریت مطبوعات و احساسات وطنپرستانه است که الحق در نظم و نثر جلوه خاصی نمود و شعرای توانای خوش قریحه و نویسندگان قابلی ظهور کرده و با بهترین الفاظ بتعبیر این سنخ افکار پرداختند حتی اینگونه افکار بلطف قریحه شاعرانه مانند عارف قزوینی بشکل تصنیف ملی در میان عامه انتشار پیداکرد از شاعران ایندوره میتوان برای نمونه از میان گذشتگان ادیب الممالک فراهانی و ادیب پیشاوری‌را نام برد و از عالم بانوان پروین اعتصامی‌را ذکر کرد و از زندگان آقای محمد تقی بهار (ملک الشعرا)را نامید که در طرز قصیده و تتبعات تاریخی و ادبی استاد است در واقع شاعران و گویندگان و نویسندگان سخنور ادب‌پرور زیادی در عصر ما ظهور کرده‌اند که الحق نظم و نثر فارسی‌را سیرا زنده نگهداشته وآنرا گویاتر و شیواتر نموده و معانی تازه در آن دمیده و خودرا اخلاف صدق صدق بزرگان قدیم نشان داده‌اند (۳) نظم و نثر فارسی از مقام شامخ ادبی قدیم که معمولاً از حیات مردم دور و از ذوق و احتیاجات عامه مهجور بود کمی بپائین آمده و بذهن و زندگی توده نزدیک شده و بر حسب احتیاجات جامعه در مضامین تازگی پیداکرده و بمطالب اجتماعی گرویده است و نویسندگان در ادای این موضوعات بیشتر از زینت الفاظ و استعمال جمله‌های دور و دراز متوجه بادای مطلب و بیان مقصود شده اند

(نا تمام)

## Exercise 31

1. The fault is not mine for the simple reason that I was not present and had nothing to do with the affair.   2. He refused to participate on the ground that he was not interested in the matter.   3. To be sure the present law has not remained in force in as much as the universities contain teachers who have never believed in these principles.   4. You can have it for a few days on condition you return it some time next week.   5. I do not attach any importance to it so long as you are satisfied.   6. Nothing would content him but I must come.   7. He was everywhere except in the right place.   8. I walk every day unless it rains.   9. Foolish though he may be he is kind of heart.   10. We sometimes expect gratitude when we are not entitled to it.   11. However we may assess (judge) the merits or defects of Greek philosophy, it must always form an interesting subject.   12. Whether he succeeds or fails, we shall have to do our part.

## LESSON XX

### Broken Plurals.

1. In addition to the sound plurals, which are used for certain forms only, there are the so-called Broken Plurals, of which there are some thirty measures.  Broken plurals maintain the radicals of the singular in their original order but change the vowel pattern. They may in addition add a consonant at the beginning or end or both. The consonants so used are أ at the beginning and ن, ‍ or ة at the end. The following table gives the plural measures from triliteral roots and the singular measures from which they are derived. Those forms which are more commonly used in Persian are marked with an asterisk.

2. Measures for Broken Plurals from triliteral roots.

\*1. فَعَل from

   \*(a) فُعْلَة        (b) فُعْلَى¹        (c) فَعْلَة

2. فُعَل from

   (a) أَفْعَل²        (b) فَعْلَاء³

---

¹ Feminine of the elative.                    ² Not the elative.

³ The feminine of أَفْعَل, not the elative.

*3. فُعَل from

    (a)* ¹فِعَال      (b)* ²فَعِيل      (c)* ³فَعِيلَة

    (d)* ³فَعُول      (e) فَعْل

*4. فِعَل from

    (a)* فِعْلَة      (b) فَعْلَة

*5. فِعَال from

    (a)* ³فَعْل      (b)* ³فِعْل      (c)* فَعَل

    (d)* ¹فَعَل      (e)* ¹فَعَلَة      (f)* ⁴فَعِيل

    (g) فُعْلَة      (h)* فَعْلَة

*6. فُعُول from

    (a)* فَعْل      (b)* فِعْل      (c)* فُعْل

    (d) فَعَل      (e)* فَعِل      (f)* ²فَاعِل

7. فُعَّل from

    فَاعِل

*8. فُعَّال from

    فَاعِل

9. فَعَلَة from

    ⁵فَاعِل

¹ Not from roots the second radical of which is doubled or the third radical of which is و or ى.

² Not from roots the third radical of which is و or ى.

³ Not from roots the first or second radical of which is ى.

⁴ Verbal adjectives not having a passive significance.

⁵ If it denotes a rational being and the third radical is not و or ى.

*10. فُعَّلَة from

فَاعِل [1]

11. فُعْلَة from

(a) فَعْل     (b) فَعَل     (c) فِعَال

(d) فُعَال     (e) فَعِيل

12. أَفْعُل from

(a) فَعْل     (b) فِعْل     (c) فُعْل

(d) from feminine words which do not end in ة and have a long vowel between the second and third radicals.

*13. أَفْعَال from

*(a) فَعَل [2]     *(b) فُعْل     *(c) فِعْل

(d) فَعَل

*14. أَفْعِلَة from

*(a) فَعَال     *(b) فِعَال     *(c) فَعِيل [3]

(d) فُعَال     *(e) فَعُول

*15. فَوَاعِلُ from

*(a) فَاعِل     *(b) فَاعِلَة

*16. فَعَائِلُ from

feminine nouns which have a long vowel between the second and third radicals.

---

[1] If it denotes a rational being and the third radical is و or ى.

[2] Especially if the first radical is و or the middle radical is و or ى.

[3] Especially adjectives the second radical of which is doubled or the third radical of which is و or ى.

17. فِعْلَان from

    (a) فَعَل     (b) فُعْل¹     (c) فُعَال

    (d) فَعَال     (e) فَعِيل     (f) فَاعَل

18. نُعْلَان from

    (a) فَعَل     (b) فَاعِل²     (c) فُعَال

    (d) أَفْعَل³

*19. فُعَلَاء from

    *(a) فَعِيل⁴     (b) فَاعِل⁴

*20. أَفْعِلَاء from

    فَعِيل⁵

21. فَعْلَى from

    (a) فَعِيل⁶     (b) فَعْلَانُ

22. فَعَالَى from

    (a) فَعْلَاء     (b) فَعْلَى

23. فَعَالَ from

    (a) فُعْلَى⁸     (b) فَعْلَانُ     (c) فَعِيلَة⁹

    (d) فَاعِلَة¹⁰

---

¹ From roots with a medial و.

² When used as a noun, but not from roots with a medial و or ى.

³ Denoting colours and physical defects.

⁴ Denoting male persons, but not words with a doubled second radical or those the third radical of which is و or ى.

⁵ Especially from roots with a doubled second radical or of which the third radical is و or ى.

⁶ Usually with a passive meaning.

⁷ In Arabic فَعَال unless preceded by the article, or in construct.

⁸ Feminine but not of the elative.     ⁹ If the third radical is و or ى.

¹⁰ From words of which the medial radical is و or of which the third radical is و or ى.

24. فُعُولَة from

    (b) فَعَل      (a) فَعْل[1]

25. فَعَالَة from

    (b) فَاعِل      (a) فَعَل

26. فَعَل from

    فَاعِل

Examples:[2]

1. (a) أُمَّت community, أُمَم ; صُورَت face, form, صُوَر ; رُتْبَه rank, رُتَب

    (b) كُبْرَى greatest (f.), كُبَر ; أُخْرَى last (f.), أُخَر

    (c) دَوْلَت state, دُوَل

2. (a) أَزْرَق blue, زُرْق

    (b) زَرْقَاء blue (f.), زُرْق

3. (a) كِتَاب book, كُتُب

    (b) طَرِيق way, road, طُرُق

    (c) مَدِينه city, مُدُن ; صَحِيفه book, page, صُحُف

    (d) رَسُول prophet, رُسُل

    (e) سَقْف roof, سُقُف

4. (a) نِعْمَت bene-ficence, plenty, نِعَم ; مِلَّت people, nation, مِلَل ; حِكْمَت wisdom, حِكَم

    (b) خَيْمه tent, خِيَم

---

[1] When the second radical is doubled.

[2] The customary spelling in Persian is used in the examples, e.g. أُمَّت for أُمَّة, but vocalization has been added.

5. (a) ثِيَاب clothes, ثَوْب ; كِلَاب dog, كَلْب

   (b) رِيَاح wind, ريح

   (c) رِجَال man, رَجُل

   (d) جِبَال mountain, جَبَل

   (e) رِقَاب neck, رَقَبَت

   (f) كِبَار great, كَبِير ; كِرَام generous, كَرِيم

   (g) قِبَاب dome, قُبّه ; رِقَاع piece of paper, رُقْعه

   (h) قِلَاع fortress, قَلْعه

6. (a) قُلُوب heart, قَلْب

   (b) عُلُوم knowledge, science, عِلْم

   (c) بُرُوج tower, sign of the Zodiac, بُرْج ; جُنُود army, militia, جُنْد

   (d) أُسُود lion, أَسَد

   (e) مُلُوك king, مَلِك

   (f) شُهُود witness, شَاهِد

7. حُكّم governor, judge حَاكِم

8. جُهّال ignorant, جَاهِل ; كُتّاب scribe, كَاتِب ; حُكّام governor, judge, حَاكِم ; تُجّار merchant, تَاجِر

9. كَتَبه scribe, كَاتِب ; طَلَبه student (of a school devoted to the study of religious sciences), طَالِب

10. وُلَات governor, وَالِي ; قُضَات judge, قَاضِي

11. (a) ثِيرَت ox, ثَور

 (b) اِخْوَت brother, (for اَخَو) اَخ

 (c) غِزْلَت gazelle, غَزَال

 (d) غِلْمَت slave, غُلَام

 (e) صِبْيَت boy, صَبِى

12. (a) اَنْفُس soul, نَفْس; اَعْيُن eye, عَين; اَبْحُر sea, بَحْر

 (b) اَرْجُل foot, رِجْل

 (c) اَقْفُل lock, قُفْل

 (d) اَيْمُن oath, يَمِين; اَذْرُع arm, ذِرَاع

13. (a) اَيَّام day, يَوْم; اَوْقَات time, وَقْت; اَشْخَاص person, شَخْص

 (b) اَرْوَاح soul, رُوح

 (c) اَجْسَام body, جِسْم; اَطْفَال child, طِفْل

 (d) سَبَب cause, reason, اَسْبَاب goods, chattels; حَال condition, state, اَحْوَال

14. (a) طَعَام food, اَطْعِمه; دَوَاء medicine, اَدْویه drugs, spice; زَمَان time, اَزْمِنه

 (b) سِلَاح weapon, اَسْلِحه; اِمَام imam, اَئِمّه; اِنَاء vessel, vase, آنیه; لِسَان tongue, اَلْسِنه

 (c) دَلِیل proof, اَدِلّه; عَزِیز dear, precious, اَعِزّه; حَبِیب friend, اَحِبّه

 (d) تُرَاب dust, اَتْرِبه

 (e) عَمُود column, اَعْمِده

15. (a) مَوَاحِل shore, سَاحِل ; فَوَارِس rider, فَارِس

(b) عَامّه common, حَوَادث happening, حَادثه ; فَوَاكه fruit, فَاكهه ;
خَوَاصّ noble, خَاصّه (عَوَامّ for) the common people; عَوَامّ
جَارِبه ; نَوَاحِى neighbourhood, نَاحِيه ;(خَوَاصِص) ; (for)
slave-girl (f.), جَوَارِى ; نَادِره rarity, نَوَادِر ; فَائده benefit فَوَائد

16. عَجُوز old woman, عَجَائز ; رِسَاله treatise, letter, رَسَائل ; عَجِيبه
wonder, عَجَائب ; جَزِيره island, جَزَائر ; وَسِيله means, وَسَائل

17. (a) نَار fire, (نَور for) نِيرَان ; أَخ brother, (أَخُو for) اخْوَان ; جَار
neighbour, جِيرَان

(b) حُوت large fish, حِيتَان

(c) غُلَام slave, غلْمَان

(d) غَزَال gazelle, غِزْلَان

(e) صَبِىّ boy, (صبيو for) صبْيَان

(f) حَائط wall, حيطَان

18. (a) بَلَد city, بُلْدَان

(b) شَابّ young man, شُبَّان ; فَارِس rider, فُرْسَان

(c) شُجَاع brave, شُجْعَان

(d) أَعْرَج lame, عُرْجَان

19. (a) وَزِير minister, وُزَرَا ; فَقِير poor, فُقَرَا ; رَئِيس head, chief, رُؤَسَا

(b) شَاعِر poet, شُعَرَا ; عَالِم learned, عُلَمَا

20. صَدِيق friend, أَصْدِقَا; طَبِيب doctor, أَطِبًّا; غَنِي rich, أَغْنِيَا; قَرِيب

وَلِي vicegerent, أَوْلِيَا; نَبِی prophet, أَنْبِيَا; قَرِيب relative, أَقْرِبَا

21. (a) قَتِيـل killed, قَتْلَى; جَرِيح wounded, جَرْحَى; مَيِّت (for مَيِّت) dead, مَوْتَى

(b) كَسْلَى lazy, كَسْلَان

22. (a) صَحْرَا plain, صَحَارَى; عَذْرَا virgin, عَذَارَى

(b) دَعْوَى dispute, claim, دَعَاوَى; فَتْوَى legal decision, فَتَاوَى

23. (a) حُبْلَى pregnant, حَبَالَى

(b) كَسْلَان lazy, كَسَالَى

(c) هَدِيَّه present, gift, هَدَايَا; رَعِيَّت peasant, subject, رَعَايَا; بَلِيَّه calamity, بَلَايَا

(d) زَاوِيه corner, angle, زَوَايَا

24. (a) عَم paternal uncle, عُمُومه

(b) عَلَف fodder, عُلُوفه

25. (a) حَجَر stone, حِجَاره

(b) صَاحِب friend, owner, صِحَابه

26. حَارِس guard, حَرَس; خَادِم servant, خَدَم

3. Broken plurals from quadriliteral roots are formed on the following measures. Nouns formed from triliteral roots by prefixing م, ت or ا form their plurals on the same measures as nouns from quadriliteral roots.

(i) فَعَالِل e.g.*

كَوْكَب star كَوَاكِب

جَوْهَر jewel جَوَاهِر

---

¹ Sometimes pronounced ro'ayā.

مَتَاجِرب ¹ experience (تجربه in Persian) تَجْرِبَة

مَنَازِل stage, resting-place (منزلت in Persian) مَنْزِلَة

مَدَارِس school (مدرسه in Persian) مَدْرَسَة

أَقْرَب nearest   أَقَارِب relations, relatives

أَكَابِر greatest   أَكْبَر

*(ii) فَوَاعِيل and فَعَالِيل from nouns which have a long vowel before the last radical, e.g.

تَصَاوِير picture   تَصْوِير

مَفَاتِيح key   مِفْتَاح

أَرَاجِيف rumour ²   إِرْجَاف

جَوَامِيس buffalo   جَامُوس

قَوَانِين law   قَانُون

دَنَانِير dinar (a coin)   دِينَار

دَوَاوِين divan (a collection of poems, etc.)   دِيوَان

تَوَارِيخ history   تَارِيخ

أَسَاتِيد master, teacher   أُسْتَاد

*(iii) فَعَالِلَة

from (a) relative adjectives, e.g.

أَرْمَنِى Armenian   أَرَامِنَة (in Persian ارامنه)

(b) from certain quadriliteral nouns (especially foreign ones) denoting persons, e.g.

تِلْمِيذ student (of a school where religious sciences are taught)   تَلَامِذَة (in Persian تلامذه).

---

¹ In Persian pronounced *tajarob*.   ² See para. 10 below.

4. In nouns that contain five or more radicals (exclusive of ة and long vowels) one of the radicals is rejected in the plural, generally the last, e.g.

عَنَاكِب spider عَنْكَبُوت

5. From the foregoing paragraphs it will be seen that some words can form their plural on more than one measure. In a few cases the meaning of the plural varies with the measure used, e.g.

عَيْن eye; spring; notable person

أَعْيُن ⎫
عُيُون ⎭ eyes; springs.

أَعْيَان notables.

بَحْر sea; poetical metre

بُحُور metres.

بِحَار ; أَبْحُر seas.

بَيْت house; couplet

بُيُوت houses.

أَبْيَات couplets.

أَمْر affair, command

أُمُور affairs.

أَوَامِر commands.

شَاهِد witness, evident example

شُهُود witnesses.

شَوَاهِد examples.

6. A number of words form their plural irregularly. Among them are:

إِبْن son بَنِى

خَلِيفَة (in Persian خليفه) caliph خُلَفَاء

ضَمِير mind ضَمَائِر

لَيْل night لَيَالِى

أَهْل people أَهَالِى

أَرْض earth أَرَاضِى fields, lands

إِنْسَان man نَاس

أفْوَاه قَم mouth

مِيَاه مَاء water

سَمَاوَات سَمَاء sky, heaven

حَوَائِج حَاجَة need (حاجت in Persian)

A broken plural خوانين xavanin is irregularly formed in Persian from خان xan 'khan' (a courtesy title).

7. A few Arabic broken plurals are used in Persian with a singular meaning, e.g.

عمله (عَمَلَجَات, pl. of عَمَلَة for) workman (pl. of عَامِل).

أرْبَاب (pl. of رَبّ) master; owner of a landed estate (pl. اربابان).

بِلَاد (pl. of بَلَد) country, region.

ادويه (أَدْوِيَجَات for, pl. of أَدْوِيَة) spice (pl. of دَوَاء).

نِيرَان (pl. of نار) fire.

فُتُوح (فُتُوحَات pl. of فَتْح) conquest (pl. of).

8. In addition to the above plurals of plurals, certain Arabic nouns are used with a double plural in Persian, a sound feminine plural being made of the broken plural, or a broken plural of a broken plural, e.g.

جَوْهَر jewel جَوَاهِر        جَوَاهِرَات

بَيْت house بُيُوت        بُيُوتَات = an office in charge of Crown property, etc.

مَكَان place أَمْكِنَة (امكنه in Persian)        أَمَاكِن

لَازِم necessary لَوَازِم necessities        لَوَازِمَات

9. Broken plurals are extensively used in Persian. The Persian plural terminations ان -an and ها -ha are also added to the singular of Arabic nouns to form the plural.

10. Certain Arabic words are used in the plural in Persian but are rare in the singular. Among them are:

مزخرفات    *moʒaxrafat*, nonsense (the singular مزخرف *moʒaxraf* is used only as an adjective 'nonsensical, absurd').

مهملات    *mohmalat*, nonsense (the singular مهمل *mohmal* is used only as an adjective 'absurd').

موهومات    *mōuhumat*, superstition(s) (the singular موهوم *mōuhum* is used only as an adjective 'fanciful, imaginary').

اراجیف    *arajif* (pl. of ارجاف *erjaf*), rumours.

اولاد    *ōulad* (pl. of ولد *valad*), children.

حشرات    *haſarat* (pl. of حَشَرَة), insects.

اسباب    *asbab* means 'utensils, goods, chattels, luggage' in the plural; the singular سبب *sabab* means 'cause'.

حکومت مرکزی

هیچ کشور و هیچ جماعتی اداره نمیشود مگر اینکه نقطه اتکاء مرکزی مقتدری داشته باشد یك معنیٔ امنیت همین است کـه حکومت مرکزی قدرت داشته باشد مفهوم مخالف این اصل نیز مـؤید و مثبت همین اصل است یعنی در هر کشور و هر جماعتی که قدرت مرکزی ضعیف گردد و آن نقطه اتکاء سست و متزلزل شود آن کشور و آن جماعت اداره نمیشود معنی اداره نشدن یك کشور یا زندگی یك جماعت و قوم هرج و مرج و عـدم امنیت است و بزرگترین وظیفه سیاسی هر دولتی در داخلـه حفظ انتظامات است عدالت و دادگستری محض حفظ امنیت است و امنیت باعتبار وجود عدالت دوام و استقرار پیدا میکند

ملاحظاتی راجع بادبیات در دوره مشروطیت

(دنباله از درس پیش)

(٤) احداث مدارس جدید و روزنامه‌ها و مجلات بتوسیع و تعمیم معارف خدمت بزرگ کرده و ادبیات نسبت به عامـه بیشتر مأنوس و در دسترس واقع گشته و توجه بعلم و ادب زیادت گرفته (٥) تمایلی در مـردم و طبقـه دانشمندان و مـؤلفان نسبت بتألیفات علمی و ادبی متقدمان ایران پدید آمـده نیز از طرف وزارت فرهنگ توجهی نسبت بتألیف کتابهای درسی و ترجمه تألیفات علمی

مغرب‌زمین پیدا شده و بخصوص تصحیح و طبع مؤلفات گذشتگان ایرانی در نظم و نثر مورد نظر خاص واقع گشته و مقدار مهمی از نوادر آثار و تصانیف گذشته باهتمام دانشمندان بطرز تصحیح جدیدی بحلیه طبع در آمده و احیا گردیده (٦) درج مطالب علمی و تاریخی بطرز تحقیقی و انتقادی و رجوع باصول و اسناد از روی نظام فکری و تتبع کامل ترق شایانی کرده و در واقع شیوه بعضی مولفان بزرگ اسلامیکه در قدیم نسبت بزمان آنان معمول بود احیا گردیده و در این امر از روش انتقادی دانشمندان مغرب‌زمین نیز استفاده کامل شده است و در حقیقت تالیفات و تحقیقات خاورشناسان مغرب‌زمین از این حیث در نهضت جدید ادبی ایران تاثیر خاص داشته و در میل و رغبت ایرانیان نسبت باحیای آثار گذشتگان نیز در سلیقه و راه و رسم پژوهش مطالب علمی عاملی مهم بوده‌است و توان گفت در میان دانشمندان ایران پیشرو عمده در این فن آقای محمد قزوینی بوده است (v) نهضتی بر ضد عبارت پردازیهای بی‌لزوم و مبالغه‌ها و مضامین و تشبیهات غیرطبیعی و پیچیدهٔ قسمتی از ادبیات قدیم شروع کرده و در این مورد برخی ترک اغلب مضامین و تشبیهات و اسلوب و معانی قدیمرا میخواهند و موضوعهای تازه پیدا میکنند و اوزان و اشکال نو بکار میبرند و در نثر مخالف جمله‌بندی تازی‌منش و استعمال کلمات زیاد عربی هستند و باحیاء شیوه ایرانی و استعمال لغات فارسی اهتمام دارند حتی بعضی دورتر رفته باستعمال جمله‌های فارسی خالص میکوشند در ضمن توان گفت ایندوره از یک لحاظ یعنی بیشتر از لحاظ موضوع و هدف و طرز تعبیرات ادبی دوره تحول و انقلاب است موازین قدیم تا حدی متزلزل شده و اصول جدید هم سر و صورتی کامل پیدا نکرده و ادبیات بطور کلی یک سیر تکامل مینماید در هر صورت برخی گویندگان جدید آثار زیبای دلربائیکه نوید سبک عالیتری را میدهد بوجود آورده‌اند

## EXERCISE 32

1. In spite of his youth he was not only fit to benefit from university education, but carried to the university a literary taste and stock of learning which would have done honour to a graduate. 2. There is not only conciseness in these lines but also elegance. 3. It will be my endeavour to relate the history of the people as well as the history of the government. 4. The wolf is hard and strong and withal one of the cleverest of animals. 5. Take a few of them, say a dozen or so. 6. How strong is the influence which universities and schools together have upon

public opinion, to what an extent their influence dominates the men who
in turn are entrusted with the administration of the country, may be
judged by the following statement.   7. He laughed so much that I could
not help laughing too.   8. Now that he is sick we shall have to do the
work.   9. What can I say but that I hope you will be happy?   10. Society
can have no hold on any class except through the medium of its interests.


# LESSON XXI

Numerals. Pronominal Suffixes. ذو . صاحب. Prepositions.
Adverbs. Conjunctions. Interjections.

1. The cardinal numbers in Arabic are as follows:

| Masculine | Feminine | Numbers | Masculine | Feminine | Numbers |
|---|---|---|---|---|---|
| أَحَدٌ } | إِحْدَى } | | أَحَدَ عَشَرَ | إِحْدَى عَشْرَةَ | 11 |
| وَاحِدٌ } | وَاحِدَةٌ¹ } | 1 | إِثْنَا عَشَرَ | إِثْنَتَا عَشْرَةَ | 12 |
| إِثْنَانِ | إِثْنَتَانِ | 2 | ثَلَاثَةَ عَشَرَ | ثَلَاثَ عَشْرَةَ | 13 |
| ثَلَاثٌ | ثَلَاثَةٌ | 3 | أَرْبَعَةَ عَشَرَ | أَرْبَعَ عَشْرَةَ | 14 |
| أَرْبَعٌ | أَرْبَعَةٌ | 4 | خَمْسَةَ عَشَرَ | خَمْسَ عَشْرَةَ | 15 |
| خَمْسٌ | خَمْسَةٌ | 5 | سِتَّةَ عَشَرَ | سِتَّ عَشْرَةَ | 16 |
| سِتٌّ | سِتَّةٌ² | 6 | سَبْعَةَ عَشَرَ | سَبْعَ عَشْرَةَ | 17 |
| سَبْعٌ | سَبْعَةٌ | 7 | ثَمَانِيَةَ عَشَرَ | ثَمَانِيَ عَشْرَةَ | 18 |
| ثَمَانٍ² | ثَمَانِيَةٌ | 8 | تِسْعَةَ عَشَرَ | تِسْعَ عَشْرَةَ | 19 |
| تِسْعٌ | تِسْعَةٌ | 9 | عِشْرُونَ | | 20 |
| عَشْرٌ | عَشْرَةٌ | 10 | أَحَدٌ وَ عِشْرُونَ | | 21 |

¹ The final *fatha* of the numerals is usually preserved in Persian (and not changed to *e*);
similarly the *kasra* of سِتَّة and تِسْعَة preserves in Persian its Arabic value, i.e. it approximates
to the vowel in the English word 'bit'.

² In Persian ثَمَانِي.

| Masculine & Feminine | Numbers | Masculine & Feminine | Numbers |
|---|---|---|---|
| ثَلَاثُونَ | 30 | مِائَتَان | 200 |
| أَرْبَعُونَ | 40 | ثَلَاثُ مِائَة (مِئَة) | 300 |
| خَمْسُونَ | 50 | أَلْفٌ | 1000 |
| سِتُّونَ | 60 | أَلْفَان | 2000 |
| سَبْعُونَ | 70 | ثَلَاثَةَ آلَاف | 3000 |
| ثَمَانُونَ | 80 | أَحَدَ عَشَرَ أَلْفًا | 11,000 |
| تِسْعُونَ | 90 | مِائَةُ (مِئَةُ) أَلْفٍ | 100,000 |
| مِائَةٌ ؛ مِئَةٌ | 100 | أَلْفُ أَلْفٍ | 1,000,000 |

2. In the case of the cardinals 3–10 Arabic uses the masculine form with a feminine noun and vice versa. The numerals 20–90 are declined as sound plurals. The oblique form is usually used in Persian, e.g.

عِشْرِين   twenty.

3. أَلْفٌ 'thousand' has two plurals آلَاف and أُلُوف; the latter is used for 'thousands' in an indefinite sense.

4. Compound numbers from twenty onwards are formed by joining the units, tens and hundreds by وَ. The largest number is put first, but the units are put before the tens, e.g.

1945.   أَلْفٌ وَ تِسْعُ مِئَةٍ وَ خَمْسَةٌ وَ أَرْبَعُونَ

5. The ordinals are formed from the cardinals on the form فَاعِل except الأَوَّل (m.) 'first' and الأُولَى (f.), e.g.

| ثَانٍ (m.) | ثَانِيَةٌ (f.) | second. |
|---|---|---|
| ثَالِثٌ | ثَالِثَةٌ | third. |
| حَادِىَ عَشَرَ | حَادِيَةَ عَشَرَةَ | eleventh. |

For the higher numbers the cardinals only are used; the ordinals of
the units are joined to the cardinal of the tens to express the compound
ordinals. If defined both parts of compound numbers take the article.

عِشْرُونَ (m. and f.) twentieth.     اَلْعِشْرُونَ the twentieth.

| | | | |
|---|---|---|---|
| حَادٍ وَ عِشْرُونَ (m.) | twenty-first. | اَلْحَادِى وَ ٱلْعِشْرُونَ | the twenty-first. |
| حَادِيَةٌ وَ عِشْرُونَ (f.) | | اَلْحَادِيَةُ وَ ٱلْعِشْرُونَ | |

6. The numeral adverbs 'first, secondly, etc.' are expressed by the
accusative of the ordinals, e.g.

أَوَّلًا first.          ثَانِيًا secondly.          ثَالِثًا thirdly.

These are frequently used in Persian.

7. The denominator of fractions when it lies between 3 and 10
inclusive is formed on the measure فُعْل except 'half' which is نِصْف, e.g.

ثُلْث a third.          رُبْع a quarter.

The plural of fractions is formed on the measure أَفْعَال, e.g.

أَثْلَاث thirds.

The Arabic fractions are used in conjunction with Persian cardinals, e.g.

دو ثلث   do sols, two-thirds.

سه ربع   se rob', three-quarters.

8. The multiplicative adjectives 'twofold, threefold, etc.' are formed on
the measure مُفَعَّل, e.g.

مُثَنَّى (in Persian مُثْنَى) twofold.

مُثَلَّث threefold; a triangle.

مُرَبَّع fourfold, square; a square.

9. Numeral adjectives expressing the number of parts of which anything is made are formed on the measure فُعَالِيّ, e.g.

ثُنَائِيّ    biliteral.

ثُلَاثِيّ    triliteral; three cubits high or long.

رُبَاعِيّ    quadriliteral; four cubits high or long; quatrain.

10. The Arabic Pronominal Suffixes are:

| | | |
|---|---|---|
| 1st pers. sing. ـِى | | pl. نَا |
| 2nd pers. sing. (m.) كَ | dual (m. and f.) كُمَا | pl. (m.) كُم |
| 2nd pers. sing. (f.) كِ | | pl. (f.) كُنّ |
| 3rd pers. sing. (m.) هِ [1] | dual (m. and f.) هُمَا [1] | pl. (m.) هُم [1] |
| 3rd pers. sing. (f.) هَا | | pl. (f.) هُنّ [1] |

e.g.      اِلٰهِى    my God.

مَوْلَانَا [2]    our master, lord.

Occasionally an Arabic Pronominal Suffix is added to a Persian word, e.g.

نور چشمى    *nure cafmi*, light of my eye (=my son).

استادى    *ostadi*, my master.

Note also the following expressions:

عَيْنَهُ himself (from عَيْن 'self, substance') used in Persian to mean 'exactly like', e.g.

شکل برادرم عینه شکل خواهرم است    *fekle baradaram ainaho* [3] *fekle xaharam ast*, My brother's appearance is exactly like my sister's.

این مملکت عینه مملکت ماست    *in mamlakat ainaho* [3] *mamlakate mast*, This country is exactly like our country.

[1] The ʒamme of هِ, هُمَا, هُم and هُنّ is changed after ـِ, ـِى and ـِىٰ into *kasre*.

[2] This is the title usually given to the poet Jalal od-Din Rumi.

[3] See Introduction to Part II, para. 12 for the pronunciation of this word.

مُشَارٌ إِلَيْهِ [1] above mentioned, aforesaid (from أَشَارَ إِلَى to indicate).

مُدَّعَى عَلَيْهِ the defendant in a lawsuit (from اِدَّعَى عَلَى to enter an action against).

11. The word ذو is used with a following noun to denote 'possessed of' the quality indicated by the noun. It is declined as follows:

Nom. sing. m. ذُو  f. ذَات  dual m. ذَوَا  f. ذَوَاتَا  pl. m. ذَوُو  f. ذَوَات

Gen. sing. m. ذى  f. ذَات  dual m. ذَوَىْ  f. ذَوَاتَىْ  pl. m. ذَوِى  f. ذَوَات

Acc. sing. m. ذَا  f. ذَات  dual m. ذَوَىْ  f. ذَوَاتَىْ  pl. m. ذَوِى  f. ذَوَات

An alternative masculine plural is أُلُو or أُولُو (nom.) and أُولِى (gen. and acc.). The first vowel of أُولُو and أُولِى is short. The vowel of ذُو and ذى before the definite article is also short. E.g.

ذُو حَيَاتَيْن  amphibious.

ذى رُوح  animate.

ذى هُوش  intelligent.

ذى نَفْع  interested in (an interested party).

أُولُو الْأَمْر  commanders.

أُولُو الْأَلْبَاب  intelligent, prudent (persons).

12. صَاحِب is also used to mean 'possessed of', e.g.

صاحب مال  sahebmal, rich.

صاحب خانه  sahebxane, owner of the house, landlord.

In the above examples صاحب saheb forms part of a compound. In the following example it does not form part of a compound and takes the ezafe, e.g.

صاحب تأليفات زياد است  sahebe talifate ziad ast, He is the author of many works.

---

[1] The tanvin is in this case pronounced in Persian, i.e. mofaron eleih.

13. اَهْل is used to denote 'capable of, possessed of, belonging to'.
It takes the *ezafe*, e.g.

اهل این کار نیستم    *ahle in kar nistam*, I am not capable of doing
this, I am not prepared to do this.

اهل فن    *ahle fann* ⎫
اهل خبره    *ahle xebre* ⎭ an expert, technician.

اهل کجائید    *ahle koja id*, Where do you come from?

اهل انگلستان هستیم    *ahle englestan hastim*, We are English.

14. Arabic prepositions are of two kinds: separable, i.e. those which
can be written alone except when followed by a pronominal suffix, and
inseparable, i.e. those which consist of one letter which is always attached
to the following word.

   (*a*) Inseparable prepositions:

ب in, by, with, e.g.

بِسْمِ ٱللّٰه    in the name of God (for باسم).

بِٱللّٰه    by God.

و by, e.g.

وَٱللّٰه    by God.

ل for, to, because of, e.g.

لِهٰذَا    therefore (for this).

ل also means 'for the benefit of' (in opposition to عَلَى 'against') and
the phrases بَر لَه and عَلَى) بَر عَلَیْه compounded with the Arabic 3rd pers.
sing. masc. pronominal suffix and the Persian preposition بر *bar*) are used
in Persian to mean 'for' or 'in favour of' and 'against' respectively, and
take the *ezafe*, e.g.

قاضی بر له او حکم داد    *qazi bar lahe u hokm dad*, The judge made an
order in his favour.

کَ like, as, e.g.

کَذَا    such like (like this).

(b) Separable prepositions:

إلَى   until, to, e.g.

إِلَى ٱلآبَد   until eternity.

حَتَّى   up to, as far as, even. In Persian it is used to mean
'even', e.g.

همه آمدند حتى بچه های كوچك   *hame amadand hatta*[1] *baccehaye kucek*,
All came, even the small children.

عَلَى   against, over, e.g.

سَلَام عَلَيكُم   peace (be) upon you.

عَلَى ٱلخُصُوص   especially.

See also (a) above under ل.

عَن   from, instead of, e.g.

رَضِى ٱللهُ عَنهُ   may God be satisfied with him.

عَنقَرِيب   shortly.

فِى   in, e.g.

فِى هٰذِه ٱلسَّنَة   in this year.

مَع   with, e.g.

مَعهٰذَا   in spite of this.

مَعذٰلك   in spite of that (= with that).

مِن   from, e.g.

أَعُوذُ بِٱللهِ مِنَ ٱلشَّرِّ   I take refuge in God from evil.

(c) Nouns or adjectives in the accusative used as prepositions. These
lose the accusative termination in Persian and are used alone or in
conjunction with a Persian preposition. They take the *ezafe* in the same

---

[1] In the phrase حَتَّى ٱلمَقدُور *hattal-maqdur* 'as far as possible' the second vowel of حَتَّى
is short and so always before a *hamzat ol-vasl*. Cf. also عَلَى ٱلخُصُوص *alal-xosus*.

way that Persian prepositions which were originally nouns take the *ezafe*,
unless they are followed by a Persian preposition:

بَعْد    after. This is usually used in conjunction with the Persian
preposition از *az*, e.g.

بعد از او    *ba'd az u*, after him.

بَیْن    between, e.g.

بین من و شما    *beine man o foma*, between me and you.

فی مَا بَیْن and مَا بَیْن are also used to mean 'between'.

تَحْت    under, and its compound درتحت *dar taht*.

عَوَض    (for عِوَض) instead of.

قَریب    near, about.

فَوْق    above.

قَبْل    before. This is used in conjunction with the Persian preposition از *az*, e.g.

قبل از ظهر    *qabl az zohr*, before midday, A.M.

وَرَاء    beyond. This is usually used in conjunction with the Arabic
pronoun مَا 'what', e.g.

مَاوَرَاء طَبِعیَّت    supernatural (what is beyond nature).

مَحْض    for, e.g.

محض خاطر شما    *mahze xatere foma*, for your sake.

مُقَابِل    and its compound در مقابل *dar moqabel*, opposite.

بَابَت    and its compounds در بابت *dar babat* and از بابت *az babat*, on
account of.

جَانِب    at the side of, and its compounds از جانب *az janeb* 'on behalf of'
and بجانب *be janeb* 'towards'.

طَرَف    at, on the side of, beside, and its compounds از طرف *az taraf*
'on behalf of' and بطرف *be taraf* 'towards'.

أطْرَاف    (pl. of طَرَف 'side'), and its compound در اطراف *dar atraf*,
about, around.

غَیْر and its compound غیر از *ɣeir az*, other than.

خارج and its compound خارج از *xarej az*, outside.

دَوْر around, round.

ضِدّ and its compound بر ضد *bar zedd*, against.

خِلاف and its compound بر خلاف *bar xelaf*, against, contrary to.

جِهَت and its compounds بجهت *be jehat* and از جهت *az jehat*, for, on account of.

سُوَی (which becomes in Persian with the *ezafe* سوای *sevaye*), apart from.

Certain Arabic compound prepositions are also used in Persian, e.g.

مِنْ قَبْل before.              مِنْ فَوْق above.

(*d*) The following are compounded with a Persian preposition. They take the *ezafe*:

با وجود    *ba vojud*, in spite of.

بوسیله    *be vasile*  
بواسطه    *be vasete*  } by means of.

از جمله    *az jomle*, from among.

در اثنا(ی)    *dar asna* (*ye*), in the course of (= in the middle of).

در ظرف    *dar zarf*, in the course of (= within the period of).

بمنظور    *be manzur*, with the intention of.

از قرا    *az qarar*, at the rate of, according to.

بقرار    *be qarar*, according to.

بعنوان    *be envan* (with the title of =) as.

بسمت    *be semat* (with the mark of =) as.

بمنزله    *be manzele* (with the rank of =) as.

15. Stress on the prepositions and their compounds listed in paras. 14 (*c*) and (*d*) above conforms to the general tendencies of Persian, i.e. it is carried on the final syllable (excluding the *ezafe*), e.g.

مقابل    *moqa'bel*, opposite.

در اطراف    *dar at'raf*, about.

از جمله    *az jom'le*, from among.

This is also the case with the majority of prepositions in para. 14 (*a*) and (*b*) above, in so far as these carry the stress, but حَتَّى, مَعْهَذا and مَعْذَلك carry the stress on the initial or the final syllable.

16. Arabic adverbs are of two main kinds, inseparable particles, which are not used in Persian, and separate particles and nouns in the nominative or accusative.

(*a*) Separate particles:

بَل usually compounded in Persian with که, thus becoming

بلکه *balke*, but, rather, on the contrary.

بَلَى yes.[1]

فَقَط only.

لا not. This is only used in Persian in compounds, e.g.

بِلا شَرْط unconditionally.

بِلا تَرْدِيد undoubtedly.

لا أَقَلّ at least.

لا بُدّ of necessity.

لا يَنْقَطِع unceasingly (lit. it does not cease).

لَمْ not. This also is only used in compounds, e.g.

لَمْ يَزْرَع uncultivated (lit. he did not sow).

بل *bal* and بلکه *balke* are used after a negative expressed or implied, e.g.

نه تنها فردا (خواهد آمد) بلکه پس‌فردا هم خواهد آمد

*na tanha farda (xahad amad) balke pasfarda ham xahad amad,*
Not only will he come to-morrow, but he will come the day after tomorrow also.

نه فقط ما بلکه همه مردم بر اثر این پیش‌آمد متاسف شدند

*na faqat ma balke hameye mardom bar asare in pifamad mota'assef fodand.*
Not only we but all the people were grieved at this event.

---

[1] In Persian this becomes *bali*; the form بله *bale* is commonly used.

بلکه *balke* is also used after a rhetorical question to mean 'on the contrary', e.g.

اشتباه یعنی چه بلکه فی‌الواقع عمداً این کاررا کرده‌اید

*eftebah ya'ni ce balke fel-vaqe' amdan in karra karde id,*

What do you mean? A mistake? On the contrary, you did it on purpose.

With an affirmative verb بلکه *balke* means 'nay rather', e.g.

این کتاب چهل ریال می‌ارزد بلکه پنجاه ریال

*in ketab cehel rial miarȝad balke panjah rial,*

This book is worth forty *rials*, nay rather fifty *rials*.

In Colloquial Persian بلکه *balke* is sometimes used in the sense of 'perhaps', e.g.

بلکه آمده باشد *balke amade bafad,* Perhaps he has come (after all).

(*b*) Many nouns can be used in the accusative as adverbs, e.g.

| | | | |
|---|---|---|---|
| أَحْيَانًا | perchance, at times. | اتِّفَاقًا | by chance. |
| جَمْعًا | together. | نِسْبَةً | relatively. |
| ٱلْآنَ | immediately, now. | فِعْلًا | at present. |

(*c*) Certain prepositional phrases are also used as adverbs, e.g.

| | | | |
|---|---|---|---|
| فِى ٱلْفَوْرِ [1] | immediately. | حَتَّى ٱلْمَقْدُورِ | as far as possible. |
| بِٱلْآخِرَه (for بِٱلْآخِرَة) | finally, at last. | مِنْ غَيْرِ رَسْم | unofficially. |

17. Stress is carried on the final syllable of the forms given in para. 16 above, except بلکه *balke* which carries it on the initial syllable, e.g.

فقط *fa'qat,* only.

دائماً *da'e'man,* continually.

18. Certain phrases compounded of Arabic and Persian words are used as adverbs, e.g.

بتدریج *be tadrij,* gradually.

Stress in such compounds is carried on the final syllable.

[1] See Introduction to Part II, para. 8 (*d*) for the pronunciation of this word.

19. Among Arabic conjunctions used in Persian are the following:

وَ    and.

إِلَّا    if not, except; and وَإِلَّا and if not, otherwise.

أَمَّا    as for; in Persian it is also used to mean 'but'.

لَكِن    and وَلَكِن and its variants لِيكِن and وَليكِن but.

20. The following phrases compounded of Arabic and Persian words are used as conjunctions:

وقتیکه    *vaqtike*, when.

مادامیکه    *madamike*, as long as (مَا دَامَ as long as it continues).

حالانکه    *halanke*, although, albeit, notwithstanding the fact that.

هر قدرکه    *har qadrke*, even if, however much that.

در صورتیکه    *dar suratike*, in the event that, although; whereas.

هر وقتیکه    *har vaqtike*, whenever.

بمجرد اینکه    *be mojarrade inke*  ⎫
بمحض اینکه    *be mahze inke*  ⎬ as soon as.

قبل از آنکه (اینکه)    *qabl az anke (inke)*, before.[1]

21. Stress is carried on the initial syllable of the forms in para. 19 above, except وَلَكِن and وَليكِن which carry the stress on the second syllable. The forms in para. 20 above carry the stress as follows:

وقتیکه    'vaqtike.

ما دامیکه    ma'damike.

حالانکه    'halanke.

هر قدرکه    'har qadrke.

در صورتیکه    dar su'ratike.

هر وقتیکه    'har vaqtike.

بمجرد اینکه    be mojar'rade inke.

بمحض اینکه    be 'mahze inke.

قبل از اینکه    'qabl az inke.

[1] This is followed by the Present Subjunctive. Cf. پیش از آنکه (اینکه) p. 74.

**22.** Various Arabic phrases are used as interjections. Among them are the following:

| | |
|---|---|
| يَاّللَّه | O God! |
| اَلْحَمْدُ لله | Praise be to God. |
| إِنْ شَاءَ اَللّه | if God wills. |
| مَا شَاءَ اَللّه | what God wills. |
| أَعُوذُ بَاّللَّه | I take refuge in God. |
| اِسْتَغْفِرُ اَللّه | I ask pardon of God. |
| بَارَكَ اَللّه | God bless (you); bravo. |

در صفت دبیر

دبیر باید پیش از همه کار و بیش از همه چیز سعی کند که دارای ملکات
فاضله و خداوند اخلاق ستوده گردد جمال صورترا بکمال معنی آراسته کند و
جامه تقوی و پرهیزکاری بر تن راست نماید و اندام اعتبار را بزیور درستی و امانت
بیاراید و گفتار خودرا با راستی و حقیقت بیامیزد و بفصاحت منطق و صراحت
لهجه زیور بخشد و زبان و قلم از ناشایست پاک دارد و در نگاهداشت رازها
کوشش فراوان بکار برد و اعتماد همگانرا بسوی خود فرا آورد و عنان قلم از
آنچه بر خلاف حقیقت است باز گیرد و کسیرا بدانچه در او نیست نستاید و از
تملق و چاپلوسی که کشنده روح ادب است بگریزد دبیر چون بدین صفتها و
زیورها آراسته باشد هر آینه قدر و بهای او نزد مردم بزرگ شود و جایگاه او در
جامعه بلند گردد و سخن او در گوشها و دلها تأثیری هرچه بیشتر بخشد و باید
دانست که دبیریرا شرایطی چند است که تا آن شرایط در وجود دبیر و
نگارنده جمع نشود نام دبیری بر وی راست نیاید و کار نگارندگیرا از عهده بر
نتواند آمد

ء آئین نگارش تالیف حسین سمیعی (ادیب السلطنه)

## معنی آزادی[۱]

برادران و هم میهنان عزیزم

بحمد الله بفضل خداوند در سایه توجه شاهنشاه جوان جوانبخت بار دیگر پا
بدایرهٔ آزادی گذاشتید و میتوانید از این نعمت بر خوردار شوید البته باید قدر
این نعمترا بدانید و شکر خداوندرا بجا آورید از رنج و محنتی که در ظرف سی
چهل سال گذشته بشما رسیده است امیدوارم تجربه آموخته و عبرت گرفته متوجه
شده باشید که قدر نعمت آزادیرا چگونه باید دانست و معنی آزادیرا در یافته
باشید در این صورت میدانید که معنی آزادی این نیست که مردم خودسر
باشند و هرکس هر چه میخواهد بکند در عین آزادی قیود و حدود لازم است
اگر حدودی در کار نباشد و همه خودسر باشند هیچکس آزاد نخواهد بود و
هرکس از دیگران قویتر باشد آنانرا اسیر و بنده خود خواهد کرد قیود و
حدودی که برای خودسری هست همان است که قانون مینامند پس مردم وقتی
آزاد خواهند بود که قانون در کار باشد و هر کس حدود اختیارات خودرا بداند
و از آن تجاوز نکند پس کشوری که قانون ندارد یا قانون در آن مجری و محترم
نیست مردمش آزاد نخواهند بود و آسوده زیست نخواهند کرد این حقیقتی است
بسیار ساده و روشن و هیچکس منکر آن نمیشود اما متاسفانه کمتر کسی باین
حقیقت ایمان دارد زیرا که غالباً می‌بینیم مردم حدود یعنی قانونرا برای دیگران
لازم میدانند اما رعایتش‌را برای خودشان واجب نمیشمارند اگر هرکس معتقد
بود که رعایت حدود قانون تنها نسبت بدیگران واجب نیست بلکه نسبت بخود
او هم واجب است تخلف از قانون واقع نمیشد و حال آنکه ما هر روز می‌بینیم
بسیاری از اشخاص از قانون تخلف میکنند و کمتر کسی است که متوجه باشد
که اگر من تخلف از قانونرا از طرف خود جائز بدانم دلیلی ندارد که دیگران هم
تخلف از قانونرا از طرف خودشان جائز ندانند در این صورت تخلف از قانون امری
رایج و شایع خواهد بود و همان نتیجه دست میدهد که گفتیم یعنی آسایش از
همه سلب میشود متاسفانه بسیاری از مردم چنین اند که هر وقت بتوانند زور
بکویند میکویند غافل از اینکه اگر بنا بزورگوئی باشد امروز من میتوانم بزیردست
خود زور بگویم اما فردا زبردستی پیدا میشود که بمن زور بگوید پس همین کس

---

[۱] نطق مرحوم آقای فروغی که در روز ۱۵ مهر ماه ۱۳۲۰ در برابر دستگاه
رادیو تهران ایراد و پخش شد

که امروز زور میگوید فردا دوچار زبردست‌تر از خود میشود آنگاه آه و ناله میکنند و باین ترتیب دنیا درست مصداق گفته شیخ سعدی میشود که میفرماید

بری مال مسلمان و چو مالت ببرند

داد و فریاد بر آری که مسلمانی نیست

پس اولین سفارشی که در عالم خیرخواهی و میهن‌دوستی بشما میکنم اینست که متوجه باشید که ملت آزاد آنست که جریان امورش بر وفق قانون باشد و بنا بر این هر کس بقانون بی اعتنائی کند و تخلف از آنرا روا بدارد دشمن آزادی است یعنی دشمن آسایش ملت است یک نکته دیگر هم در این باب میگویم و بمطلب دیگر میپردازم و آن اینست که شما شنوندگان من یقین دارم بسیار شنیده اید که از تمدن و توحش و ملل متمدن و وحشی سخن میگویند آیا درست فکر کرده‌اید که ملت متمدن کدام است و ملت وحشی چیست گمانم اینست که بعضی از شما خواهند گفت ملت متمدن آن است که راه آهن و کارخانه و لشکر و سپاه و تانک و هواپیما و از این قبیل چیزها دارد و ملت وحشی آنست که این چیزها ندارد و یا خواهند گفت ملت متمدن آنست که شهرهایش چنین و چنان باشد خیابانهایش وسیع و اسفالته خانه‌هایش چند اشکوبه باشد و قس علیهذا البته ملل متمدن این چیزها دارند اما من بشما میگویم بدانید که این چیزها فروع تمدنند اصل تمدن نیستند اصل تمدن این است که ملت تربیت داشته باشد و بهترین علامت تربیت داشتن ملت اینست که قانونرا محترم بدارد و رعایت کند اگر این اصل محفوظ باشد آن فروع خود بخود حاصل میشود اما اگر ملتی قانونرا محترم ندارد هر قدر از آن چیزها داشته باشد نمیتوان گفت تربیت دارد و نمیتوان گفت متمدن است آن چیزها هم عاقبت از دستش میرود پس از این مقدمات که گمان میکنم قابل انکار نباشد میپردازیم باصل مطلب و یادآوری میکنم که وجود قانون بسته بدو چیز است یک قانونگذاری و یکی مجری قانون و جمع این دو چیزرا حکومت یا دولت میگویند و چون ملتهای مختلف‌را در زمانهای مختلف در نظر میگیریم میبینیم حکومتهای آنها همه و همیشه یکسان نبوده و نیستند گاهی از اوقات قانونگذاری و مجری قانون یکنفر بوده و گاهی چند نفر معدود و بعضی از ملتها هم بوده و هستند که قانونگذاری و اجرای قانونرا تمام ملت بر عهده گرفته است قسم اول حکومت انفرادی و استبدادی است قسم دوم حکومت خواص و اشراف است و قسم سوم‌را حکومت ملی میگویند که اروپائیان دموکراسی مینامند و هریک از این سه قسم هم

اشکال مختلف داشته و دارد کـه چون مقصود مـن ایـن نیست کـه بشما علم حقوق درس بدهم داخل این بحث نمیشوم و همین قدر میگویم مـلـتـهـا هـرچـه دانـاتـر و برشد و بلوغ نزدیکتر میشوند بقسم سوم یعنی بحکومت ملی متمایلتر میگردند جز اینکه ملتها چون غالباً دارای جعیت فراوان و کشـور پهناورند نمیتوانند هر روز یـک جا جمع شـونـد و وظیـفـه قانونگذاری و اجرای قانونرا خودشان مستقیماً بجا بیاورند بنا براین بهترین ترتیبی کـه پیـدا کرده‌اند این است کـه ملت جماعتی‌را نماینده خود قرار دهد کـه بنام او قانونگذاری کـنـنـد و مجمع آن نمایندگانرا ما مجلس شورای ملی نامیده‌ایم و مجلس هم چند نفررا برای اجرای قانون آختیار میکند کـه هیئت وزیران نامیده میشود و ایـن هر دو جماعت در تحت ریاست عالیه یکنفر هستند کـه اگر او انتخابی بـاشـد رئیس جمهوری نامیده میشود و اگر دائمی و موروثی باشد پادشاه است شما ملت ایران بموجب قانون اساسی کـه تقریباً سی و پنج سال پیش مقرر شده است دارای حکومت ملی پادشاهی هستید اما اگر درست توجه کـنیـد تصدیق خواهید کـرد کـه در مدت این سی و پنج سال کتر وقتی بوده‌است کـه از نعمت آزادی حقیقی یعنی مجری و محترم بـودن قانون بر خـوردار بوده باشید و چندین مرتبه حکومت ملی یعنی اساس مشروطیت شما مختل شـده است آیا آیا فـکـر کرده اید کـه علت آن چیست من برای شما توضیح میکنم علت اصلی این بـوده است کـه قدر این نعمت‌را بدرستی نمیدانستید و بوظایف آن قیام نـمیـکـردیـد و بسیاری از روی نادانی و جماعتی از روی غرض و هـوای نفس از شرایطی کـه در حکومت ملی باید ملحوظ شود تخلف میکردند شرایطی کـه در حکومت ملی باید ملحوظ باشد چیست فراموش نکنید کـه معنی حکومت ملی اینست کـه اختیار امور کشور با ملت باشد و البته میدانید کـه هرکس اختیاراتی دارد در ازای آن اختیارات مسئولیتی متوجه او میشود پس اگر بمقتضای اختیارات خود چنـانـکـه وظیفه وجدانی حکم میکند عمل نکند مسئول واقع میشود و معنی مسئول واقع شدن همیشه این نیست کـه کسی از او سئوال و بـاز خواست کند مسئول واقع شدن غالباً باینست که شخص گرفتار عاقبت وخیم میشود اگر مخلوق نباشد کـه از او بـاز خواست کند خالق از او بازخواست خواهد کرد باز خواست خالقرا هم همیشه بروز قیامت نباید محول نمود غالباً بـاز خواست خالق در همین زندگانی دنیا واقع میشود و شخص جزای عمل خودرا میبیند و چنانکه گفته‌اند

از مکافات عمل غافل مشو

گندم از گندم بروید جو ز جو

اکنون ببینیم اگر ملت در اختیارات خود بمقتضای وظیفه قانونی و وجدانی عمل نکند چگونه مسئول واقع میشود طبقات ملت مختلفند و هر کدام در عمل حکومت ملی وظیفه خاص دارند عامه مردم موظفند که در انتخاب نمایندگان خود برای مجلس شورای ملی اهتمام داشته و نمایندگان صالح انتخاب کنند و پس از انتخاب مراقب رفتار آنان باشند و افکار صالح یعنی عقاید آزادیخواهی یعنی قانونخواهی یعنی میهن‌دوستی نمایش دهند و معتقد باشند که خیر عموم خواستن بر اعمال اغراض شخصی مقدم است و هر فرد از افراد ملت مکلف است شغل و حرفه مشروع آبرومندی مطابق استعداد خود اختیار کند و در انجام آن بکوشد نمایندگان ملت موظفندکه در قانونگذاری و نظارت در اجرای قانون اهتمام ورزند و نمایندگی ملت‌را وسیله پیشرفت اغراض وهوای نفس و جاهطلبی ندانند وظیفه وزیران اینست که خودرا مجری قانون و خدمتگذار ملت بدانند و در پیشنهاد قوانین بمجلس و اجرای آن قوانین همواره خیر و صلاح ملت‌را در نظر داشته باشند وظیفه مستخدمین و کارکنان دولت اینست که در اجرای قوانین از روی صحت و درستی وسیله پیشرفت کار وزیران باشند و موجبات آسایش ابنای نوع خودرا که مخدومین ایشان هستند فراهم آورند وظیفه روزنامه‌نگاران اینست که هادی افکار مردم شوند و ملت و دولت‌را براه خیر دلالت کنند وظیفه پادشاه اینست که حافظ قانون اساسی و ناظر افعال دولت باشد و افراد ملت‌را فرزندان خود بداند و بمقتضای مهر پدری با آنها رفتار کند و گفتار و کردار خودرا سر مشق مردم قرار دهد روی هم رفته وظیفه جمیع طبقات ملت اینست که گفتار و کردار خودرا با اصول شرافت و آبرومندی تطبیق کنند چنانکه یکی از حکمای اروپا گفته است اگر بنیاد حکومت استبدادی بر ترس و بیم است بنیاد حکومت ملی بر شرافت افراد ملت است و مخصوصاً اگر متصدیان امور عامه شرافت‌را در اعمال خود نصب العین خویش نسازند کار حکومت ملی پیشرفت نمیکند و بالاخره جمیع طبقات باید دست بدست یکدیگر داده در پیش بردن حکومت ملی متفق و متحد باشند که بزرگترین آفت حکومت ملی اختلاف کلمه و نفاق است پس اگر افراد ملت فقط ملاحظات و منافع شخصی‌را منظور بدارند و حاضر نشوندکه یک اندازه از اغراض‌جوئی خودرا فدای منافع کلی کنند و از راه صلاح خارج شده بجای اشتغال بامور شرافتمندانه برای پیشرفت اغراض خصوصی وسایل نامناسب از تزویر و نفاق و فتنه و فساد و دسته‌بندی و هوچیگری بکار برند و اگر نمایندگان ملت در قانونگذاری یا اجرای قانون اهتمام

لازم ننمایند و نمایندگی ملترا وسیله تحصیل یا حفظ منافع شخصی بدانند و
عوام فریبی‌را پیشه خود بسازند و دسیسه‌کاری‌را شعار خود کنند یا معنی
نمایندگی ملترا فقط مدعی شدن با دولت بدانند و اگر وزیران وزارترا فقط مایه
تشخیص و جلب منافع شخصی فرض کنند و اگر روزنامه نگاران بجای حقیقت
گوئی و رهبری ملت براه خیر روزنامه‌را آلت هتاکی و پیش بردن اغراض فاسد
قرار دهند و اگر پادشاه حافظ قوانین نباشد وافراد ملترا فرزندان خود نداند
و سلطنترا وسیله اجرای هوای نفس بسازد و اگر طبقات ملت از طریق شرافت
پا بیرون گذارند یا راه اختلاف و نفاق پیش گیرند گذشته از اینکه شخصاً
مسؤل یعنی گرفتار عاقبت وخیم میشوند باید حتم و یقین دانست که باز اوضاع
این سی و پنج سال گذشته تجدید خواهد شد کشور و ملت هر روز گرفتار
مصیبت و فتنه و فساد میشود و نه تنها آزادی تباه خواهد شد بلکه بدار فنا و
نیستی خواهیم رفت و اگر ملت عبرت گرفته باشد و بوظیفه وجدانی خود عمل
کند امیدواری میتوان داشت که روزگار محنت و ذلت سپری شود و دوره شرافت
و سعادت و سرافرازی برسد

# APPENDIX I

## Irregular Verbs.

The following is a list of the main irregular verbs. A few verbs of rare occurrence have been omitted. The verbs have been arranged in alphabetical order. The meanings of the verbs will be found in the vocabulary. Obsolete verbs are put in square brackets.

| Present Stem | | Infinitive | |
|---|---|---|---|
| (ajin) | آجین | (ajidan) | آجیدن |
| (aʒ) | آز | (axtan) | آختن |
| (ara) | آرا | (arastan) | آراستن |
| (aʒar) | آزار | (aʒordan) | آزردن |
| (aʒma) | آزما | (aʒmudan) | آزمودن |
| (asa) | آسا | (asudan) | آسودن |
| (aʃub) | آشوب | (aʃoftan) | آشفتن |
| (aɣar) | آغار | (aɣeʃtan) | آغشتن |
| (oft) | افت | (oftadan) | افتادن |
| (afraʒ) | افراز | (afraxtan) | افراختن |
| (afraʒ) | افراز | (afraʃtan) | افراشتن |
| (afruʒ) | افروز | (afruxtan) | افروختن |
| (afarin) | آفرین | (afaridan) | آفریدن |
| (afʒa) | افزا | (afʒudan) | افزودن |
| (afʃar) | افشار | (afʃordan) | افشردن |
| (agin) | آگین | (agandan) | آگندن |
| (ala) | آلا | (aludan) | آلودن |
| (ama) | آما | (amadan) | آمادن |
| (a) | آ | (amadan) | آمدن |
| (amuʒ) | آموز | (amuxtan) | آموختن |
| (amiʒ) | آمیز | (amixtan) | آمیختن |
| (ambar) | انبار | (ambaʃtan) | انباشتن |
| (andaʒ) | انداز | (andaxtan) | انداختن |

| Present Stem | | Infinitive | |
|---|---|---|---|
| (anduz) | اندوز | (anduxtan) | اندوختن |
| (anda) | اندا | (andudan) | اندودن |
| (engar) | انگار | (engaʃtan) | انگاشتن |
| (angiz) | انگیز | (angixtan) | انگیختن |
| [1](ar) | آر | (avordan, avardan) | آوردن |
| (aviz) | آویز | (avixtan) | آویختن |
| (ahiz) | آهیز | (ahextan) | آهختن |
| (ist) | ایست | (istadan) | ایستادن |
| (baxʃa) | بخشا | (baxʃudan) | بخشودن |
| (bar) | بر | (bordan) | بردن |
| (band) | بند | (bastan) | بستن |
| (baʃ) | باش | (budan) | بودن |
| (biz) | بیز | (bixtan) | بیختن |
| (pala) | پالا | (paludan) | پالودن |
| (paz) | پز | (poxtan) | پختن |
| (pazir) | پذیر | (paziroftan) | پذیرفتن |
| (pardaz) | پرداز | (pardaxtan) | پرداختن |
| (pandar) | پندار | (pandaʃtan) | پنداشتن |
| (pēivand) | پیوند | (pēivastan) | پیوستن |
| (pēima) | پیما | (pēimudan) | پیمودن |
| (taz) | تاز | (taxtan) | تاختن |
| (tab) | تاب | (taftan) | تافتن |
| (tavan) | توان | (tavanestan) | توانستن |
| (jah) | جه | (jastan) | جستن |
| (ju) | جو | (jostan) | جستن |
| (cin) | چین | (cidan) | چیدن |
| (xiz) | خیز | (xastan) | خاستن |
| [(xosb) | خسب | (xoftan) | خفتن] |
| (xah) | خواه | (xastan) | خواستن |

[1] The Present Stem can also be formed regularly, آور avar.

| Present Stem | Infinitive |
|---|---|
| (deh) ده | (dadan) دادن |
| (dar) دار | (daʃtan) داشتن |
| (dan) دان | (danestan) دانستن |
| (duʒ) دوز | (duxtan)¹ دوختن |
| (duʃ) دوش | (duxtan)² دوختن |
| (bin) بین | (didan) دیدن |
| (roba) ربا | (robudan) ربودن |
| (rah) ره | (rastan) رستن |
| (ru) رو | (rostan) رستن |
| (ris) ریس | (reʃtan) رشتن |
| (rav-, rōu) رو | (raftan) رفتن |
| (rub) روب | (roftan) رفتن |
| (ʒan) زن | (ʒadan) زدن |
| (ʒada) زدا | (ʒadudan) زدودن |
| [(ʒi) زی | (ʒistan) زیستن |
| (saʒ) ساز | (saxtan) ساختن |
| (separ) سپار | (sepordan) سپردن |
| (setan) ستان | (setadan) ستادن |
| (seta) ستا | (setudan) ستودن |
| (seriʃ) سریش | (sereʃtan) سرشتن |
| (sara) سرا | (sorudan) سرودن |
| (somb) سنب | (softan) سفتن |
| (suʒ) سوز | (suxtan) سوختن |
| (ʃetab) شتاب | (ʃetaftan) شتافتن |
| (ʃav-, ʃōu) شو | (ʃodan) شدن |
| (ʃu) شو | (ʃostan) شستن |
| (ʃekan) شکن | (ʃekastan) شکستن |
| (ʃomar) شمار | (ʃomordan) شمردن |
| (ʃenas) شناس | (ʃenaxtan) شناختن |
| (ʃenav-, ʃenōu) شنو | (ʃenidan) شنیدن |

¹ To sew.      ² To milk.

| Present Stem | Infinitive |
|---|---|
| (ferest) فرست | (ferestadan) فرستادن |
| (farma) فرما | (farmudan) فرمودن |
| (foruʃ) فروش | (foruxtan) فروختن |
| (farib) فریب | (fariftan) فریفتن |
| (feʃar) فشار | (feʃordan) فشردن |
| (kah) كاه | (kastan) كاستن |
| (kar) كار | (kaʃtan) كاشتن |
| (kon) كن | (kardan) كردن |
| (kar) كار | (keʃtan) كشتن |
| (kub) كوب | (kuftan) كوفتن |
| (godaʒ) گداز | (godaxtan) گداختن |
| (goʒar) گذار | (goʒaʃtan) گذاشتن |
| (goʒar) گذر | (goʒaʃtan) گذشتن |
| (gir) گير | (gereftan) گرفتن |
| (goriʒ) گريز | (gorixtan) گريختن |
| (geri) گرى | (geristan) گريستن |
| (goʒin) گزين | (goʒidan) گزيدن |
| (gosel) كسل | (gosestan) گسستن |
| (gosel) گسل | (gosixtan) گسيختن |
| (goʃa) گشا | (goʃadan) گشادن |
| (gard) گرد | (gaʃtan) گشتن |
| (goʃa) گشا | (goʃudan) گشودن |
| (gu) گو | (goftan) گفتن |
| (gomar) گمار | (gomaʃtan) گماشتن |
| (lis) ليس | (leʃtan) لشتن |
| (mir) مير | (mordan) مردن |
| (neʃin) نشين | (neʃastan) نشستن |
| (negar) نگر | (negaristan) نگريستن |
| (navaʒ) نواز | (navaxtan) نواختن |
| (nevis) نويس | (neveʃtan) نوشتن |
| (nama) نما | (namudan) نمودن |
| (neh) نه | (nehadan) نهادن |
| (hel) هل | (heʃtan) هشتن |
| (yab) ياب | (yaftan) يافتن |

# APPENDIX II

## Interjections.

The following is a list of some of the interjections in common use:

آفرین    *afarin*, bravo!

افسوس    *afsus*, alas!

به به    *bah bah*, bravo!

حیف    *heif*, what a pity!

خوش بحال او    *xoſ be hale u*, lucky fellow!

راستی    *rasti*, really!

اینك    *inak*, lo! behold!

زنهار    *ʒenhar*, beware! have a care! mind!

The two last are used in Classical rather than in Modern Persian.


# APPENDIX III

## The Calendar.

The Muslim era is used in Persia. It dates from the morning after the flight (or *hejre*) of the Prophet Mohammad from Mecca to Medina on the 16th of July, A.D. 622. For civil purposes a solar year is in use. It begins with the 1st of Farvardin, which falls on the 20th, 21st, or 22nd of March. There are twelve months, the names of which are:

| | | | |
|---|---|---|---|
| فروردین | *farvardin*. | مهر | *mehr*. |
| اردی بهشت | *ordi beheſt*. | آبان (ابان) | *aban* (*aban*). |
| خرداد | *xordad*. | آذر | *aʒar*. |
| تیر | *tir*. | دی | *dei*. |
| مرداد | *mordad*. | بهمن | *bahman*. |
| شهریور | *ſahrivar*. | اسفند | *esfand*. |

The first six months have thirty-one days and the last six thirty days, except Esfand, which has twenty-nine days. Every fourth year is a leap-year (کبیسه *kabise*) in which Esfand has thirty days.

The civil day begins at sunset.

The present year (1952) is, according to the Persian solar year, 1330/31.

The Muslim lunar year, by which religious holidays are reckoned, consists of six months of thirty days and six months of twenty-nine days as follows:

| | |
|---|---|
| محرم | moharram. |
| صفر | safar. |
| ربيع الاول | rabi' ol-avval. |
| ربيع الاخر (ربيع الثانى) | rabi' ol-axer (rabi' os-sani). |
| جمادى الاولى (جمادى الاول) | jomadi ol-ula (jomadi ol-avval). |
| جمادى الاخرى (جمادى الثانى) | jomadi ol-oxra (jomadi os-sani). |
| رجب | rajab. |
| شعبان | ʃa'ban. |
| رمضان | ramaʒan. |
| شوال | ʃavval. |
| ذو القعدة (ذى القعدة) | ʒol-qa'da (ʒel-qa'da). |
| ذو الحجة (ذى الحجة) | ʒol-hejja (ʒel-hejja). |

In a period of thirty years an intercalary day is added to the last week of the year eleven times.

The following formula[1] gives the A.H. lunar year ( = Anno Hegirae, or year of the Hejre) equivalent to the A.D. year:

$$(\text{A.D.} - 621 \cdot 54) \div \cdot 970225.$$

The following formula gives the A.D. year equivalent to the A.H. lunar year:

$$(\text{A.H.} \times \cdot 970225) + 621 \cdot 54.$$

The present year (1952) is, according to the lunar year, 1371/2).

Popularly the year is divided into a number of periods, which include forty days known as the چله بزرگ celleye boʒorg at the summer solstice when the heat is at its height, and forty days at the winter solstice when the cold is at its maximum. The celleye boʒorg is followed by the چله کوچك celleye kucek, a period of twenty days when the heat and cold respectively are still considerable. There is also a period at the end of the winter known as the سرماى پيرزن sarmaye pire ʒan.

---

[1] This formula is given by Duncan Forbes, *Grammar of the Persian Language* (Calcutta, 1876), p. 60.

# PUBLIC HOLIDAYS

The weekly holiday is celebrated on Friday.

A period of three to five days' holiday is observed at the New Year. The 13th of Farvardin, known as سیزده بدر *sizdah be dar*, is also observed as a public holiday. The anniversary of the Constitution, to commemorate the Grant of the Constitution by Mozaffar od-Din Shah in 1906, is a public holiday; it falls on the 14th Mordad.

The official religion is the Ja'fari or the Ithna 'Ashari rite of Shi'ism.

The chief religious holidays are the 10th Moharram, known as عاشورا *afura* or روز قتل *ruze qatl*, the day on which the Imam Hosein was killed[1]; the 20th Safar, forty days after *afura*, and hence known as اربعین *arba'in*; the 27th Safar, in commemoration of the martyrdom of the Imam Reza; the 28th Safar, in commemoration of the martyrdom of the Imam Hasan; the 29th Safar, in commemoration of the death of Mohammad, known as رحلت حضرت رسول *rehlate hazrate rasul*; the 17th Rabi' I, in honour of the birthday of Mohammad; the 13th Jomadi I, in commemoration of the death of Fatima, the daughter of Mohammad, and the 20th Jomadi II, in celebration of her birthday; the 27th Rajab, known as عید مبعث *ide mab'as*, the anniversary of the day Mohammad began his mission; the 15th Sha'ban, the anniversary of the birthday of the twelfth Imam, Hazrate Hojjat; the 19th Ramazan, in commemoration of the day on which Ali was fatally wounded, and the 21st and 23rd Ramazan, in commemoration of the death of Ali; the 1st Shavval, known as the عید الفطر *id ol-fetr*, when the fast of Ramazan is broken; the 10th Zol-Hejja, known as the عید قربان *ide qorban*, the day on which pilgrims to Mecca make a sacrifice; and the 18th Zol-Hejja, known as the عید غدیر *ide yadir*, the anniversary of the day when Ali became Caliph.

---

[1] The first ten days of Moharram are regarded as days of mourning in commemoration of the martyrdom of the Imam Hosein. The 9th Moharram is known as تاسوعا *tasu'a*.

# APPENDIX IV

## Currency, Weights and Measures.

### 1. CURRENCY

The monetary unit is the *rial* (ریال).[1] A *rial* is equal to 100 *dinars* (دینار).
The following terms are also used:

| | |
|---|---|
| 1 *shahi* (شاهی) | = 5 *dinars.* |
| 1 *sannar* (صنار) | = 10 *dinars.* |
| 1 *abbasi* (عباسی) | = 20 *dinars.* |
| *yak haₓar* (یك هزار) | = 1 *qeran* (which was formerly equal to 1000 *dinars*). |
| 1 *qeran* (قران) | = 1 *rial* or 1·25 *rials.* |
| 1 *toman* (تومان) | = 10 *rials.* |

Thus ده تومان و سه عباسی *dah toman va se abbasi* means 100 rs.
60 *dinars*; هفت ریال صنار کم *haft rial sannar kam* means 6 rs. 90 *dinars.*

### 2. WEIGHTS

| | |
|---|---|
| 16 *mesqals* (مثقال) | = 1 *sir* (سیر). |
| 10 *sirs* | = 1 *carak* (چارك). |
| 4 *caraks* | = 1 *mane tabriₓ* (من تبریز). |
| 100 *mane tabriₓ* | = 1 *xarvar* (خروار). |

1 *mesqal* is equal to 71·6 grains or 4·64 grams.
1 *sir* is equal to 2 oz. 185 grains or 74·24 grams.
1 *mane tabriₓ* is equal to 6·5464 lb. or 2·97 kilos.
1 *xarvar* is equal to 654·64 lb. or 297 kilos.

The *man* varies from town to town. The one most commonly used in
North Persia is the *mane tabriₓ*. The *mane fah* is equal to two *mane tabriₓ*.
The *mane rēi* is equal to four *mane tabriₓ*. The *mane noh abbasi* is equal to
7 lb. 5½ oz.

---

[1] In 1959 the rate of exchange to the pound sterling was 210 rs.

### 3. MEASURES

4 gerehs (گره) = 1 carak (چارك).

4 caraks    = 1 ẓar‘ (ذرع).

6000 ẓars    = 1 farsax (فرسخ).[1]

1 gereh is approximately 2½ ins.

1 ẓar‘ is approximately 41 ins.

1 gaẓ (گز) is approximately 1 metre.

The term angoʃt (انگشت) is used for a finger's breadth.

1 jarib (جريب) is, in some areas, approximately 1 hectare but it varies considerably in different parts of the country.

In certain parts of the country land is measured in qafiẓ (قفيز), approximately ⅒ of a jarib; the qafiẓ, like the jarib, varies in extent in different parts of the country. سنگ sang, طاق taq, جره jorre, سرجه sareje and سبو sabu are terms used in different parts of the country in measuring water. The quantity of water represented by these terms varies from district to district.

The metric system is also used, and is tending to supersede the local measures.

# APPENDIX V

## Abjad.

Certain numerical values are assigned to the letters of the alphabet. The arrangement of the letters of the alphabet in numerical order is known as *abjad*, so called from the first of a series of meaningless words, which act as a mnemonic to the numerical order:

ضَظَّغْ ثَخَّذْ قَرَشَتْ سَعْفَصْ كَلَمَنْ حُطّى هَوَّزْ أَبْجَدْ

---

[1] The length of the *farsax*, however, tends to vary in different parts of the country. It approximates in some parts to 3½ miles. It tends to be used to express the distance normally covered by a mule or on foot in an hour. In certain parts of the country the distance of the *farsax* is double the normal *farsax*, i.e. some 7 miles, in the same way as the *mane ʃah* is double a *mane tabriẓ*.

A doubled letter (i.e. a letter with a *taſdīd*) has the value of a single letter only.

پ has the value of ب.                    ژ has the value of ج.

چ has the value of چ.                    گ has the value of ك.

Thus, the death of the poet Ahli which took place in A.H. 942 is recorded as follows:

پادشاه شعرا بود اهلی   Ahli was the king of poets (= A.H. 942).[1]

# APPENDIX VI

### Intonation.

1. Rules for word stress have been given in the relevant sections in the *Grammar*. Word stress is, however, usually subsidiary to sentence stress, as will be shown in the following examples. The sentence can be divided into a series of Intonation Groups, which conform acoustically to certain patterns. It is not unusual to find these groups composed, on the one hand, of a single word, or, on the other, of several words. Each Intonation Group contains one prominent syllable, which is differentiated from the other syllables of the Intonation Group by breath-force or stress. This breath-force or stress is also accompanied by tonal prominence due to a change of intonation direction or glide.

2. If the sense of an Intonation Group is not complete it conforms to a certain tone pattern which indicates that there is more to follow. This can be called a Suspensive Intonation Group. If the sense is complete the Intonation Group conforms to another type which can be called a Final Intonation Group.

3. The intonation of Persian falls between two principal tone levels. There is a rise to the high tone level on a syllable on which there is breath-force or stress, and if the stress is final either there is a downward glide on it to the low tone level or a gradual descent to the low tone level begun on the final stress and continued on the remaining words or syllables in the Intonation Group.

4. Sometimes, in order to break the monotony of an Intonation Group, a glide from the high tone level to the low tone level is introduced; this is usually unaccompanied by breath-force and is thereby differentiated

---

[1] See Duncan Forbes, *Grammar of the Persian Language* (Calcutta, 1876), p. 24.

from the downward glide on a prominent syllable or word in a Final
Intonation Group. Such internal glides are only used, however, on
syllables which can carry word stress.

5. There are, of course, many variations of tone in addition to the
two main tone levels, and the actual division of sentences into Intonation
Groups varies from speaker to speaker. In order to make the general
pattern clearer a graphical method has been adopted in the following
examples. This, in attempting to bring out the general tendencies of
Persian intonation, will inevitably make Persian intonation appear more
stereotyped that it is in actual practice. The prominent syllable in each
group is marked by a vertical stroke preceding it, thus *kar'dan*. A thick
line —— represents a stressed syllable containing a long vowel or
diphthong and a thick dot • a stressed syllable containing a short vowel.
A thick curved downward stroke ⌐ represents a downward glide or
a final stress; a thick downward stroke equal to approximately half the
foregoing, thus ⌐, represents a downward glide on a final stress, followed
by a gradual descent on the remaining syllables in the Intonation Group.
A thick upward stroke ⌐ represents an upward glide to the high tone
level used in questions (see below, para. 9). A thin line —— represents
an unstressed syllable containing a long vowel or diphthong and a thin
dot • an unstressed syllable containing a short vowel. A vertical stroke |
represents the end of a Suspensive Intonation Group and a double
stroke || the end of a Final Intonation Group.

6. The English student should be careful to give each syllable its
full value and not to clip his words as is often the tendency in English.
Vowels do not lose their quantity in unstressed syllables. A long
unstressed passage tends to be articulated more quickly, but the relative
length of the vowels remain the same. The English student should also
remember to give a double consonant its full value.

7. Final Intonation Groups. In Final Intonation Groups the unstressed
syllables preceding the final stress are on the low tone level. There is
a rise to the high tone level for the final stress, on which there is either
a downward glide to the low tone level or a gradual descent spread over
the unstressed words or syllables which follow the final stress. The
descent tends to be gradual if the unstressed syllables following the final
stress exceed two in number, e.g.

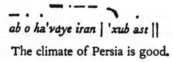

*ab o ha'vāye iran* | '*xub ast* ||

The climate of Persia is good.

*in dokkan'dar | aj'nase xodra | be qēi'mate monaseb | 'miforufad ||*

This shopkeeper sells his goods at a reasonable price.

*dar tabes'tan | 'namifavad inja ʒendagi kard ||*

In summer it is impossible to live here.

If the finite verb is not in a final position there tends to be only a slight rise of tone in the final Intonation Group followed by a downward glide on the final stress, e.g.

*fo'ru' kardand | be xandī'dan ||*

They began to laugh.

8. Suspensive Intonation Groups. The unstressed syllables preceding the stressed syllable are on the low tone level. There is a rise to the high tone level on the stress and the high tone level is then maintained to the end of the group, e.g.

*vasa''ele tahsil | dar ta'mame fahrhaye boʒorge iran | fara'ham mibafad ||*

Facilities for study are available in all the large cities of Persia.

*aha'liye esfahan | dar saxtane anva' va aqsame ʒorufe noqre'i | os'tad and ||*

The people of Isfahan are masters in making different kinds of silver vessels.

The following would be a possible alternative version if the internal glides in the second suspensive Intonation Group were omitted:

*aha'liye esfahan | dar sax'tane anva' va aqsame ʒorufe noqrei | os'tad and ||*

If a subordinate clause precedes the principal sentence, there tends to be a rise to the high tone level on the last syllable of the final word of the subordinate clause and this is accompanied by breath-force, which, even if it would normally fall elsewhere, is moved to the final syllable of the clause, e.g.

*har ce aʒ qodrat va qovveye doulate markaʒi mika'had | dar at'raf va aknafe*
As the power of the central government decreases people in the distant

*mamlekat | mar'dom | gar'dan aʒ eta'at | bi'run kafide | toyi'an mikonand ||*
parts of the country, having thrown off its allegiance, rebel.

In the above example the stress in the word *mikahad* is shifted from the first syllable to the final syllable.

If a subordinate clause follows the principle sentence, it sometimes begins on the low tone level and gradually descends below that level, e.g.

*efte'ha | 'nadaram | ke ciʒi 'bexoram ||*
I have no appetite to eat anything.

In the case of auxiliary verbs such as *tavanestan* 'to be able' and *xastan* 'to want' there is usually a rise to the high tone level on the auxiliary verb while the following dependent subjunctive clause or clauses descend gradually to the low tone level. If the initial syllable of the auxiliary carries the stress, the descent begins on the immediately following unstressed syllables of the auxiliary, e.g.

*'namitavanad | tasmim 'begirad | ke 'beravad ||*
He cannot make up his mind to go.

*aʒ inke ba adab va rosume mamlekat afna na'bud | natavanest jehate*
Because he was unacquainted with the customs of the country, he could not

*doulate matbu'e 'xod | ahdnameye tejara'ti | mon'a'qed namayad ||*
conclude a commercial agreement for his sovereign government.

9. Interrogative Sentences.

(a) Sentences containing an interrogative word such as *ce* 'what'. Stress is usually carried on the interrogative word, which rises to the high

tone level. There is either a downward glide on the interrogative word
to the low tone level or a gradual descent beginning on the syllable
carrying the stress and continuing throughout the remaining words or
syllables of the Intonation Group. The tonal pattern of interrogative
sentences of this type does not, therefore, materially differ from that of
statements, e.g.

*ko'ja mixahid beravid* ‖

Where do you want to go?

*esme in aba'di* | *cist* ‖

What is the name of this village?

If the emphasis is not on the interrogative word but on some other
word in the sentence, the stress will be carried on this word and not the
interrogative, thus

*esme 'in abadi cist* ‖

What is the name of *this* village?

(*b*) Sentences without an interrogative word. In sentences of this
kind, the interrogation is marked by an upward glide to the high tone
level on the final syllable of the last word in the sentence, or by a rise
to the high pitch level on the final stress; the remaining words or syllables
continue on the high tone level or there is a very slight fall on the final
stress, e.g.

*aqabe 'kasi* | *'migardid* ‖

Are you looking for someone?

*aʒ 'in* | *'meil* | *'mifarmaid* ‖

Would you like some of this?

*aʒ' in* | *baraye fo'ma* | *'beyavaram* ‖

Shall I bring you some of this?

Questions introduced by the particle *aya* are treated in the same way as questions which contain no interrogative word, e.g.

*'aya | in | male ſomast ||*

Is      this      yours?

*'aya | far'da | 'miravid ||*

Are you going to-morrow?

# KEY

## Key to *Persian Grammar*

### EXERCISE 1 (p. 8)

The book is here — The pencil is there — That is a (the) table and this is a (the) chair — This is the pen — Where is he (she, it)? — He (she, it) is not here — What is this? — This is a book — What book is it? — He (she) gave a book to me — He (she) gave the pen to me — Where did he (she) see you? — He (she) saw him (her) here — He (she) gave the pencil to me — He (she) saw the table, chair and book — He (she) gave the pencil and pen to him (her) — He (she) gave the table and chair to you — He (she) saw us — The chair is not here.

### EXERCISE 2 (p. 8)

۱ این کتاب است — ۲ کتابی دید — ۳ قلم و مدادرا کجا دید — ٤ کتابی بمن داد — ٥ میز اینجاست — ٦ این چیست — ۷ این قلمی است — ۸ قلم و مدادرا بشما داد — ۹ کتاب اینجاست و مداد آنجاست — ۱۰ آن چیست — ۱۱ آن صندلی است — ۱۲ کتابرا کجا دید — ۱۳ آنرا اینجا دید — ۱٤ شمارا دید

### EXERCISE 3 (p. 15)

This is our house — Whose is that garden? — That garden is mine — Where is the father of this child? — This room has a window (windows) — Your book is on the table — A man came to our house — His (her) son is outside — My daughter has a cat — He (she) saw them in the garden — This woman gave a book to me — Where did he (she) go? — He (she) went to the town — The book and the pencil are on the table — Your mother came to our house — His (her) horse is in the garden — This house is ours.

### EXERCISE 4 (p. 15)

۱ اطاق در و پنجره دارد — ۲ این باغ مال کیست — ۳ باغ مال اوست — ٤ اسبی دارد — ٥ زنی باطاق ما آمد — ٦ اسب و ماده گاو در باغ است — ۷ بچه در اطاق شماست — ۸ قلم و مداد روی میز است — ۹ بمنزل شما آمد — ۱۰ برادر شما بشهر رفت — ۱۱ بچه را در باغ دید — ۱۲ کتاب شمارا بمن داد — ۱۳ این منزل آنهاست

### EXERCISE 5 (p. 24)

Where did you go? — We went to your house — How much did you buy this book for? — I bought it cheaply — This man sold the garden

to that woman — I wrote a letter to him (her) — Whom did you see?
— I saw your son and daughter — We reached the town — How much
did you sell this ox for? — I sold it for a high price — They were
walking slowly — He (she) gave the book to him (her) — They came
to our house — He (she) saw the horse in the garden — They came here
and saw me — Your daughter is the smallest (youngest) of all — We
worked more yesterday than today — We went to the town the day
before yesterday — Where is your house? — Our house is in the town
— We were at home yesterday.

### EXERCISE 6 (p. 24)

۱ کتاب بزرگی بمن داد — ۲ بشهر رفت — ۳ اورا پریروز دیدم — ٤ منزل
و باغرا خریدند — ٥ یواش آمد — ٦ اینرا چند خریدید — ۷ آنرا ارزان خریدم —
۸ مرد و زن و بچهها را دیروز دیدیم — ۹ نامه (نامهای) بمن مینوشت — ۱۰ در
باغ راه میرفتیم — ۱۱ دیروز کجا بودید — ۱۲ منزل بودم — ۱۳ زن از مرد
مسنتر است — ۱٤ بیشتر اسب دارید تا او — ۱٥ زود آمد — ۱٦ دیر کردیم

### EXERCISE 7 (p. 36)

This water is cold — Bring me (some) warm water — Where are you
going? — Give me the key of the garden door — He (she) went to the
town with his (her) son and daughter — Put the book on the table —
Take the children with you — That boy is drinking water and the girl
tea — Take the black book from the table and give it to him (her) —
He (she) sold his (her) house and garden — He (she) bought tea, coffee
and meat in the town — I saw that very man in the town yesterday —
They went themselves — Nobody was in the garden — I do not like
him (her) very much — He (she) said nothing to me — I have never
been in Persia — He (she) will come this very day.

### EXERCISE 8 (p. 37)

۱ بچهرا در باغ دید — ۲ نامه (نامهای) با قلم من مینویسد — ۳ اسب
خودرا دیروز فروخت — ٤ در اطاق من چای میخورند — ٥ فردا بشهر خواهم
رفت (میروم) — ٦ این کتابرا بر دارید و بآن مرد بدهید — ۷ بچهها در باغ
میدویدند — ۸ اسبهای زیاد دارد — ۹ این کتاب گران بود — ۱۰ اینرا بمن
خواهد فروخت — ۱۱ گل صورتی از گل زرد بزرگتر است — ۱۲ برگهای درخت
سبز است — ۱۳ کتاب چندان خوبی نبود — ۱٤ هیچ بچه ندارد — ۱٥ کسی
ندیدم — ۱٦ هیچ وقت آنجا بودهاید — ۱۷ هیچ وقت آنرا بمن نگفت

## Exercise 9 (p. 52)

How long were you there last year? — I stayed (lit. remained) six
months last year but this year I shall stay only five months — He (she)
bought five books last Wednesday — We will go to the town the day
after tomorrow in the morning — He (she) set out at ten in the morning
— The winter of the year before last was very cold — One third (two
*dangs*) of this house belongs to my brother and one third belongs to
each of my sisters — They came forward one by one — This house has
many rooms — Get another horse ready for me — We were with him
(her) (i.e. we went to see him, her) on Thursday — Several persons were
there but I did not know (lit. recognize) any of them — This book
is worth nothing — Your watch is half an hour slow — I waited until
2 p.m. for you — He (she) came three days ago and will go after three
more days — They separated from one another in the town — He (she)
returned after a few minutes — He (she) brought ten eggs for me.

## Exercise 10 (p. 52)

۱ زن ظهر با دو دختر خود بر گشت — ۲ دیشب زود خوابید — ۳ آفتاب
نزده راه افتادیم — ٤ تا ساعت ده برای من صبر کنید — ٥ پسر بزرگش نه سال
دارد و پسر کوچکش هفت سال (دارد) — ٦ یکی از آن مدادها را بمن
بدهید — ۷ بعد از یک ساعت و نیم منزل بر گشتیم — ۸ پریروز یک دست
لباس خرید — ۹ باغ شما از باغ ما بزرگتر است — ۱۰ ساعت من ربع ساعت
جلو است — ۱۱ هفته آینده آفتاب ساعت پنج و نیم طلوع خواهد کرد و هفت
ربع کم غروب خواهد کرد — ۱۲ دیروز زود بر خاستیم

## Exercise 11 (p. 60)

Perhaps he (she) will come tomorrow — I want to go to Tehran next
year — He (she) cannot come today but perhaps he (she) can come
tomorrow — I shall not believe this until I see it — He (she) wanted to
sell this garden but it was not possible — We will wait until you come —
We must start before sunrise tomorrow — He (she) wants to go after
four more days — Three men were killed in the town the day before
yesterday — It has rained very little this year — On Monday we walked
about for two or three hours in the town — I cannot wait until he (she)
comes — Your watch must be broken (out of order) because it is half
an hour slow — Although I wanted to see him (her) I could not wait
until he (she) came — The hours of work were increased in order to put

up the factory's power of production — The exports of this country consist more of (are more) agricultural products than industrial [goods] — The exports of this country consist of wheat, wool and dried fruits and its imports consist mainly of sugar, tea, cotton piece goods and machinery.

## EXERCISE 12 a (p. 60)

۱ تا بچه‌ها اینجا باشند باید بمانید — ۲ با اینکه میخواست برود نمیتوانست برود — ۳ نمیشود رفت — ٤ باید دیروز رفته باشد — ٥ پس‌فردا باید برود بچه‌های خودرا ببیند — ٦ تا بمن ننویسید نمیایم — ۷ پدرش اورا خواست — ۸ زودتر از این (پیش از این) نمیتوانست بیاید — ۹ میبایست پیش از ما رفته باشد — ۱۰ میبایست پریروز رفته باشیم — ۱۱ میخواست ببرادر خود بنویسد — ۱۲ تا منزل برسید شب میشود — ۱۳ دیروز توفان شدیدی بود — ۱٤ کتاب خودرا باو دادم تا بخواند — ۱٥ میخواهد شمارا ببیند

## EXERCISE 12 b (p. 60)

۱ صادرات این مملکت عبارت است از مواد زراعتی — ۲ سطح زندگی این مملکترا باید بالا برد — ۳ حالا باید بروم زیراکه دیر شده است — ٤ تولید این کارخانه کم شده است — ٥ با اینکه ناشتائی خیلی دیر خوردیم گرسنه شده‌ام — ٦ با اینکه خسته شده بود تا بعد از نصف شب با برادر خود در شهر ماند — ۷ دیروز خیلی باران آمد و صبح زود توفان شدیدی بود — ۸ تاجر تجارتخانه در شهر باز کرد میخواهد اجناس صنعتی وارد کند و خشک بار و پشم صادر کند — ۹ وقتیکه وارد شدم هیچ کس در اطاق نبود — ۱۰ اورا هیچ وقت ندیده‌ام ولی میخواهم اورا بشناسم — ۱۱ شاید رفته باشد نیم ساعت پیش ساعت خودرا حاضر میکرد — ۱۲ تابستان گذشته هر روز گردش میرفتم (پیاده راه میرفتم) — ۱۳ نمیگذارم که بروید — ۱٤ اینرا نمیشود خواند — ۱٥ امروز صبح کجا میرفتید

## EXERCISE 13 (p. 69)

The capital of this country is a large town — If you see my sister give her this letter — If you had come earlier I would have taken you there — When he (she) was going to the town with his (her) sister and brother he (she) saw us — Persia has many mountains — He (she) is studying as hard as he (she) can (with the greatest possible effort) — If we had set out earlier we should not have arrived so late — It has not yet rained this year — Perhaps he (she) has gone — You must ask your sister this — If he (she) is at home we will ask him (her) — He (she) must have

come — If the weather is fine (good) tomorrow we will go to the town —
If you have read this book you do not need it any more — This boy
always studies; he is always early at school; he studies very well and is
never lazy; he works for the most part and seldom speaks; he is polite
to all and always tries to know his lessons fluently.

## EXERCISE 14*a* (p. 70)

۱ اگر بشهر رفتید (بروید) قدری چای و قهوه برای من بخرید — ۲ اگر
برادرتان منزل برود همراه شما را همراه خود میبرد — ۳ اگر هفته گذشته رفته بودید
بهتر بود — ٤ باکشتی بایران رفتند ولی از راه خشکی بر گشتند — ٥ اگر فردا
بروم همراه من میائید — ٦ این مملکت بسیار قصبه و ده دارد — ۷ اگر امشب
سرد بشود ممکن است که یخ ببندد — ۸ اگر برف زیاد ببارد (بیاید) ممکن است
راه بسته شود — ۹ این دست کم بیست ریال میارزد — ۱۰ هر سال بپایتخت
میرویم — ۱۱ وقتیکه اورا دیدم در باغ تند راه میرفت — ۱۲ اگر دو هفته پیش
میامدید تابستان هنوز تمام نشده بود

## EXERCISE 14*b* (p. 70)

۱ نگذاشت که باهم برویم — ۲ اینرا باو گفتم و بس — ۳ روی هم رفته
کتاب بدی نبود — ٤ ناگاه بلند شد و از اطاق بیرون رفت — ٥ هر هفته مبلغی
پول باو میدهند — ٦ هر سال بشهر میرفتیم و دو ماه آنجا میماندیم — ۷ ایران
بیشتر کوه و بیابان است — ۸ دویست و پنجاه بچه در مدرسه هستند و سن هر
یکی از آنها کمتر از پانزده سال است — ۹ همراه شما میایم تا راهرا گم نکنید —
۱۰ اینجا بنشینیم زیراکه خسته شدهام — ۱۱ اگر بخواهید سر وقت برسید بهتر
است که حالا بروید — ۱۲ باید حالا بروید و الا دیر میکنید

## EXERCISE 15 (p. 84)

Show me the book which you bought yesterday — The boy who came
to our house is the brother of that girl — Whoever wants to come must
come quickly — The children who were with him (her) were small —
He (she) heard what was said — The New Year, which occurs at the
beginning of spring, is the greatest national festival of Persia — On some
days in summer it is very hot — When it is spring most people go to
summer quarters — Persons who would like to receive the newspaper
regularly can remit (lit. transfer) to the account of the newspaper at the
National Bank 180 *rials* for the period of one year and 100 *rials* for six

months and send (lit. write) their full address to the newspaper office so
that one copy may be sent regularly every day — Beware of whoever
tells you of the faults of others because he will also tell your faults to
others — Acquire (lit. learn) knowledge[1] as long as you can because the
benefit thereof will accrue to you — There is a great difference between
words and actions — I shall have prepared my lesson by the time you
return — Whether he (she) says so or not I shall do this — What have
you done that you are so regretful? — Accept the advice of wellwishers
because whoever does not listen to advice suffers loss.

## EXERCISE 16 (p. 84)

۱ این همان مردی است که دیروز اینجا بود ــ ۲ برای آن مردیکه در باغ
دیده‌بودم صبر کرد ــ ۳ شاید پسریکه در باغ بود دررا باز کرده باشد تا
خواهرش وارد شود ــ ٤ دیشب وقتیکه منزل بر گشتم تاریک بود ــ
٥ نمیتوانست بیاید زیراکه مریض بود ــ ٦ پسر تا پدرش بر نگردد نمیتواند
بیاید ــ ۷ با اینکه زود رفتیم تا بشهر رسیدیم تاریک شده بود ــ ۸ اندکی فکر کرد
پس جواب داد ــ ۹ وقتیکه رسیدیم همه رفته بودند ــ ۱۰ این قدر دیر کردید
که ترسیدم مبادا فراموش کرده باشید ــ ۱۱ پیش از آنکه بروید نامه‌را
بنویسید ــ ۱۲ بعد از آنکه رفتید (رفته بودید) زیاد نماندم ــ ۱۳ فائده ندارد
که بیائید (آمدن ندارد) مگر اینکه بخواهید بیائید ــ ٤۱ هر وقت که آنجا
میروم میخواهم بمانم

## EXERCISE 17 (p. 85)

۱ دیروز بعد از آنکه شمارا دیده‌بودم اورا دیدم ــ ۲ تا باران آمد بر گشتیم ــ
۳ میخواستم سایر کتابهارا بخرم ــ ٤ در ایام نو روز که بزرگترین عید سال
ایران میباشد مردم بدیدن هم دیگر میروند و دست کم پنج روز عید میگیرند ــ
٥ اگر بخواهید روزنامه‌را مرتب دریافت کنید باید دویست و پنجاه ریال بدفتر
روزنامه بفرستید ــ ٦ اگر بحسن ظن آنها اعتماد کنید پشیمان میشوید ــ ۷ اگر
نتوانید بیائید عیب ندارد ــ ۸ اگر حل این مسئله‌را میدانستم بشما میگفتم ــ
۹ ترسید مبادا مادرش مریض شده باشد ــ ۱۰ اگر بتهران رفتید (بروید) نامه
(نامه‌ای) برای من بنویسید ــ ۱۱ اگر نرفته باشد باو میگویم ــ ۱۲ فراموش
کرد بشما بگوید ــ ۱۳ میخواهم با شما بایران بیایم زیراکه هیچ وقت آنجا
نبوده‌ام ــ ٤۱ بعقیده من اگر این موضوعرا حالا مطرح کنیم بهتر است ــ
٥۱ چه بروید چه نروید هیچ فرق نمیکند ــ ۱٦ این کتاب بدرد شما بیخورد

*The Mongol Conquest of Persia* (p. 95)

The two hundred years' period of history of the Mongols, the conquest of Tamerlane and other events which happened in Persia before the Safavids, each in their own turn, were the cause of murder, plunder, bloodshed and innumerable acts of destruction in Islamic countries generally and in the country of Persia in particular. In these attacks Persia suffered injury more than any other and having entered upon a period of extraordinary decline (having fallen into a precipice of strange decline) trod a descending arc. Another thing which contributed to (aided) the decline and decay of Persia and which day by day closed the doors of progress upon her was, in addition to the superstitions and fancies which resulted from the conquest of the Mongols and Turks, the ignorant fanaticism of the people and the fixing of the centre of civilization in Western Europe and America. In view of the internal obstacles which prevented her relations with foreign countries, Persia was unable to adopt civilization easily from Europe or, like European countries, to advance along the road of progress.

## EXERCISE 18 (p. 95)

۱ زمستان که سرد میشود یخبندان میشود — ۲ دیروز صبح بیرون شهر گردش کردیم (پیاده راه رفتیم) — ۳ آنچه را که گفتیم بآنها بر خورد — ٤ پیش از آنکه بر گردید باید بآنچه میخواهم بگویم گوش بدهید — ٥ هنوز از اطاق خود بیرون نیامده است — ٦ مدتی است که مرده است — ۷ این کتابرا باو نسبت میدهند — ۸ تصمیم گرفت که بایران برود — ۹ بیست سال پیش مرد — ۱۰ وقتیکه وارد شد کتابی میخواندم — ۱۱ شکست خورد — ۱۲ دهرا غارت کردند — ۱۳ مصلحت دیدیم که برویم زیرا که دیر شده‌بود و میخواستیم پیش از آنکه تاریک بشود بمنزل برسیم — ۱٤ استیلای مغول که در قرن سیزدهم اتفاق افتاد باعث خرابیهای زیاد در ایران شد (خسارات زیاد بایران وارد آورد) و سالهای سال طول کشید تا خرابیهائیکه از استیلای مغول نتیجه شده بود جبران شود بسیاری از مراکز علم و تمدن نابود شد و هزاران نفر کشته شدند

*Persia's Relations with Europe** (p. 109)

In the time of Shah Tahmasp an Englishman called Antony Jenkinson set out for Persia in A.H. 969 (A.D. 1561–2) on a mission on behalf of Elizabeth, the queen of England. He brought a letter for Tahmasp I, the

Safavid king, from the aforementioned queen relating to the creation of friendly relations and the preservation of the well-being (lit. interests) of humanity and the interests of the two parties. The aforementioned envoy came to Qazvin, the capital of Shah Tahmasp, in the month of Zol-Hejja 969 (August 1562); but since he was not acquainted with the manners and customs of Persia he was not able to conclude a commercial treaty on behalf of his sovereign government. Having no alternative (lit. remedy) he returned. The same envoy (representative) came once more to Persia in the year A.H. 970 (A.D. 1562-3) on behalf of the Russian government; and (but) on this occasion also he returned without obtaining any result. In the year A.H. 972 (A.D. 1564-5) another group came to Persia on behalf of the Moscow Company and the shah treated this group also with kindness. He gave permission for English and Russian merchants to trade and travel freely in Persia.

* Taken from Reza Pazuki, *Tarikh-e Iran az Moghol ta Afshariyyeh.*

## EXERCISE 19 (p. 109)

۱ از خواهر خود خبر دارد — ۲ مدت مدیدی است که بانگلستان نرفته‌ام — ۳ بیش از این نمیشد ماند — ٤ مردی که امروز صبح با او صحبت میکردید همشهری من است — ٥ خیلی اعتماد بنفس نشان داد — ٦ پسر خودرا خوب بار آورد (پرورش داد) — ۷ تمام سال در دهات زندگی میکنیم — ۸ میل دارد بیرون شهر زندگی کند — ۹ من همعقیده شما هستم — ۱۰ تصمیم گرفتیم اینجا بمانیم زیراکه باصفاتر است — ۱۱ مصمم شد هفته گذشته بطرف هندوستان حرکت کند — ۱۲ اگر با کشتی برود مسافرت او سه هفته طول خواهد کشید — ۱۳ پدر شوهر خودرا بیشتر دوست دارد تا مادر شوهر خودرا — ١٤ سعی کردم زودتر بیایم ولی با اینکه تصمیم داشتم ساعت ده راه بیفتم تا حاضر شدم حرکت کنم ساعت یازده شد و در نتیجه وقتیکه رسیدم دیر شده بود و منزل رفته بودید — ۱٥ روابط تجارتی بین ایران و اروپا در زمان صفویه بر قرار شد سفرای زیاد از اروپا بایران آمدند و سعی کردند عهدنامه‌های تجارتی از طرف دولتهای خودشان با دولت ایران منعقد و روابط دوستانه بر قرار کنند بعضی از آنها موفق شدند و برخی از آنها بدون حصول نتیجه باروپا بر گشتند

## The Coming of the Sherley Brothers to Persia (p. 122)

The Sherleys were two brothers, called Antony and Robert, who in A.D. 1597 (A.H. lunar 1007), coming through Ottoman territory and

Western Persia, reached Qazvin with twenty-five Englishmen for the purpose of [concluding a] union with European countries against the Ottoman state and the acquisition of concessions for British merchants. Among their companions were a number of soldiers and artillerymen, who were well informed about the military situation of Europe; and Antony Sherley himself had done military service and taken part in the wars between Spain and Holland towards the end of the sixteenth century A.D. At this time Shah Abbas was busy in Khorasan repelling the rebellion of the Tartars (i.e. the Uzbegs). When news of the arrival of the English envoys (representatives) reached the shah he sent a message saying, 'Let our foreign guests be received with full honour and what they require by way of horses, servants and such like be provided [for them]. The life of anyone who acts contrary to this order will be in danger and if anyone treats the lowest of their attendants badly his head will be cut off.' (To be continued)

## EXERCISE 20 (p. 123)

One can recognize the friendship of men by two things; first if, when the friend is afflicted by straitened circumstances, they do not withhold bounty from him; and secondly they do not flee from him when in straitened circumstances — We enjoyed this journey very much — The policeman began to investigate the matter — He (she) was transferred from the ministry of war to the ministry of the interior — Your younger brother resembles your mother more than your father — They quarrelled over this affair — Although you are in the right, you must ask his pardon — This matter has nothing to do with that matter — Yesterday I was with one of your friends and he (she) praised you very much — After I crossed the bridge I met a large number of people — Avoid indolence and bodily ease because indolent people given to bodily ease are in need of this [person] and that [person] — Strength lies in knowledge not in wealth and greatness in intelligence not in years — Act upon your own words so that others (lit. they) may act upon your words — One cannot judge (lit. recognize) people by their clothes — To die in honour is better than to live in ignominy — It is not fitting to rely upon the friendship of kings — Do not act with such mildness that people (lit. they) become audacious towards you or with such severity that they become disgusted (fed up) with you — He who is a man never opens his mouth in evil — Do not rely upon anyone until you have tried him several times — Do not make one enemy in the hope of a thousand friends — Whenever anyone speaks badly of you consider him (her) more excused than that person who repeated (lit. transmitted) those words to you.

EXERCISE 21 (p. 123)

۱ با من بشهر آمد و آنجا از هم جدا شدیم — ۲ منزل بر نگشت زیراکه از
پدر خود میترسید — ۳ بعنوان نماینده کشور خود بانگلستان فرستاده شد —
٤ ارتش بر دشمن حمله کرد و آنهارا شکست داد — ٥ اگر آنجا بود از او
میپرسیدیم — ٦ پس از آنکه دشمنان خودرا مغلوب کرده بود (کرد) بر تمام
مملکت فرمانروائی کرد — ۷ سعی کرد از ما دوری کند — ۸ از او استدعا کردیم
که بماند — ۹ دارائی او عبارت است از سه باب خانه و دو باغ — ۱۰ با هم
مشورت کردیم و تصمیم گرفتیم که برویم — ۱۱ شروع کرد بخندیدن —
۱۲ بعقیده من اگر از نوشتن این نامه صرف نظر کنید بهتر است — ۱۳ بین
اولین مسافرین انگلیسی که بایران آمدند دو برادر بنام شرلی بودند بامید
تحصیل امتیازات تجارتی بدربار شاه عباس آمدند چند سال در ایران ماندند و
داخل خدمت شاه عباس شدند یکی از آنها در چندین جنگ اروپا شرکت جسته
از امور نظامی آگاهی داشت

*The Coming of the Sherley Brothers to Persia* (p. 141)

(Continued from the previous lesson)

In accordance with this arrangement the governor of Qazvin gave him
a fitting welcome and provided every means for the repose of that company until news reached the town of the arrival of the shah in the vicinity
of Qazvin. The Sherley brothers and their companions went out with the
controller (superintendent) and governor of Qazvin to give the shah a
ceremonial welcome. The shah kissed the two brothers on the face,
welcomed them with full respect and gave them and their companions
many gifts and presents (one hundred and forty horses with golden
bridles, one hundred mules, one hundred camels and a large amount of
money). Then he went with them to his capital, Isfahan, and entertained
them for six months in that town. He treated them with such favour that
they considered themselves the sincere servants of the shah; and Antony,
during his sojourn in Isfahan, convinced the shah of his devotion and
sincerity. With the help of Allahverdi Khan, the commander of the
Persian army, he took much trouble in learning Persian arts of war while
the Persians learnt the arts of war from Sherley and trained (lit. made
ready) regular soldiers and assembled five hundred cannon and twenty
thousand muskets. Antony then proposed to Shah Abbas that he should
send an envoy to the courts of the rulers of Europe and become allied
to them against the Ottoman state.                    (To be continued)

## Exercise 22 (p. 142)

Do not be deceived by the lying words of flatterers and beware of listening to them so that you do not become grieved or regretful (lit. do not bite the finger of regret) — Whoever speaks evil behind the backs of others is in no way worthy of friendship — Whoever does not good work in his (her) lifetime will not have a good name after death — Men are superior to animals by virtue of good conduct and good actions — Someone brought Anushiravan the Just good news saying, 'I have heard that God most high has removed such and such an enemy.' He replied (lit. said), 'Have you ever heard that He will leave me? I have no grounds for rejoicing at the death of my enemy because our life is also not eternal.'

## Exercise 23 (p. 142)

۱ ببازار رفته است کتابی بخرد — ۲ بعد از آنکه دو سال در ارتش بود افسر شد — ۳ این حکایت شنیدنی است — ٤ این نوع کتاب‌را دوست ندارم — ٥ انواع و اقسام سیوه در ایران بعمل میآید — ٦ مردم شروع کردند بجمع شدن در میدان مرد و زن و بچه‌ها آنجا بودند و تا بعد از غروب متفرق نشدند — ۷ زنها بچه‌هایشانرا روی دوششان میبردند — ۸ کتاب هم خواندنی است و هم خوب نوشته شده است — ۹ میروم و هیچ کس از رفتن من نمیتواند جلوگیری کند — ۱۰ نه برای من زیاد فائده داشت نه برای هیچ کس دیگر — ۱۱ روز و شب وسایل استراحت برای همه کارگران فراهم است — ۱۲ هیچ وقت با او صحبت نکرده‌ام و هرگز باو ننوشته‌ام — ۱۳ یا او باید برود یا من — ۱٤ نمیتواند بیرون رفته باشد والا بمن میگفت

### The Coming of the Sherley Brothers to Persia (p. 164)

(Continued from the previous lesson)

The shah, who wished at this time to embark upon (lit. come out from the door of) war with the Ottoman state and retake those provinces which he had surrendered at the beginning of his reign to that state, accordingly (according to this arrangement) sent some envoys to the courts of all the Christian sovereigns of Europe. Among them he sent Antony Sherley accompanied by Hosein Ali Bak (Beg) Bayat to Europe as an envoy. They reached (lit. entered) Italy by way of the Caspian Sea, Moscow, the White Sea, the North Sea and Germany. In all the countries on the way they presented friendly letters from Shah Abbas on the subject of alliance

with Persia against the Ottoman government and the opening of commercial relations for the sale of Persian silk together with the presents
which Shah Abbas had given. A quarrel broke out between Hosein Ali
Bak Bayat and Antony Sherley in Italy; Antony separated from him and
went to Spain. He did not return to Persia. But Robert Sherley, Antony's
brother, who had remained in the service of Shah Abbas, became the
object of his favour, but, when there was no news of the coming of
Antony, Shah Abbas' favour towards him ceased. Robert Sherley, however, since he was a young man of determination and good conduct,
again attracted the love of the shah towards himself. The first charge
which was given by Shah Abbas to Robert Sherley was his choice as the
leader of a group of the army and his despatch to make war on the
Ottoman government. Similarly he took part in the wars which Shah
Abbas undertook in the years A.H. 1013 (A.D. 1604–5) and A.H. 1014 (A.D.
1605–6) with the Ottoman government. He was wounded three times.
In one engagement he killed a large number of the Ottoman army and
took their leaders prisoner. And in one battle when he came face to face
with the Ottomans, after drawing up his own force, when he saw that
his soldiers were in fear at the large number of the enemy, he turned
towards them, addressed some words [to them] and then himself first
attacked the enemy. Having given courage to his soldiers and in this way
defeated the Ottomans, he became the object of Shah Abbas' favour. Subsequently he was sent by Shah Abbas in A.H. 1016 (A.D. 1608) from Isfahan
to Europe. After a long journey and the carrying out of his mission he
went to England in A.H. 1020 (A.D. 1611–12) and finally after eight years'
travelling he returned to Persia in A.H. 1024 (A.D. 1615).        (The end)

## EXERCISE 24 (p. 165)

An ungrateful peasant was criticizing God most high saying, 'Why
has He made a marrow to grow (lit. become green) on a slender bush and
made the small acorn to grow on a tall tree? If I were the Creator of
created things I would act differently to this.' The peasant was thinking
thus when an acorn from the top of the tree hit his nose so that blood
flowed. The peasant said to himself, 'See the weakness of my judgement
and counsel. If this acorn had been a marrow it would have killed me.'
Then he asked forgiveness and pardon for his boldness.

## EXERCISE 25 (p. 166)

۱ نمیفهم چطور اتفاق افتاد — ۲ حتی دشمنانش با او نامهربانی نکرده‌اند تا
چه رسد بدوستانش — ۳ منزل در تابستان غیر قابل سکونت است تا چه رسد

بزمستان — ٤ فرصترا غنیمت بشمارید و الا پشیمان میشوید — ٥ با اینکه دلم
برای او تنگ شده است باز باخوشوقتم که رفته است — ٦ همیشه مریض است با
این همه همواره بشاش است — ٧ در نهایت سختی زندگی میکند در صورتیکه
برادرش درکمال راحتی زندگی میکند — ٨ دیشب کارخانه آتش گرفت بکلی
نیست و نابود شد و در نتیجه کارگران زیاد بیکار میشوند — ٩ کاررا میبایست
کرد پس ما آنرا انجام دادیم — ١٠ هیچ کس آنجا نبود پس رفتم — ١١ بهتر
است که برود — ١٢ بهترین دوستانش انکار نمیکنند که در اشتباه بود —
١٣ تنها ترس من این است که پدرم دنبال من بیاید — ١٤ احتمال دارد که
امروز بیاید — ١٥ معلوم نیست که از چه راهی رفته است — ١٦ چه بیاید چه
برود فرق نمیکند — ١٧ این قبیل کتاب و این نوع آدم کمیاب است

### *Persia and England* (p. 175)

After [the reign of] Shah Abbas the Great the English East India Company received in A.H. 1038 (A.D. 1628–9) a new *farman* concerning the silk trade from Shah Safi, his successor. But they could not obtain again all the concessions and rights which they had acquired in the time of Shah Abbas. Although an envoy from Charles I of England came in the month of Sha'ban 1039 (April–May 1630) with a letter to Shah Safi [asking] for help and assistance to English merchants and nationals in Persia, which expression of love and friendship was well received by the ruler of Persia, in the time of this king the most important part of the Persian trade was in fact (lit. essentially) in the hands of Dutch merchants. On a second occasion Charles I sent another letter to Shah Safi [asking] for help for the British East India Company. This letter was also well received by the Safavid ruler and he sent a friendly letter to the king of England. Finally in A.H. 1053 (A.D. 1643) the English East India Company founded a factory for themselves in Basra. Meanwhile, the trade of the Dutch in Persia daily increased and they engaged in rivalry with the English.

### *A General Amnesty for the Tribes* (p. 176)

In accordance with the proposal of the [chief of] staff of the southern division, approved by his Imperial Majesty, an order for a general amnesty for all the tribes of Fars has been issued. This order has been transmitted by the commander of the division to the chiefs of the tribes. According to information [received] from the general staff it was announced in the course of the transmission of this order that the tribes could keep their arms with them and remain armed provided that they received a special permit. In addition to the transmission of the general amnesty to all the tribes, assurances on every account were given by the government [to the tribes] and they were encouraged to hope for the necessary measures of assistance from the government.

## *Desire** (p. 176)

I was a child. We had gone in summer to summer quarters. Every day in the afternoon, the children used to come down from the mountain behind the sheep and goats. They used to say that there was a green meadow near the top which had much water and that from that high place one could see the town and the [whole] world, and that unless one saw it one could not describe it. I wished (lit. my heart wished) that I was as fearless and strong as they were. Perhaps they also wished that they had the facilities for being lazy which I had. One day I said to the village headman, 'I am going with the children tomorrow to the meadow. How far is it to there?' He laughed and said, 'You have to go a long way to get there and you will get very tired.' I said, 'If the meadow is behind this mountain its no distance for me. How far is it really?' He said, 'One has to go up for five hours.' My heart sank in fear but there was nothing for it. The next day I set out with firm steps for my objective with the village headman and the children. I said to myself that as long as I had life in me I would not show I was tired. I was still in the full ardour of my determination when the village headman said, 'We have arrived. Here is the meadow.' Out of happiness I ran a few steps and said, 'I am ready to go to the summit. But you said it was five hours' walk. It is only two and a half hours since we set out.' He said, 'If I had said it was two hours' walk you would have arrived here tired. I said five hours so that you would do the two hours' walk easily.'

* Taken from Mohammad Hejazi, *A'ine.*

## EXERCISE 26 (p. 177)

۱ بارها اوقاتش تلخ میشود با این همه اورا دوست داریم و صفات خوبی دارد — ۲ هیچ شك نبود كه بر علیه او سوء قصد كنند — ۳ در هر بابی صحبت بكند (هر چه بگوید) جالب توجه خواهد بود — ٤ چه خودش بیاید چه كفیلی بفرستد فرق نمیكند — ٥ اورا همیشه بهترین دوست خود میدانستم — ٦ ترس وبا باعث قرنتینه شدیدی شدهاست كه تمام روابط تجارتیرا مختل كردهاست تا چه رسد بقطع آمدوشد مسافرین — ۷ بهیچ وجه كاررا تمام نكردهام بر عكس تازه شروع كردهام — ۸ این اصطلاح بر خلاف قواعد صرف و نحو است با وجود این

جزو زبان رایج شده است — ۹ در هر جامعه هر قدر ظاهراً فاسد شده‌باشد هستند آنهائی که بعناصر بد تن در نداده‌اند — ۱۰ از چند سال پیش که این شرکت تأسیس شده‌است سود زیادی کرده است — ۱۱ کاشکی دیروز می‌آمدید آنوقت برادر مرا پیش از آنکه راه بیفتد میدیدید

*Persia and England* (p. 195)

(Continued from the previous lesson)

During the reign of Shah Abbas II the influence of the English became appreciably less than formerly whereas (lit. but on the contrary) the domination and influence of the Dutch in Persia and the Persian Gulf was increasing, and they had become so emboldened by the progress of their affairs in Persia that their warships even destroyed the factories of the English in Basra. But subsequently as a result of a war which took place in Europe between the two aforementioned governments their commercial relations in India and Persia were interrupted and the Persian government benefited from the opportunity to lessen the influence and concessions of the two governments in Persia. Among other things the Persian government refrained from paying the sum which was paid annually to the English on account of the customs' revenue of Bandar Abbas. The East India Company had recourse to the English king, who at that time was Charles II; and he wrote a letter to Shah Soleiman on this matter in the year A.H. 1081 (A.D. 1671–2). Until towards the end of the twelfth century A.H. the influence of the Dutch was appreciably greater than that of the English in the Gulf; but towards the end of this century certain new events which occurred in Europe weakened (lit. were the cause of weakness to) the Dutch. At the same time also the English government, because of differences which had broken out between the East India Company shareholders, united all the old companies in the year A.H. 1120 (A.D. 1708) and founded a big company called the Company of English Merchants for Trade with the East Indies. The king of England also meanwhile gave the factors (lit. heads) of the company consular and diplomatic rank at the courts of the rulers of India and their influence increased.                                                     (The end)

*Tehran* (p. 195)

Tehran had not yet become as large as it is today; and most of the avenues which are the glory of the capital and the names of which everyone in the city knows had not yet come into existence; and at the time of the sunset call to prayer the gates of the city would be shut. Traffic from inside the city to outside and within the city itself would be stopped at nightfall. In winter when the sun set earlier the doors in the gates would be closed earlier. It was in these days that one of the foreign envoys remained outside the gates until morning and passed the night among the muleteers. It was in these same times that robbers would cut off people's heads for a few *tumans* a few steps from the gates.

## EXERCISE 27 (p. 196)

۱ از نخست وزیر هم تنفر دارند و هم اورا حقیر میشمارند — ۲ با من بدرفتاری کرده است با این همه میخواهم نسبت باو منصف باشم — ۳ او دشمنی دارد یعنی برادر خودش — ٤ قسمت زیادی از جنگل مغرب خالصه است و دولت حکم داده است که هیچ کس بدون اجازه حق ندارد درختهارا قطع کند تا از اتلاف آن جلوگیری شود — ٥ گفت هر چه دارم در اختیار شماست — ٦ همان بود که اورا کشت — ۷ همیشه آنچه را که اقتضای وقت است انجام میدهد نه آنچه را که خودش میخواهد — ۸ آن تغییراتی که بنظرم رسید دادهام — ۹ همان مردیست که دیروز باو بر خوردیم — ۱۰ این است علتی که مانع موفقیت اوست — ۱۱ میدانم که آمده است — ۱۲ ترسیدم مبادا که اوقات اورا تلخ کند — ۱۳ پولرا بگیرید معلوم نیست که آنرا لازم نداشته باشید — ۱٤ هیچ کس شك ندارد که او موفق خواهد شد

## The Government's Programme (p. 202)

The government's programme, which was discussed in the national consultative assembly, is as follows: (1) taking into full consideration the interests of the country, the government considers it expedient in foreign policy to have close cooperation with those states with whose interests the interests of Persia are connected; (2) to reform the judicial laws and remove their deficiencies in order to give full legal security and also review other laws which are not in keeping with the exigencies of the day; (3) to review the structure of the security forces and to provide full means for [the maintenance of] law and order; (4) [to exert] special care in the provision of the foodstuffs needed for the country; (5) to review the civil service laws; (6) to reform the economic and financial affairs of the country, by such means as a modification of taxation in order to reduce the burden of taxation and when the budget for next year is prepared to prevent [the inclusion of] expenses which are not in keeping with the existing conditions of the country; to review commercial regulations; to abolish unnecessary monopolies which have not yet been abolished; and to strive to reduce the cost of living; (7) to pay special

attention to the progress of agriculture, the improvement of the conditions of life of the peasants, the extension of irrigation and the gradual
prevention of the cultivation and use of opium; and to review the laws
for agricultural development and the execution of the programme for
agriculture; (8) [to pay special attention] to the development (lit. progress
and perfecting) of industries as far as possible with a preference for the
running of factories by individuals belonging to private companies; and
to strive to improve the conditions of life of the workers; (9) to develop
(lit. make perfect, complete) roads and railways within the limits of the
country's means; (10) to reform the administrative divisions of the
country and to give attention to participation by the people in the
running of local affairs; (11) to develop educational establishments and
to exert care in the reform of public morals; and (12) to extend public
health organizations and to pay special attention to public health.

### The Mixing of Tongues* (p. 203)

There is no language in the world which can keep itself free from an
admixture of other languages, except the language of a people who never
mix with other people. But this is impossible because words from one
people penetrate into [the language of] another people through trade,
travel and intercourse and even through the hearing of the fables and
traditions of other peoples. All the languages of the world in this way have
loan words. One must consider what are the results achieved through the
mixing of one language with another. The mixing of languages comes
about in several ways (lit. is of several kinds). One way is that a language
naturally takes whatever it has not got from its neighbour or from further
afield and adapts it to its own pronunciation and taste, i.e. it swallows the
word, chews and digests it, and divests it of its original forms and peculi-
arities; and even according to its own inclination sometimes inverts the
letters, alters them, or changes the meaning. If the word is primitive it
makes it derivative and if derivative primitive and so on *ad infinitum*,
just as the Arabs did and still do with foreign words. We also have done
this with some Arabic, Turkish and European words; but with us this
was not general practice.

* Mohammad Taqi Bahar (Malek osh-Sho'ara), *Sabk-shenasi.*

### EXERCISE 28 (p. 203)

۱ تغییراتی که در برنامه‌هایمان میدهیم بعداً اعلام میشود — ۲ دشمن در
موقع عقب نشینی کشوررا ویران میکرد — ۳ شما بایستی اینرا بمن گفته باشید

(میگفتید) نه اینکه من بشما — ٤ هر چه بیشتر پول کسب میکند بیشتر میخواهد —
٥ تا ملتی قدرت خودرا حفظ میکند زبان آن هیچ وقت کهنه نمیشود — ٦ شك
دارم که آنجا بود — ٧ نمیدانم که حال او بهتر شده است یا بدتر — ٨ از او
پرسیدم که خودش میاید یا کفیلی میفرستد — ٩ بهیچ وجه پیشبینی نمیکرد که
این چقدر فرق میکند — ١٠ اصرار میکنم که برود — ١١ تا آنرا شنیدم آمدم —
١٢ هر چه زودتر خواهم آمد — ١٣ وقتیکه کارتان تمام شد بمن خبر بدهید —
١٤ تا بر گردید حاضر خواهم شد

## The Railway Health Service (p. 207)

In construction works as in every other great or small work attention
must be paid from the beginning to the health and physical well-being
of the workers. After much experience (lit. many tests) it has been realized
that if all the tools and implements for work are available but the engineers,
master-craftsmen, supervisors, foremen and workmen are weak and sick
matters will not progress. For this very reason the question of the health
of the workers is regarded as one of the effective factors in the progress
of construction work. Large construction concerns which are engaged
in work in towns are perhaps not greatly in need of health organizations
because municipal health organizations and others watch over the physical
well-being of the townspeople; but workmen who are engaged in road
construction work on the roads and in locations far from inhabited places
have no access to medicines and treatment. For this reason if there is the
slightest negligence concerning the health of such workers, affairs cease
to progress in an orderly fashion and the physical well-being of thousands
of persons is endangered. The health department of the railway construction department, which was founded for the comfort of the railway
workers, guarantees their physical well-being. The administration of this
department, with the help of special branches which it has for the preservation of the physical well-being of the workers, takes action along
three lines: (i) precautionary measures for the prevention of the spread
of infectious diseases, (ii) the care (treatment) of sick workers, and (iii)
help to the injured. Since contractors for constructional work are bound
by the contents of their undertakings to make available (ready) for the
workers houses, drinking water and foodstuffs in accordance with the
principles of hygiene, the department of health watches over the per-
formance of these undertakings to protect the workers from contagious
diseases and carries out at the proper time the necessary inspections by
means of technical officials and inspectors. In addition in time of necessity
it inoculates with serums workers who are engaged in operations near

places where there are infectious diseases and by the distribution of
quinine takes steps to assure (lit. to prepare the causes of) their physical
well-being.

### The Science of Belles Lettres* (p. 208)

Poetry and prose, or to use another expression, words joined [in a
special sequence] and words dispersed [in any order], are the subject of
the science of *belles lettres*. The object of this science is that words in
poetry or prose should be written on whatever subject it may be with
proper regard to the principles of eloquence and rhetoric and formed
according to the style adopted by eloquent and learned men; and that
the level of prose and poetry of a man of letters or poet should be such
that it gives delight and enjoyment to the intelligence and imparts gladness and happiness (lit. expansion) to the heart. The advantages of the
science of *belles lettres* are that it keeps men from offences due to ignorance, smooths the roughness of their nature, gives polish (lit. brightness)
and purity to their character, arouses emotions of chivalry and manliness,
directs their zeal towards the acquisition of honour, and guides them
towards good actions and noble ends, because the man of letters cannot
do other than investigate and research deeply into the literary remains of
great men and masters and the words of philosophers and learned men,
and gather an ear from every heap of corn. Thus, he obtains some good
advice from every word and derives some benefit from every fine point;
and if he acts in this way an imprint of what he has acquired inevitably
remains in his soul, a joy and happiness appear in his heart, and a fitting
impress is made on his character and a polish given to it.

* Husein Sami'i (Adib os-Saltaneh), *A'in-e Negaresh.*

### EXERCISE 29 (p. 208)

۱ هر چه بتوانم بدیدن او میروم ـ ۲ هر قدر که ثروتمندتر میشود بهمان
اندازه جاه‌طلبی او بیشتر میشود ـ ۳ بهمان نسبت که هدف نویسنده نه تنها
ترسیم عالم وقایع محض بلکه درك او از آنهاست هنرمندش توان خواند و
کارشرا هنر ـ ٤ مساعی او تا آن حد بنتیجه رسید که تعداد آنهائیرا که مبتلا
بامراض مسری بودند کاسته است ـ ٥ این پیشنهاد تا آن اندازه که با مصالح
عمومی ارتباط دارد (مورد علاقه عموم است) روشن است ـ ٦ هر چه تندتر تا
آنجا بدوید ـ ۷ آنقدر اوقاتش تلخ نشد که حقش بود ـ ۸ بهتر است که ده
نفر جانی خلاص شوند (فرار کنند) تا اینکه یك نفر بیگناه‌را بدار کشند ـ ۹ حال
او از دفعه آخر که بشما نوشته بودم بهتر شده‌است ـ ۱۰ انگلیسها آزادی

خودرا حتی بیش از پادشاهان خود دوست دارند ــ ۱۱ جرأت نداشت تکان
بخورد مبادا اورا ببینند ــ ۱۲ البته اگر ثروتمند بودم مسافرت میکردم ــ ۱۳ اگر
تصادمی نمیکردیم زودتر میرسیدیم

## Education Today (p. 213)

One of the outstanding characteristics and excellent features which distinguishes education today is the existence of the laboratories of various educational institutions. Formerly what students of schools and universities learnt in different subjects was confined to those points and problems found in their textbooks or in printed books. But the principles and system of education today differ from the past and are, indeed, in this respect superior because the students observe with their own eyes and test the practical operation of that which they read in books and commit to memory. This new method has induced the leaders of pedagogy to adopt these principles even in the teaching of the principles of history and knowledge of the ancient history (periods) of nations and peoples[1] and to take the students to museums and excavations (subterranean ruins) in order to substantiate historical theses.

## On the Art of Writing* (p. 213)

Now let us say a little about what pertains to the art of writing and of a literary man, reveal what composition is and show what is demanded of it. In dictionaries [the word] *enṣa* is defined as 'to begin' and 'to bring into existence', and as a technical term it is the science by which is made known the way to the understanding of the meanings [of language] and the interpretation of those meanings by means of pleasant and agreeable words and phrases, such as are acceptable to the nature and close to the understanding of the reader and make clear the object of the writer. This is the art of writing. A man of letters inevitably needs to become thoroughly versed in many branches of knowledge. In his work as a writer he must make use of and seek help from various arts, because the eloquent writer does not always write about one subject or write in one way: on the contrary the variety of his words is in proportion to the variety of the subjects and matters which occur to him. He has no alternative but to have an adequate knowledge (lit. a fitting portion) of everything so that he can embark on every kind of discussion and express himself on every subject. Syntax, grammar, logic, rhetoric,[2] history, stories [of the pro-

---

[1] I.e. archaeology (for which the current term is باستانشناسی).

[2] بدیع and بیان, معانی are different branches of rhetoric.

phets], lexicology, proverbs, ethics, biography, genealogy, disputation and many other branches of knowledge, all are considered to be among the things which belong to the science of *belles lettres* and especially to be among the tools and instruments of the writer. He has no choice but to acquire them. He cannot, having embarked upon the art of writing, write about whatever he wants without these branches of knowledge.[1]

Since my object in laying (spreading out) this compendium [before the reader] is not to discuss and investigate the science of *belles lettres* and its roots and branches, and I am merely concerned with a part of it, namely the art of a literary man and writing, I shall not enter upon a discussion and description of the aforementioned branches of knowledge and their connection with the science of *belles lettres*; and I shall pass over what the masters of the craft have written in this respect: which of these sciences belongs to the roots of *belles lettres*, which to the branches, to what extent each one affects literature, and which has the greatest influence. I will merely say this much so that from these indications the extent of the relationship and connection of the science of *belles lettres* to all branches of human knowledge may be fully (lit. well) grasped and the great services which it performs to all branches of positive and speculative knowledge known. 　　　　　* *A'in-e Negaresh.*

## EXERCISE 30 (p. 214)

۱ تا توانستم آنرا تحمل کردهام حوصلهام اکنون بسر رسیدهاست (طاقتم طاق شدهاست) — ۲ تا پول در میاورد آنرا خرج میکند — ۳ از این که بـایـد بـروم هـیـچ بـرای مـن نـمیـتـوانـد نـاگوارتـر بـاشد — ٤ نمیگویم که بهیچ وجه غفلت کردهاست یا ناصالح بودهاست — ٥ چنان بلند حرف مـیـزنـد کـه حـتی از اینجا صدای اورا میشنوم — ٦ چنان سخت زخمی شدهاست کـه حـتّاً میمیرد — ۷ چنان سخت زخمی شدهاست کـه احـتـمـال دارد کـه بـمیـرد — ۸ چنـان سخت زخمی شدهاست که مـمکن است کـه بمیرد — ۹ محصول بعمل نیامد زیراکه خشکسالی بود — ۱۰ ممکن نیست که خسته شده باشد زیرا کـه فقط کـمی راه رفتـهاست

### The [*Experimental*] Agricultural Garden (p. 217)

At a distance of two kilometres from the town of Ahvaz on the west side of the R. Karun a very large garden, which has different kinds of trees suitable to the climate of Khuzistan, has been founded. Steps have been taken to irrigate that extensive garden by means of motor-pumps

١ دانشها and آگاهیها appear to be used synonymously here.

[pumping water] from the Karun in order that the trees shall be watered. Different kinds of date palms, pomegranates, olives, and bananas, etc., have been planted in that garden; and even tropical grasses and cuttings have also been sown in the cultivated part (lit. sown fields) of the above-mentioned garden by way of experiment (lit. examples). Millions of *tumans* have been spent on the garden, the purchase of necessities and implements for agriculture and the import of saplings from abroad.

### Some Observations concerning Literature during the Period of the Constitution* (p. 217)

A series of political, scientific and literary events, to describe and expand on which a separate book would be necessary, prepared the way for the appearance of the constitution, the imperial rescript for which was issued in A.H. lunar 1324 (A.D. 1906). In brief it can be said that Persian literature, as well as carrying on the old themes and styles, also acquired in this period certain new features. It is possible to summarize them as follows: (i) foreign languages, especially French, which had begun to spread in Persia from the beginning of the Qajar period, became current and intercourse between Persia and Western Europe became greater than it had been formerly. The literary compositions of those regions, poetry and prose, stories and novels, became well known in this country. As a result of this mixing not only were a number of foreign books translated and a number of foreign words incorporated into the Persian language but also some modern writers, both in concept and form, adopted to a certain extent the style and method of thought of the west. Sometimes they went [even] further in this course and departed from the style of Persian. (ii) Liberal thoughts, social and political ideas, the idea of equality of political rights, the problem of freedom of thought and the freedom of the press, and patriotic sentiments, were among the new subjects which came into [Persian] literature, and had in truth, in poetry and prose a special éclat. Able and talented poets and skilful writers appeared and occupied themselves in interpreting these thoughts in the best possible words. Ideas of this sort were even spread among the common people in the form of popular ballads by the grace of poetical talent such as [that possessed by] Aref of Qazvin. Among the poets of this period one can mention, by way of example, Adib al-Mamalek Farahani and Adib Pishevari among the deceased and Parvin E'tesami in the world of women; and among the living Mr Mohammad Taqi Bahar (Malek osh-Sho'ara), who is a master in the *qasideh* (a kind of ode) and in historical and literary research. In truth, many eloquent and skilful poets and writers have appeared in our age, who have indeed kept Persian poetry and prose alive, made it more eloquent and expressive, breathed into it new meanings, and shown themselves to be the true successors of the great men of ancient times. (iii) Poetry and prose have abandoned something of their ancient lofty, literary status, which was usually far removed from the life of the people and separated from the tastes and needs of the common people and come nearer to the mind and life of the masses. In keeping with the needs of society new features (lit. freshness) have appeared in its subject matter and poetry and prose have become occupied with (lit. turned towards) social subjects, and writers, in developing these subjects, have paid attention more to the subject matter and to expressing their meaning than to verbal ornament and the use of long sentences. (To be continued)

\* Dr Rezazadeh Shafaq, *Tarikh-e Adabiyyat-e Iran.*

## EXERCISE 31 (p. 219)

۱ تقصیر من نیست باین جهت که حضور نداشتم و در این امر هیچ دخیل نبودم — ۲ از شرکت کردن امتناع کرد چونکه باین امر علاقه نداشت — ۳ البته قانون فعلی تا آنجا که معلمینی در دانشگاهها هستند که اصلاً باین اصول معتقد نیستند از اعتبار خود افتاده‌است — ٤ بشرط اینکه در عرض' هفته آینده آنرا پس بدهید میتوانید چند روز داشته باشید — ٥ تا وقتیکه راضی باشید اهمیتی بآن نمیدهم — ٦ هیچ چیز اورا قانع نمیکرد مگر آمدن من — ۷ همه جا بود جز آنجا که باید باشد — ۸ هر روز پیاده راه میروم مگر اینکه باران بیاید — ۹ بر فرض که احمق باشد آدم خوش قلبیست — ۱۰ گاهی با اینکه مستحق آن نیستیم انتظار حقشناسی داریم — ۱۱ بهر نحوی در باره مزایا یا نواقص فلسفه یونانی قضاوت کنیم همیشه موضوع جالبی خواهد بود — ۱۲ چه موفق بشود چه نشود ما کار خودمانرا انجام میدهیم

## The Central Government (p. 231)

No country and no community can be administered unless it has a strong central point of support. One meaning of security is just this that the central government should have power. The meaning of the opposite to this also confirms and substantiates this same principle: that is to say no country and community in which the central power is weak and whose point of support is unstable and tottering, will be [properly] administered. A failure to administer a country or the life of a community or people [properly] means anarchy and lack of security. The greatest internal

¹ در عرض ‎*dar arz(e)*, in the course of.

political duty of every government is to preserve order. Justice and the administration of justice are merely for the preservation of security and security acquires permanence and stability by virtue of the existence of justice.

### Some Observations concerning Literature during the Period of the Constitution (p. 231)

(Continuation from previous lesson)

(iv) The creation of new schools, newspapers and periodicals, performed a great service to the extension and spread of (lit. making general) education. Literature became more adapted to the common people and within their reach and attention to science and *belles lettres* increased. (v) An inclination towards [a study of] the scientific and literary works of the classical (lit. ancient) writers of Persia appeared among the people and scholars and writers as a class; and also attention on the part of the ministry of education was paid to the composition of textbooks and the translation of the scientific works of the west; and in particular special attention was given to the editing and printing of the poetical and prose works of Persian writers of the past. A large number of rare works and compositions of the past were printed and edited by the endeavour of scholars according to the new methods and revived. (vi) Striking progress was made in the critical inclusion of scientific and historical matter and reference to principles and documents on the basis of intellectual discipline and full research. In fact, the style of some great Islamic writers, which, each in its own time, was customary in the classical age, was revived; and in this full use was made of the critical method of western scholars. Indeed the writings and researches of Western orientalists had in this respect a special effect on the modern literary movement in Persia and were an important factor in [encouraging] the taste of Persians and [influencing] their methods of scientific research in their wish and desire to revive the literary remains of the writers of the past. It can be said that the great pioneer among Persian scholars in this technique was Mr Mohammad Qazvini. (vii) A movement against unnecessary wordiness and hyperbole and the forced and complicated subjects and similes of a part of classical literature began; and in this respect some seek to abandon most of the classical subjects, similes, style and rhetoric, to find new subjects and to use new metres and forms. In prose they oppose the formation of sentences on the model of Arabic and the use of large numbers of Arabic words. They endeavour to revive a Persian style and to use Persian words. Some have even gone further and try to use sentences of pure Persian. Meanwhile it can be said that the present age in one respect, namely in respect of the subject matter and purpose [of literature] and the method of literary interpretation, is a period of transition and revolution. The classical metres have been to a certain extent shaken but the new principles have not yet been fully established and literature in general is passing through a period of evolution. In any case some modern writers have produced lovely and attractive works which give promise of a finer style.

EXERCISE 32 (p. 232)

۱ با اینکه جوانی بیش نبود نه تنها شایسته این بود که از تعلیم و تربیت دانشگاه استفاده کند بلکه ذوق ادبی و مایه علمی که با خود بدانشگاه برد باعث افتخار یك نفر فارغ التحصیل بود — ۲ این جمله نه تنها موجز¹ است بلکه زیبائی هم دارد — ۳ کوشش من این خواهد بود که هم تاریخ ملت و هم تاریخ دولترا بنویسم — ٤ گرگ حیوانی است سبع و قوی با این همه یکی از زرنگترین حیوانات میباشد — ٥ چند تا از اینهارا بر دارید مثلاً ده دوازده تا — ٦ از بیانات ذیل بر میاید که نفوذ دانشگاه‌ها و مدارس در افکار عمومی تا چه اندازه قوی است و تا چه حد کسانیراکه سازمان اداری مملکت بنوبت بآنها سپرده میشود تحت تسلط خود در آورده است — ۷ آنقدر خندید که من هم نتوانستم از خنده خودداری کنم — ۸ اکنون که مریض شده است باید کاررا انجام دهیم — ۹ چه بگویم غیر از اینکه امیدوارم که سعادتمند بشوید — ۱۰ جامعه بر هیچ طبقه نمیتواند اعمال نفوذ کند جز از راه جلب منافع آن

*On the Qualities of a Writer** (p. 245)

A writer must before all else strive to be the possessor of excellent qualities and a praiseworthy character. He should adorn the beauty of form with the perfection of meaning; cloak the body in the garment of piety and abstinence; adorn the form of authority (lit. credit, standing) with the ornament of honesty and good faith; mix his discourse with uprightness and truth and give it beauty by the clearness of his logic and the frankness of his words; keep free his tongue and pen from that which is unseemly; exert abundant efforts in the keeping of secrets; attract to himself the confidence of all; restrain his pen from what is contrary to the truth; and he must not praise anyone for what is not in him; and must flee from flattery, which is fatal to the spirit of *belles lettres*. If a writer is endowed with these qualities and adorned with these ornaments,

¹ موجز‌ *mujez*, concise.

his rank and worth will indeed be great in the eyes of men, his position in society will be high, and his words will have the greatest possible effect on the ears and hearts [of men]. It must be realized that several conditions are necessary [of fulfilment] for a writer and unless these conditions are fulfilled in the person of the writer, the title of writer cannot be applied to him, and he cannot carry out the responsibilities imposed by the work of a writer.

\* Hosein Sami'i (Adib os-Saltaneh), *A'in-e Negaresh.*

## The Meaning of Freedom\* (p. 246)

My dear brothers and fellow-countrymen:

Praise be to God you have once more by the grace of God under the shadow of the care of [our] young and auspicious sovereign stepped into the ring of freedom and you can enjoy this gift (lit. bounty). Of course you must realize the value of this gift and give thanks to God for it. I hope that you have learnt and taken warning from the trouble and toil which you have suffered during the last thirty or forty years and that you know how to recognize the value of the gift of freedom and have understood its meaning. If this is so you know that the meaning of freedom is not that men should be self-willed and that everyone should do whatever he wants. Constraints and limits are necessary to the essence of freedom. If there are no limits set and everyone is self-willed, no one will be free and whoever is the strongest will make others his captives and slaves. The constraints and limits which are set to self-will are what is called the law. Thus, men will be free when the law is operative and everyone knows the limits to his authority and does not transgress them. A country, therefore, which has no law, or in which the law is not put into execution and respected, its people will not be free and will not live at ease. This is a very simple and obvious truth; and nobody denies it. But unfortunately few people believe this truth because usually we see that people consider limits, i.e. the law, necessary for others but do not hold the observation of the law incumbent upon themselves. If everyone believed that the observation of the limits set by the law was not only incumbent with reference to others but also with reference to himself, transgression of the law would not occur, whereas every day we see many people transgressing the law. Few people understand that if they consider it permissible for themselves to transgress the law, there is no reason why others also should not consider transgression of the law permissible for themselves. In this event transgression of the law will become common and widespread and the result will be as we said, namely all will be deprived of ease. Unfortunately it is the nature of many people to exert undue force whenever they can, neglecting the fact that if there is to be the exertion of force, while one may be able to overpower one's subordinate today, tomorrow some stronger person will appear who will exert undue force against one. Thus that same person who exerts force today will tomorrow meet someone stronger than himself. Then there will be sighing and lamenting; and in this way the world will exactly bear out the words of Sheikh Sa'di who wrote:

> You are carrying off the goods of the Muslims but when
>      your goods are carried off
> You complain and lament that 'the religion of Islam does
>      not exist'.

Accordingly the first recommendation which I make to you in a spirit (lit. the world) of well-wishing and patriotism is that you should understand that a free people is one the course of whose affairs proceeds in accordance with the law. Thus anyone who treats the law with contempt and considers its transgression permissible is an enemy of freedom, i.e. an enemy of the ease of the people. I would like to make one further point in this connection and then occupy myself with another matter. It is this: you, my listeners, I am certain, have often heard people speak about civilization and barbarism and civilized and uncivilized peoples. Have you ever really thought which is a civilized people and which an uncivilized people? I fancy that some of you will say a civilized people is one which has railways, factories, soldiers, armies, tanks, aeroplanes and such like while an uncivilized people is one which has not these things. Or it will be said that a civilized people is one whose cities are like this and like that, its streets wide and asphalted, its houses of several storeys and so on. Of course civilized peoples have these things. But I say to you: realize that these things are the accessories of civilization. They are not the essential part. The essential part of civilization is that a people should be educated and the best proof (lit. sign) of a people being educated is that it respects and observes the law. If the essential part is preserved the accessories will automatically be obtained. But if a people does not respect the law however much it may have of those things, it cannot be said that it is educated and it cannot be said that it is civilized. Those things will in the end be lost to it. After these preliminaries, which I do not think can be denied, we will occupy ourselves with the essential part of the matter. I would remind [you] that the existence of the law depends on two things: one the legislature and the other the executive, which together are called the government. If we consider different peoples in different ages we shall see that their governments were not and are not all or always of one kind. Sometimes the legislative and executive power reside in one person and sometimes in a limited number of persons; and there were and are some peoples among whom responsibility for the legislative and executive power is accepted by the whole people. The first type of government is called autocratic and despotic government; the second aristocratic government and the third popular government which Europeans call democracy. Each of these three types had and have different forms, into a discussion of which I shall not enter, since it is not my purpose to give you a lesson in political science. I shall merely say this that peoples as they become more learned and mature incline more towards the third type, namely popular government, except that since usually large populations and extensive countries are involved, peoples cannot every day assemble in one place and exercise legislative and executive duties directly. Accordingly the best way which they have devised is for the people to make a group of persons their representatives to legislate in their name. We call the collectivity of such representatives the national consultative assembly. The assembly also chooses a few people to execute the law, who are called the council of ministers. Both these two groups are under the supreme leadership of one person who, if he is elected, is called the president of the republic and, if he is permanent and hereditary, the king. You, the Persian people, by virtue of the fundamental laws which were established about thirty-five years ago have a representative monarchical government. But if you consider [the matter] carefully you will agree that during these thirty-five years you seldom enjoyed the gift of true freedom, namely [a state of affairs in which] the law was executed and respected. Several times representative government, i.e. the basis of your constitution, was disrupted. Have you ever thought what was the reason for this? I will tell you. The fundamental reason was this that you did not rightly know the value of this gift and you did not exert yourselves to perform the duties imposed by it, and many out of ignorance and some because of ulterior motives and personal desires transgressed those conditions which must be observed in representative government. What are the conditions which must be observed in representative government? Do not forget that the meaning of representative government is that authority over the affairs of the country rests with the people. And of course you know that whoever has powers also has in return for those powers a responsibility. Therefore, if he does not act according to the exigencies imposed by his powers as his conscience dictates, he will be answerable; and to be answerable does not always mean that some one will call him to account. To be answerable usually amounts to this that a person suffers a terrible end: if there is no creature who will call him to account, the Creator will do so. Being called to account by the Creator cannot always be deferred until the day of resurrection. Usually being called to account by the

Creator takes place in the life of this world and a person receives the reward of his actions. As has been said:

> Do not be careless concerning the retribution [which you will receive] for your actions.
> Wheat grows from the wheat [seed] and barley from the barley [seed].

Now let us see how does a people become answerable if it does not act with regard to its powers in accordance with its legal duties and the demands of its conscience? A people consists of different classes. Each one has a special duty in the matter of representative government. It is the duty of the common people to exercise care in the election of their representatives to the national consultative assembly, to elect honest representatives, to watch over their conduct after their election, to give evidence of sound thoughts, that is liberal beliefs, which mean law-abidingness, that is patriotism; and to believe that to desire the well-being of the public takes precedence over the pursuit of selfish personal interests. It is incumbent upon every individual of the community to choose a respectable and lawful occupation and craft in accordance with his talents and to strive to carry that out. It is the duty of the representatives of the people to exercise care in passing laws and supervising their execution and not to consider the function of representative of the people as a means for the furtherance of selfish interests and desires or ambition. The duty of ministers is to consider themselves the executors of the law and the servants of the people and always to have in mind the well-being and interests of the people when proposing laws to the assembly and when carrying out the laws. The duty of government servants, in executing the laws with integrity and uprightness, is to facilitate the work of the ministers and to bring about the ease of their fellow-men, whose servants they are. The duty of pressmen is to guide the thoughts of the people and to lead the nation and the government along the path of well-being. The duty of the king is to defend the fundamental laws, to watch over the actions of the government, to consider all individuals among the nation his children, to treat them in accordance with fatherly love and to make his words and actions an example for the people. Altogether, the duty of all classes of the nation is to make their words and actions compatible with the principles of honour and reputation because, as one of the wise men of Europe said, if despotic government is founded on fear, representative government is based on the honour of the individuals of the nation. And it is especially the case that if those who are in charge of the affairs of the common people do not in their actions make honourable conduct their aim, representative government will not progress. Finally, all classes must co-operate with each other and be united in bringing about the advance of representative government, because the greatest calamity in representative government is discord and disunity. Thus, if the individuals of a nation consider only their personal considerations and interests and are not prepared to sacrifice one jot of their personal seeking to the common interest, turn aside from the path of what is right and, instead of occupying themselves with honourable matters, adopt unfitting means such as hypocrisy, discord, sedition, corruption, connivance [for evil ends] and demagogy in order to further private interests; and if the representatives of the people in passing or executing laws do not exercise the necessary care, and consider the function of representative of the people a means for the acquisition or preservation of personal advantages and make demagogy their occupation and intrigue their practice, or consider the function of representative of the people to consist merely in making claims against the government; and if the ministers suppose the position of minister to be merely a means for the recognition and acquisition of personal advantages; and if pressmen make the newspapers into instruments of abuse and means for the furtherance of corrupt desires instead of speaking the truth and leading the people along the path of well-being; and if the king does not defend the laws or consider all individuals of the people his children but makes sovereignity a means for the execution of personal desire; and if all classes of the people depart from the path of honour or follow the road of discord and disunity, apart from the fact that they will be personally accountable, i.e. they will suffer a terrible end, they can be certain that the conditions of the last thirty-five years will be renewed. The country and the nation will be afflicted every day by calamity, sedition and corruption; and not only will freedom be lost but we shall enter the world of annihilation and non-existence. But if the nation has taken warning and acts according to its conscience one can hope that the day of toil and ignominy will pass and the day of honour, happiness, and holding one's head high will come.

* A speech by the late Mr Forughi, which was broadcast by radio Tehran on 15 Mehr 1320 (7 October 1941).

## ADDITIONAL EXERCISES

### EXERCISE 14c

1. It is not necessary for you to tell him to come because I have written to him. 2. It is possible that he has gone. 3. If you have not read this book I think that you ought to read it. 4. I shall try to finish this work by this afternoon. 5. If he had not been lazy he would have learnt Persian more quickly. 6. If the journey to Persia by land did not take so long, I would go by land. 7. If they wish to raise the standard of living in this country it will be necessary to increase the exports of the country; otherwise it will not be possible. 8. In spite of the fact that the agricultural production of the country has increased, the country cannot yet export agricultural goods. 9. I shall not go out until the rain stops. 10. I was very thirsty by the time I reached the town. 11. As soon as the sun rises we must start. 12. As soon as I got to the door I remembered that I had left my key on the table in my room. 13. I told the boy to bring you some eggs today. 14. Do not take any of these books away. 15. If you had not known Persian better than I, I should not have given you this letter to translate: I should have done it myself.

### EXERCISE 16c

1. There is no difference between these two cloths. They are both very dear; neither of them is worth 30 *rials* a metre. 2. He stayed such a long time with his brother that I thought he had forgotten he had said he would come with me to the town. 3. It is no good your going now; it is too late. All the people whom you want to see went an hour ago. 4. The newspaper is published every day except Friday and each number costs one and a half *rials*. 5. I handed the money over to him and I asked him to give me a receipt. 6. If he had had greater experience he would not have made this mistake. 7. Although the style of Persian writers of earlier centuries differs from the style of writers of the present day, it is not difficult to understand their works. 8. I forgot to tell him that I was not coming. 9. I shall finish the work before you return. 10. By the time you finish this it will be dark. 11. Take him into the next room and give him a seat until the minister is ready to receive him.

### EXERCISE 17a

1. It would have been better if you had gone to see him instead of writing to him. 2. Instead of visiting Shiraz this spring as I had planned

I shall stay at home. 3. I went straight home from the office yesterday instead of going for a walk as is my custom. 4. I shall not go without telling you. 5. When he had finished his work he went home without telling his brother. 6. It is difficult to find the way without a map. 7. He suddenly got angry without the slightest reason. 8. Other than him I knew no one there. 9. I do not know what to do other than to tell him. 10. If I had thought that it was possible to do other than pay his fine I would not have paid it. 11. I wrote the letter before I knew that he was coming. 12. The cost of living was not so high before the war as it is now. 13. Will you buy some cheese on the way home if you go before me? 14. He looked so happy that I knew before he began to speak that he had good news. 15. There was no one there but him. 16. They will not come unless you invite them. 17. After he had read the letter he gave it to me to read. 18. I would have told him what you told me if I had seen him after I had seen you. 19. If you still want to see me after you have seen him, let me know.

## Exercise 18a

1. Please tell your brother to come here as quickly as possible. 2. If we go now perhaps we shall get to the station before the train starts. 3. The building of the factory was finished the year before last and it began production last year. 4. We were listening to the radio when suddenly the telephone bell rang. 5. If you had listened to what I said you would not have made so many mistakes in your work. 6. If you listen carefully to what I say the matter will be clear to you. 7. He asked me to come for a walk with him. 8. While we were going for a walk yesterday it began to rain. 9. When I saw him he was bargaining with a draper in the bazaar. 10. I do not know whether he has returned or not. 11. I went to see my brother yesterday afternoon; if you had returned yesterday I would have asked you to come with me to see him. 12. If he has returned from the village I will give him your message. 13. We shall return before it gets dark. 14. I do not know whether he can help me or not.

## Exercise 21a

1. My object in asking you to come to see me today was to transmit to you the new orders which have arrived from Tehran. 2. You cannot go without obtaining his permission first. 3. If he has not already decided to come, I shall try to persuade him to come. 4. As soon as the battle began it was clear that the enemy would be defeated. 5. I shall not only write a letter to him but I shall also go to see him. 6. As I

was going home I suddenly remembered that I had forgotten to lock the door of my office; I returned and as I was going up the steps I saw that I had not only left the door open but had also left the light on.  7. As I told you yesterday what you suggest is impossible.  8. As I crossed the bridge it began to snow.  9. This morning as I was going along the street I saw a man selling apples. I went up to him and asked how much the *mann*. He said 7 *rials*. I said that was too dear and asked what his lowest price was. He replied that he would not sell for less than 7 *rials*. Finally after much argument I persuaded him to let me have them at 5 *rials* the *mann*.

### Exercise 23 a

As I was crossing the bridge over the river I met one of my former colleagues. I had not seen him for years and wondered (thought to myself) whether he would recognize me, let alone speak to me. When he saw me he stopped and greeted me warmly. It was impossible for us to exchange[1] more than a few words because I was on the way to my work and it was growing late and he had business in the city. Accordingly we parted having first arranged[2] to meet on the following evening when we hoped that we would both have more leisure.

### Exercise 25 a

I pushed back[3] the crowds and passing from the rear, walked down the living avenue of people until I came in front of a group of Arabs where stood the white man with the grey beard. I would have run to him only I was a coward[4] in the presence of such a mob, and would have embraced him, only being an Englishman, I did not know how he would receive me, so I did what cowardice and false pride suggested,[5] walked up to him, took off my hat and said, 'Dr Livingstone, I presume?'

### Exercise 26 a

1. If the man from whom I bought the horse had not been so ready to sell it for such a low price I should never have bought it. I wish I had not bought it so hastily; if I had waited a little I might have found a much better horse to buy.  2. As the demonstrators passed through the centre of the town they were joined by a large number of the towns-

---

¹ رد و بدل کردن‎ *radd o badal k.*      ² قرار گذاشتن‎ *qarar goɀaʃtan.*

³ عقب زدن‎ *aɀab ɀadan.*      ⁴ واهمه داشتن‎ *vaheme d.*, to be frightened.

⁵ تلقین کردن‎ *talqin k.*

people. They intended to hold a meeting[1] at the entry to the bazaar but before they reached the bazaar they were dispersed by the police. 3. If you see the village headman will you tell him that I should like to see him as soon as possible. A new circular has arrived from Tehran with instructions for the calling up of those liable[2] to military service. I wish to give him copies of this circular to put up[3] in public places[4] in this village and the neighbouring villages. A new law has been passed according to the provisions[5] of which a large number of men will be exempt from military service.

## EXERCISE 27a

After finishing our meal we were about to resume our journey when our hostess said, 'I should be very grateful if you would say a few words to my son before leaving. We lead such a lonely[6] life here that the arrival of two travellers is an event for him.' She took us into the garden where her son was sitting, doing nothing. He talked to us about the countryside which he seemed to know well. We had been chatting for a quarter of an hour when he turned to me. Then only did I notice[7] he was blind.

## EXERCISE 28a

Near the village I met several unknown[8] persons. They began to talk and one of them said to me that it would be a good thing if I was to be their guest that night. Although I did not know them and was somewhat suspicious of them, since I was a stranger and had no accommodation and it was night, I accepted their invitation. They took me through the middle of the village to a large house which was situated beside the river. As soon as I entered the house an old man came to me quietly and said, 'Would that you had not come here; I fear that you will never leave here alive. Flee from here as quickly as possible, otherwise they will kill you.' However much I thought the meaning of the old man's words was not clear to me, but in any case I had no alternative but to pass the night in the house. There was nothing for it. Accordingly with firm steps I went forward and entered a large room. I had hardly sat down when another person came into the room, and as soon as I saw him I knew that I was in a dangerous place and that the old man was right and that I must flee as quickly as possible.

| | |
|---|---|
| [1] میتنگ miteng. | [2] مشمول maʃmul. |
| [3] نصب کردن nasb k. | [4] اماکن عمومی amakene omumi. |
| [5] مقررات moqarrarat. | [6] تنها tanha. |
| [7] متوجه شدن motavajjeh ʃ. | [8] ناشناس naʃenas. |

## Why the Jackals Howl Outside the Town

And now, just outside the walls surrounding the telegraph office, rose a prolonged and dismal[1] howl,[2] followed by another and yet another; while from the city, like an answer, came back the barking[3] of the dogs. 'Are those jackals howling outside?' I asked, 'and do they come so close to the town?' 'Yes,' answered the Khán, 'they always do so, and the dogs always answer them thus. Do you know why? Once upon a time the jackals used to live in the towns, just as the dogs do now, while the latter dwelt outside in the desert. Now, the dogs thought it would be much nicer to be in the town, where they would be sheltered from the inclemency of the weather, and would have plenty to eat instead of often having to go without food for a long time. So they sent one of their number to the jackals with the following message: "Some amongst us," they said, "are ill, and our physicians say that what they need is a change of air, and that they ought if possible, to spend three days in the town. Now, it is clearly impossible for us dogs and you jackals to be in one place at the same time, so we would ask you to change places with us for three days only, and to let us take up our quarters in the city, while you retire into the desert, the air of which will doubtless prove very beneficial[4] to you also." To this proposition the jackals agreed, and during the following night the exchange was effected.[5] In the morning, when the people of the city woke up, they found a dog wherever there had been a jackal on the previous night. On the third night the jackals, being quite tired of the desert, came back to the gates of the town filled with pleasant anticipations[6] of resuming their luxurious city life. But the dogs, being very comfortable in their new quarters, were in no hurry to quit them. So after waiting some time, the jackals called out to the dogs, "*naxofha-ye foma xub fode*", ending up with a whine, just such as you heard a minute ago and (as Mírzá 'Abdu'lláh, who is a native of Isfahán, will tell you) just such as you may hear any day in the mouth[7] of an Isfahání or a Yezdí. But the dogs, who are Turks and speak Turkish, only answered "*Yokh! yokh!*" ("No! no!"), and so the poor jackals had to go back into the desert. And ever since then they come back at night and hail the dogs with the same question, as you heard them do just now; and the dogs always give the same reply, for they have no wish to go back to the

---

[1] غم انگیز yamangiz.

[3] عوعو ōuōu.

[5] صورت گرفتن surat gereftan, to take place.

[7] گلو galu, throat.

[2] زوزه zouze.

[4] سازگار sazgar, salubrious.

[6] انتظارات entezarat, expectations.

desert. And that is why the jackals come and howl round the town after dusk, and why the dogs always answer them.'

(E. G. Browne, *A year among the Persians*, Cambridge, 1927, pp. 199–201)

### The Persian Plateau[1]

Villages cluster round the foothills,[2] wherever water exists, or can be found, but are seldom less than five miles apart. Towns of importance are anything from one to two hundred miles distant from each other. Mountain ranges are never far distant: salt marshes, and a few large expanses of salt water lie at their feet.[3] Such wild vegetable and animal life as exists is that of the desert, though wherever man has settled the mulberry, walnut and other fruit trees thrive. The heat in summer is very great, rising to 140 degrees in the sun; in winter the thermometer may fall below zero, the cold being more formidable[4] because it is ushered in[5] by freezing[6] sand-storms, lashing tiny pebbles like hail into the traveller's face, thereby increasing his misery and that of his mount.[7] But when the traveller is fortunate enough to be able to travel by caravan and not by car the desert has its compensations: in summer the long, cool night is the best time to travel. At dusk[8] the sky is illumined with rainbow tints along the unbroken horizon: within an hour of sunset it is dark; the blue turns to lapis lazuli, till it merges[9] into the deeper purple of the dark horizon and the Milky Way[10] appears overhead.

(A. T. Wilson, *Persia*, London, 1932, p. 7)

### Shiraz

The capital of the province of Fars is Shiraz, famous for its wine and honey, the home and the grave of the two most famous poets of Persia, Hafiz, the contemporary of Dante, and Sa'di. It has been laid in ruins more than once by earthquakes, but can still show noble[11] mosques and fine bazaars. The city lies in the midst of a long plain, some twelve miles across, terminating towards the east in a salt lake, the home[12] of countless water fowl. In spring the plain is green with heavy crops of cereals and

---

[1] فلات *falat.*

[2] کوه‌پایه *kuhpaye.*

[3] دامنه *damane*, skirt (of a mountain, etc.).

[4] هیبت *heibat*, formidability.

[5] طلیعه *tali'e*, vanguard.

[6] پر سوز *por suz*, biting (of cold, or wind).

[7] مرکب *markab.*

[8] هوای گرگ و میش *havaye gorg o miš.*

[9] محو شدن *mahv f.*, to be obliterated.

[10] کهکشان *kahkašan.*

[11] معظم *mo'azzam* ( =great, fine).

[12] مسکن *maskan*, dwelling-place.

of cotton; the hillsides bright with the foliage of vines, grown for the raisin crop rather than for wine, which is not as in France, a staple beverage... South of Shiraz extends a long series of great limestone ranges, between which lie fertile valleys, descending in a series of steps to the sea coast. Locusts and drought are the great enemies of the farmer. The nomad is poorer but less dependent on weather and insect pests,[1] for if grazing in one part of the province is bad he can usually transfer his flocks to a far-off region, perhaps three hundred miles away, which has not been stricken. The nomads are unruly[2] neighbours, but they have their place in the economy of the country and have in recent years been brought under effective control.[3]          (*Ibid.* pp. 11–12)

### Bandar Abbas and Hormuz

At the entrance of the Persian Gulf, by which until recent years the great majority of travellers have entered Persia, lies Bandar Abbas, named after the great king who was to Persia what his contemporary, Elizabeth, was to England. It has an evil reputation[4] for heat and bad water. Hormuz, once an emporium[5] comparable to modern Bombay, and repeatedly mentioned by Milton as the source of fabulous[6] wealth, is now almost uninhabited. 'It has no fresh water,' wrote the incomparable Thomas Herbert, 'save what the fruitful[7] clouds weep over her, in sorrow of her desolation, late so populous', and its sole commerce today is red oxide[8] and rock salt for local use. But it was the scene of great adventures, when the British and the Portuguese fought in the sixteenth century for the mastery[9] of the Eastern Seas. Here it was that the discoverer of Baffin Bay met his death. 'Master Baffin went on shoare with his Geometricall Instruments,' says Purchas, 'for the taking of the height and distance of the Castle wall, for the better leavelling[10] of his Peece to make his shot: but as he was about the same, he received a small shot from the Castle into his belly and died immediately.'[11]

(*Ibid.* p. 14, slightly adapted)

[1] آفات afat (pl. of آفت afat).    [2] ناراحت و متمرد narahat va motamarred.
[3] تسلط tasallot.    [4] بناحقی معروف بودن be nahaqqi ma'ruf b.
[5] دار التجاره dar ot-tejare.    [6] شگفت‌انگیز Jegeftangiz.
[7] جانبخش janbaxJ, life-giving.    [8] خاك سرخ xake sorx.
[9] تفوق tafavvoq.    [10] تراز کردن taraz k.
[11] جا در جا مردن ja dar ja mordan.

### The Beginning of the Movement for Constitutional Reform in Persia

The Persian constitutional movement of the early twentieth century was the result of a process which had been going on in Persia, largely silently, throughout the nineteenth century. Up to this time the basic theories of the state and of life generally were set in the frame[1] of Islam. The intrusion[2] of the West into Persia in the nineteenth century perhaps more than any other single event led Persian thinkers[3] to question the old theories and bases of the state and to seek some new or additional base for it. The disastrous[4] wars with Russia in the early part of the century concluded by the Treaty of Turkomanchay in 1828 convinced[5] Persians of the need of reform, military and otherwise. Further, it was through the various military missions which came to Persia from 1807 onwards that Persians had first become acquainted with modern military and scientific techniques and with the political changes[6] which were taking place in Europe. Mīrzā Ṣāleḥ, the first Persian known to have written an account of British parliamentary institutions, was sent to England in 1815 in pursuance of plans for military reform. He also visited Turkey and Russia. Writing in his diary of the *tanẓīmāt* he castigates obscurantist[7] mullas who opposed them. He gives in his diary what is probably the first account by a Persian of the French revolution. Diplomatic travel also played an important role in the dissemination[8] of knowledge of western institutions. Abu'l-Ḥasan Shīrāzī, who was sent on a mission to England by Fatḥ 'Alī Shāh, wrote in his *Ḥayrat-nāmeh* an account of the justice and security which he found in England, comparing it with the tyranny which prevailed in his own country. Nāṣir al-Dīn himself made three journeys to Europe, the first in 1873. The Persian merchant communities, both inside and outside Persia, were another important channel through which modern ideas spread. The Persian press published by members of the Persian communities in Istanbul, Calcutta and elsewhere also did much in the latter part of the nineteenth century to encourage reform.

(The Encyclopedia of Islam, Leiden–London, new
ed. 1960– , art. on *Dustūr*)

[1] چهار چوبه *caharcube.*  [2] نفوذ *nofuẕ.*
[3] متفکرین *motafakkerin.*  [4] مخرب *moxarreb.*
[5] معتقد کردن *mo'taqed k.*  [6] تحولات *tahavvolat.*
[7] کهنه پرست *kohnehparast.*  [8] بسط *bast.*

### The Evolution of the Landowning Class in Persia

With the rise of Islām and the incorporation of Persia into the Islamic empire, land ownership was of two main kinds: on the one hand was private property, and on the other was land which had no private owner, the ultimate ownership of which came to be vested in the Muslim community and in the *imām* as its representative. With the division of the *dār ul-islām* into a number of semi-independent and independent kingdoms, at times at war with each other, there was inevitably a modification in the theory that all land which had no private owner was held by the *imām* for the people, and the tendency was for the rights of the *imām* in this respect to pass to the temporal ruler. Under the Seljūqs there was a re-integration of the eastern part of the Abbasid Caliphate. Ultimate ownership of such land which had no private owner came to be vested in the Seljūq people and the *sulṭān* as their representative. The *imām*, meanwhile, played an uneasy part in the background. He no longer delegated his temporal power to the *sulṭān*, but was required merely to give legal and religious sanction to the activities of the 'ruling *khān*'. The conception of 'the people' was never very strong and tended to be overshadowed by the elements of absolutism which gained ground as the traditions of the steppe weakened. The Mongol position was broadly similar, but the element of consultation was weaker and the break-up on the fall of the Mongol Īlkhān dynasty greater because of the weakening and ultimate disappearance of the caliphate. With the disintegration of the Īlkhān kingdom and its break-up into constantly warring principalities, the emphasis came to be laid on the individual ruler. Under the Ṣafavids there was to some extent a reaffirmation of the idea of 'the people', not as a conquering horde who were the owners in common of their conquests, one group of whom or one of whose number was by common consent their leader, but as a national group ruled over by the *shāh*. Ultimate ownership and all rights vested in him, not as the representative of the people, but as a divinely appointed ruler, or, according to his more extreme followers, as an emanation of the Godhead. His rule, therefore, could not be other than absolute, and submission to his government could not involve any measure of consultation with the ruled, nor did it require their freely accorded consent. Under the Qājārs the religious element was considerably weakened, but the element of absolutism remained and was untempered by any element of responsibility. This increase in the element of absolutism ran right through society and affected the general attitude to land and also the position of the peasants on the land.

In so far as the landowning classes were concerned, the feudal landed aristocracy of Sasanian Persia disappeared after the Arab conquest. The *dihqāns*, on the other hand, continued to be responsible for local administration and the collection of tribute from the protected communities, and after conversion to Islām they largely retained their lands and furnished one of the main sources of supply for recruits to the bureaucracy. Meanwhile, a new class of landed proprietor grew up, drawn originally from the Arabs who acquired large landed estates partly by grant from the *imām*, partly by conquest and partly by purchase. To them were added in the course of time converted non-Arabs. This class differed from the feudal landed aristocracy of Sasanian times in that its members did not hold their land in return for military service, and from the *dihqāns* in that they were not primarily either the representatives of the government *vis-à-vis* the peasants or tax-collectors, though such functions were often in the course of time taken over by them. With the rise of Turkish military government a new class was interposed between the state and the landowner, and the state and the peasant, i.e. the *muqṭaʿ*, to whom was assigned first the right to collect the revenue and eventually the right to the land itself. In the settled areas the old landowner was probably largely driven out by or, in so far as he accepted government service, assimilated to the *muqṭaʿ*. In the tribal areas and the more inaccessible districts such as the Caspian provinces, local leaders probably in large measure retained both their lands and their influence. Broadly speaking, the rise of new dynasties did not materially alter the structure of landowning classes, though it altered their personnel, and, to some extent, the relative importance of the different sections of the landowning class.

Throughout the pre-Mongol period a striking feature is the recuperative power of agriculture. This can in part probably be explained by the fact that the local village communities formed relatively stable and to some extent self-governing communities, under their own *kadkhudās*, who acted as middlemen between the village communities and the government, or the *muqṭaʿ*. Although large-scale resettlement sometimes took place there was on the whole little movement from one village to another. Neighbouring villages, indeed, often spoke different dialects. When one cultivator fell out his land was in all probability taken up by his fellow villagers. The main contact with the outside world was through the tax-collector. On the other hand, it is true that the villagers were, in many cases, virtually tied to the land and subject to heavy dues of one kind and another. It would seem, however, that as long as the various classes retained some sort of independence and corporate sense, as long as all power was not concentrated in the hands of one person or group of persons, and some degree of local self-government was preserved, there was a possibility of obtaining redress, or in the last resort of taking refuge with neighbouring princes or landowners, while the need to maintain economic well-being broadly speaking set a limit to the exactions of the landowners and government officials upon the peasants, though many instances of places being ruined by over-taxation can be cited. With the rise of the Mongols the restraint afforded by Islām was temporarily at least removed, nor was there any longer a limit set to taxation by considerations of economic self-interest. Local communities were further subject to a greater degree of interference by the civil and military officials than heretofore, and this involved a corresponding weakening in local self-government. Further, certain practices, which had formerly been customary only, received the sanction of law through imperial decrees. The peasant as a result, became more effectively tied to the land than was the case before. This dependence was further increased when military service under the Qājārs became a charge on the land and not on the individual.

As long as the peasant could appeal to a court presided over by the qāẓī which was independent of, or, at least not entirely subordinate to, the landowner, muqṭaʿ, or tuyūldār, he had some possibility of redress. This was to some extent the case under the Seljūqs. The religious institution, it is true, had been virtually incorporated into the general structure of the state, but there was still some balance between the various organs of the administration. Under the Mongols land disputes in some cases were still referred to courts presided over by qāẓīs. Under the Ṣafavids a change occurred. On the one hand, the independence of the qāẓīs was reduced, while, on the other, in so far as they tended to become assimilated to the landowning class, they were less likely to support the claims of the peasants against their lords. Moreover, both the tuyūldārs and the holders of hereditary soyūrghāls were in many cases given full powers to decide all cases in the area granted to them, to the exclusion of the officials of the central or provincial government. This tendency to extend the jurisdiction of the local landowner and tuyūldār and to concentrate all power in their hands continued in Qājār times. The result was a further weakening in the element of local self-government and an increase in the dependence of the peasant.

Meanwhile, however, other influences began to be felt. Contact with foreign countries was increasing. Military reverses, especially at the hands of Russia in the early part of the nineteenth century, had already shown that some change was needed if Persia was not to be left behind by the technical superiority of certain European countries; in the latter part of the nineteenth century the Young Turk movement and the movement for reform headed by Jamāl ud-Dīn Asadābādī (Afghānī) had a profound influence. Further, the ever-growing financial stringency was exercising the minds of both the ruling classes and the intellectuals: but whereas the former were looking for ways to provide themselves with better military forces and more money to pay for the extravagances of the royal courts, the latter resented the tendency of their rulers to attempt to solve financial difficulties by the grant of commercial concessions to foreigners, on the grounds that such grants would reduce Persia to the economic and political tutelage of foreign powers. They sought rather a larger share in the government of the country, and looked to the acquisition of the technical knowledge of western European countries to provide them with greater material ease. These various and conflicting movements and tendencies came to a head in the Constitutional Revolution of 1905–6 and resulted in the grant of the Constitution by Muẓaffar ud-Dīn Shāh in 1906. With this began a new period in the history of Persia. In so far as land tenure is concerned, the break in legal theory was perhaps greater than the change in practice and in the general attitude to land, which in some ways remained essentially medieval. Power, moreover, still largely remained in the hands of the landowners and tribal *khāns*, and it was not till the reign of Riẓā Shāh that this was materially altered.

(A. K. S. Lambton, Landlord and Peasant in Persia,<br>Oxford, 1953, pp. 173–7)

## KEY TO ADDITIONAL EXERCISES

### EXERCISE 14c

۱ لازم نیست که باو بگوئید که بیایید زیراکه باو نوشته‌ام — ۲ ممکن
است که رفته باشد — ۳ اگر این کتابرا نخوانده باشید فکر میکنم که آنرا باید
بخوانید — ٤ سعی میکنم این کاررا تا امروز عصر تمام کنم — ٥ اگر تنبلی
نمیکرد زبان فارسی‌را زودتر یاد میگرفت — ٦ اگر مسافرت بایران از راه خشکی
این قدر طول نمیکشید از راه خشکی میرفتم — ۷ اگر بخواهند سطح زندگی این
مملکترا بالا ببرند لازم است که صادرات مملکترا زیاد کنند و الا ممکن نخواهد
شد — ۸ این مملکت با اینکه محصولات زراعتیش زیاد شده‌است باز نمیتواند
مواد زراعتی صادرکند — ۹ تا باران بند نیاید بیرون نمیروم — ۱۰ تا بشهر
رسیدم خیلی تشنه شدم — ۱۱ تا آفتاب طلوع کند باید راه بیفتیم — ۱۲ تا دم در
رسیدم یادم آمد که کلید خودرا روی میز اطاقم گذاشته‌ام — ۱۳ پسر گفتم
امروز چند دانه تخم مرغ برای شما بیاورد — ۱٤ هیچ یکی از این کتابهارا
نبرید — ۱٥ اگر زبان فارسی‌را از من بهتر بلد نبودید این نامه‌را بشما نمیدادم
که ترجمه کنید خودم ترجمه میکردم

### EXERCISE 16c

۱ بین این دو پارچه فرقی نیست هر دو خیلی گران است هیچ یک از آنها
متری سی ریال نمی ارزد — ۲ آنقدر پیش برادر خود ماند که فکر میکردم
فراموش کرده که بمن گفته‌است که با من بشهر میاید — ۳ هیچ فائده ندارد
که حالا بروید زیاد دیر شده‌است همه آنهائیکه میخواستید ببینید یک ساعت
پیش رفته‌اند — ٤ روزنامه هر روز غیر از جمعه منتشر میشود و قیمت هر شماره
یک ریال و نیم است — ٥ پولرا باو تحویل دادم و از او خواهش کردم که
رسیدی بمن بدهد — ٦ اگر تجربه بیشتری داشت این اشتباها را نمیکرد —
۷ اگر چه سبک نویسندگان ایرانی قرنهای پیش با سبک نویسندگان امروز فرق
دارد مشکل نیست که تألیفات آنهارا بفهمیم — ۸ یادم رفت باو بگویم که
نمیایم — ۹ تا بر گردید کاررا تمام میکنم — ۱۰ تا اینرا تمام کنید هوا تاریک
میشود — ۱۱ اورا بآن اطاق (باطاق پهلوئی) ببرید و اورا بنشانید تا بحضور
وزیر برسد

## EXERCISE 17a

۱ اگر بجای اینکه باو بنویسید بدیدن او میرفتید بهتر بود — ۲ امسال بهار
بر خلاف تصمیم قبلی بجای اینکه بشیراز بروم منزل میمانم — ۳ دیروز بجای
اینکه مطابق معمول پیاده گردش کنم از اداره مستقیماً بمنزل رفتم — ٤ بدون
اینکه بشما خبر بدهم نخواهم رفت — ٥ وقتیکه کارشرا تمام کرد بدون اینکه
برادر خود بگوید بمنزل رفت — ٦ پیدا کردن راه بدون نقشه مشکل است —
۷ ناگاه بدون کوچکترین علتی اوقاتش تلخ شد — ۸ غیر از او هیچ کسی‌را
آنجا نمیشناختم — ۹ نمیدانم چه کنم جز اینکه باو بگویم — ۱۰ اگر فکر
میکردم جز اینکه جریمه اورا بدهم راه دیگری هم بود آنرا نمیپرداختم —
۱۱ نامه‌را پیش از آنکه بدانم که میاید نوشتم — ۱۲ قیمت زندگی آنقدر که
حالا بالا رفته‌است پیش از جنگ بالا نبود — ۱۳ اگر پیش از من بروید خواهش
میکنم در بر گشتن قدری پنیر بخرید — ۱٤ آنقدر خوشحال بنظر میامد که پیش
از آنکه شروع کند بحرف زدن میدانستم که مژده دارد — ۱٥ غیر از او هیچ
کس آنجا نبود — ۱٦ نخواهند آمد مگر اینکه آنهارا دعوت کنید — ۱۷ پس از
آنکه نامه‌را خواند آنرا بمن داد که بخوانم — ۱۸ اگر اورا بعد از آنکه شمارا
دیده‌بودم میدیدم آنچه‌را که بمن گفته‌بودید باو میگفتم — ۱۹ اگر پس از آنکه
اورا دیدید باز بخواهید مرا ببینید بمن خبر بدهید

## EXERCISE 18a

۱ خواهش میکنم ببرادرتان بگوئید که هرچه زودتر اینجا بیاید — ۲ اگر
حالا برویم شاید پیش از آنکه ترن حرکت کند بایستگاه برسیم — ۳ بنای
کارخانه پیرارسال تمام شد و سال گذشته شروع کرد بتولید — ٤ برادیو گوش
میدادیم که ناگاه تلفون زنگ زد — ٥ اگر بآنچه میگفتم گوش میدادید در
کارتان اینقدر اشتباه نمیکردید — ٦ اگر با دقت بآنچه میگویم گوش بدهید
مطلب برای شما روشن میشود — ۷ از من خواهش کرد که با او گردش بروم —
۸ دیروز وقتیکه گردش میکردیم باران گرفت — ۹ وقتیکه اورا دیدم با بزازی
در بازار چانه میزد — ۱۰ نمیدانم بر گشته است یا نه — ۱۱ دیروز بعد از ظهر
بدیدن برادرم رفتم[1] اگر دیروز بر میگشتید از شما خواهش میکردم که با من
بدیدن او بیائید — ۱۲ اگر از ده برگشته باشد پیغام شمارا باو میدهم —
۱۳ پیش از آنکه هوا تاریک شود بر میگردیم — ۱٤ نمیدانم که میتواند بمن
کمک کند یانه

---

[1] For this use of the infinitive see Grammar, Lesson XIII, para. 1b.

## Exercise 21a

۱ مقصود من از اینکه از شما خواهش کردم که امروز بیائید مرا ببینید این بود که دستورات تازه‌را که از تهران آمده‌است بشما ابلاغ کنم — ۲ بدون اینکه اول از او اجازه بگیرید نمیتوانید بروید — ۳ اگر هنوز تصمیم نگرفته باشد که باید سعی میکنم اورا قانع کنم که باید — ٤ تا جنگ شروع شد معلوم بود که دشمن شکست میخورد — ٥ نه تنها نامه باو مینویسم بلکه بدیدن او هم میروم — ٦ موقعیکه منزل میرفتم ناگاه یادم آمد که فراموش کرده‌ام در اداره‌امرا قفل کنم بر گشتم و موقعیکه از پله‌ها بالا میرفتم دیدم که نه تنها دررا باز گذاشته‌ام بلکه چراغرا هم خاموش نکرده‌ام — ۷ بطوریکه دیروز بشما گفتم آنچه‌را که پیشنهاد میکنید غیر عملی است — ۸ موقعیکه از پل عبور میکردم شروع کرد برف آمدن — ۹ امروز موقعیکه در خیابان راه میرفتم مردی‌را دیدم که سیب میفروخت پیش او رفتم و از او پرسیدم که منی چند میفروشد گفت منی هفت ریال گفتم زیاد گران است و پرسیدم که آخرین قیمت چیست جواب داد که کمتر از هفت ریال نمیدهد بالاخره بعد از چانه زدن زیاد اورا راضی کردم که منی پنج ریال بمن بفروشد

## Exercise 23a

موقعیکه از پل عبور میکردم بیکی از همکاران سابقم بر خوردم سالها بود که اورا ندیده بودم و پیش خود فکر میکردم که شاید مرا نشناسد تا چه رسد باینکه با من صحبت کند وقتیکه مرا دید ایستاد و بگرمی با من سلام علیک کرد ممکن نبود بیش از چند کلمه رد و بدل کنیم زیرا که من سر کار میرفتم و دیر میشد و او در شهر کار داشت بنا بر این پس از اینکه قرار گذاشتیم که شب بعد هم دیگررا ملاقات کنیم باین امید که فراغت بیشتری داشته باشیم از هم جدا شدیم

## Exercise 25a

توده مردمرا عقب زدم و از پشت سر آنها جلو آمده بین مردمیکه صف کشیده بودند آمدم تا بجلو یک دسته عرب رسیدم که یک نفر سفیدپوست با ریش سفید آنجا ایستاده‌بود دلم میخواست پیش او بدوم ولی در حضور آنقدر جمعیت واهمه داشتم و میخواستم اورا در آغوش بگیرم ولی چون یک نفر انگلیسی بود نمیدانستم چطور مرا میپذیرد پس آنطوریکه ترس و تکبر بمن تلقین کرد رفتار نمودم یعنی پیش او رفتم و کلاه خودرا بر داشته باو گفتم تصور میکنم که شما دکتر لیونگستون هستید

## EXERCISE 26 a

۱ اگر آنمردیکه اسبرا از او خریدم چنان حاضر نبود بچنین قیمت کم بفروشد
هیچ وقت آنرا نمیخریدم کاشکی آنرا اینقدر با عجله نخریده بودم اگر قدری صبر
میکردم شاید اسب خیلی بهتری پیدا میکردم که بخرم — ۲ موقعیکه
تظاهرکنندگان از وسط شهر عبور میکردند عده زیادی از اهالی شهر بآنها ملحق
شدند قصد داشتند دم دروازه بازار میتنگ بدهند ولی پیش از آنکه ببازار برسند
پاسبانها آنهارا متفرق کردند — ۳ اگر کدخدای دهرا دیدید بی زحمت باو
بگوئید که میخواهم هرچه زودتر اورا ببینم بخشنامه تازه با دستورات برای
احضار آنهائیکه مشمول نظام وظیفه هستند از تهران رسیده است میخواهم
رونوشت این بخشنامه‌را باو بدهم که در اماکن عمومی چه در این ده و چه در
دهات مجاور نصب کند قانون تازه وضع شده است که مطابق مقررات آن عده
زیادی از مردم از نظام وظیفه معاف خواهند شد

## EXERCISE 27 a

پس از آنکه غذارا تمام کردیم میخواستیم دوباره راه بیفتیم که میزبان ما
گفت اگر پیش از آنکه بروید چند کلمه با پسرم حرف بزنید خیلی ممنون میشوم
(مزید تشکر خواهد شد) ما اینجا چنان تنها هستیم که آمدن دو نفر مسافر
برای پسرم اتفاقی است مارا باغی برد که پسر او آنجا بی‌کار نشسته‌بود با ما
در باب دهات اطراف که ظاهراً آنرا خوب میشناخت صحبت میکرد ربع ساعت
گفتگو کرده‌بودیم که روی خودرا بطرف من کرد و تازه آنوقت متوجه شدم
که او کور است

## EXERCISE 28 a

نزدیک ده بچند نفر ناشناس بر خوردم شروع کردند بحرف زدن و یکی از
آنها بمن گفت که خوب است امشب مهمان ما باشید با اینکه آنهارا نمیشناختم
و نسبت بآنها قدری مظنون شدم از اینکه غریب بودم و جائی نداشتم و شب
شده‌بود دعوت آنهارا قبول کردم مرا از وسط ده بمنزل بزرگی که کنار رود خانه
واقع شده‌بود بردند تا وارد منزل شدم پیر مردی یواش پیش من آمد و گفت
کاشکی اینجا نیامده‌بودید میترسم که هیچ وقت زنده از اینجا بیرون نروید هرچه
زودتر از اینجا فرار کنید و الا شمارا میکشند هر قدر فکر کردم معنی حرفهای
پیر مرد بر من روشن نشد و در هر صورت چاره نداشتم غیر از اینکه شبرا در آن
منزل بگذرانم کار از کار گذشته‌بود بنا بر این با قدمهای محکم جلو رفتم و

وارد اطاق بزرگی شدم تازه نشسته‌بودم که کسی دیگر داخل اطاق شد تا اورا
دیدم فهمیدم که در جای خطرناکی هستم و حق با پیر مرد است و هر چه
زودتر باید فرار کنم

## شغالها چرا بیرون شهر زوزه میکشند

اینک زوزه غم‌انگیز کشیده درست پشت دیوارهای تلگرافخانه بلند شد و پست
سر آن زوزه دیگری بگوش رسید و هی تکرار میشد و صدای عوعوی سگها مثل
اینکه جواب باشد از شهر شنیده میشد در خان از خان پرسیدم که شغالها هستند که
بیرون زوزه میکنند و بشهر اینقدر نزدیک میشوند جواب داد بلی همیشه این
کاررا میکنند و سگها هم همواره اینطور جواب میدهند میدانید چرا وقتی شغالها
مثل سگهای امروزه در شهر زندگی میکردند و اینها بیرون شهر در صحرا زندگی
میکردند سگها فکر کردند که خیلی بهتر است که در شهر باشند که از بدی
هوا محفوظ بمانند و بجای اینکه بارها برای مدتی مدید بدون غذا بمانند غذای
فراوان داشته باشند پس یکی را از بین خود با این پیغام پیش شغالها فرستادند
که بعضی از ما مریض هستند و پزشکان ما گفته‌اند که احتیاج بتغییر آب و
هوا دارند و باید چنانچه ممکن باشد سه روز در شهر بگذرانند ولی واضح است
که غیر ممکن است که ما سگها و شما شغالها در آن واحد در یک جا باشیم
بنا بر این از شما تقاضا داریم که جایتانرا فقط برای سه روز با ما عوض کنید
و بگذارید که ما در شهر اقامت کنیم و شما بصحرا بروید که آب و هوای آنجا
برای شما هم بدون شک خیلی سازگار خواهد بود شغالها این پیشنهادرا قبول
کردند و شب بعد این تغییر جا صورت گرفت صبح که اهالی شهر بیدار شدند
دیدند که هر جا که شب پیش شغالی بود اکنون سگی هست شب سوم شغالها
که کاملاً از صحرا خسته شده‌بودند با انتظارات خوش از تجدید زندگی پر
تجمل شهری خود بدروازه شهر بر گشتند ولی سگها از اینکه در جای تازه خود
بسیار راحت بودند عجله نداشتند که شهررا ترک کنند شغالها پس از آنکه مدتی
صبر کردند بسگها بانگ زدند که ناخوشهای شما خوب شده و حرفشانرا با ناله
تمام کردند مثل همان ناله که یک دقیقه پیش شنیدید و یا بطوریکه میرزا
عبدالله که اهل اصفهان است برای شما تعریف خواهد کرد مثل ناله که هر
روز از گلوی یک نفر اصفهانی یا یزدی میشود شنید ولی سگها که ترک هستند
و ترکی حرف میزنند فقط جواب دادند که یوخ یوخ یعنی نخیر نخیر و شغالهای
بیچاره مجبور شدند بصحرا بر گردند و از آنموقع ببعد هر شب بر میکردند و
همانطوریکه الآن شنیدید همان سوآلرا از سگها میکنند و سگها همیشه همان

جوابرا میدهند زیراکه بهیچ وجه نمیخواهند بصحرا برگردند و بهمین جهت است که شغالها بعد از غروب میایند و دور شهر زوزه میکشند و سگها همیشه بآنها جواب میدهند

## فلات ایران

دهات متعدد که عموماً بیش از یك فرسخ و نیم از هم دور نیست در کوهپایه‌ها هر جا که آب هست یا میشود پیداکرد نزدیك هم واقع شده است ولی فاصله بین شهرهای معتبر بتفاوت از سی تا شصت فرسخ است سلسله کوه‌های بزرگی که در دامنه آنها نمك زارها و چند دریاچه نمك واقع شده است همیشه جلو چشم است گیاه‌ها و نباتاتی که وجود دارد گیاه‌های صحرائی و بیابانی است و همچنین حیواناتی که پیدا میشود حیوانات صحرائی و بیابانی است ولی هر محلی که انسان برای خود اختیار کرده است درختهای توت و گردو و سایر درختهای میوه‌دار در آن بخوبی بعمل میاید گرمای تابستان خیلی شدید است و درجه حرارت در آفتاب تا ۱٤۰ درجه میرسد در زمستان هم ممکن است زیر صفر برسد و طوفان ریگهای پر سوز که بطلیعه سرما ریگهای کوچك مثل تگرگرا بصورت مسافر میبارد و بر بدبختی او و مرکبش میافزاید مزید بر هیبت آن میشود ولی وقتیکه مسافر فرصت اینرا دارد که بجای مسافرت با اتومبیل با کاروان برود لذتی که در صحرا دست میدهد این همه سختیهارا تلافی میکند در تابستان شبهای بلند خنك بهترین موقعی است برای حرکت الوان قوس قزحی در هوای گرگ و میش خط ممتد افقرا روشن میکند تا یك ساعت بعد از غروب تاریك میشود رنگ نیلگون آسمان بلاجوردی تبدیل میگردد تا بالآخره در ارغوانی پررنگ افق تیره محو میشود و کهکشان بالای سر مسافر نمایان میگردد

## شیراز

شیرازکه شراب و عسلش شهرت دارد مرکز استان فارس است و زادگاه و مدفن دو تن از معروفترین شعرای ایران یعنی حافظ و سعدی است که اولی با دانته معاصر بود با اینکه زلزله بیش از یك دفعه شهررا خراب کرده‌است هنوز دارای مسجدهای معظم و بازارهای زیبا است شهر شیراز در وسط دشت طویلی واقع شده است که پهنای آن در حدود چهار فرسخ است که بطرف مشرق بدریاچه نمك که مسکن مرغابیهای بیشمار است محدود میشود در فصل بهار این دشت با کشتزارهای فراوان از غله و پنبه پوشیده میشود و تماماً سر سبز بنظر میرسد و موستانها که آنهارا بیشتر برای کشمش میکارند تا برای شراب که اینجا بر

خلاف فرانسه نوشیدنش عمومیت ندارد در تپه‌ها برق میزند رشته‌های ممتد
کوه‌های آهکی بزرگ که دره‌های حاصلخیز در لابلای آنها واقع شده‌است
بجنوب شیراز بصورت پله بسوی ساحل خلیج پائین میاید ملخ و خشکسالی
دشمن بزرگ زارع است چادرنشینها از زارعین فقیرترند ولی باندازه آنها دستخوش
آفات سماوی و طبیعی نیستند زیراکه اگر در یك قسمت استان علف كم باشد
عموماً میتوانند گله‌های خودرا بمنطقه دیگری که شاید نود فرسخ از آنجا دور
باشد و دچار کمی علف نشده باشد ببرند چادرنشینها همسایه‌های ناراحت و
متمردی هستند ولی موقعیت آنها در اقتصاد کشور بی اهمیت نیست و دولت
آنهارا در سنوات اخیر تحت تسلط خود در آورده است

## بندر عباس و هرمز

بندر عباس که بنام آن پادشاه بزرگی است که مقام او برای ایران و ایرانیان
همان اهمیترا دارد که مقام الیزابت ملکه معاصر او در انگلستان در مدخل خلیج
فارس واقع شده است که اغلب مسافرین تا این سنوات اخیر از آن راه وارد
ایران میشدند شدت گرما و بدی آب و هوای آن بناحقی معروف است و آنرا
بدنام کرده‌است هرمز که روزی دار التجاره‌ای بود که با بمبئی امروز میشود
مقایسه کرد و شاعر انگلیسی میلتون مکرر اسم آنرا بعنوان منبع ثروت
شگفت‌انگیزی ذکر کرده‌است اکنون تقریباً خالی از سکنه است [جهانگرد] بی‌نظیر
توماس هربرت نوشته است که هرمز هیچ آب شیرین ندارد مگر آب بارانی‌که
ابرهای جانبخش بر آن از غم خرابیهایش که تا این اواخر چنان آباد بود
میریزد و تنها تجارت آن امروز خاك سرخ و نمك سنگ برای استفاده محلی است
ولی حوادث بزرگ موقعی که انگلیسها و پرتغالیها در قرن شانزدهم میلادی با
هم برای تفوق در دریاهای مشرق‌زمین جنگ میکردند در آنجا صورت گرفت
اینجا بود که کاشف خلیج بفین وفات یافت پرچاس نوشته است که استاد بفین
با آلات هندسی خود بساحل رفت تا ارتفاع و فاصله دیوار قلعه‌را اندازه‌گیری
کند باین مقصود که بهتر بتواند توپ خودرا تراز کرده تیراندازی کند ولی
موقعی که مشغول آن کار بود تیری از قلعه بشکم او خورد و جا در جا مرد

## آغاز نهضت مشروطیت در ایران

نهضت مشروطیت اوایل قرن بیستم میلادی در ایران نتیجه یك سلسله
حوادث و احوالی بود که در تمام مدت قرن نوزدهم بیشتر بدون سر و صدا انجام
میگرفت تا آن زمان عقاید اصلی که مردم نسبت بملك و ملکداری و یا بطور

كلی نسبت بزندگی افراد داشتند در چهارچوبه اسلام قرار گرفته بود نفوذ ممالك
اروپای غربی در ایران در قرن نوزدهم شاید بیش از هر واقعه دیگری باعث
شده است كه متفكرین ایرانی تردیدی نسبت بعقاید قدیمی راجع بدولت و اساسی
كه بر آن بنا شده بود پیدا كنند و جویای اساس جدید یا متفاوتی برای آن
بشوند جنگهای مخرب با روسیه در اوایل قرن نوزدهم كه با عهدنامه تركمانچای
در سال ۱۸۲۸ خاتمه یافت ایرانیهارا معتقد كرد كه اصلاحات اعم از نظامی
و غیرنظامی¹ لازم است بعلاوه ایرانیها در بدو امر بوسیله هیئتهای نظامی
مختلفی كه از ۱۸۰۷ ببعد بایران میامدند با فنون نظامی و علمی جدید و
تحولات سیاسی كه در اروپا صورت میگرفت آشنا شدند میرزا صالح كه بقرار
معلوم اولین ایرانی است كه شرحی از مؤسسات پارلمانی انگلستان نوشته است
در سال ۱۸۱۵ در طی اجرای طرحی برای اصلاحات نظامی بانگلستان اعزام
شد بتركیه و روسیه هم رفت در سفرنامه خود تنظیمات عثمانیرا توضیح داده
بملاهای كهنه پرست كه مخالف آن بودند سخت حمله كرده‌است شرحی كه او
در سفرنامه خود از انقلاب فرانسه نوشته‌است احتمالاً اولین شرحی است از
انقلاب فرانسه كه بقلم یك نفر ایرانی تحریر یافته‌است² مسافرتهای مأمورین
سیاسی هم در بسط معلومات راجع بمؤسسات مغرب‌زمین سهم بزرگی داشت
ابوالحسن شیرازی كه از طرف فتحعلی شاه بعنوان سفارت بانگلستان فرستاده
شده‌بود شرحی از عدالت و امنیتی‌را كه در انگلستان دیده‌بود در حیرت‌نامه
نوشته‌است و با ظلم و ستمی كه بر مملكت او حكمفرما بود مقایسه كرده‌است
خود ناصر الدین شاه سه دفعه كه اولین بارش در سال ۱۸۷۳ میلادی بود باروپا
مسافرت كرد جماعتهای تجار ایرانی چه در داخله چه در خارجه هم در پخش
افكار جدید عامل مهمی بودند مطبوعاتی كه ایرانیان مقیم استانبول و كلكته و
نقاط دیگر بزبان فارسی چاپ میكردند هم در اواخر قرن نوزدهم بسیار مشوق
اصلاحات بود

تحول طبقه زمیندار در ایران

پس از ظهور اسلام و منضم شدن ایران بممالك اسلامی مالكیت زمین بدو
نوع تقسیم شد یكی املاك شخصی و دیگری املاكی كه مالك خصوصی نداشت
و مالكیت نهائی آنها بجامعه اسلامی و به امام كه نماینده آن جامعه بود تعلق
میگرفت با تقسیم دار الاسلام بعده از ممالك نیم‌مستقل و مستقل كه گاهی با هم

---

¹ اعم از... و, a'amm az ... va, whether ... or.

² تحریر كردن tahrir k., to write.

میجنگیدند ناگزیر در این نظریه که همه زمینهائی که مالك خصوصی ندارد باما م تعلق میگیرد و او اینها را برای مردم نگاه میدارد تعدیلی حاصل شد و این تمایل بوجود آمد که حق امام در این باره بفرمانروایان دنیوی انتقال یابد در زمان سلجوقیان ممالك قسمتهای شرقی قلمرو خلفای عباسی از نو وحدت یافت و مالکیت نهائی زمینهائی که مالك خصوصی نداشت بقوم سلجوقی و بسلطان که نماینده آنان بود تعلق گرفت در ضمن امام تحت الشعاع قرار گرفته و مقام او مبهم بود دیگر قدرت دنیوی خود را بسلطان تفویض نکرد بلکه تنها چیزی که از او میخواستند این بود که بر اعمال خان فرمانروا یعنی خانی که بسلطنت رسیده‌بود از نظر شرعی و مذهبی صحه بگذارد کلمه مردم هرگز مفهومی بسیار قوی نداشت و بتدریج که عوامل حکومت مطلقه بر اثر ضعیف شدن سنن صحرانشینی سلجوقیان پیشرفت حاصل میکرد مفهوم کلمه مردم را تحت الشعاع خود قرار میداد وضع مغول از این حیث بطور کلی شبیه بوضع سلجوقیان بود اما تمایل بمشاوره ضعیفتر بود و تجزیه‌ای که پس از بر افتادن سلسله ایلخانان مغول در ممالک آنان روی داد بر اثر ضعف و انقراض نهائی دستگاه خلافت قطعیتر بود با تجزیه ممالك ایلخانان و تقسیم آن باما رتهائی که دائم باهم در جنگ بودند موضوع روی کار آمدن فرمانروای واحد اهمیت حاصل کرد در زمان صفویه دوباره مفهوم کلمه مردم تا حدی مصداق یافت این لفظ دیگر بمعنی قبایل مستولی ترك و مغول که مالك مشترك متصرفات خود بودند (و یك دسته یا یك تن از میان آنان با رضایت عامه رهبر قوم میشد) نبود بلکه بمعنی مجموع افراد ملتی بود که شاه بر آنان فرمان میراند مالکیت نهائی و هر حقی که بود باو میرسید اما نه بعنوان نماینده مردم بلکه بعنوان سلطانی که از جانب خدا معین شده بود یا بقول آن عده از پیروان شاه که بیشتر غلو میکردند تجلی ذات الهی بود بنا بر این حکومت او چیزی جز حکومت مطلقه نمیتوانست باشد و اطاعت از او مستلزم هیچ مشورتی با افرادی که در زیر حکم وی بودند نبود و لازم نبود که این افراد آزادانه و باتفاق رضایت خود را ابراز کنند در زمان قاجاریه جنبه مذهبی حکومت بمقدار معتنابهی ضعیف شد اما استبداد آن باقی ماند و هیچ مسئولیتی در کار نبود که آن را بکاهد این قوت یافتن عامل حکومت مطلقه در جامعه ریشه دواند و در طرز تفکر عامه نسبت بمسئله زمین‌داری و همچنین در وضع رعایائی که زندگی آنان وابسته بزمین بود مؤثر افتاد

در مورد طبقه زمین‌دار باید دانست که اشراف «فئودال»، ایران دوره ساسانی پس از غلبه عرب منقرض شدند اما از طرف دیگر دهقانان (بمعنی اخص کلمه) همچنان مسئول اداره امور محلی و جمع خراج از جوامع مورد حمایت مسلمین

بودند و پس از آنکه اسلام آوردند بیشتر زمینهای خودرا حفظ کردند و از همین طبقه بیشتر کارگزاران دیوان استخدام میشدند در ضمن طبقه جدیدی از مالکین بوجود آمد هسته اصلی این طبقه تازیانی بودند که یا عده‌ای از املاك زراعتی وسیع خودرا بعنوان عطیه از امام گرفته بودند و یا بعضی‌را بر اثر فتح و غلبه مالك شده و یا برخی‌را از راه خرید بدست آورده بودند بمرور دهور افراد غیر عربی که باسلام گرویده بودند باین طبقه افزوده شدند فرق این طبقه با اشراف فئودال دوره ساسانی در این بود که افراد دسته اول زمینرا در مقابل خدمات نظامی نمیگرفتند و اما فرقی که با دهقانان داشتند این بود که اصولاً در برابر اینان نه نماینده حکومت بشمار میرفتند و نه عامل خراج اگر چه بمرور دهور در غالب موارد این اموررا بر عهده گرفتند با ظهور حکومت لشکری ترکها طبقه جدیدی میان حکومت و طبقه زمین‌دار و همچنین میان حکومت و رعیت قرار گرفت و آن عبارت بود از مقطع که نخست حق جمع خراج و سر انجام حق استفاده از خود زمین باو واگذار شد در نواحی غیر ایلی محتملاً مالك قدیم جای خودرا بیشتر بمقطع داد و در صورت قبول خدمت دیوانی در طبقه مقطع مستحیل شد و اما در نواحی ایلی و در جاهای دوردست یعنی جاهائی مانند ولایات متصل بدریای خزر حکام محلی تا حدود معتنابهی هم املاك خودرا حفظ کردند و هم نفوذ خودرا بطور کلی ظهور سلسله‌های جدید تغییر اساسی در ماهیت طبقه زمیندار نداد هر چند اعضاء و کارگزاران آن و تا حدی اهمیت نسبی دسته‌های مختلف طبقه زمین‌دار‌را تغییر داد

یکی از خواص بارز سراسر دوران پیش از مغول نیروی باز یافته کشاورزی است در توجیه این معنی شاید تا حدی بتوان گفت که مردم دهنشینی که تابع کدخدایان خود بودند نسبةً دارای وضع ثابت و تا حدی حق خود مختاری داشتند و کدخدا واسطه‌ای بود میان مردم ده و دیوان یا مقطع اگرچه گاهی عده کثیری از مردم دهنشین در نقاط تازه‌ای سکونت مییافتند با اینهمه بر روی هم انتقال از دهی بده دیگر کمتر صورت میگرفت در واقع مردم دهات مجاور بسا بلهجه‌های مختلف سخن میگفتند هنگامی که برزگری از کار خود بعللی باز میماند زمین او بظن غالب بدست همروستائیان او می افتاد مهمترین وسیله ارتباط روستائیان با دنیای خارج محصل مالیات بود از طرف دیگر این نکته نیز درست است که دهقانان در بسیاری از موارد اصولاً بزمین وابسته بودند و مشمول پرداخت انواع و اقسام عوارض سنگین میشدند با این همه چنین مینماید که تا هنگامی که طبقات مختلف قادر بحفظ نوعی استقلال بودند و حس میکردند که نوعی همبستگی دارند و تا زمانی‌که همه قدرت

در دست یك فرد یا یك دسته از افراد متمركز نبود و مردم محلی تا
درجهای بر امور خود حاكم بودند امكان دادخواهی برای دهقانان باقی بود
اگر هم از همه جا ناامید میشدند میتوانستند بامرا یا مالكان نواحی مجاور
پناه برند در ضمن احتیاج حكومت باستقرار وضع اقتصادی بطور كلی سبب
میشد كه اخاذی مالك و عمال حكومت از حد معین تجاوز نكند گرچه بنقل
مواردی میتوان پرداخت كه بسیاری از جاها بر اثر وضع مالیات زائد ویران
شده است با ظهور مغول آن قیودی كه ناشی از دین اسلام بود لا اقل
موقتاً بر طرف گشت و دیگر از نظر تأمین منافع شخصی حدی برای وضع
مالیات قائل نشدند بعلاوه كار مداخله مأموران لشكری و كشوری
در امور مردم محلی بمراتب بیش از حدی شد كه تا آن هنگام معمول بود
و این نكته باعث میشد كه بهمان نسبت از میزان خودمختاری هر محل
كاسته شود از این گذشته روشهائی كه سابقاً فقط رنگ عرف وعادت داشت
بوسیله فرمانهای سلطنتی قوت قانونی حاصل كرد در نتیجه زارع بنحوی مؤثرتر و
بیش از پیش بزمین وابسته شد و این وابستگی در زمان قاجاریه باز هم بیشتر شد
زیرا در این دوره آماده كردن افراد برای خدمت نظام بستگی بزمین داشت نه بافراد

ما دام كه رعیت میتوانست از محكمهای داد خواهی كند كه رئیس آن
قاضی بود (و این قاضی یا مستقل بود یا دست كم یك باره تابع مالك و مقطع
و تیولدار نبود) تا حدی امكان داشت كه بشكایت او برسند و این مطلب تا
اندازهای در زمان سلجوقیان مصداق داشت راست است كه دستگاه مذهبی
اصولاً ضمیمه تشكیلات كلی حكومت شده بود اما هنوز میان دستگاههای مختلف
اداری موازنهای بر قرار بود در حكومت مغول مرافعات ملكی در پارهای از موارد
هنوز بمحاكمی كه قاضی بر آنها ریاست میكرد ارجاع میشد در روزگار صفویه
تغییری در این وضع پدید آمد كه از یك طرف از میزان استقلال قاضیها كاسته شد
و از طرف دیگر چون رفته رفته طبقه قضات در طبقه زمیندار مستحیل میشد
كمتر محتمل بود كه قضات از دعاوی رعیت علیه ارباب حمایت كنند از این
گذشته در بسیاری موارد هم بتیولدداران و هم بصاحبان سیورغالهای موروثی
اختیارات كامل داده میشد تا بهمه قضایائی كه در زمینهای اعطائی اتفاق
میافتاد رسیدگی كنند و در این مورد مأموران حكومت مركزی و محلی اختیاری
نداشتند این تمایل یعنی توسعه اختیارات مالك و تیولدار محلی و تمركز تمام
قدرت در دست آنان همچنان در دوره قاجاریه دوام یافت در نتیجه عامل خود
مختاری محلی بیشتر دچار ضعف و فتور و رعیت بزمین بیشتر وابسته میشد

با این همه در طی این احوال تأثیرات دیگری احساس میشد ارتباط ایران با

کشورهای بیگانه رو بـفـزونی نـهـاده بـود شکستهای نظامی ایران مخصوصاً از
روسیه که در اوایل قرن نوزدهم وقوع یـافت ثـابت کرده بود که اگر ایران
نخواهد از بعضی ممالک خارجی بسبب برتری فـنی (تکنیکی) آنـان عقب بماند
محتاج تغییری در اوضاع است در نیمه دوم قرن نوزدهم نهضت جوانان ترک و
نهضت اصلاح طلبی کـه سـیـد جمال الدین اسدابادی (افغانی) در رأس آن قـرار
داشت اثری عـمـیـق در ایرانیان کرد از این گذشته وخامت روز افزون اوضاع
مالی هم ذهن طبقه حاکمه و هم ذهن طبقه درس خوانده‌را بخود مشغول کرده
بود اما در حالی که اولی در جستجوی راه‌هائی بر آمده بود که خودرا با قوای
نظامی بـهـتـر مجهز کند. و پول بیشتری برای ولخرجی دربارهای سلطنتی بدست
آورد دوبی از تمایل طبـقـه حاکمه که میکوشید مشکلات اقتصادی‌را از طریق
اعطای امتیازات ببیگانگان حل کند خشمگین و بیـزار بود زیرا این کار باعث
میشدکه ایران از نظر اقتصادی و سیاسی تحت قیمومیت اجانب در آیـد طبقـه
درس خوانده میخواست که سهم نسبةً بیشتری در اداره امور مملکت بدست آورد
و امیدوار بود که با کسب معلومات فنی ممالک اروپای غربی بتـواند آسایش
بیشتری بـرای آنـها فراهم کـند این جنبشها و تمایلات مختلف و متخالف در
انقلاب مشروطیت ۱۹۰۵-۶ (۱۳۲٤) بـاوج خود رسید و در ۱۹۰٦ مـنـجـر
باعطای مشروطیت از طرف مظفر الدین شاه شد با این ترتیب دوره جدیدی در
تاریخ ایران آغاز گشت در مورد زمین‌داری شاید بتـوان گفت که نقض نظریه
شرعی بیش از تغییری بـود کـه در روش زمین‌داری و هـمـچنیـن در طرز تفکر
عمومی نسبت بـایـن مطلب پـدیـد آمـد و مسئله مالکیت و زمین‌داری اصولاً از
بعضی جهات بهمان حالی که در قرون وسطی داشت باقی مـانـد از ایـن گذشته
قسمت اعظم قدرت همچنان در دست مالکان و خوانین عشایر بـاقـی ماند و تا
روی کار آمدن رضاشاه تغییر مهمی در اوضاع داده نشد
(از مالک و زارع در ایران ترجمه منوچهر امیری بنگاه ترجمه و نـشر کتاب
تهران ۱۳۳۹ ص ۳۲۲-۳۲۸)

## ADDITIONAL VOCABULARY

A اجانب   ajaneb (pl. of اجنبی ajnabi), foreigners.
A اخاذی   axaẓi (pl. of اخذ axẓ), exactions.
A اخص   axass, more or most special.
A ارجاع   erja', reference (for consideration, decision, etc.).
A اصولاً   osulan, essentially, fundamentally.

A   اعطاء   *e'ta*, granting, bestowing.

A   امارت   *emarat*, emirate.

A   امرا   *omara* (pl. of امیر *amir*), amirs.

A   انتقال   *enteqal*, transfer; انتقال یافتن *enteqal yaftan*, to be transferred.

A   انقراض   *enqeraz*, extinction.

اوج   *ouj*, zenith.

بیزار   *bizar*, disgusted, wearied.

پاره   *pare*, part, portion; some.

پیرو   *peirou*, follower.

A   تابع   *tabe'*, subject.

A   تجزیه   *tajzie*, fragmentation, break-up.

A   تجلی   *tajalli*, emanation.

A   تعلق   *ta'alloq*, belonging; تعلق گرفتن *ta'alloq gereftan*, to belong.

A   تفکر   *tafakkor*, thought, meditation.

A   تفویض   *tafviz*, delegation, entrusting (of authority).

A   توجیه   *toujih*, explanation.

A   جنبه   *jambe*, side, aspect.

A   حمایت   *hemayat*, protection.

خشمگین   *xafmgin*, angry.

A   خواص   *xavass* (pl. of خاصه *xasse*), properties, qualities.

A   دهور   *dohur* (pl. of دهر *dahr*), times, periods.

دیوان   *divan*, government office (especially dealing with finance).

ریشه   *rife*, root; ریشه دواندن *rife davandan*, to take root.

A   زائد   *zaed*, superfluous; excessive.

سر انجام   *sar anjam*, in the end.

A   سکونت   *sokunat*, dwelling, residence.

A   سنن   *sonan* (pl. of سنت *sonnat*), traditions.

A   صحه   *sehheh*, endorsement; صحه گذاشتن *sehheh gozaftan*, to endorse.

A   ضمیمه   *zamime*, enclosure, appendix; ضمیمه شدن *zamime f.*, to be included (in).

A   ظن   *zann*, بظن غالب *be zanne yaleb*, in all probability, presumably.

A   عرف   *orf*, custom, customary law.

A   عطیه   *atiye*, gift, grant.

A عمیق *amiq,* deep, profound.

A غلبه *γalabe,* conquest.

A غلو *γolovv,* exaggeration.

فزونی *fozuni,* increase, abundance.

A قادر *qader,* powerful; able (= having the power to).

A قضیه *qaziye,* case, instance, circumstance.

A قطعی *qat'i,* definite, ultimate.

A. کثیر *kasir,* numerous.

کشوری *kefvari,* civil (as opposed to military).

A ماهیت *mahiyat,* quiddity, essence, nature.

A متخالف *motaxalef,* conflicting.

A متصرفات *motasarrefat* (pl. of متصرفه, *motasarrefe*), possessions.

A متمرکز *motamarkez,* centralized.

A محدود *mahdud,* limited.

A محصل *mohassel,* tax-collector.

A مستحیل *mostahil,* transmuted, transformed; absorbed (into), assimilated (to).

A مستلزم *mostalzem,* necessitating, requiring; involving.

A معتنابه *mo'tanabeh,* considerable.

A مقام *maqam,* status.

A منضم *monzamm,* annexed, joined.

A موازنه *mavazene,* balance, equilibrium.

A موقةً *movaqqatan,* temporarily.

A ناشی *nafi,* growing, arising (from).

A نسبی *nesbi,* relative, proportional.

A نظریه *nazariye,* theory.

A نهائی *nehai,* definite, ultimate.

A واقعی *vaqe'i,* true, real.

A وخامت *vaxamat,* critical condition.

A وضع *vaz',* situation, position.

A وقوع *voqu',* happening, occurrence; وقوع یافتن, *voqu' yaftan,* to happen.

هسته *haste,* core, kernel.

# INDEX

*h* (cont.)
  used to form diminutives, 100; the
    past participle, 16; verbal nouns,
    96
  *See also* •
*hamze*, xv, xxi, 3, 6, 9, 12, 17, 182–5,
  205
Holidays, public, 257

Indefinite adjectives, nouns and pro-
  nouns, 80–1
Indirect speech, 156
Interjections, 255
  Arabic phrases used as, 245
Interrogative sentences, 5, 263–5
Intonation, 260–5

*jazm*, xxi

*kasre*, xxi

Letters:
  of prolongation, 182
  'moon' letters, 181
  'servile' letters, 181, 188
  'sun' letters, 181
  'weak' letters, 182

Measures, 130, 259

Negative:
  with verbs of prohibition, 159
  with نا, 158
  with قدغن, 159
  with هرگز, 61
  with هیچ, 33, 34
  *See also* the Verb
Nouns:
  of Multitude, 133
  used as adjectives, 136
  used generically, 128, 134–5

Abstract nouns, 96
Collective nouns, 134
Compound nouns, 102-4, 106–7
Diminutives, 100
formation of nouns, with suffixes,
  97–100
Generic nouns in relative clauses, 77
plural of nouns, 8, 133
plural termination, omission of, 135
Verbal nouns, 96–7
Nouns, Arabic:
  of Instrument, 198
  of Place, 198
  of professions and trades, 198
  Abstract nouns, 198–9
  declension of nouns, 196–7
  Diminutives, 199
  Diptotes, 196
  gender of nouns, 197–8
Numerals, 37–44
  addition, 41
  Approximate numbers, 40
  Cardinals, 37–9, 42
  Classifiers used with numerals,
    43–4
  Distributives, 40
  division, 41
  Fractions, 41
  multiplication, 41
  Multiplicatives, 40
  Ordinals, 37–9, 42
  percentage, 41
  Recurring numerals, 40
  subtraction, 41
Numerals, Arabic, 233–5
  Fractions, 235
  Multiplicative adjectives, 235
  Numeral adjectives, 236
  Numeral adverbs, 235

Object, the direct, 4

# PERSIAN INDEX

the 'Indefinite' ی, 3–4, 6–7, 20,
   77, 81, 125–8
the 'Relative' ی, 75–8, 128
the 'Verbal' ی, 128
يا, 136
يار-, 102
يافتن, 85, 92
ـبه-, 100
يچه-, 100

ـبزه-, 100
ـيژه-, 100
يك, 45
يك خرده, 81
يك ديگر, 45
يكی, 45
يكی ديگر, 45
ـن-, 42, 101
ـينه-, 63, 101